AN OVERVIEW OF EXTRATERRESTRIAL RACES

Trafford rev. 11/17/2022

 www.trafford.com

North America & international
toll-free: 844-688-6899 (USA & Canada)
fax: 812 355 4082

AN OVERVIEW OF EXTRATERRESTRIAL RACES:

Who Is Who
In the
Greatest Game
Of History

Rolf Waeber

Artwork and Poems by Yeva

Foreword by Yeva

The Earth is only a tiny cell within the body of the universe. There are billions of galaxies, each with billions of stars; we call our star - the Sun. One can only wonder what other names were given to the billions of suns out there. One wonders how many billions of planets support life, as we know it, or lives beyond our imagination.

"Where the suns shine there is life" - reads the inscription on a circular bronze object dated 1122 - 1236 BCE (Chou Dynasty). Even though time is the greatest enemy of history, from which a huge chunk is missing, still there is enough information to put the jigsaw puzzle together. The ancient scriptures of many cultures, the artifacts, the paintings, and prehistoric cave art provide an abundance of proof. What about the stories passed on from generation to generation of the ancient tribes? How on Earth did so called primitive people from the Dogon tribe know and worship for thousands of years the visitors from the distant star that was only "discovered" decades ago. All of the above and more open the pages of a book filled with overwhelming evidence, that the planet Earth was visited by super intelligent extraterrestrial races since the beginning of times. The ancients knew it, saw it, and some could even explain it, all those magical encounters, unbelievable technology, amazing and unfamiliar appearances of the visitors, beguiling those who witnessed, they saw a glorious mighty power and worshipped it. The god has arrived! The stories multiplied and changed with the speed of light. Some ancients worshipped the Sun - the life giver, it literally is. I wonder where from they got that accurate information?! Hmm.... It is a fact that the star started it all and sustained it for billions of years. We are all so different; the human people, the alien people, all of the animal and plant kingdom, the planets, the stars, the objects around us, all so different in appearance, yet, all made practically of the same. We are and everything else visible and invisible truly the stardust. We are one.

With all the information that is available, how ignorant it would be to think that the Earth is the only planet in the infinite universe that contains life. If it could happen here, it could and did happen on countless other planets, we just didn't find them yet. They found us instead.

Not so long ago the belief was that Earth is the center of the universe, flat as a pancake supported by giant turtles. It is laughable now, but then, if anyone would try to question that ludicrous theory, one would die by the sadistic and brutal hand of the church. Millions forced to die in agony, in the fire of hate, ignorance and lie. Giordano Bruno (1548-1600), one of the most brilliant and progressive minds of his time, was one of the many to die for the truth. If only a few like Giordano were given a chance to live, think and speak out then... our world would most probably be a better place now.

The humans should learn from history, so not to repeat the same shameful mistakes, but do they?! Instead of creating wonders, the human mind is capable of, they savagely kill each other for money, oil, power, or land, which gets destroyed day by day, polluting the air, flattening the rain forests, contaminating the water etc... And after all this, they call themselves civilized. The human species have yet far to go to earn this title, and then maybe they will be ready for acceptance by an intergalactic community. Yes, the humans are still a primitive species, but one can't be too hard on them, as they are only in their infancy; some only a few hours in life, some weeks or months, in a cosmic scale. The advanced ones don't get burned at the stake anymore, but they suffer for the truth, by being ridiculed and sometimes even silenced. Who knows how long it will take for the human species to face the truth, decades, centuries, millennia, that is, if they don't destroy one other in the mean time.

Maybe with ETs intervention the humans will learn how to live in harmony with each other and nature. After all, everything and everyone is interconnected in the universe. One day, when the humans are fully grown, they will reach the distant worlds and maybe even help some beginners of the cosmic family and become a contributing factor in their development, as we were helped once by our star cousins back in a distant past. Then we will become the gods, but for now the humans are still in their nappies. Well, one has to crawl before one walks, running and flying comes later, much later. Despite it all, look what the humans achieved in only the last 100 years and the possibilities lying ahead.

Imagine other civilizations which are thousand or even millions of years older than ours! What are they capable of? Growing artificial planets? Creating the atmosphere in a world where there's none? Defying gravity? Finding cosmic shortcuts and traveling from star to star which are light-years apart? Living in peace???

So it's best to leave all these questions open and just wonder.

...And that is where this book takes you, the compendium to introduce the others, ET beings, those who came down and have gone, those who came down and stayed and those who are yet to come. This book offers a unique perspective to the wondering ones, those with an open mind, heart and soul.

INTRODUCTION

This book is the result of many years of search for answers.

This book intents to give an overview about all the different alien/extraterrestrial races which were and are in contact with the many civilizations on planet Earth. This is a huge collection which will be useful to every person who wants to know more about UFOs, alien visitors, celestial beings and much more. It is not intended to give the last truth. But it is a wonderful dictionary for each person who wants to know more. You can start searching; therein you will find many applicable internet addresses and important information about people who work in this fascinating field. You will have data about space beings from the Pleiades, Lyra, Tau Ceti, Andromeda, Sirius, Aldebaran, Betelgeuse, Venus, Mars, Arcturius and many more. You will hear from extraterrestrial races like the Greys, Zetas, Arcturians, Pleiadians, Sirians and about 200 more races.

Astronomers calculate that there exist at least 1,000,000,000 galaxies, each galaxy having an estimate of about 50,000,000,000 planets.

Over 10,000 UFO sightings are reported annually around the world.
About 200 extraterrestrial races are known to be in contact with Earth and millions of people have met or seen extraterrestrials.
The following list of races inhabiting this universe is by no means complete. The names given to the various groups are the names which are already in use to describe them. Names used herein are the most common ones.
Sometimes there are controversial statements, but today it isn't possible to check all of them if they are true or not.
This work gives a synopsis of what's going on and what was going on on planet Earth and in deep space.
These specifications are from experiencers, abductees, contactees and channeler from many different countries, like Australia, Brazil, Canada, France, Germany, Great Britain, Mexico, New Zealand, South Africa, Switzerland, United States and many more.

Our current understanding of the history of military UFO investigations is that they began in 1941 with the first crash recovery of a flying saucer in Cape Girardeau, Missouri. It is known that there exist many paintings from the Middle Ages with spaceships.

Perhaps some of you, dear readers, have insider knowledge that can serve to confirm or refute some of these claims. If so, then please share your data with the author of the book. Please contact the author in care of Trafford Publishing.

Critics are welcome and help to improve the quality of this dictionary. It is not intended to insult anybody or critic religion beliefs, but it is important not to exclude information.

LIST OF PAINTINGS

All paintings by Yeva.

I am terrestrial
With extraterrestrial … soul
And celestial mind
Travel through space and time
Quantum reality
Nine dimensions so hard to define
With words and on paper
Impossible task
Though it's all out there
Under ethereal mask
Black and white holes, shortcuts
And so much more
Right around the corner
Behind the cosmic door
Won't mention non-mentionable
Embrace inter-dimensional
ET's blood spilling out of my veins
Sub-Atomic particles
Jumping up in ecstasy
Splitting atoms in my busy brains.

Dedication

This book is dedicated to all extraterrestrials.

Acknowledgements

To Yeva for her beautiful paintings and poems, and for believing in me.

Thanks to Sylvia and Marcus, founder of Alienalley.com, an outstanding website.

Thanks to Alien, Brian Wilson, E.A. Karvovski, Jelaila Starr, Tina.

To all channelers, researchers, investigators, lightworkers for their encouragement.

Thanks to the extraterrestrial beings for giving me inspiration.

Without them this book wouldn't exist.

–

They Are

So there, somewhere,
Up there they are,
Upon the invisible star
They are,
Upon the unapproachable
Time and space,
Untouchable place... They are.

So give me the answer
Show me the sign,
Free over-time working
Mind of mine,
Open the windows
Of truth to face,
For all human race
Oh what a waste!

Table of Contents

1. RACES

1.1 Basic Alien Classes of the Milky Way Galaxy

Humanoids / Mammalians:

Adam Kadmon, Adamu, Aldebarans, Alpha Draconians, Aryans, Atlans, Bernarians, Biaviians, Blond Nordic Humanoids, Catlike Lyrans, Centaurians, Cetaceans, Cetians, Dals, Darker Skinned Lyrans, Dinoids, Dorians, Earth Humans, Erranians, Felines, Fomalhautians, Greens, Hubrids, Humans, Hybrids, Ikels, Janosian, Jargans, Jupiterians, Koldasians, Korendians, Kumaras, Lulus, Lyran Giants, Lyran Humans, Mayans, Mothmen, Mushaba, Nibiruans, Nordics, Nors, Nyptonians, Ogattans, Old Ones, Orange, Orion Humans, Paschats, Pegasians, Pleiadians, Procyonans, Pshaat, Pteroids, Sasquatch, Semites, Sirians, Solarians, Stagyians, Suernis, Tall Whites, Tau Cetians, Telosians, Teros, Terrans, Terrians, Ummites, Vedrians, Vegans.

Reptilians:

Altairians, Amphibians, Aquillians, Arcathians, Ari-An, Aurigan Dracos, Booteans, Burrowers, Capellan Dracos, Capellans, Carians, Centaurians, Ciakars, Draco-Reptilians, Draconians, Dracos, Dracs, Fomalhautians, Hubrids, Hybrids, Lizards, Mintakans, Nagas, Nibiruans, Orions, Procyonans, Red Dracs, Reptiles, Reptilian Crossbreeds, Reptilians, Reptiloids, Reptoids, Reptons, Rigelians, Saurians, Sauroids, Serpent Race, Shapeshifter, Shetis, Snakes, Targs, Targzissians, Vegans, Winged Dracos.

Insectoids (Greys):

Antaris, Ataien, Bernarians, Blues, Delphohims, Dows, Eban, Grays, Greys, Insectillians, Orion Greys, Plusadians, Reticulans, Rutilias, Skreeds, Vegans, Visitors, Zeta Reticulis, Zetas.

Nonphysical/Etheric Beings:

Andromedans, Arcturians, Betelgeusians, Etheric Sirians, Kantarians, Lyrans, Neptunians, Pleiadians, Plejarans, Saturnians, Ultra Terrestrials, Venusians, Vortex Collective.

1.2 Detailed Overview of Races in the Milky Way Galaxy

ABBENAKI   Inhabitants of Marduk.

ABERNACHE   Race from planet Maldek.

ADAM KADMON   Human looking race.

ADAMIC RACE   → Jupiterians.

ADAMU   Earth humans created by the Elohim.
Annunaki, Collective, Elohim.

AGHARIANS   → Aghartians.

AGARTHIAN GIANTS   → Agarthians.

AGHARTHIANS   Many Agarthian Giants stay long periods and operate in Nibiru.
Tamlris, YaPool.
→ Agartha.
→ Agartha Network.

AKONOWAI   Race of Sirians of the 3rd planet of Sirius B.

ALCYONES   → Alcyons.

ALCYONS   A genetically conglomerate race.
Do not necessarily adhere to the non-intervention ethics of certain group in the Taygeta system.
→ Damsowzulvitz.

ALDEBARANS   Human militarists who are working with the Dracos and Greys.
They have a large underground facility below Egypt, base of a secret Kamagol-II cult which has connection to the Bavarian Thule Society and the Montauk time-space projects.

ALIENS   Extraterrestrials have been visiting planet Earth since the beginning of time.
They come from many different galaxies.
About 95 % of all extraterrestrials are of a positive nature. One of the basic laws is the Law of Non-Interference.
There are many types of extraterrestrials, some of them are from the Adamic Race (Adam Kadmon type), similar to Earth humans.

There are about 200 known different extraterrestrial races that have been monitoring the Earth. The negative experiences seem to be from only 6 planets.

ALPHA DRACONIANS

Home of green and brown skinned, 7 to 8 ft tall Reptilian Humanoids.

Many of them have assimilated human DNA to enhance their emotional centers.

They are controlling a large number of other races by a massive computer network and sub-space transceiver that exists at some undisclosed location near their home system. It operates simultaneously on the 3rd and 4th dimension.

These Dracos are said to serve an elite class of Reptilians, the White Dracos (Beige Dracos) and dark-skinned winged Dracos called Ciakars. Were the first race to have space travel in our galaxy, 4 billion years ago.

They believe that this universe was here for them.

A reptilian race composed of master geneticists.

Created the primate race, which was first brought to Mars and then to Earth.

The primate race was then tinkered with by many other different races (21).

The primate race became Homo Sapiens.

We used to have 12 strands of DNA, 10 strands were taken out by a group from Orion in order to control us.

→ Ciakars.

ALTAIRIANS

Alleged reptilian inhabitants of the Altair system in the Aquila constellation.

They collaborate with Nordic humans, Greys and Earth military presence.

Headquarters of the "Corporate", which maintains ties with the Ashtar and Draconian Collectives.

Humanoids: There are 2 variants:

>>   Nordic looking,

>>   Semitic looking
            Landed at Holloman AFB, New Mexico in the 1960's.

→ Anon Sa Ra.

ALTEANS

From Altea.

They are reputed to have links with demons and the Oogons.

AMPHIBIANS

Similar to the Saurians or Reptiloids, yet being hominoid creatures with reptilian as well amphibian-like features.

They are semi-aquatic in nature.

A race lives in the Alcyone star system in the Pleiades.

ANAKIM

Elder race.
Also called "Giants". Alleged from 9 to 11 ft tall.
They have allegedly been encountered in deep and extensive cavern systems in North America.
They are believed to have interstellar traveling capabilities.

ANDROMEDANS

4th and 5th dimensional beings.
Are a very old telepathic race and live to an average age of 2,007 years.
A non-physical race of purely awesome ancient angelic beings from the Andromeda galaxy.
Humanoid, Caucasian type, oriental type.
Small white translucent skinned people with a crystal visible in their third eye.
They have no fat, are all slim, they know no age (all look the same age).
Have light green to yellow blood. They don't have a reproductive system.
Skin color light blue, eyes are slightly larger than those of Earth humans, lips are thin & light pink, ears slightly smaller, long fingers & toes.
They've blue blood because their blood is copper-based, they are 7 to 9 ft tall, look similar like us, they are hairless.
Children go to school from 150 to 200 years.
They don't have a military, they are scientists.
They have no financial system.
They have 3 sexes: male, female, androgynous.
Male vary in height from 1.70 to 2.12 m, female from 1.63 to 1.93 and have alluring energies and quite buxom figures.
They can transport themselves through their mind.
They are governed by a Council of Seven.
Member of the Galactic Federation.
Can travel outside of space-time.
They are working with the Americans.
→ Year 1997.09.
→ Moraney, Morenae, Vasais.

ANNANNUKI

Transformed name for the Annunaki.

ANNUNNAKI

"Astronauts".
Now they call them Annunaki.
They are metallic consciousness, they can use the electrical equipment for surveillance.
Tehuti was one of them.
→ An, Cain, Isis, Luluwa, Ninti, Tehuti.
→ Elohim, Seeders.

ANTARIS
Race from the Antares star system.
Look similar to the Zetas, but appear much taller, much longer elongated neck, long spindly arms and fingers.
They are Star Beings.
They are the higher selves of the Zetas.

APA-MUS
Created on Earth an ape-beast hybrid.
→ Ninhursag.
→ Sheti.

AQUILLIANS
Reptilian race.

ARCATHIANS
Reptilian race.
Relatives of the Aquillians.
They came to the planet Mars and absorbed the energy of all humanoid beings, only a few of the Martians survived beneath the surface of Mars.

ARCTURANS
→ Arcturians.

ARCTURIANS
One of the most advanced civilizations.
4th and 5th dimensional beings from the Arcturian Star System in the Bootes Constellation.
They work with the Ascended Masters, whom they call Brotherhood of the All, in close connection and with the Galactic Command.
Arcturian society is governed by the elders.
Travel the universe in their starships, which are one of the most advanced in the entire universe.
3 to 4 ft tall, slender, skin is a greenish color, very large almond-shaped eyes, only 3 fingers, eyes are dark brown or black, they don't have ear lobes, a slightly larger cranium, lifespan from 350 – 400 years, semi-physical.
There are no male & female.
The information about the Arcturians is very confusing and contradictive.
6 to 7 ft tall, humanoid form, eyes are black with no visible pupils (three times human's), their bodies have a luminous white glow, no ears, a tiny nose, a small narrow mouth, some have wings.
Skin color from vanilla to very dark brown, possess a mane on the back of the neck and an extremely thin tail, 4 very long fingers, eyes are pale blue or dark brown and much bigger than human eyes.
Male vary in height from 2.31 to 2.64, females from 2.11 to 2.49.
There is no sickness.
They live in crystal domes.
Sleep only a short time once a week.
Are able to time travel.
Have been working with Earth since life first started on this planet.

They have many bases on Earth (many of them inside mountains) and 3 bases on the Moon.
Have bases all over the universe.
Guardians and protectors of higher consciousness in the universe.
Channel: Dr. Norma Milanovich, David K. Miller, Patricia L. Pereira.
→ Athena (starship).
→ Helio-ah, Malantor,Juliano, Palpae, Quaker, Quantra, Quoarts, Tomar.

ARI-AN

Is one of the oldest Reptilian races which descended from dinosaur ancestors in the Orion system.
They created the most powerful empire in this galaxy.
Crop Circles from the Ari-An often have a snake-like form, they are designated to their descendants on Earth that they haven't been forgotten.

ARYANS

"Good" extraterrestrial race.
Tall blond Nordic Humanoids who work with the Greys.
Allegedly invited to work in the Nevada Military Complex.
Also live in the Antarctica.
Have access to UFO type craft, utilize the symbol of the Swastika.
Are presently in conflict with the Greys.
→ Sumerian Empire.

ASVINS

Indians called the Atlanteans Asvins.
Highly technology advanced.

ATAIEN

Race from Epsilon Eridani.
They look like gigantic praying mantises.
They have wings, height over 6 ft, coloring ranges from light grey to gold.

ATLANS

Benevolent humans, descendants of Atlanteans, who are said to inhabit vast and complex cavern cities beneath Southern Brazil and surrounding regions.
Were once part of the Atlantean Empire.

ATLANTEANS

→ Atlans.

AURIGAN DRACOS

→ Year 1997.09.

AVYONIANS

Race of planet Avyon.

BAAWI

A group of extraterrestrials according to Billy Meier.

BELLATRICIANS

Former member of League of Orion.

By-pedal being, upper head surrounded by large bony crest, large red or dull yellow eyes, very small nose, thin lips that ride from one side of head to other, no ears, scaly skin in green, yellow, brown or red color, crest that runs up middle of the back up to top of the head, hand with 6 long, clawed fingers, feet with 5 toes ending in small very sharp claws, very thick small tail which extends to the feet.

Males vary in height from 2.44 to 3 m, females from 2.60 to 3.12 m.

BERNARIANS

Inhabitants of the Bernard's Star System.

Human beings along with the Orange control this star system.

BETELGEUSIANS

They live in spiritual form.

They manifest on Earth as beautiful humans with blond hair, gold colored skin.

BIAVIIANS

Extraterrestrial race. Was in contact with Riley Martin. One of their motherships was stationed close to Saturn. They have been here on Earth since before Atlantis.

Beings: Nela, O-Nee-Sayer-Wann Nela, O-Qua Tangin Wann Tan, Tan.

BIGFOOT

The Bigfoot and the Yeti are not the same.

They are of average intelligence and peaceful by nature. The Sasquatch are interdimensional & psychic, they can slip into an invisible state.

BIRDLIKE LYRANS

Very different from humanoid, very thin, birdlike. Are very cool & intellectual.

Scientists, explorers, philosophers.

They were in the Indus Valley.

BIRDMEN

→ Mothmen.

BLONDE NORDIC HUMANOIDS

→ Nordics.

BLUES

Star warriors.

Optical similar to the Grays.

Apparently they have translucent skin, large almond shaped eyes and are small of stature.

In Florida arrived, offered advice, not to deal with the Greys, it would only lead to disaster, the military said no deal!

BLONDS	Tall Telosian Blonds, who have been known to have some connection with the underground networks of Nevada and the South-West. → Telos
BOOTEANS	Reptilian race from the Bootes System. These and the Alpha Draconians are allegedly involved with the Dulce scenario.
BURROWERS	Mutation of Saurian or Serpent race that is capable of burrowing through the Earth.
CAPELLAN DRACOS	→ Year 1997.09.
CAPELLANS	Formerly independent bluish-skinned Reptiloids. Female dominated warrior society who were drawn under Draconian domination after the Greys approached them a few centuries ago claiming to be fleeing from Draco overlords, asking the Capellans for help. But in reality the deceitful Greys were working fully for the Dracos and used the Capellans collaboration to betray and conquer them. In recent times they liberated themselves and joined the Federation of Worlds in their efforts to blockade the Solar System from Draconian interventionists.
CARIANS	"Bird People". Parent Race of the Reptilians. Humans with eagle-like features & colorings. The Founders gave the Carians a new planet in the Orion Constellation. The Carians were a more evolved race than the Felines for a long time. Like the Felines they were etheric. They can be 12 ft tall or only a few inches in height. They began genetic crossing with certain reptiles, the result was a new hybrid race known to us as the Draconians, they were part Carian and part reptile. The Carians are known for their sharp analytical abilities and organizational skills. They have the most advanced starships in the universe.
CASSIOPAEANS	They live in omnipresence (in all realms).
CATLIKE LYRANS	Catlike nose, gentle & small mouth, large & catlike eyes with a second lid.

CENTAURIANS

Allegedly have bases in the Maldives Islands.
Humanoid Centaurians:
Very similar to Earth people.
Very muscular with blonde, brown, black or red hair, eyes Asian in shape or rounded and are brown, black, blue, green or hazel in color, skin color dark brown or slightly tanned white color.
Males vary in height from 1.80 to 2.40, females from 1.65 to 2.10 m.

Reptoid Centaurians:
Very scaly, lizard-like, muscular body, skin color is green/blue or red/green, hands contain 6 digits which end in razor sharp claws, eyes are rounded with a vertical slit and are bright red or golden, no tail, feet have 5 long toes ending in razor sharp claws, about 2.40 m tall.

CENTRAL RACE

Are the creators of all human races in the universe.
They create planets and star systems.

CETACEANS

Mermaids, mermen, porpoises, whales.
They have finger & toe bones in their fins. They have a rudimentary humanoid skeleton that has been adapted for their Earth environment.
They are positive spiritual beings.
Also known as:
>>   Dolphin Race,
>>   Dolphins.
→ Sirians.

CETIANS

→ Tau Cetians.

CHANEQUES

Veracruz, Mexico.
Mexican gnomes or interplanetary visitors.
Diminutive mutation of the human family?
Height about 2 feet, light brown complexion, black hair.
Ability to appear suddenly before the viewer's eyes.
They are like small children.

CHANGELINGS

Other name of the Shapeshifter.

CHUPACABRAS	"Goatsuckers".

4 to 5 ft tall, small tan colored, glowing red eyes (large slanted?), small holes for a nostril, small slit-like lipless mouth, no visible ears, on the oval head which has an elongated jaw sit 3 large horns, two small arms, clawed hands with three fingers, two long hind legs with 3 claws, no tail, fine grey fur with dark spots, spine-like appendages running from the top of the head down to the bottom of their backbone, the spines are said to be phosphorescent and multicolored, they may have wings.
Said to give up a strange ammonia smell.
First seen in Brazil, but many sightings in Central America.

CIAKARS

Royal reptilian race of the Alpha Draconians from Rigel in Orion.
They apparently were brought by someone to our time & space, and dumped here.
They range from 14 to 22 ft tall & can weigh up to 1,800 pounds.
They have wings and a very long tail.
They life 4,100 years.
The most are Service-to-Self.
They state that our solar system belongs to them.
They are a different race than the Alpha Draconians.
Their genetics have been kept totally intact.
There are approx. 20 of the royal Draconian line in the planet at this time, an underground facility was apparently built for them in Madagascar.
→ Asaru.
→ Alpha Draconians, Mothmen.

CORTEUM

Alien race that works with the ACIO.
According to Dr. Anderson, the Corteum are benevolent.
Most ACIO personnel were unaware of their existence.
→ ACIO.

COUNTERFEIT RACE

→ Controllers.

CRYSTAL PEOPLE

Race on planet Ishna in the (White) Sirius System evacuated the Paschats from their dying (Yellow) Sirius star system.
Is an intellectual, cerebral and creative race, which is highly ingenious.
Their bodies are of crystalline substance, very light, fine and fragile.   They are egg breeder, all children are twins. They are very beautiful people.

CYAKARS

→ Ciakars.

DALS   Race of Nordic types who come from the DAL
                              universe, they are a brand of the Lyrans.
                              They are helping the Pleiadians.
                              The "brown Greys".
                              → Greys.

DARK LORDS   Evil, manipulative beings.
                              Also known as satanic beings.

DARKER-SKINNED LYRANS
                              More rare. Caucasian in feature, light chocolate skin,
                              brown eyes, some have green eyes, dark brown hair.
                              Influenced the area of Pakistan, India.

DELPHOHIMS   Other name of the Greys.
                              Partner of the Collective.
                              → Collective, Greys.

DERO   Demonic group of Skymen?
                              They've good guys and bad guys in the cavern.
                              Subterranean dwellers.
                              → Controllers.

D'NAAR   Very dark race from Orion.

DINOIDS   From the Bellatrix System in the Orion Constellation.
                              Very similar to Humans, 7 to 10 ft tall, various skin
                              colors.
                              Came to Earth approx. 26,000,000 B.C.E.

DJINN   → Jinn.

DOLPHIN RACE   Cetaceans.

DOLPHINS   Are a very old race.

DORIANS   Extraterrestrial race who was in contact with Riley
                              Martin.

DOWS   The white Greys.
                              Genetically engineered race with an Insectoid genetic
                              base, assimilated Reptilian DNA and other types of
                              DNA.
                              They have large heads, thin bodies, grey-white skin.
                              Serve the Dracos.
                              Are in war since several generations with the Tau
                              Cetians.
                              → Greys, Tau Cetians.

DRAC-ORANGE   (No soul-energy matrix).
                              Live below Nevada Military Complex.

DRACO MOTHMEN   → Mothmen.

DRACO-REPTILIANS   → Draconians, Dracos, Shapeshifter.

DRACONIANS   Hybrid race created by the Carians.
Sub race of the Ciakars.
Oldest reptilian race in this universe, their forefathers came from an other universe.
Soulless entities.
Cold-blooded beings that prefer the warm climates.
They have conquered many star systems and have genetically altered many of the life forms.
Royal line of the Reptilians.
The highest order of the Draco caste is the white skinned Draco beings.
They have wings, made of long thin bony spines or ribs that protrude out of their backs, the ribs are adjoined by flaps of leathery blackish-brown skin, whereas the Reptoids do not have wings.
Some of the Dracos have conical horns that develop midway between the brow and the top of the skull and are blunt at the tips.
Their upper torsos are extremely lean and their neck muscles splay out from the base of their jaw to their shoulder blades. Usually 7 to 12 ft tall.
Average life span from 1,800 to 4,100 years.
The area most densely populated with Draconian sub-races is the Orion system & systems in Rigel & Capella.
The major Draconian base is in New Mexico.
They don't like the Human beings.
Not all of them are bad.
They can literally create a solar system, they can move planets and take moons and put them wherever they want.
→ Alpha Draconians.

DRACOS   They had come from Capella in the constellation Auriga.
Dracos are the hybrids created by the white Nordics.
Dracos are a genetic mixture of white Nordics and alligators, they were originally created as military warriors to protect Atlantis and Earth from other aliens as well to explore parallel dimensions.
Are subservient to the Orion Greys, even though they have greater military power & greater force.
Have two hearts, (*15 – 22 ft tall*), strength of 8 to 16 men, have no compassion.
8 ft tall, *soulless entities.*
Were once the most feared warriors in this part of the universe.
They particularly like eating human children (tens of thousands from NY alone).
→ Lucifer.

→ Year 1997.09.
→ Rigel.
→ Draconians, Mothmen, Reptiloids.

DRACS   Also called Draconians.
                             → Arimanius.
                             → Draconians.

DRAGONWORMS   Subterranean creatures, allegedly very intelligent.

EATA   One of the four old races on Sirius' old Yellow sun
                             system, before it collapsed.
                             The Eata were very strong physically. They have a
                             mixture of colors and striped people.
                             → Paschats.

EBAN   The larger Greys call themselves Eban.
                             They have two brains that are not connected.

EEKENESE   Inner-Earth race, resemble a blending of human and
                             insect and are very trustworthy.

ELOHIM   The rulers of the Annunaki call themselves Elohim.
                             The word"Elohim" is the plural of God & Goddesses.
                             The Elohim are the humans who came from the
                             Collective and created the Earth humans (Adamu) by
                             genetically altering the pre-humans.
                             Elohims are: Marduk, Tiamat.
                             → Collective.
                             → Jesus.
                             → Ascended Master.

EPSILON ERIDANIANS   → Eridanians.

EPSILON ERIDANIS   → Eridanians.

ERIDANIANS   From Epsilon Eridani.

ERRANIANS   Inhabitants of planet Erra in the Plejaren System.
                             → Erra.

ESTEKNAS   Intraterrestrial race, part of the Cosmic White
                             Brotherhood.
                             → Great White Brotherhood.

ETHERIC SIRIANS

The Etheric Sirians are the soul group that were given Earth as their new home when their former home planet Sirius B imploded.

Many of the Etheric Sirians in aquatic forms are beaching themselves. They are returning to the Nommos home world for training on being in a human body for returning to Earth as land guardians.

The majority of Etheric Sirians are found among the black, red & brown races of Earth.

→ Nommos, Sirians.

EVE-ORANGE

(Soul-energy matrix).
Live below the Nevada Military Complex.

EXTRATERRESTRIALS

→ Aliens.

FELINES

"The Lion People".

The Felines are one of the two primary races in our universe.

Parent Race of the Humans.

Bi-pedal race that stand 12 to 16 ft tall, skin is covered by a sort of soft fuzz, they do have manes, males and females have long hair, eye color ranges from blue to gold, golden brown color to white.

As part of the Universal Game the Founders gave the Felines a new planet in the Lyra Constellation, the Felines named it Avyon, when the Felines arrived, they were in etheric form.

After numerous crossings and genetic updates, the Adamic Human was made.

FOMALHAUTANS

Humanoids:

Human rebel group from the Pleiades that colonized Fomalhaut 250,000 years ago and are now found on Fomalhaut's 3rd & 4th planets.

Muscular Nordic type, usually blonde with very blue, hazel or steel-grey eyes.

Males are about 1.85 m tall, females are very buxom and from 1.68 to 1.83 m tall.

There is a second type which is dark skinned with dark hair and brown, gray or black eyes.

Reptoids:

Smaller dinoid-reptoid hybrid groups from Bellatrix in Orion that colonized the second planet some 200,000 years ago.

Very scaly & bony, upper head is surrounded by large bony crest, large red or dull yellow eyes, very small nose, thin lips that run from one side of head to other, no ears, green, yellow, brown or red colored skin, small crest runs up middle of back up to top of the head, bi-pedal, 6 long fingers ending in very sharp claws, very small tail extends to feet.

Males vary from 2.44 to 3 m, females from 2.60 to 3.12 m.

GARGOYLES   Is there a connection to the Reptilians?

GIZANS   There is allegedly a huge cavern beneath Egypt which is inhabited by people with close ties with the Secret Government.

The Giza (Gizeh) people may be under Reptilian control.

GIZAHNS   → Gizans.

GRAYS   → Greys.

GREENS   Humans with an olive-green skin color.

They claim to be from the subterranean realms beneath Europe, called St. Martin's Land.

GREYS   There are many different kinds of grey beings. There are many variations in size and color.

They are genetic engineers.

Mercenaries are experts in psychic warfare, infiltration and manipulation.

They were no more than 30,000,000 people.

There are over 18,000 Greys living on Mars (underground and on the surface).

Silvery grey colored people are benign and call themselves Zetas, dull brownish grey people are bad.

The short Greys (3 to 5 ft) are mercenaries of the taller (from Orion) are about 7 to 8 ft tall.

Reticulans are about 4.5 ft tall.

Greys from Bellatrix are about 3.5 ft tall.

Greys from Orion range in height from 6 to 9 ft.

Zeta Reticulans are only 4 % of the ETs around the Earth & the solar system.

Many of them are androids.

They clone themselves because they are unable to sexually reproduce.

Communicate telepathically. Emotionless beings.

Have a slit for a mouth, nose and ears are indentations, webbed hands with 4 fingers, large head, thin body.

Their huge black eyes receive also infrared and ultraviolet light.

5th density beings have no body, 4th density Greys can transit between 3rd & 4th density.

Some of them are loving spiritual beings, most of them aren't!

Their symbol is the equilateral triangle.

Signed treaty with president Eisenhower.

Gave the US government 9 crafts which duplicated & created 53 crafts.

Today over 25,000,000 citizens have been contacted/abducted. At least one in every 40 Americans have been implanted with alien devices that are used to control/protect them.

By 1989, over 3,000,000 Greys were occupying these deep multilevel underground complexes.

Level 7 at Dulce is called "Nightmare Hall".

The Hubble Space Telescope was created to keep a watchful eye on the invasion fleet.

There are only 2,000 real Greys left, all the rest are clones (organic robots).

The Greys are responsible for Fatima, where the Virgin Mary supposedly spoke to the children: All the people there were implanted by the Greys.

→ Kolta, Krill.

→ Dals, Delphohims, Dows, Grays, Little Greys, Orion Greys, Reptilian Crossbreeds, Reticulans, Rigelians, Tall Greys, Zeta Reticulans, Zetas.

→ Controllers.

→ Bellatrix, Orion, Phobos.

→ Year 1931.

HAV-MUSUVS

→ Suvians.

HOOVIDS

They are reputed to be bringers of healing and enlightenment, and to be the original designers of the universe.

HUBRIDS

Reptilian/Human hybrids possessing a human soul-matrix.

HUMANS

Earth is the only planet in the Solar System which has humanoid inhabitants. There was a human form on Mars long ago.

A soul can be removed from humans in about 4 seconds.

→ Earth.

HYADEANS

Refugees in the Hyades (Taurus Constellation) from the ancient Lyran wars.

HYBRIDS

34,000,000 hybrid kids are "made" by the Grays, they live in space ships (space stations?).

Type1: >> *almost reptilian:*

Made of Human egg and sperm and Alien genetics (Grey). Possess no soul matrix, look like Greys, black eyes, no white in eyeball, slit vertical pupils, small body, legs, arms, tiny mouth, no hair, four fingers, greenish fluid instead of blood, internal reproductive organs, no external sexual organs, they eat through the skin.

Type2: >>   *more reptilian*:
Made of Human egg and sperm and Hybrid genetic material type 1. Possess no soul matrix, very similar to the Greys, little amount of white in eyeball, thin hair, lean body, four fingers, clearly bigger than type 1, no external sexual organs.

Type3: >>   *more humanoid*:
Made of Human egg and sperm and Hybrid genetic material type 2. Similar to Earth Humans, black eyes, sometimes missing eyebrows and eyelashes.

Type4: >>   *almost humanoid*:
Nordic type. Made of Human egg and sperm and Hybrid genetic material type 3. Eyes normally looking, round, but bigger pupils, five fingers, seldom body hair, crimson blood, full normal external reproductive organs. Have mental abilities of the Greys.

All hybrids are sterile and unable to reproduce, however, have well-developed digestive systems. Appearance of human children with usually large heads and eyes, fine sparse hair.

IARGANS   → Jargans.

IGIGIS   → Zetas.

IGUANOIDS   Approx. 4 to 5 ft. tall, humanoid appearance with iguana-like parts.
Have been reported to be extremely dangerous. They are utilizing black witchcraft, sorcery and other forms of mind control against their enemies.

IKELS   Small hairy humanoids with cloven hoofs inhabiting caverns beneath South America.
They have been known to kidnap women and children through the ages.

INEXTRIANS   From the star Mirach in the Andromeda system.

INSECTILLIANS   They are known as scientists.

JANOSIAN   Their ancestors lived on Earth thousands of years ago.
They are like Earth humans, somewhat oriental and slender.
They came back to Earth seeking contact with Earth governments to exchange technology for a place to live.

JARGANS   A very silent and peaceful race from Iarga.
Technologically developed 3rd dimensional beings.
Similar to Earth humans, but taller and very stocky.
They make very little contact with Earth Humans.

JINN

The Jinn from the Inner Earth are manipulating the surface population. They dwell on a parallel level and normally are invisible to us. They are able to materialize and disappear at will.
They are not immortal.
Also known as:
>>   Djinn,
>>   Genie,
>>   Jinni.

JINNI

→ Jinn.

JUPITERIANS

Has the oldest native race in the Solar System and is known as Adamic Race.
They have a gold-colored complexion.
The people are present in the physical and the etheric dimension.
There's a reptile species:
Kangaroo like with pointed scales down the back & tail, 2 arms folded upward like a praying mantis, long thin hands, claws, 3 slightly webbed slender fingers with curving nails, opposing thumb near the wrist, long brain capacity.
They live in modern space colonies.
They have bases on many planets and satellites in the Solar System.

KANTARIANS

Interdimensional beings from Sirius.

KARIDEL

One of the four old races on Sirius' old Yellow sun system, before it collapsed.
The Karidel were rulers and philosophers. Fawn colored with bright blue eyes.
→ Paschats.

KOGI

Primarily etherical physical beings.

KOLDASIANS

Look like Earth humans.
They were involved in the South Africa case around 1960 and have allegedly a base there.
Were involved in Operation Fireball.
Negative aliens recently invaded their territory in an interplanetary war.
→ Carl Vlierden.

KORENDIANS

Humans living on the colonized planet Korender.
4 to 5 ft tall (or 3 to 4 ft tall?), look exactly like Earth humans.
They have a large underground facility in Massachusetts.
They have an alliance with the Arcturians.
→ Bob Renaud.

KRYONS
Inner-Earth race, average height 8 to 10 ft, white skin, blue eyes, some have blond hair, most have white hair. They are slender, intelligent, telepathic.

KUMARAS
The Kumaras are an extremely ancient and vast soul lineage that originated outside of this local universe. They were among the first souls to occupy a humanoid form which was reptilian. This was before the creation of humans. The Kumaras have engineered many forms of life. The planet Venus isn't their only home, but simply one of the countless bases throughout the omniverse.
The Kumaras founded the Galactic Federation.
The Kumaras are like Warrior-Priests.
→ YaPool.

LEMURIANS
Commonly described as graceful, at least 7 ft tall, long flowing hair, long slender necks, a walnut sized organ that protrudes from the center of their foreheads, some of them have the third eye open. They dress in white robes and sandals. It's said that they possess the ability to disappear at will.
There have been stories from credible witnesses who insist the Lemurians have the power of invisibility.

LIQUIDIANS
They can shapeshift easily.
Also known as Liquids.
→ Nibiru.

LIQUIDS
→ Liquidians.

LITTLE GREYS
→ Greys.

LIZARDS
Sub race of the Reptilians.
Also known as Lizzies.

LIZZIES
→ Lizards.

LULUS
Primitive worker-race, created 250,000 B.C.E.
→ Ninhursag.

LYRAENS
→ Lyrans.

LYRAN GIANTS
Caucasian in type, exist in the 3rd and 4th dim.
Light skin, eyes, hair, muscular body, 6 - 9 ft tall.

LYRAN HUMANS
The portion of the Lyran Humans from a planet that orbited Sirius B chose to remain incarnated instead to ascend to etheric form.

LYRAN REDHEADS
Red hair to strawberry blonde, very fair skin tone, green eye color.

LYRANS

They are 3rd and 4th dimensional beings.
Eyes are accentuated.
Ancestors are creators of Earth people.
Are the forefathers of the Zeta Reticulis (Greys).
They destroyed them several times.
They've now reached a higher level of spirit.
Had larger eyes than the Earth humans.
Races: Birdlike Lyrans, Catlike Lyrans, Darker-Skinned Lyrans, Lyran Giants, Lyran Redheads.
Some incarnate into human form on Earth.
The most common symbols they use were of birds & of cats.
Inhabitants: Alena, Talida.
Allegedly have bases below Egypt.
→ Sirians.
Race from the former planet Maldek.
→ Maldek.

MALDEKIANS

Former inhabitants of the destroyed planet Maldek.

MARTIANS

There was living a humanoid race about 77,000 B.C.E. They were banished to another part of the universe because of misuse of energy.
Their average life span was 2,500 years and they procreated no more than three times.

MAYANS

Inner-Earth race, short in stature, look like Mexicans.

MINTAKANS

Formerly part of the Orion League.
Primarily Amphitoid species, plus a few Reptoid & Dinoid hybrids.
Froglike, mainly bi-pedal, skin smooth and hairless with iridescent colors in bright reds, oranges, yellows or browns, eyes are quite large, wraparound and bright red, orange or greenish yellow in color, nose consists of 2 small slits, very thin lips, very large mouth and frog-like, ears are 2 small round circles, large head, neck seems non-existent, very muscular body, arms and legs, 4 long thin toes are webbed, toes have small claws.

Males vary from 2.13 to 2.44 m, females from 2.29 to 2.59.

MORONTIA

Extraterrestrial race.
→ Michael Odell.

MOTHMEN

Dark nocturnal aliens, 8 ft tall, humanoids with bat-like wings.

Very intelligent and extremely malignant.

Also called:

>> Birdmen,

>> Ciakars,

>> Pteroids,

>> Winged Dracos.

They have been encountered in several underground bases:

>> Dulce, New Mexico,

>> Montauk Point, Long Island,

>> Point Pleasant, West Virginia.

→ Draconians.

MUONS

Race from planet Myton in the Pleiades.

MUSHABA

Dark skinned race from planet Mushaba in the Alcyone Star System in the Pleiades. They exist simultaneously on the 3rd and 5th dimension.

NAGAS

Very advanced Serpent/Reptilian race, with a Humanoid form, about 7 to 8 ft tall, of various colors, oftentimes scaled skin.

Children of goddess Kadru.

A reptilian race based in Antarctica lost a battle against a race from the Gobi region and were driven into underground.

Have a major base or lair beneath the mountains adjacent to Lake Manosowar in Tibet.

The Nagas have an affinity with water.

→ Serpents.

→ Snakeworld.

→ Agartha, Patala.

NEPHILIM

The fallen angels of Lucifer.

NEPTUNIANS

The native race has evolved to the etheric state, living in the planets atmosphere.

They create physical art forms which are known throughout many galaxies.

Whenever they want they can materialize a physical body.

NIBIRIANS

→ Nibiruans.

NIBIRUANS

Are from Nibiru.

They are a reptilian-human hybrid race.

They disguised themselves as bird-humans, fish-humans, lion-humans,...

Controlled the Sumerian Empire.

The Great Flood was an attempt to destroy the slave races y the Nibiruans, because they have rebelled against their gods.

The Hebrews are descendants of the Nibiruans.

Also known as Nibiruans.

NOBOA

Civilization from the 5th dimension of Sirius.

NOMMOS

Race on a planet in the Sirius star system.

They are known for their highly advanced use of sound.

Play an important role in the Earth's evolution.

Race of beings that takes the physical form of dolphins, whales, mermaids, mermen on planet Earth.

→ Etheric Sirians, Sirians.

NORDICS

Humanoid race from the Pleiades.

Home planet is Altaira from star system Altair.

5 to 6.5 ft tall, blonde hair, pale white skin. More muscular and taller than the average human, males and females.

Communicate telepathically.

→ Nors.

→ Procyon, Rigel.

NORS

Are the Nordics?

Elder race. Etheric mortal beings that can change to any life form on Earth.

They live in several solar systems and have bases and colonies on Mars, Venus and the Moon.

Member: Borealis.

NYPTONIANS

Extraterrestrial race who was in contact with Riley Martin.

OGATTANS

Short humanoid bird-like species, extremely friendly and spiritually oriented from a planet of prismatic domed communities of crystalline material surrounded by crystal forests emanating rainbow colored auras.

They are said to be helping small numbers of Earth humans with divine guidance.

They have taken many small children to their home planet for schooling.

There was a contact with them in North Carolina.

OLD ONES

An ancient humanoid race that populated the surface world millions of years ago and then moved underground. An immensely scientifically advanced race. Extremely long-living people.

OOGONS

They claim to have been around at the time of the last"Big Bang".

ORANGE

Hybrid type of alien of humanoid form and possess reptilian characteristics yet with human-like reproductive organs and capable of breeding with human beings.
Head very large, brain has 4 lobes, eyes big and dark with no iris and whites, hands and feet with 6 digits, digestive system sponge like.
They oftentimes have been described as having course yellow, orange or reddish hair that stands upright in stalk-like fashion.
Live below Nevada Military Complex.

ORBS

They appear as spherical energy patterns, glowing balls of light in a rainbow of colors.
They live in collectives.

ORION GREYS

Hold control over the Draconians & the Zeta Reptilians.
Have the economic & political control.
A huge underground city, built by negative aliens from Orion exists beneath Iraq.
→ Greys.
→ Orion Empire.

ORION HUMANS

They left Sirius B and traveled to a planet in the Orion constellation to make a new home.
Sanat Kumara was/is the leader of the Orion Humans.
→ Ascended Masters, Sanat Kumara.

ORIONS

4th and 5th dimensional beings.
There are two distinctly different races:
>>   Reptilian race from the Rigel star system (they are not the Lizards).
→ Orion Greys, Rigelians.
>>   Shapeshifter race.
They are not Reptilian and hate all Reptilian races for aeons.
They are masters at Black Magic and mind control.
→ Orion Humans.
The Orion civilization is primarily 89% Vegan in nature, 75% is of the human type, 11% are of a Lyran stock.
The ones with very sharp blue eyes are priests.
The Greys make up the Orion Empire.
Dominated Asia, Germany.

OROTHETA

One of the four old races on Sirius' old Yellow sun system, before it collapsed.
The Orotheta were protectors and warriors. They have orange eyes.
→ Paschats.

PAA TALS

The Paa Tal created life forms that could evolve on their own, with free expression, not like the Draconians.
"Paa Tal" is a Draconian word.

PAETRI

One of the four old races on Sirius' old Yellow sun system, before it collapsed.
The Paetri were artists and skilled workers. They have white or greyish fur/skin and green eyes.
→ Paschats.

PASCHATS

Old feline race of Sirius includes the races:
Eata, Karidel, Orotheta, Paetri. A cross between cat and lion, but their jaw is less elongated, their ears less round than lions, stand on two tall legs (similar to Earth-human legs), their paws have evolved to more useful shape, they have ails, they have different colors and eyes, they don't speak, they use telepathy, the are all twins.

PEGASIANS

Sirius B Human Colonist:
There is a white skin type and a blue skin type.
Males vary from muscular to child-like bodies, blond to light brown hair, light blue to green colored eyes, from 1.98 to 2.24 m tall.
Females are extremely pale or have light blue skin, are extremely voluptuous in appearance, from 1.88 to 2.03 m tall.
Human type with red or orange skin:
Similar to the first type, skin & hair is light red or dark orange, eyes are more cat-like & iris is either red or dark blue.
This group originally came from some of the more distant stars in the Lyra Constellation.

Hybrid formed from the dinoid & the second Human race:
Scaly skin with pronounced cat-like eyes that are either red, brown or pale yellow, more muscular than a human, 4 thin long fingers or toes with a small claw,
Males vary from 2.13 to 2.44 m, females from 2.08 to 2.31 m.

PELEGAIANS

(Avyons) Race on starship Pelegai.

PLEIADIANS 3rd, 4th or 5th dimensional beings.

Their civilization is over 100,000 years old. They came from the Old Universe.

Some of them are ancestrally Altairians.

Are primarily vegetarians, average age 700 years, whiter and smoother skin than Earth humans.

Pleiadians don't have blood.

Children are educated 60 to 70 years.

They call their spacecrafts beam ships.

They have been involved in our solar system for a long time and are still active.

They used symbols at times which are birds or winged figures, symbol of the seven stars.

Are from Alcyone, Taygeta.

There are many different types of Pleiadian races.

It doesn't mean that they are here to help us.

Sponsored the Hebrews.

Races:

>> 1.   tall, straw blonde hair, hands have 6 digits, their eyes have a yellow striated iris & copper pupil, skin is translucent ash pale with a hint of pink in the lips.

They are loving & benign of nature.

They wear silvery robes and a sash decorated with hieroglyphs.

>> 2.   orange skin, amber-gold eyes, streaked blonde hair, slim athletic built, very tall (male at least 6, 5 ft), have a hypnotic gaze.

Maybe they are time traveler from the 35th century?

>> 3.   the more commonly seen Pleiadians are almost white haired, intense blue eyes, bronze tan complexion, between 6,5 & 7 ft tall, long ear lobes, ears are somewhat lower than Earth human ears.

Sometimes called Tall Blondes or Nordics.

Wear deep blue one-piece jumpsuits / flight suits.

They also have taken Earth children without permission.

Part of the Andromedan Council.

They were involved in the 3rd Golden Age of Egypt attempting to end the worship of the many Nibiruan and Sirian gods with the one-god concept.

Interacted with the ancient Hawaiians.

Also known as Plejarans.

Known Pleiadians: Mira, Semjase.

Channel Barbara J. Marciniak, Lia Shapiro.

→ Pelghi, Pleiades.

→ 196,000 B.C.E., 225,000 B.C.E., 228,000 B.C.E.

PLEJARANS   Other name of the Pleiadians.

PLUSADIANS   → Zeta Reticulians.

PRAYING MANTIS	Race similar to the praying mantis on Earth, ant-like. Huge bulging eyes like an ant located on the head's side. Some fly-like hairs which are stiff, blacky-brown, straight and brittle. No chest. Long, frail, gangly-like arms. Tall like a human but not human-like, drab colored. There is a similar looking race which is called by some people "Walking Sticks". → Mars. → Croesus. → Ataien, Jupiterians.
PRE-CETACEAN	Race who lived on land on planet Earth, 8,000,000 B.C.E. Ancestors of the Whales and Dolphins.
PROCYONANS	<u>Pure Lyran-Sirian Humanoid:</u> Blue or white skinned and look like Earth humans, eyes are much larger and have a color of blue, green or brown, smaller ears, brain is larger, males vary from 1.98 to 2.24 m, females are well proportioned, from 1.93 to 2.13 m. <u>Amphitoid-Reptoid Hybrid:</u> Green, brown or blue-colored scaly skin, lizard-like body, bulgy brown, yellow or red eyes, very thin nose with small slit-like nostrils, eyes can move independently for each other, oval ears, mouth is a thin slit that runs from ear to ear, almost round head, small neck, very muscular body, 4 thin nail-less fingers, 3 long toes with long sharp claws, very small tail, males vary from 2.13 to 2.34 m, (larger) females from 2.13 to 2.44 m.
PSHAAT	Race in Sirius A. Highly sentient beings who, in size and appearance, closely resemble the African lion and dwell only on two inner water planets.
PTEROIDS	→ Mothmen.
RED DRACS	Reside in Sirius B.
REPTILES	→ Reptilians.

REPTILIAN CROSSBREEDS

There are many other various reptilian physical types that have been encountered through the ages.

>>   Grey-Crossbreeds:

4 to 4.5 ft tall, oversized craniums, large black eyes with vertical slit pupils, thin torsos, arms, legs.

They have 3 or 4 fingers, short claws or no claws, short and stubby feet with no toes.

>>   Greenish-Tanned Crossbreed:

Greenish-tan skin, large almond shaped eyes that are golden in color with a dark, metallic green vertical slit pupil.

Have same physical construct as a Grey.

REPTILIANS

Over 7 billion years old.

The Dragon, Snake and Lizard People.

The Reptilians are the creation of their parent race, the Carians.

The Reptilians are second class genetic mixture between the White Dracos and alligators.

They evolved on a planet in the Alpha Draconi star system of the Orion Constellation.

The royal line of Reptilians are the Draconians, the winged dragons.

The Reptiles have two other sub races, known as the Winged Serpents (Snakes) and the Lizards (Lizzies).

The Reptilians are less emotional than the Humans, they have a highly knowledge of universal physics and laws.

The Reptilians are responsible for the Mystery Schools on Earth.

The Reptilians represent the Dark in the Polarity Integration Game while the Humans represent the Light. (Sauroid races) don't have soul-energy matrix.

No true hybrid can exist between the sauroid and human races.

Reptilian races fighting for control.

They have taken over millions of worlds in the Local Cluster of Galaxies, there are only some hundred worlds left that are free from their control.

Reptilians rape Earth-people.

They maintain bases on Venus and on some of the moons of the outer planets.

General description: Body size from 4 to 8 ft. They have no hair, rough textured skin almost like scales, large eyes, slit-like pupils, for a nose nostrils, shell-like ears (can hear a wider range than humans), very small mouth, three, four or six lizard-like fingers. Most have separate sexes, they bear eggs.

6 to 7 ft tall, greenish to brownish in color, claw like four-fingered webbed hands, faces are a cross between a human and a snake with a central ridge coming down

from the top of the head to the snout, eyes have vertical slits in their pupils and golden irises.

They are all cold-blooded, they have no sweat glands, they have 3 fingers with an opposing thumb, eyes are catlike & large, they have teeth, they are mostly meat eaters.

They are high-testosterone beings without any feminine characteristics.

They don't possess a soul-matrix.

Some Reptilians eat humans like we eat chicken.

They have insignias of a Flying Serpent.

There are over 1833 reptilians living in our planet (1998).

→ An, Belsazar, Sansiruous, Senayaga.

→ Aquillians, Arcathians, Gargoyles, Reptilian Crossbreeds.

→ Alcyone, Moon of Earth.

REPTILOIDS

→ Reptilians.

REPTOIDS

From the Sagittarius Constellation.

Came to Earth 26,000,000 B.C.E.

From 5,5 to 9 (7 – 10?) ft tall, powerful arms and legs, large tail, long arms with three long fingers and an opposable thumb, the claw are short & blunt, they don't have a navel, greenish-brown skin, wide lipless mouth with teeth very similar to Earth reptiles , large black eyes with vertical slit pupils, heads are slightly conical in shape and have two bony ridges riding from their brow toward the back of the head, small flattened nose, no body or facial hair.

More muscular than Dinoids.

→ Reptilians, Zetas.

REPTONS

→ Reptilians.

RETICULANS

Alias of the Greys.

Dying race, the height was reduced from around 7 ft.

Some 40,000 years ago, the Grey have become as we know them today.

The rogue Greys (still 7 ft tall) have survived and formed an alliance with the Illuminati family on Earth, and other alien races.

The benign Reticulans are preparing places on Earth and other planets, to be the homes of their hybrid offspring.

There are 3 main groups of Greys:

Rogue Greys: often hostile.

Appear very robotic, like to manipulate their human subjects through biochip implants.

They are supposed to be responsible for animal mutilations.

Treaties with certain Earth governments.

Skin is dull brownish-grey.

Neutral Greys: often benevolent.
Scientific and very dependant on technology.
Apparently they can detach the soul of a biological life
form and bind it to a machine.
Benign Greys (Zetas):
Love humanity, rely more on consciousness than
technology.
Creators of Essassani and other hybrid colonies.
They are the most advanced in hybridization and have
already established several colonies.
The Reticulans also have a council, called Nebulus.
Color is silvery-grey.
→ Luanda.
→ Greys, Zetas.
→ Essassani.
→ Illuminati, Nebulus.

RIGELIANS

Reptilian race that is different from the Dracos.
The only Reptilian race in Orion.
Small, yellowish-green skin, sometimes grayish.
Almost entirely devoid of emotions.
Have the ability to disintegrate matter to energy.
They use telepathic hypnosis in abductions.
They are not connected to the Illuminati.
→ Greys, Orion Greys, Orions.

Root Races

1st Polarian:
The only continent was on the North Pole.
Totally sexless, immortal.
People from Imperishable Sacred Land.
2nd Hyperborean:
The 1st & 2nd root race were not completely
physical.
→ Hybornea, Hyperborea.
3rd Lemuria:
First race physicalized.
Original name was"Land of Shalmali".
→ Lemuria.
4th Atlantis:
→ Atlantis.
5th Aryan:
Has been in existence for over a million years.
Homo Sapiens.
Sub races:

1st	60,000 B.C.E.	Hindu
2nd	40,000 B.C.E.	Arabian
3rd	30,000 B.C.E.	Iranian
4th	20,000 B.C.E.	Celtic
5th	20,000 B.C.E.	Teutonic
6th		will emerge in America
7th		will emerge in a new
		continent in the Pacific.

6th Meruvian:
Is just beginning.
People of New Lemuria.
Muvarians and descendants of the present human races live in Zeta ruled society controlled by frequency fence and Holographic Insert Technology.
In 1986 Zetas began losing control over their future human populations.
→ Year 1986.
7th Paradisian:
Tara is the name of the new continent that hasn't emerged yet.
A race of super beings.

RUTILIAS

Zeta-Draco hybrids.

SANTINIANS

4th and 5th dimensional beings.
Race from Alpha Centauri, home planet is Metharia.
Member of the Ashtar Command.
Member of the Interplanetary Federation.
Incidentally maintain bases on Venus.

SASQUATCH

Large hairy humanoids, 6 to 9 ft tall.
They have the ability to spontaneously induce invisibility through producing an electromagnetic psychic shield around themselves.
They come from Uranus.

SATURNIANS

The native have a balanced mentality.
A transparent green etherical energy form has visited Earth.

SAURIANS

→ Burrowers.

SAUROIDS

→ Reptilians.

SEEDERS

They exist outside of time.
They created many races of the same genetic blueprint:
>>   Annunaki,
>>   Earth humans (Terrans).

SEMITICS

Humanoid race.

SERPENT CULT

The Illuminati and the Serpent Race.

SERPENT RACE

→ Burrowers, Reptilians.

SHAPESHIFTER

The majority of shapeshifters are female.

All have a long tongue with hair-like protrusions, claws, scales, a tail, large round eyes, eye color is beige, yellow, yellow-green with a black vertical slit for a pupil. Some have wings.

Draco-Reptilians in disguise.

→ Draco-Reptilians, Illuminati, Reptilians.

SHETIS

Inner-Earth Reptilian (Lizard) race at the time of Ninhursag.

Used mind-control and programming techniques to control the Apa-Mus race on Earth.

SIRIANS

4th and 5th dimensional beings.

Sirian souls come in many fashions, most as dolphins & whales (Cetaceans). Sirians are spiritual warriors and strong connected to life forms of dolphins & whales.

Primary genetics of Sirius is of Vegan stock.

They took a lot of Lyran qualities.

They were interbreeding with the Lyrans and got so mixed that the only way to denote a Sirian would be through their belief structure rather than their physical appearance.

The ultimate attempt was to join the royal houses of Sirius and Lyra.

Sirians were of Vegan heritage.

Taller than Earth humans, larger brains, live much longer than Earth humans, very light brown to very dark brown skin, very pronounced eyes, large slightly angled eyes.

They can see inside of an object, have telepathic & psychic abilities.

Sirians are on many different levels, mostly existing in the Light realms.

Sirius was in power in Egypt and controlled Meso-America.

Allegedly have bases below Egypt.

The Sirian control over the Roman Empire was immense.

Peru has been territory of the Sirians & the Lyrans.

They are working with the Japanese.

Usually they used symbols of serpents & dogs.

The Sirian Masters from the White Lodge established:

>> the mystery schools,

>> Knights of Templar,

>> Masons,

>> Teutonic Knights,

>> and much more.

Member of the Galactic Federation.

The Sirian have waged war in the past with the Orion Empire (Unholy Six / Reptilian star systems).

The dispute between the Sirians and Orion Reptiloids dates back to the ancient invasion of Orion by the Draconian Empire, where many Nordics escaped to Procyon, Sirius, Sol System.
→ Senayaga.
→ Etheric Sirians, Nommos.

From Sirius A:
Great Lion Beings, 7 to 8 ft high, smart.
They look very humanoid but are covered with cat-like fur.
Have played an important part in our history.

From Sirius B's 3rd planet:
There lives the race of the Akonowai.
They call the Creator by Ja Ta.

SNAKES → Winged Serpents.

SOLARIANS Human residents of the Solar System.

SOULLESS ONES → Controllers.

STAGYIANS Extraterrestrial race who was in contact with Riley Martin.

SUERNIS Race of Atlantis who incarnated as the Israelites.

SUVIANS Live in vast underground cities beneath the Panamint Mountains of California.
This huge facility is now operating as a major Galactic Federation base on Earth.
Established interstellar travel, exploration and colonization.

TALL GREYS → Greys.

TALL WHITES Race from near Arcturus.
Humanoid features, 6 ft tall, blond hair, large blue eyes, chalky-white skin, four-fingered hands without nails but two inch long claw-like appendages. Have advanced technology, very high intelligent.
They live on Earth close to the mountain of Indiana Springs Auxiliary Air Force Station, Nevada.

TARGS Also called Dracos by humans.
Ancestors of the Nagas.
Their logo is the flying dragon.
→ Targzissians.

TARGZISSIANS

Extraterrestrial race who was in contact with Riley Martin.
Also known as:
>> Dracos
>> Targs.

TAU CETIANS

Also called Cetians.
Muscular built body, about 5 ½ ft tall, somewhat broad faces, slightly pointed eyes, hair in a crew style cut.
They have been at war with the Dows for several generations. The Dows kidnapped a large number of Tau Cetian children.

Humanoids:
Males vary from 2.13 to 2.59 m, females from 1.98 to 2,40 m.

Brown-skinned Humans:
Light brown to copper colored hair or black to red-orange hair, eyes are green, blue, brown or gray.

Green-skinned Humans:
Light green, blonde or brown hair, eyes are green, hazel or steel-blue.

Red-skinned Humans:
Red, orange or blonde hair, eyes are red, brown or dark blue.

Bear-like Mammaloids:
Brown, black or blonde furry beings with small furry tails, teeth are Earth-Human like, eyes are brown, blue or black, ears are bear-like, walk on two legs, muscular arms with paw-like hands with 5 stubby claw-laden fingers, very muscular legs with very short feet with 5 stubby toes, vary from 2.74 to 3.66 m.
→ Epsilon Eridani, Tau Ceti.
→ Dows.

TAYGETIANS

→ Year 1997.09.
→ Pleiadians.

TELOSIANS	Tall, blond inhabitants beneath Mt. Shasta in Northern California. Allegedly possess interstellar vehicles. Brand of the Agartha Network. Part of the Melchizedek spiritual order with connections to Arcturus, Ashtar Command, Saturn, Sirius. Claim to have connections with South America, especially the Mato Grosso region to their underground sister city Posid. → Telos. → Adama, Sharula.
TEROS	Various human groups who inhabit the cavern system and reestablished antediluvian cities beneath North America. There was a NASA satellite photograph clearly indicating a huge circular opening in the icecap near the South Pole. Is said to be ultra modern with conveyor belts, crystal buildings, domes, electromagnetic vehicles, monorails, spaceports.
TERRANS	Earth humans.
TERRIANS	Other name for Earth Humans. → Terrans.
ULTRA-TERRESTRIALS	Come from the Universe of the Metatronic Light Spiral.
UMMITES	Scandinavian appearing race from planet Ummo in the Epsilon Eridani (Wolf 424 system) system. Similar to humans in appearing, have extremely delicate fingertips. They're light sensitive and almost completely telepathic. In the 1930's, a Norwegian vessel on the high seas had conducted an experiment in the upper reaches of radio frequency (400 megacycles). Established bases on Earth in 1950. Landed at San Jose de Valderas in 1967. Some of their ambassadors work closely with French and Spain Government Scientists. They reportedly work closely with the Vegan humanoids. → Ummo, Wolf424.
URANIANS	They have an unusual sense of direction, they have exceptional navigators for the starships of many worlds.

VEDRIANS

From planet Vedra in the Sutarus system in the Andromeda galaxy.
Short statured, dark haired, tan or yellowish skin.
They created two new species and many small tribes, each separated by vast distances, on Earth.
Blood types "0 Rh neg" are related to them.
➔ 2,500,000 B.C.E.

VEGANS

3rd and 4th dimensional beings.
Peaceful humans descended from refugees from the Lyran Wars (attacked by Draconians), work closely with other refugee-colonists now living in the Pleiades, Wolf424,...
There are human and nonhuman types (insect or reptilian like, but mammals).

Humanoid-Type Vegans:
6 to 7 ft tall, males & females, darker skin, non-Caucasian type, tough skin, primarily black hair, skin tone from light brown (beige) to very dark brown, very striking eyes, very large dark pupil & iris.

Nonhuman-Type Vegans:
(Because of appearance)
The appearance can either be insect like or reptilian, some have a greenish tinge to the hair & skin, eyes are very large and may have a second lid, depending of the planet of origin, very small nose.
Some incarnate into human form on Earth.
Most of the current Vegans are humans who are similar to dark skinned Orientals like those of India.
Inhabitants: Menara, Solar.
Maintain a base beneath Furnace Creek, California.
➔ Vega.

VENATICIANS

Race from the Canus Major area.

VENUSIANS

Venusians exist at the astral-body level.
Their hands are more pointed than on Earth people (like a flame).
Allegedly have bases in Brazil, Nevada and Tibet.
➔ Venus.

VERDANTS	They have colonized roughly 246,000 formerly uninhabited planets. Some of these are in the Milky Way galaxy, but the vast majority are scattered all over the universe.
	Estimated population of about 500 trillion on all their planets.
	Have been observing Earth for 1,000 years.
	Average lifespan up to 19,787 years.
	A female can produce only one offspring in her lifetime.
	They eat in a 36-hour cycle and are strictly herbivores.
	→ Verdant.
	→ Phillip H. Krapf.
	→ Goodwill.
	→ Gretcheenyal.
VISITORS	Alias of the Greys.
VORTEX COLLECTIVE	Is a race of hyper-intelligent, pan-dimensional entities. They have no true form, but can become whatever they choose to be in a given moment.
	→ Vortex.
"WALKING STICK RACE"	Similar to the Praying Mantis race. Like giant bugs/insects. Dark colored. Long body, great big eyes, feeler-type things like insects.
WATCHERS	They have been coming here for many thousands of years.
WINGED DRACOS	→ Mothmen.
WINGED SERPENTS	Sub race of the Reptilians.
	Also known as Snakes.
	→ Draconians.
YETI	The Bigfoot and the Yeti are not the same.
	The Yeti is a being of moderate intelligence.
	They lived upon a small planet that doesn't exist anymore. Their lifespan was approximately about 400 years, but now significantly less.
ZARDANIANS	Race.
ZENETAENS	Race from Andromeda.
	They were living in hollowed-out asteroids and moons.
	Skin color is blue, but was red about 2,500,000 years ago, like the Lyrans and Vegans.
	They are 5th dim. beings.
ZETA RETICULINS	→ Plusadians.

ZETA RETICULIS

3rd and 4th dimensional beings.
They share a group mind.
There are benevolent and malevolent beings (Greys).
The Lyrans were their forefathers.

ZETA types

127. Zeta Reticulum.
Some are living in cavern in Mongolia.
Zetas from Zeta I Reticuli:
Greys and Hybrids with assimilated human DNA.
Some of them work with Federation Worlds and tend to resist the Zeta II Reticulians and Draconians.
Zetas from Zeta II Reticuli:
Grey skinned, large heads, slanted dark eyes, thin bodies.
They have a Reptilian DNA base with assimilated Insectillian and plant-based genetics, which provides a greenish chlorophyll-based circulatory system.
They don't have a working digestive tract.
They are mostly clones.
The original Greys are far more scarce.
They must apply vital fluids from other life forms or vegetable juices to their skin through which it is absorbed.
They are controlled by the Dracos.

ZETAS

The Zeta form was created by the Nibiruans, they're a cross between the Reptilians, Humans and in some cases Inscetillians. They were in essence created as androids.
Were known in ancient times as the Igigi.
Some are working with the group of 4 dimensional Reptilians, formerly under Marduk's command.
An other group has evolved through beneficial exchange with humans.
The third group are those who believe that mankind will not ascend.
They come from a binary star where they live on planets close to the 2 rotating stars in heat & desert areas.
The Draconians helped to rescue the Reticulians from their dying planet (from excessive exposure to radiation) some hundred thousand years ago.
The Zetas support the Reptoids & the Reptoids support & derive authority from the Orion Empire.
Silvery grey colored people are benign beings, they never abducted and tortured Earth people, they are well on their way to become like the Arcturians, they are now part of the Ashtar Command.
Allegedly have bases in Nevada and New Mexico.
→ Kolta, Oris, Raechel.
→ Michael Wolf.
→ Greys, Plusadians, Reticulans.

2. ORGANIZATIONS

2.1 Federations, Organizations, Councils, Networks and Groupings of the Milky Way Galaxy and in various dimensions

16 GROUP

Group target is Globalization.
They think they own the planet.
They work with extraterrestrials and are being supervised from Mars.
Member:

>>	Australia:	Collins, Andrew, Sidney,
>>	Belgium:	Bonucar Phil, Brussels,
>>	Brazil:	Milahe, Franco, Recife,
>>	Canada:	Rulky, Alex, Montreal (Swiss native from Bern),
>>	China:	Chi-Wa-Yin, Beijing,
>>	Colombia:	Ruiz, Edgar Maldonado, Bogota,
>>	Germany:	Sibernich, Johan, Regensburg (member of the Trilateral, his alias is Bernard Hauptmann),
>>	India:	Al Muhir, Ben, Delhi,
>>	Italy:	Cinconti, Amada, Rome,
>>	Japan:	Wadi Wan, Tokyo (member of the Trilateral),
>>	Mexico:	Van Melbruck, Jacobo, Mexico City (member of the Trilateral),
>>	Russia:	Maljich, Sergin, Leningrad,
>>	Saudi Arabia:	Am-Al-Shanal, Abdulah, Mecca,
>>	Switzerland:	Bulweicht, Heinrich, Olten (he is an alien),
>>	USA:	Lonick, John, N.Y, "The Professor", Washington D.C.

24 ELDERS

Cosmic Masters.
→ Galactic Council.

ACIO

Advanced Contact Intelligence Organization.
Secret organization of the NSA.
Former simply called NSA Special Projects Laboratory.
They have 15 distinct security clearances. Those at level 12 and above are aware of the Corteum Technology Transfer Program (TTP), they are about 120 people and are primarily in India, Belgium and the United States.
There are only 7 who have level 7 clearance.
→ Corteum.

ADVANCED CONTACT INTELLIGENCE ORGANIZATION
→ ACIO.

AETHERIUS SOCIETY

Founder was George King.

AGARTHA EMPIRE

Other name of Shamballa Empire.
→ Shamballa Empire.

AGARTHA NETWORK

Vast system of caverns below the region of the Gobi desert.
Seat of government for the inner world.
Language: Solara Maru.
Member of the Confederation of Planets.
Space travel has been perfected.
Average height 12 ft., age unlimited.
There are about 120 subterranean cities.
Capitol Cities:

Mt TELOS: Average height 6 ft 5 inches to 7 ft 5 inches.

POSID: Primary Atlantean outpost, located beneath the Mato Grosso region of Brazil.
Population 1.3 million.

RAMA: Located near Jaipur.
Population 1 million.

SHINGWA: Remnant of the Uighurs, located on the border of Mongolia & China with a small secondary city in Mt Lassen, California.
Population 1.5 million.

SHONSHE: Refuge of the Uighur culture, a brand of the Lemurians who formed their Colonies 50,000 years ago.
Population: ¾ million.
(Sharula Dux, Ra of Telos, Rana Mu of Telos).

ALLIANCE & BROTHERHOOD of INTERPLANETARY FELLOWSHIP

ALLIANCE of the GALAXIES
Member: Klala.

ALPHA ONE   → Black Monks.

ALPHA TWO   Is Majestic 12.
                               → Black Monks, MJ-12.

ALPHA-OMEGA   Council of the Life Bearers.

ANCIENT ONE   → Nibiruan Council (9D).

ANDROMEDA COUNCIL   → Andromedan Council.

ANDROMEDAN COUNCIL
Is a group of beings from 139 different star systems.

ANDROMEDAN FEDERATION
Based in:
>> Alpha Centauri,
>> Epsilon Eridani,
>> Iumma (Wolf 424),
>> Procyon,
>> Tau Ceti,
>> Taygeta (Pleiades),
>> Vega (Lyra,
>> ...

APRO   Air Phenomena Research Organization founded by Jim
                               and Coral Lorenzen.

ARCTURIAN CONFEDERATION
→ Arcturians.

ARCTURIAN COUNCIL   Channel is Judith Moore.

ARI-AN EMPIRE   Feared the Kanus Empire.
                               → Ari-An (race).

ASHTAR COLLECTIVE   → Ashtar Command.

ASHTAR COMMAND   Is part of the Great White Brotherhood.
                               The Ashtar Command includes etheric energies and it
                               also includes people who are living on Earth.
                               Main focus is intellectual advancement.
                               Founder & director Mikael Ashtar.
                               Lord Monka is now Commander of the Ashtar
                               Command.
                               To oversee all rebellion forces.
                               Primarily in the Southern Americas.
                               There's a medical team & a tactical team.

Enormous fleet of interplanetary space crafts (13 (1?) million) from all over the universe.

10 million men surrounding this hemisphere.

Function on the fifth-dimensional level.

"We are the ETHERIANS".

The Ashtar / Astarte collective is a massive electronic collective mind or intelligence with a nerve centre rumored to be based within a 20 mile long computer into which numerous space cultures are tied via electro telepathic implants.

This collective has long since infiltrated by the Draconian collective at various levels and can no longer be trusted.

The Ashtar collaboration and the rebel angels which manipulate much of this collective by masquerading as Ascended Master, eventually establish a large network based in Sirius-B.

The command is comprised of:
>> Angelic Messengers,
>> Ascended Masters,
>> extra-galactic beings,
>> White Brotherhood,
>> Aldebaran, Altair, Arcturus, Sirius-B, Zetas.

Member: Adoniesis, Aldelan, Aleva, Alisha, Alphon, Andromeda Rex, Anton, Ashtar, Avalon, Awaana, Ballerian, Cassion, Cetti, Elys, Galimai-A, Hatonn, Hilarion, Ithacar (Ithakar), J.W., Joshua, Jycondria, Korton, Kuthumi, Lady Athena, Lytton, Matton, Mirvin, Monka, Rigel, Sananda (Jesus), Soltec, St. Germaine, Theodora, Venajoa, Voltra, Xyletron, Yuminale.

Also known as:
>>   Ashtar Space Command,
>>   Galactic Command,
>>   Starfleet.

Channel: Yvonne Cole.

→ 1952.

→ Telosians.

ASHTAR SPACE COMMAND
                                  → Ashtar Command.

ASTARTE COLLECTIVE   → Ashtar Command.

AUM   Japanese sect. Leader is the bearded guru Shoko Asahara.
                                  Involved in E/M weapons technology.

AVIARY   Top Secret group of individuals who have obtained more complete information about UFOs.

BABYLONIAN BROTHERHOOD

→ Azazael.

BASILIDEANS

A Gnostic sect founded by Basilides of Alexandria. Existed during the 2nd century. They worshipped Abraxas as Supreme Being.

BAVARIAN ILLUMINATI

Founder is Adam Weishaupt.
Controls the Bilderbergers group through which it coordinates the activities of the three world power structures:
>> Black Nobility,
>> Maltese Jesuits,
>> Wycca Masons.
Is also active in Utah.
→ CIA, Illuminati.

BILDERBERG

→ Bilderbergers.

BILDERBERG GROUP

→ Bilderbergers.

BILDEBERGERS

→ Bilderbergers.

BILDERBERGERS

Who are referred to as Bilderbergers, only because Bilderberg was the first known meeting place in modern history.
Part of the Secret Government created at World War II by a War Criminal.
(39 members) consists of:
>>   13 Black Nobility members,
>>   13 Maltese Jesuits,
>>   13 Wicca Masons.
Prince Bernard of the Netherlands was the founding chairman of the Bilderbergers.
Ultimately controlled by the Bavarian Illuminati through the Scottish Rite.
This group is carrying out, in secrecy, the global plans for dealing with the aliens.
The headquarters is in Geneva, Switzerland.
The most important and powerful is the Policy Committee. Policy meetings are held on a nuclear submarine beneath the polar icecap.
The international steering committee includes:
>>   Bentson, Lloyd
>>   Black, Conrad
>>   Clinton, Bill
>>   Jordan, Vernon
>>   Kissinger, Henry
>>   Mitchell, George
>>   Prince Hans Adam of Liechtenstein
>>   Prince Bernard of the Netherlands

>>   Rockefeller, David.
The first meeting (annually in May/June) took place in May 1954.

BILDERBURGERS   → Bilderbergers.

BLACK LEAGUE   Resistance movement of the Orion Humans to fight their reptilian overlords.
A Pleiadian underground peace corps.
Their skin is bluish-copper.
The symbol of their struggle became the black dragon.

BLACK MONKS   Implanted human beings that are no longer considered to be Earth humans.
Underneath the Black Monks is a project called Blue Moon which primarily deals with the lunar bases.
Under Blue Moon are 2 groups called:
>>   Alpha One
>>   Alpha Two (is MJ-12).
→ MJ-12, NSA.

BLACK SUN   Secret Society within the Thule Society.

BLUE LODGE   Located between Sirius A and Sirius B.

BLUE LODGE of CREATION
                           → Blue Lodge.

BLUE STAR COUNCIL

BROTHERHOOD   → Great White Brotherhood.

BROTHERHOOD of ADEPTS
                           The Mahatmas of wisdom formed the Brotherhood of Adepts.
                           → Mahatmas.

BROTHERHOOD of LIGHT
                           One dimension of the Brotherhood of Light consists of the Ascended Masters.
                           Member: El Morya.
                           Channel: Christine Bearse, Fernella Rundell.
                           → Great White Brotherhood.

BROTHERHOOD of MOUNT SHASTA
                           Member: Saint Germain.

BROTHERHOOD of the ALL
                           Are the Ascended Masters.

BROTHERHOOD of the ROYAL TETON
                           Member: Saint Germain.

BROTHERS of the GOLDEN ROBE
Head is Kuthumi.

CARPOCRATIANS   A Gnostic sect founded by Carpocrates of Alexandria.
The sect endured until the 6th century.

CENTRAL SUN COUNCIL

Representatives for Sirius are:
>> Aumtron,
>> Metatron (Head of the council).

CENTURIA COMMAND   Primarily in the North America area.

CFR   → Council on Foreign Relations.

CHARIOT of the SUN   MERKABAH Group of Thoth.

CHRISTOS ALLIANCE   Head is Sanat Kumara on planet Venus.

CIA   Founded in the year 1947.
Today the CIA controls all the world's illegal drug
markets. The drug money was used to finance the deep
underground alien bases.
The CIA has an inner-core who work for Bavarian
Intelligence.
→ Bavarian Illuminati.

CO-MASONRY   Also known as adoptive Masonry, allowing for the
admission and initiation of women.

COLLECTIVE   The Collective is comprised of many different human
races and a cetacean-based race (Greys, also called
Delphohims).
The humans are the same genetically as those found on
Earth.
They are from the three main colony zones:
>> Orion,
>> Pleiades,
>> Sirius.
The Elohim are the humans who came from the
Collective and created Earth people.
→ Elohim.

CONFEDERATION of FOMALHAUT
Founded 20,000 years ago after very destructive wars.
→ Fomalhautans.

CONFEDERATION of FREE WORLDS
Other name of Galactic Confederation of Light.

CONFEDERATION of HUMANS

Other name: Intergalactic Confederation.

Headed by the Ashtar Command.

CONFEDERATION of PLANETS

Council of Nine.

Council of Twelve.

Member: Agartha.

CONFEDERATION of STARS

(Orion).

CONTROLLERS

They have been known by different names:

- the Soulless Ones,
- the Elders,
- the Dero,
- the Greys,
- the Illuminati,
- the Counterfeit Race.

Yet, very few know the real identity and purpose of **THE CONTROLLERS**, a strange, parallel race that is metaphysically programmed to do evil and, according to authorities, has complete control of our education process, major philanthropic foundations, the banking system, the media, as well as dominant influence over all worldly governments.

Since the down of recorded history, these negative forces have kept us in human bondage by:

- controlling our minds,
- planting imperfect thoughts in our heads,
- kidnapping humans,
- impregnating women,
- causing global warfare and ethnic hatred,
- creating a false economic system,
- assassinating or replacing our most trusted spiritual leaders, rulers, and elected officials with **android "duplicates"**.

CORPORATE COLLECTIVE

Humanoids, Reptiloids & Ashtar Collective based in:

Aldebaran,

Altair (Aquila),

Arcturus,

Bernard's Star,

Bootes Centaurus,

Sirius-B,

Zeta I Reticuli,

...

Cosmic Beings

Non-individualized energies perceived as personified presences.

COSMIC CONFEDERATION COUNCIL of PLANETS
2 to 3 million civilizations in the Milky Way galaxy.

Cosmic Virgins   Lady Mary, Yuminale from Alpha Centauri.

COSMIC WHITE BROTHERHOOD
Other name of the Great White Brotherhood.

COUNCIL of 4   Helping people to become conscious of their own unique gifts.
Bi-La, Melora & Ocala have merged.
Members:
>>   Bi-La, a Tibetan guide,
>>   Melora,
>>   Ocala, an angelic guide,
>>   Pallas Athena.

COUNCIL of 6   Originated in the Andromeda galaxy.

COUNCIL of 9   Governing body of our local universe.
9 councilors represent 9 dimensions of life form.
They manifest the Sacred Blue Light of Creation in physicality. In this galaxy that Light has chosen to shine upon the Sirius star system.
They are led by Lord Aescapulus.
Guardians of the Great Blue Lodge, one of the Chief Councils of Lord Siraya, is housed in the Sirius-B star system.
Headquarter is in Miztitlan, Titicaca, Peru/Bolivia.
Members:
>>   Colarion,
>>   Maitreya.
Channel: André.
→ Colarion.

COUNCIL of 12   Controlled by the Scottish Rite "Council of 50".

COUNCIL of 12   Lady Masters of Karma.
Member: Isis, Lady Portia.

COUNCIL of 48   Located in the galaxy of Andilla.
The Council of 48 has a large supervision of a lot of the different commands in the different galaxies.
They're like news reporters.
Chief Councilor: Lord Hatonn.
Members: Dr. Rayness.

COUNCIL of 50   → Scottish Rite.

COUNCIL of ABORAHA   Channel: Judith Moore.

COUNCIL of AIN SOPH   Member: Ariel.

COUNCIL of ELDERS   Many different races are presented.

COUNCIL of LIGHT   Multidimensional & spiritual council.
Is comprised of Ascended Masters and the Angelic Realm. A collective of extraterrestrial and Interdimensional energies.
Also known as the Great White Brotherhood.
Channel: Jennifer Shepherd.
→ Great White Brotherhood.

COUNCIL of SOL   Channel: Gillian Mac Beth-Louton.

COUNCIL of the INTERGALACTIC SPACE CONFEDERATION
Representative: Andromeda Rex.
→ Intergalactic Space Confederation.

COUNCIL of the MASTERS
A great many of those councils of Masters are within Michael's Legions, and also another great many are involved with the Ashtar Command. There are councils within councils, there are a whole society set up of organizations and councils.

COUNCIL of the RAINBOW BRIDGE
Member: Shamra Talia.

Council on Foreign Relations
(CFR), part of the Secret Government.
Chairman: Rockefeller, David.
→ 16 Group.

COUNCIL on UNIVERSAL UNDERSTANDING
Channel: AsariA.

CSETI   Centre for Study of Extraterrestrial Intelligence. Director Dr. Steven Greer.

DARK ALLIANCE   Dark Forces. Most of them are Reptilian / Reptoid / Dinoid races. Opponent of the Galactic Federation of Light.

DEEP FREEZE   → Operation Deep Freeze.

DEMONS   Demons aren't fallen angels!
They usually leave us alone, if we don't invoke them.

DIVINE COALITION   Includes members of nearly all the top world backing families in effort to improve the world rather than to destroy it.
Includes some members of the Bilderberger Group, government officials.

DRACONIAN COLLECTIVE
→ Draconian Empire.

DRACONIAN EMPIRE
Main focus is material conquest.
Mostly excluded to reptiloids.
Has a base beneath Dulce, New Mexico.
Is also active in Utah.
Based in:
>> Alpha Draconis,
>> Bellatrix (Orion),
>> Capella,
>> Epsilon Bootes,
>> Polaris,
>> Rigel (Orion),
>> Zeta II Reticuli,
>> ...

DULCE BASE
There are over 18,000 aliens at the Dulce Base.
→ US-Alien Bases.

EARTH's SPIRITUAL HIERARCHY
Member: Hilarion, Kuthumi, St. Germain.

ECHELON
NSA spy system that is able to intercept, record and
translate any electronic communication:
>> cellular
>> data
>> email
>> fax
>> telephone
>> telex.

EGYPTIAN MASONIC RITE
Count Cagliostro did admit women into his sacred
Freemasonry organization.

ELOHIM
Creator Gods, Beings of Love.
The Elohim are pure unmanifest energy.
They are travelers of the universe and in service to the
Light.
Were last on Earth in great numbers at the time of
Abraham. As the Elohim departed from this universe
they activated a nuclear holocaust at the place known as
Sodom to destroy all the people with low vibrations.
Abraham and the people who didn't lower their
vibrations survived.
Are known as:
>> ancient Greek Gods,
>> Archangel Sandalphon,
>> Hathor,
>> Melchizedek,

>> Ptah,
>> Purity,
>> Ra,
>> Sanat Kumara,
>> Sananda,
>> YHWH.
1st Ray: Amazonia, Hercules.
2nd Ray: Apollo, Lumina.
3rd Ray: Amora, Heros.
4th Ray: Astrea, Purity.
5th Ray: Cyclopea, Virginia.
6th Ray: Aloha, Peace.
7th Ray: Arcturus, Victoria.
→ Kumaras.
→ Vywamus.

EMERALD CITY   Home of Hilarion.

EMERALD RAY   Hilarion.

FEDERATION   Abbreviation of the Interdimensional Federation of Free
Worlds.
Is made up of the highest beings of representation of the
Universal Government.
Each of the 12 regions of the Federation are individually
governed by a command, headed by a Supreme
Commander whose responsibility encompasses
universes.

FEDERATION OF PLANETS
Isn't the Galactic Federation.

FEDERATION OF THE DRACONIAN REPTOIDS
The Lizzies are members of the Federation of the
Draconian Reptoids.
They work together with the Orion Empire.

FLORIDIAN MOUNTAINS COMMUNICATION CENTER
Representative for the Southwest. Captain Avalon.

FORCES of LIGHT   Consist of the benevolent human race that reside on
Andromeda, Antares, Arcturus, Lyra, Pleiades, Sirius,
Vega, ...

FOUNDERS   Council of 12 beings who have come
together to create their own universe   and game.
They are souls who have completed more than one
universal game in other places.
90 people were invited from the Founders in this
universe (45 Carians, 45 Felines).

FREEMASONRY   Is an international fraternity for men, Traditionally women were not admitted.
Christians, Hindus, Jews, Moslems and even various Neo-Pagans are members.
In 1717, several Masons met in London to form the first United Grand Lodge of England, as a governing force over   British Masonry.
Religion and politics are forbidden topics in any lodge.
In spite of popular belief, Masonry isn't a secret society.
There is no Masonic Conspiracy to control the United States or the world.
The secret password is Tubal Cain.
→ Knights Templar, Masonry, York Rite of Freemasonry.

GALACTIC ASSOCIATION of WORLDS
Consists of some 360 member civilizations.
Representatives: Bashar.
→ Year 2827.

GALACTIC CENTER   Members: Averran, Nascia.

GALACTIC COMMAND   Is composed of:
>> Arcturians,
>> Lyrans,
>> Pleiadians,
>> Sirians,
>> Vegans.
→ Arcturus.
→ other name of the Ashtar Command.

GALACTIC CONFEDERATION
Is dwelling on the frequency levels of the 5th dimension and above.
Seat of government for our local Vega galaxy and is located in the Pleiades star cluster of systems.
The purpose of the Galactic Confederation Forces of Light is to assist the spiritual hierarchy.
→ Forces of Light.

GALACTIC COUNCIL of LIGHT
Is in charge of overseeing the development of all galactic civilizations. Is led by the 24 Elders.
Also known as Confederation of Free Worlds.
→ 24 Elders.

GALACTIC FEDERATION

Spiritual confederation of advanced beings centered in light and love.

Founded by the Kumaras, Sirius B inhabitants 4,300,000 B.C.E. with help of Sirius A inhabitants.

Tens of thousands of worlds.

About 40% are Humans.

They have (about 20,000,000?!) starships around Earth.

Member:

>> Pegasians   3,780,000 B.C.E.
>> Arcturians   3,750,000 B.C.E.
>> Andromedans   3,500,000 B.C.E.
>> Procyonans   3,500,000 B.C.E.
>> Tau Cetians   2,500,000 B.C.E.
>> Centaurians   1,100,000 B.C.E.
>> Bellatricians recently
>> Fomalhautans   recently
>> Mintakans   recently
>> Alpha Centaurians
>> Bernardians
>> Cassiopeians
>> Nibiruans
>> Pegasians
>> Perseus
>> Pleiadians
>> Sirians.

>> Long ago Earth was member and soon will be again an active member.

A principal base on Earth is in Gran Sabana, Venezuela.

Has a major base beneath Furnace Creek, California.

Secondary bases are in many places, especially inside mountains or underground.

Headquarter is in Agam Des.

The 4th dimension is also more the frequency of the Galactic Federation.

Also known as Galactic Federation of Light.

→ Alystar, Atmos, Diane, Helena, Joysia, Sa Lu Sa.

→ Panamint Mountains.

GALACTIC FEDERATION COUNCIL

Head of it is Metatron.

Meeting in the Great Hall on Sirius B.

→ Nibiruan Council.

GALACTIC FEDERATION FORCES of DARKNESS

Orion, Zeta Reticuli.

Dinoids, Draconians, Reptoids have some competition with earthlings.

GALACTIC FEDERATION NIBIRUAN COUNCIL

Head is Devin, a 9 dimensional being.
→ Nibiruan Council.
→ Devin, Jelaila Starr, Jonathan Starr.

GALACTIC FEDERATION of LIGHT

Created over 4,500,000 years ago.
Subdivided in 24 regional councils.
"Our" council is located on the 4th planet of the Sirius B star system.
Membership has been augmented from approx. 100,000 members to over 200,000 councils; most of the new members coming from the Dark Alliance, about 40% are humanoids.
The main headquarters are located in the Vega solar system.
Commander is Sananda.
→ Galactic Federation.

GALACTIC FEDERATION of PLANETS

Formed by the Ashtar Command.
Oversees everything.
Ties together human colonies:
- Epsilon Eridani,
- Erra-Taygeta (Pleiades),
- Hyades (various colonies),
- Iummo (Wolf424),
- Koldasian System,
- Lyra (Vega),
- Pleiades (Erra-Taygeta),
- Saturnian Tribunal,
- Tau Ceti,
- Vega (Lyra),
- WOLF424 (Ummites of IUMMO).
The Pelegaians compose the oldest Council, oftentimes called the 9D Lyran and Orion Councils since all four of the primary races are represented.
→ Alystar, Hatonn, Joysia.
→ Sirian A Council.

GALACTIC FEDERATION of WORLDS

Located in the Sirius star system.
Large federation of civilizations from many different planets, galaxies and universes working together.
There are thousands of councils under the Galactic Federation.
The Galactic Federation has one major overseeing council which has representatives of each member council; this council meets in the Great Hall.
But each council has it's own Great Hall.
→ Milky Way Galactic Federation.

GALACTIC FEDERATION'S SIRIAN A COUNCIL
→ Sirian A Council.

GALACTIC PACT The Galactic Federation of Planets formed the Galactic Pact.

GALACTIC TRIBUNAL Located around the star Aldebaran.
Head is Kla-La, President is Kadar.
Member: Sutko.

GIZEH EMPIRE → Gizeh Intelligence.

GIZEH GROUP → Gizeh Intelligence.

GIZEH INTELLIGENCE Is a renegade group of human extraterrestrials, predominantly Pleiadians.
They are working with secret societies in an effort to dissolve all national sovereignties into a global political order.
Were headquartered under the Gizeh plateau in Egypt.
The Germans were involved with the Gizeh Group in the 1930's.
The Germans were given a lot of technology including free energy devices, anti-gravity technology.
Also called Gizeh Empire, Gizeh Group, Kamagol-II cult.

GLAY COMMAND Primarily in the Europe area.

GOETIAN SPIRITS The Goetian Spirits are all aliens and/or angels.
There are 72 spirits:
Amon, Amy, Andromalius, Asmodai, Barbatos, Beal, Beleth, Belial, Botis, Buer, Dantalion, Decarabia, Focalor, Forneus, Gaap, Gusion, Lerie, Marbas, Paimon, Ronove, Seere, Sitri, Skeleton, Valefor, Vepar, Zepar.

GRAN HERMANDAD BLANCA
→ Great White Brotherhood.

GREAT BLUE LODGE The Great Blue Lodge of Creation is located in the Sirius B star system.
→ Council of 9.

GREAT CENTRAL GOVERNMENT
The destruction of planet Earth is not permitted.

GREAT CENTRAL SUN Is the source & the centre of a galaxy & a cosmos.
Origin of all physical & spiritual creation.
Also known as:
>>   Great Central Source,
>>   The Great Hub,
>>   The Heart of God,
>>   The Source.

GREAT CENTRAL SUN GOVERNMENT
Member: Kuthumi.

GREAT CENTRAL SUN HIERARCHY
Ambassador: Ashtar.

GREAT COSMIC GOVERNMENT
Voice is Lord Maitreya.
Member: Ashtar, Soltec.

GREAT KARMIC BOARD
Member: Saint Germain.

GREAT STAR UNION of CENTAURUS
→ Centaurians.

GREAT TRIBUNAL Representative of Earth is Kadar Monka.

GREAT WHITE BROTHERHOOD
Founded by Sanat Kumara.
Allegedly established by the Lemurians before the cataclysm.
For millions of years.
A multi-dimensional, intergalactic, interplanetary spiritual organization of beings who choose to serve the divine cosmic plan in this universe that include:
>> Ascended Masters who have arisen from Earth into immortality and remain to assist their sisters & brothers,

>> many energies of Love & Light,
>> members of the Heavenly Host,
>> the Spiritual Hierarchy,
>> beneficent members from other planets,
>> certain unascended Chelas, people who are now living on Earth.
>> the Ashtar Command.
Member race: Esteknas.
Members: Cassion, Cetti, Djwhal Khul, El Morya, Goo Ling, Hatonn, Jesus, Jokhym, Korton, Lord Buddha, Monka, Sananda, Sarna, Soltec, St. Germain.
Extraterrestrial Masters: Aeb, Aldrix, Amaru, Anahuac, Anitac, Anrar, Antar, Antarel, Astar (is not Ashtar), Atunez, Ceres, Dracel, Erjabel, Etel, Godar, Icu, Kulba, Lertrad, Meth, Oesceve, Olea, Oletamo, Olmex, Omen,

Omuni, Oniac, Ordelat, Ossim, Oxalc, Oxiram, Oxlam, Oxmalc, Rampiac, Reges, Rosinac, Rumilac, Sampiac, Semun-Iac, Serionac, Solitum, Soloviac, Sordaz, Sum, Terec, Titinac, Xendor, Xenialac, Xenon, Xozian.
<u>Intraterrestrial Masters:</u> Abudamir, Alcir, Aminael, Azur-Mah, Cecea, Etnakiel, Mulla, Solmen, Soriam, Soromez.
Also known as:
>> Brotherhood,
>> Brotherhood of Light,
>> Cosmic White Brotherhood,
>> Council of Light,
>> Gran Hermandad Blanca,
>> Hermandad Blanca,
>> La Gran Hermandad Blanca,
>> Mahatmas,
>> White Brotherhood of Light,
>> White Lodge.
→ Lemuria.

GREATER NIBIRUAN COUNCIL
→ Nibiruan Council.

GROUP OF NINE
Sananda isn't member

GROUP OF FORTY
David K. Miller.

HAARP
Is being designated for capturing and modulating electromagnetic fields for the purpose of total control of brain ware patterns in order to establish a system of complete "order on the surface of the planet" in either 3rd or 4th density.
It has nothing to do with weather or climate.
These things are emanating from 4th density.
They are working on this since the 1920's.

HATONA COUNCIL
Council in the Andromeda galaxy.
Head is the Krel group.

HERMANDAD BLANCA
→ Great White Brotherhood.

HERMETIC ORDER of the GOLDEN DAWN
Its key founder was Dr. William Wynn Westcott, a London Rosicrucian.
The secret chiefs of the Third Order were equivalent to the Mahatmas (of the Theosophical Society), who could also be contacted in the astral plane.

HIGH COUNCIL of MELCHIZEDEK
Ambassador: Ashtar.

HIGHEST CELESTIAL GOVERNMENT

HIGHEST COUNCIL of the SOLAR SYSTEM

HIGHEST TRIBUNAL of the INTERPLANETARY COUNCIL

HOLY FOUR

Group of Masters.
>>   Sanaka,
>>   Sananda,
>>   Sanat-Kumara,
>>   Sanatana.

HORLOCKS

Other name of the Men in Black.

HOUSE of ALN

(Dark Forces).
Began in the Orion Constellation, later established on a neighboring planet in the Lyran Constellation. Later returned to the Orion Constellation.
The House of Aln was peopled more by the flying serpents (Snakes), than Carians.
By the time of the first Earth, the House of Aln was headed by a winged serpent known as Cobazar, father of Jehovah.
The royal line of Reptilians are the Draconians, the winged dragons.
Jehovah is the reigning patriarch of the 9D House of Aln. Enki is the reigning patriarch of the 4D House of Aln.   Enki has become the reigning patriarch of the 5D House of Aln.
→ Cobazar, Enki, Jehovah.

HOUSE of AVYON

(Light Forces).
(Feline) Devin is the reigning patriarch of the 9D Royal House of Avyon.
(Human) Anu is the reigning patriarch of the 5D Royal House of Avyon at this time.
→ Anu (5D), Devin (9D), Joysia (9D).

ILLUMINATI

(Orion).
Term first used in the late 15th century.
The founder was the Bavarian professor Adam Weishaupt in 1776. A decree in Bavaria in 1784 banned all secret societies, by the turn of the 20th century occultists Leopold Engel and Theodor Reuss revived it.
Controls the direction of the world. The centre of power is in the lower 4th dimension (lower astral).
The Illuminati is made of a group of about 20 men, all are white and of an older age of about 70 (in reality they could be much older). They are genetic hybrids, the result of interbreeding between Reptilians & Humans many thousand years ago. They are all shape shifters (reptilians).
Fighting for central control with the Greys; love-hate relationship with the Greys for world domination.

>> Bavarian Illuminati.
>> Bilderberg Group.
>> Club of Rome.
>> Council of Foreign Relations (CFR).
>> (Freemasons).
>> Jehovah's Witnesses (Charles Taze Russel).
>> Mormon Church.
>> Reptilians.
>> Rothschilds.
>> Round Table of Nine.
>> Royal Institute of Internal Affairs.
>> Trilateral Commission.
>> United Nations (U.N.).
>> Vatican City.
→ Reptilians, Rigelians, Shapeshifters.
→ 1994.

INTERDIMENSIONAL FEDERATION of FREE WORLDS
→ Federation.

INTERGALACTIC BROTHERHOOD OF LIGHT
5th- and 6th-dimensional extraterrestrials from many galaxies.

INTERGALACTIC COUNCIL
→ Channel Valerie Donner.

INTERGALACTIC COUNCIL of the SPACE CONFEDERATION
→ Intergalactic Space Confederation.

INTERGALACTIC COUNCIL of TWELVE
Is a group of interplanetary representatives composed of beings from the Angelic and Extraterrestrial realms.
Channel: Shaari.
→ Veyares.

INTERGALACTIC FEDERATION
Other name: Confederation of Humans.
Includes: Arcturus, Centaurians, DAL, Lyra, Pleiades, Sirius, Vega.

INTERGALACTIC FEDERATION of PLANETS
Organization within the Solar System.
Members are all planets without Earth.
Representative for Earth is Cdr. Monka of the Ashtar Space Command.
Also known as Solar System Federation.

INTERGALACTIC FEDERATION of SOVEREIGN PLANETS

A consortium of approx. 27,000 species scattered throughout the universe.
Member planets: Verdant.

INTERGALACTIC FLEET

Presently (2000.12.31) there are over 33 battle planetoids in the fleet. Each of them is over 1,600 km (1,000 miles) in length. They ensure that no manned craft leaves Earth and lands on the Moon.
Commander Alphon.
Member: Xyletron.

INTERGALACTIC LEGION of SPECIAL VOLUNTEERS
For the Ashtar Command.

INTERGALACTIC SPACE CONFEDERATION
Andromeda Rex, Ashtar.

INTERGALACTIC UNION

Future Galactic Headquarters will be in the Solar System.

INTERGALACTIC UNION of FREE WORLDS
Includes members from many galaxies within our own universe and other universes.

INTERPLANETARY ALLIANCE
Within the Solar System.

INTERPLANETARY FEDERATION
Is a union of about 7 million planets.
Member: Archos.

INTERPLANETARY PARLIAMENT
Headquarters on Saturn.

JASON SOCIETY   Part of the Secret Government.

JERUSALEM COMMAND

In charge of Sirius 1, 2, 3.
→ Sananda.

KACHINA   → SUN BOW CLAN.

KAMAGOL-II CULT   Secret cult beneath Egypt, also called Gizeh Empire, Gizeh Intelligence.
→ Gizeh Intelligence.
→ Aldebarans.

KANUS EMPIRE	Warriors from Sirius, a doglike race (similar to wolves). Vicious and barbaric Sirian warriors. There was (is until now?) a war between the Kanus Empire and Ari-An; entire worlds were totally destroyed.
KARMIC BOARD	All life streams pass before the Karmic Board before each incarnation on Earth to receive their assignment and karmic allotment for that lifetime. They pass before the Karmic Board again at the end of each lifetime to review their performance. Members: >> Cyclopea (Elohim of the 5th Ray), >> Goddess of Liberty, >> Great Divine Director, >> Kuan Yin (Goddess of Mercy), >> Lady Master Nada, >> Pallas Athena Goddess of Truth), >> Portia (Goddess of Justice).
KKK	Ku Klux Klan. In the early 1900's was the popularity of the KKK with Masons. Although no reliable figures exist, the KKK appears to have been very successful in recruiting Masons into it's ranks. One former Klansman claimed that 50-60 percent of the first Klansman in Oregon were Masons.
KNIGHTS TEMPLAR	Forerunners of the Knights of Malta. The only order of Masonry strictly for Christians, was founded in the 11th century. Is a part of the Masonic structure known as the "York Rite of Freemasonry". Over 200,000 members in the U.S.A., Mexico, Germany and Italy. → Masonry.
KOR	Great Communications Center on Mars (for the Solar System) for Ashtar Command. Member: Alta-Zar, Amor, Atrica, El-Tar, Elexar, Erisa, Gor-Ed, Jenis, Ka-L-Lia, Korton, Le-Ar, Lotan, Zo.
KU KLUX KLAN	→ KKK.
KUMARAS	Sanat Kumara, Sananda were originally of the Elohim. → Seven Holy Kumaras.
LA GRAN HERMANDAD BLANCA	→ Great White Brotherhood.
LABYRINTH GROUP	A super secret sub-group of the ACIO.
LADIES of SHAMBALLA	Are Ascended Masters.

LASMURIAN BROTHERHOOD
Of planet Lasmur in the Orion constellation.

LEVERONS   Other name of the Orion Alliance.

LORDS of KARMA   Member:
>>   Lady Nada,
>>   Pallas Athena,
>>   Portia,
>>   Quan Yin,
>>   Vista.

LORDS of SHAMBALLA   Are Ascended Masters.

LYRAN GALACTIC FEDERATION
It was a Carian commander that ruled over the vast fleet of star ships and cruisers for the Lyran Galactic Federation and the Royal Houses of Avyon and Aln.

MAHIKARI   Japanese sect.

MAHATMAS   Masters (teachers) of Wisdom.
Also called the Great White Brotherhood.
Most of the Mahatmas lived in remote regions:
>>   India,
>>   Mongolia,
>>   Tibet (Himalaya).
The Mahatmas dictated various materials which Madame Blavatsky wrote into her books.
→ Madame Helena Petrovna Blavatsky.

MAJESTIC TWELVE   → MJ-12.

MAJIC-12   → MJ-12.

MAJORITY TWELVE →   MJ-12.

MARCAB EMPIRE   210,000 B.C.E.

MASONIC CONNECTION
→ Masons.

MASONRY   It is said Saint Germain is the inventor of Masonry.
The Knights Templar is a part of the Masonic structure.
→ Freemasonry, Knights Templar.

MASONs	Connected to KKK. Norman Vincent Peale was a 33rd degree Mason, as were the founders of the Jehovah's Witnesses, Scientology, Theosophy and Unitarianism.
MELCHIZEDEK ORDER	Brotherhood. Is active within the Mormon Church, the Masonic Lodge and the Mt. Shasta Community. Part of them are the Telosians. Also called Order of Melchizedek. Member: Sanat Kumara. → Telosians.
MEN in BLACK	A MIB is a Draco created robotic sentinel in order to protect the interests of the Dracos. Also called Horlocks. Have several origins: >> human incarnations from Orion, >> negatively oriented Sirius energy, >> Orions who time-traveled. Have been on Earth since 1600 C.E. Ancient underground Atlantean complexes are occupied by the MIB's, beneath the Eastern U.S. seaboard. Operatives steal and recover wrecked UFO vehicles or their fragments. Also frighten and harass UFO witnesses and hush them up. Some UFO witnesses disappear after reporting UFO activity and Men in Black encounters. They silence some of these witnesses by killing them. They wear thick black sunglasses, black suits, black 1930 FBI type hats, brightly shined black shoes and black socks. They have olive complexions or pale-greyish skin, thin lips, a pointed chin, mildly slanted eyes, black hair. They carry black briefcases; also they have sometimes shown CIA or Air Force identifications. Both agencies deny that they are affiliated. They have a behavior like androids or robots and speak in monotone with no facial expressions or emotions. They drive black vintage luxury cars, the license plates always unidentifiable. Sometimes use black helicopters without any identification. It is thought that they are alien or government agents. The first occurrence of MIB's was traced to Albert K. Bender (editor of Space Review) in 1953.
MIB	→ Men in Black.

MILKY WAY GALACTIC FEDERATION

The Milky Way Galactic Federation is the oldest galactic federation in this universe.

The Galactic Federation was established after the first Galactic War between Humans, Reptilians, Felines and Carians.

Was established with the founding members of Lyra and Orion.

Flagship was Pelegai, one of the few ships intact after the war.

Now there are millions of members from across our galaxy.

MISSION RAHMA   Spaceships landed in the desert of Chilca, south of Peru on Jan 22, 1974.

MJ-12   Majestic-12 is a Top Secret Research and Development/Intelligence operation responsible directly and only to the President of the United States.

Part of the Secret Government, established Sept. 24, 1947. It ceased to exist in 1969 and became a private concern.

Is now called NSC SSG (1998)

Eisenhower established a permanent committee to oversee and conduct all covert activities with the aliens.

This included FBI director Edgar Hoover and six leaders of the "Council on Foreign Relations" known as the "Wise Men" and others from the "Trilateral Commission".

MJ-12 plans to make soon an "official" announcement under controlled conditions, probably Area 51. Network TV will tell us they are the "Saviors of Humanity" who have come to defend the earth against an invasion of man-eating aliens called Reptoids. The story is a lie! They already work for the Reptoids!

Also known as:

>> Jehovah,

>> Majestic Twelve,

>> Majic-12,

>> Majority Twelve,

>> National Security Council,

>> NSC SSG,

>> Zodiac.

➔ 16 Group.

MOST HIGH INTERPLANETARY HIERARCHY

Member: Ashtar, Soltec.

MUFON   Mutual UFO Network Inc. in Canada and U.S.A.

NATIONAL SECURITY AGENCY
→ NSA.

NATIONAL SECURITY COUNCIL
→ NSC, NSC SSG.

NEBULUS   Council of the Reticulans.

NEPHILIM   Fallen Lords.

NEW WORLD ORDER   (NWO).
The Reptilians are the principal architects behind the NWO.
It is going to manifest itself, but it is going to be very short-lived.
Denver is apparently scheduled to be the headquarters of the Western Sector of the United States, Atlanta is said to be the centre for the Eastern Sector. Colorado is a major centre of the NWO   and the Queen of England has been buying upland there. Denver, Colorado is a major satanic centre.
Time-space forces are currently involved with the New World Order scenario, attempting to carry out their dictatorship from their base in the Aldebaran system in an other time-space dimension.

NIBIRUAN COUNCIL   Main administrative arm of the Galactic Federation.
Work with other Galactic Federation Councils.
Overseeing the Divine Contracts of every soul residing in the galaxy.
The Council has many smaller councils.
There are hundreds of thousands of beings in the Council.

NIBIRUAN COUNCIL (3D)
Was begun in January 1997 in Kansas City, Missouri. Jelaila established the Nibiruan Council with partners; Terry Spears and Dermot Kerin, head is the walk-in Jelaila. In July 1998 moved to Los Angeles.
Represents the 9D and Greater Nibiruan Councils on Earth.

NIBIRUAN COUNCIL (4D/5D)
They were involved with Earth (Egypt, Sumeria, Babylon, Atlantis and Lemuria).

NIBIRUAN COUNCIL (5D)
Enki has become Head of the 5 dim.
Nibiruan Council, representing the Dark.

NIBIRUAN COUNCIL (9D)

Elder Council of the Greater Nibiruan Council.
Other names: The Ancient One, Pelegaians.
Comprised of members from the 2 royal houses of Aln and Avyon. Not all of them are of Human origin. Devin & Jehovah are the Heads of the 9D Nibiruan Council.
The 9D members are part of the original "Game Players" of the Polarity Integration Game on the First Earth. Their flagship is the Pelegai. They oversee the ascension projects for all planets and races that are ready for ascension.
→ Devin, Jehovah.

NICAP

National Investigations Committee on Aerial Phenomena, Washington, D.C.
Most important civil UFO group in the 1960's.

NINE

→ Group of Nine.

NSA

(National Security Agency).
Headquarter is at Fort Meade, Maryland.
NSA was created as the agency in America that would handle the alien problem.
The NSA established radio contact with the Greys (operating within 2 stationary asteroids) and this led to the 1954 AFB landings (under the Eisenhower administration). Even though previous treaties were signed (Truman, etc.) with the humanoid groups under Mt. Shasta, California. (Telos, Ashtar, Agartha, Melchizedek).
The NSA has (1995) 53 UFO-type craft that are situated on the Moon.
Inside the NSA there is a group called Black Monks.
Member: Menzel, Donald M.
→ ACIO, Black Monks.

NSC

National Security Council.
Reports directly to the President.
Includes:
>>   Secret 5412 Committee which directs covert (black) operations.
>>   PI-40 Subcommittee (aka MJ-12) which exercises control of the UFO Cover-Up.

NSC SSG

National Security Council Special Study Group.
New name of MJ-12.
They know that there are 7 large motherships in our Solar System.
Member: Dr. Michael Wolf.

NWO	Currently has 53 Earth built UFO-type spacecraft on the Moon. There is a working colony on the Moon since 1961. → New World Order.
OLIN	One Language Intelligent Networks.
OHERA Group	Group of Light Beings. Channel: Amber Leigh.
OPERATION DEEP FREEZE	The way it works is that members of the CIA, FBI, NSA, KGB and MOSSAD are declared dead and given false identities. They have total anonymity & are outside all laws. Today there are over 26,000 of them. They are in charge of the doubles and clones.
OPHITES	A Gnostic sect which evolved during the 2nd century and existed for several centuries.
ORDER of MELCHIZEDEK	Other name of Melchizedek Order.
ORION ALLIANCE	Also known as Leverons.
ORION COMMAND SECURITY UNIT	→ Jonathan Vallance.
ORION CONSORTIUM	Consisting of 19 different races from the Orion constellation.
ORION COUNCIL of LIGHT	6th dimensional beings.
ORION EMPIRE	The Orions are made up of two opposed races: >> "The Council of Light" at Betelgeuse. >> evil Orions were based at Rigel. The Greys make up the Orion Empire. The Federation of the Draconian Reptoids works with the Orion Empire. The Greys would like to be free of the Orion Empire. The Greys are training humans to fight their war against the Draconians when they arrive here.
ORION GROUP	Major Orion influence in the Middle East about 3,600 B.C.E.). Orion Groups leaves Earth (3,000 B.C.E.)
ORION LEAGUE	Former members are: Bellatricians, Mintakans.
PEGASUS STAR LEAGUE	→ Pegasians.

PELEGAIANS   → Nibiruan Council (9D).

PI-40   (Jan. 1995). Is on top of MJ-12.

PLANETARY COUNCIL   → Solaris Kumara.

	SUN:	*Horus* coordinates with the higher Intergalactic Council.
	MERCURY:	*Hermes* directs interplanetary, Intergalactic communication.
	VENUS:	*Adonis*, directs the evolution of love and beauty.
	EARTH:	*Enoch*, directs prophetic communication.
	MARS:	*Croesus*, coordinates activities with the Ascended Masters in the Brotherhood of Light.
	ASTEROID BELT:	*Athena*, defends truth & justice.
	JUPITER:	*Jove*, maintains the balance of the planet's magnetic fields.
	SATURN:	*Zoroaster*, concerned with order, structure & destiny.
	URANUS:	*Quetzalcoatl*, works for religions & philosophical change.
	NEPTUNE:	*Merlin*, focuses upon scientific discoveries.
	PLUTO:	*Lao-Tzu*, contributes detached wisdom.
	PHOENIX:	*Apollo*, the catalyst for change.

PLANETARY COUNCIL of LIBERATION
Commander is Unixitron.

PLEIADIAN COUNCIL of LIGHT
Channel Gillian MacBeth-Louton.

PLEIADIAN HIGH COUNCIL
Channel Valerie Donner.
→ Mira.

RADIANT ONE   The Light of the Radiant One.
(Ashtar Command).
Planet Shan rejected it.

ROSICRUCIAN ORDER   AMORC is internationally known as the Ancient
Mystical Order Rosae Crucis. The Rosicrucian Order
consists of thousands of men and women in over 100
countries.

SAN TAM   University of Spectrology & Universality in the city of Ziconia on the planet Yore in the galaxy of Glay in Pacifica. University of Colors.
→ Goddess Princess Osanta, Oaspe, Ronald Claymore, Dr. Norman Watson, Dr. Zel.

SATANISTS   Their headquarters is in Belgium. The Brotherhood created Belgium just for this reason in 1831.

SATURNIAN-COUNCIL   Member: Philip.

SATURN-TRIBUNAL   The great administrative center of the Solar System.
Representatives from all the Solar planets are present at the Saturn Tribunal sessions.
Member: Kadar-Monka.

SCOTTISH RITE   "Worship of the Serpent".
(Wicca Mason).
Headquarter is in Washington D.C.
Branch of the Illuminati.
The Scottish Rite was created by Jesuits and Masons at the Parisian college of Clermont.
Mormonism became a hybrid religion between Christianity and Gnostic Scottish Rite Masonry.
Episcopalians, Methodists, Southern Baptists have fallen under the control of the Scottish Rite.
→ Illuminati.

SECRET SOCIETY of SCIENTISTS
→ Ciudad Subterraneo de los Andes.

SECRET GOVERNMENT   - The Bilderbergers,
- The Council on Foreign Relations (CFR) and
- The Trilateral Commission are the Secret Government and rule this nation through MJ-12 and the study group known as the Jason Society.

SEVEN HOLY KUMARAS

The Lords of the Flame from Venus.
Over millions of years have given much of their Light, Love & Life to assist in the forward evolution of Earth into Freedom's Star.
The name "Kumara" is a title.
Also called The Seven Sons of Brahma.
The activity of the Kumaras is distinctly different from that of the Masters from the Central Sun.
Member:

>>   *Sanatka*   1st Ray, Blue Flame,
                    Will   of God,

>>   *Sa Ananda*   2nd Ray, Yellow Flame,
                    Wisdom of God,

>>   *Sa Na Tana* 3rd Ray, Pink Flame,
                    Love of God,

>>   *Sujata*   4th Ray, White Flame,
                    Purity of God,

>>   *Kapila*   5th Ray, Green Flame,
                    Science of God,

>>   *Sa Na Kumara*

                    6th   Ray,   Purple-Gold-Ruby
                    Flame, Peace of God,

<<   *Sanat Kumara*

                    7th Ray, Violet Flame, Freedom of God.

→ Holy Four, Kumaras.

SEVEN KUMARAS   → Seven Holy Kumaras.

Seven Rays of the Christ Word

Ashtar, Cassiel.

SHAMBALLA EMPIRE   Former Yu daughter empire of the Lemurian Empire founded a surface empire in India. The prince of Agartha was named Rama.
Originally situated in the Indus river valley of India.
Also known as Agartha Empire.

SILVER FLEET   Fleet Cmdr. is Anton.

SIRIAN A COUNCIL   Council of the genetic engineers of the Galactic Federation.
Joysia is Chief Genetics Engineer.

SIRIAN CENTRAL SUN COUNCIL
Head is Metatron.

SIRIAN HIGH COUNCIL   Channel is Patricia Cori.

SIRIAN SOLAR BREEDS   → Tamlris.

SIRIUS ALLIANCE

Provides genetic engineers.
The most of them are Felines who live on the planet Sirius A.
They work out of the 6th dimension.
Some were known as Sekmet, Seshat, Atum Ra (Aton).
Joysia was chosen to head the DNS Recoding program for Earth.

SIRIUS COMMAND

In the north & very cold areas.

SISTERHOOD

→ Brotherhood.

SOLAR CROSS

Light bearers.
Intergalactic organization of man, about 15,000 members in this sector of space. They are working with KOR. Al of them are also members of the Universal Confederation of Planets. It's headquarters is in Trantor.
Member: Alta-Zar, Amor, Atrica, Bellarion, Dar-Nell, Eia, El-Tar Jenis, Elan, Elexar, Erisa, Gor-ed, Hatonn, Ka-L-Lia, Katonis, Kla-La, Korton, Lactu, Lalur, Le-Ar, Lotan, Meck-Tau, Merku, Mon-Ka, Mora, Myl-La-N-Trok, Sig-Mar, Soltec, Surnia, Sutko, Voltra, Zo, Zolgus.

SOLAR SYSTEM FEDERATION

Other name of the Interplanetary Federation of Planets.

SOLAR TRIBUNAL

On the moons of Saturn.
Thalaro is one of the 12 Elders at the Solar Tribunal on Saturn; governing this solar system; Head is Mon-Ka.
Part of the Galactic Federation.
Part of the Space Federation.
Member: Saint Germain, Thalaro.

SOLARIANS

Lords of Light.

SPACE ALLIANCE

Member: Andromeda Rex.

SPACE BROTHERHOOD

Channel: Diane Tessman.

SPACE COMMAND

Member: Lady Athena.

SPACE COUNCIL

SPACE FEDERATION

Member: Kadar-Monka, Soltec.
Speaker: Hatonn.

SPACE VOLUNTEERS

They are coming from the whole universe.

SPECIAL VOLUNTEERS

They are coming from the whole universe.

SPIRITUAL HIERARCHY   Supreme spiritual council in service to the ascension of Earth.
Member: Esola, Esu, Glund-Oyarsa, J.W., Joshua, Lurga, Malacandra, Oxoh, Perelandra, Veritilbia,
>>   archangels
>>   ascended masters
>>   Brotherhood of Light
>>   Intergalactic Brotherhood of Light
>>   Humans.

STAR COMMAND   Is a group of interplanetary   representatives composed of extraterrestrials from many universal cultures.
→ Mishar, Shaari, Veyares.

STARFLEET   "Federation of Free Worlds".
Other name is Ashtar Command.
Prime Directive is: Law of non-interference in the development of class M planets.
Large bases are in Norway & Sweden.
→ Ashtar Command.

Starseeds   Galactic beings on Earth from Arcturus, Orion, Pleiades, Sirius and many more..

SUBUD   Spiritual movement that evolved around the Indonesian mystic Muhammad Subuh, also known as Bapak (spiritual father).
Latihan is the basic spiritual exercise of the Subud movement. The object of the Latihan is the worship of God.

SUMERAN EMPIRE   In Aldebaran there lived a race of Aryans and some different color races.
The Sumerian Aldebaran race were the white Gods in Sumeria in Mesopotamia.
The Sumerian language is identical to the Aldebaran language and the speaking frequency of the German language and the Sumerian language is almost identical.
→ Aldebaran.

SUN BOW CLAN   Name in the Hopi-prophecy KACHINA.
Master builders sent from the Confederation of Stars (Orion), but primarily they came from the blue star "RIGEL".

Supreme Creative Force   → God.

THEOSOPHICAL SOCIETY

Founded in the 19th century by:

>>   Djwhal Khul,

>>   El Morya,

>>   Kuthumi,

>>   Serapis Bey,

>>   & other masters.

Was formed in September 1875 by Henry Steele Olcott and William Q. Judge, its secretary was Helena Petrovna Blavatsky.

In 1882 the international headquarters was established in Adyar, Madras, India.

The real founders were:

>> Kuthumi (Koot Hoomi Lal Singh),

>> El Morya.

TIME LORDS

They are the divine shepherds of "physical creation".

When the Supreme Creative Force first began the physical creation, the Time Lords were created.

"Light" and "Time" compose Creation.

They had to create the eight dimensions of physical creation.

The Time Lords had to construct the three dimensional galaxy, to accomplish this task, the Time Lords were given the creative "pulse of time".

They are in charge of time.

Keepers of time of Earth, they answer only to the Creator.

Great Beings of Light whose orders are represented by many Divine Councils.

Channel: Karen Angel.

TIME MASTERS

The Time Masters are responsible for the vocational speed of cosmic substrata comparable to the Akashic fields.

THULE SOCIETY

The elite of the Thule Society is the Black Sun secret society.

TWELVE CIVILIZATIONS

24 civilizations = 24 dimensions = 24 levels of consciousness.

The Group of Nine is the head of the 24 civilizations.

They are in an other galaxy, in the cold zone.

Tom is the speaker of the group of nine (not physical).

ALTEA:

50 million light-years from Earth, 52 times the size of Earth, 144,000 habitants.

(technology).

People have no voice, 1 sex, blue eyes, no hair, communication to Earth by computer box.

Ancestors of Atlantis and time before.
Joseph of Aramaea
ARAGON:
Chief is Joseph,
(science, medicine)
ASHAN:
People have no nose, no eyes, no hands.
(color, sound, arts).
Ancestors of Scandinavians, Phoenicians.
Moses came from Ashan
ELARTHIN:
In other galaxy
HOOVA:
56 times light velocity,
(Jehovah), chief is Jesus.
16000 times the size of Earth.
Physical, small, dark skin, dark hair, 3 sexes, live 500,000
to 1.5 million years, different voice,
5 million habitants.
People of Hoova visited Earth 3 times.
(Hebrews, Nazarenes, Chinese), 6 million Jews of World
War II returned to Hoova
MORA-TRIOMNE:
MYREX:

TWELVE PARTNER CIVILIZATIONS

ANCORE:
Partner of Aragon.
SPECTRA:
Partner of Hoova.
ZENEEL:
Most obedient, people not equal like earth people.
(alchemy).
→ ZEEMED:
Civilization under ZENEEL.
→ ZENTHORP:
Civilization under ZENEEL.

UNHOLY SIX

Other name of the Orion Empire.

UNITED FEDERATION   Main focus is on spiritual development.
>> Alpha Centauri,
>> Andromeda Constellation,
>> Epsilon Eridani,
>> Hyades cluster,
>> Iummo / Ummo (Wolf424),
>> Pleiades cluster,
>> Procyon,
>> Tau Ceti,
>> Tay Geta (Pleiades),
>> Vega (Lyra),
>> ...
Is also active in Utah.

UNITED NATIONS   Under control of the international Illuminati.
→ Illuminati.

UNIVERSAL CONFEDERATION
A confederation of over 680 planets.
Planet Centurus in Alpha Centauri belongs to the Universal Confederation.
→ Soltec.

UNO   → United Nations.

UNIVERSAL CONFEDERATION of PLANETS
Member: Alta-Zar, Amor, Atrica, Bellarion, Dar-Nell, Eia, El-Tar Jenis, Elan, Elexar, Erisa, Gor-ed, Hatonn, Ka-L-Lia, Katonis, Kla-La, Korton, Lactu, Lalur, Le-Ar, Lotan, Meck-Tau, Merku, Mon-Ka, Mora, Myl-La N-Trok, Sig-Mar, Soltec, Surnia, Sutko, Voltra, Zo, Zolgus.

UNIVERSAL SPIRITUAL SUN
→ Solaris Kumara.

VIOLET RAY   → St. Germain.

VORTEX   The Vortex is a part of all universes in which all points in the multiverse collide, but is in itself no universe and belongs to none. The Vortex is devoid of all space and time.
→ Vortex Collective.

VRIL COMPANY   Founded 1919 in Germany.
Their medium Maria Orsitsch had telepathically contact to the Sumerian (Aldebaran) Empire.
They gave the Vril Company the correct plans (telepathically) to build the first Flying Saucers on Earth in the year 1922 with implosion technology.
The first German UFO was built in the year 1934, elevated 60 meters, then was without control, and was destroyed.

The 2nd German UFO was built in the same year and was photographed in the South Atlantic close to the Antarctica.

In the year 1942 they built 17 VRIL-1 UFOs with speeds up to 12,000 km/hour, diameter 11.5 m.

They built 1942 the HAUNEBU-III Flying Disc, diameter 71m, crew 32, duration of flight until 8 weeks, velocity 7,000 km/hour (until 40,000 km/h).

In 1944 they have planned to visit the Aldebaran star system with the huge spaceship VRIL-7.

It is said that at least one VRIL-7 spaceship with the name „ODIN" left to Aldebaran, from Brandenburg in Germany.

→ Peenemünde.

Walk-ins   Walk-ins are people from other dimensions who have walked into the body of a person here on Earth. Walk-ins usually carry the Crystal Gene.

WHITE BROTHERHOOD

→ Great White Brotherhood.

WHITE BROTHERHOOD of LIGHT

→ Brotherhood of Light.

WHITE KNIGHTS   Include many people from every race, religion, ethnicity, bankers, military leaders, politicians.

WHITE LODGE   → Great White Brotherhood.

WHITE SISTERHOOD   Member: Isis, Lady Mary, Lady Nada.

YORK RITE of FREEMASONRY

Other name for the Knights Templar.
→ Knights Templar.

3. PLANETS, STARS, STARSYSTEMS, GALAXIES, UNIVERSES

10th PLANET   Also called Nibiru, Planet-X will pass Earth in Spring 2003 after 3600 years.

11th PLANET   Is Maldek.

12th PLANET   Is Nibiru.

2001 KX76   Kuiper Belt object.
                         Diameter: approx. 960 – 1270 km.
                         → 10th Planet.

2002 AW197   Kuiper Belt object.
                         Diameter: approximately 540 miles (900 kilometers).

2004 DW   Kuiper Belt object, larger than Quaoar.
                         Diameter: approx. 1400 km,
                         Orbit: 4.4 billion miles.

AARMON   Small planet in the Pleiades.
                         → Cmdr. Aldelan.

ACHID   Star in Cassiopeia.

ACITARES   Planet in the Pleiades in the 5th dimension.
                         Also known as Akitares.

ADALIA   Planet in the Bootes Constellation.
                         Very strongly elevated in the 7th interdimension.

ADRASTEA   One of the four inner moons of Jupiter.
                         Orbit: 129,000 km,
                         Diameter: 20 km (23 x 20 x 15),
                         Radius: 10 km (6 miles),
                         Discovered: 1979.
                         Is one of the smallest moons in the Solar System.

AKITARES   → Acitares.

AKONOWAI   Sirian name of the Sirius B solar system.
                         → Sirius B.

AL MANKIB   Other name of Betelgeuse.

ALCIONE   → Alcyone.

ALCOR SYSTEM   Home of Korton.

ALCYONE	Huge central star in the Pleiades star cluster. Approx. 400 light-years from Earth.

Home of:
>>   a warrior Reptilian race,
>>   an Amphibian race,
>>   Aryan Human race.
A photon belt encircles the Pleiades, our sun is entering the Photon Belt between now & the year 2011.
Planets: Mushaba.
→ Photon Belt, Pleiades.
→ Alcyons, Pleiadians.

ALDEBARAN

(Arab.: the Follower).
Star in the Taurus constellation, also called Alpha Tau.
13ᵗʰ brightest star in the sky.
Distance from Earth 68 light-years.

Nearest star system with intelligent life form. 2 inhabited planets which build the Sumerian Empire.
Seat of the Galactic Tribunal around this mighty star.
There are no Greys in Aldebaran. There are human Terran colonies.
Apparently a space force may have helped to colonize that system by sending time-space forces back into the distant past to inhabit the 4ᵗʰ dimensional realm.
There are also Insectoid forces involved with Aldebaran.
→ Corporate Collective, Sumerian Empire.
→ Aldebarans.

ALDEBARAN

Planet in the Pleiades.
Beings: Amor.

ALDEBARAN-3

Beings: Kla-La, Sutko.

ALDERON

Planet in the Pleiades.
Very earthlike, has a blue atmosphere.
Distance to sun is 93,000,000 miles.

ALMACH

Star in the Andromeda constellation.
355 (+/- 28) light-years from Earth.
Also known as:
>>   Alamak,
>>   Almaach,
>>   Almaak,
>>   Almak.

ALNILAM

Blue super giant star in the Orion constellation.
Diameter: about 30 Suns,
Distance: 1340 light-years from Earth,
Brightness: 250,000 times brighter than our sun.
Means „String of Pearls".

ALNITAK   Triple star system in the Orion constellation.
                          Blue super giant star.
                          Diameter: about 15 Suns,
                          Distance: 820 light-years from Earth,
                          Brightness: at least 11,000 times brighter than the Sun.
                          Means „Belt, Girdle".

ALNITAK B   One of the 2 companion stars of Alnitak in the Orion
                          constellation.

ALNITAK C   One of the 2 companion stars of Alnitak in the Orion
                          constellation.

ALPHA CENTAURI
                          Other name is Rigel Kentaurus.
                          3 star system in the Centaurus constellation: Alpha Centauri A,
                          Alpha Centauri B, Proxima Centauri.
                          3rd brightest star in the sky.
                          Distance from Earth: 4.36 to 1,000 light-years.

                          Master Chiron is another who is returning from the Alpha
                          Centaurian complex.
                          Base of Ashtar.
                          Belongs to the Universal Confederation.
                          There is a Human Colony.
                          Planets: Centurus, Proximo Centauri.
                          → 25,000 B.C.E.
                          → Centaurians, Santinians.
                          → Andromedan Federation.
                          → Elizabeth Klarer.
                          → Musline, Soltec, Yuminale.

ALPHA DRACONI   Star system in the Orion Constellation.
                          37 light-years from Earth.
                          Also called Thuban.
                          Reptiloids are on the way to Earth.
                          Planets: Tiphon.
                          → Draconian Empire.
                          → Alpha Draconians.

ALPHA DRACONIS
                          → Alpha Draconi.

ALPHERATZ   Star in the Andromeda constellation.
                          97.1 (+/- 2.1) light-years from Earth.
                          Also known as:
                          >>   Alpherat,
                          >>   Sirah,
                          >>   Sirrah.

ALTAIR

Brightest, variable double star in the Aquila constellation.
15.7 light-years from Earth.

The 4th and 5th planet are inhabited.
Home of humans and Greys who have collaborated in the past.
They colonized the Pleiades long ago.
There was a contact with an Earth woman in the 1950s.
There is a small Earth Human military colony, containing families with children. They have enslaved the beings of that planet. They got there with the Montauk experiment.
Planets: Altaira.
→ Altairians.
→ Corporate Collective.

ALTAIR 4

There lives a race that visits Earth.

ALTAIR 5

There lives a race that visits Earth.

ALTAIRA

4th planet from the sun called Altair.
The atmosphere is controlled.
Home planet of the Nordics, there live also Greys.
Two moons: Alta One, Alta Two.
→ Greys, Nordics.

ALTEA

Planet.
→ Twelve Civilizations (Altea).
→ Alteans.

AMALTHEA

One of the four inner moons of Jupiter.

Orbit:	181,300 km (112,468 miles),
Diameter:	189 km (270 x 166 x 150),
Radius:	86.2 km (98 km) (54 miles),
Length:	270 km (168 miles),
Width:	about half of length,
Discovered:	1892.

Rotates synchronously.
Is the reddest object in the Solar System.
Radiates more heat than it receives from the Sun.
Amalthea consists of water ice and rock and the overall density is close to the density of water ice.

AMAZON STAR

Other name of Bellatrix.

ANANKE

One of the eight outer moons of Jupiter.

Orbit:	21,200,000 km,
Diameter:	30 km,
Radius:	15 km,
Discovered:	1951.

One of the smallest moons in the Solar System.
Ananke's orbit is retrograde and unusual.

ANDILLA   Galaxy.
                         → Council of 48.

ANDROMEDA   (M31) galaxy, 2,600,000 light-years from Earth.
                         It is in many respects similar to our own Milky Way.
                         2 million light-years from Earth.
                         Nearest major galaxy to the Milky Way.
                         The black hole in Andromeda's center is 30,000,000 times more
                         massive than our sun.

                         Stars: Sutarus.
                         Planets: Eritera, Mushaba.
                         → Council of Six.
                         → Andromedans.
                         → Islanda.

ANDROMEDA CONSTELLATION
                         Is not the Andromeda galaxy!
                         Stars: Almach, Alpheratz, Mirach, Tishtae, Zenatae.
                         → Mirach.
                         → Andromedans.

                         Home of the Orange race.

ANOVA   Planet, oldest inhabited world of Satania.

ANTARES   Star system.
                         → Antaris.

APAXEIN-LAU   Planet of the Zeta/Zephelium race.

AQUILA   Constellation.
                         Stars: Altair.
                         → Altairians.

ARAY   Planet in Cassiopeia.
                         They have many similarities with Earth people.
                         They are between 2,10m & 2,70m tall.
                         → Antonni.

ARCANNA 12   In the 12th interdimensionality.
                         From there came the "Gods".

ARCTURIA   Planet.
                         → Isross, Zoltar.

ARCTURUS	Cool orange (red) super-giant star in the Bootes Constellation. 4th brightest star, magnitude zero.
	Brightest star of the northern hemisphere.
	18 times larger than the sun, 4 times the sun's mass.
	Surface temperature of 4,290 degrees Kelvin.
	36 (37?) light-years from Earth.
	Also known as: Haris-el-sema, Alpha Boötis.
	→ Bootes.
	→ Corporate Collective.
	→ Tall White race, Telosians.
	They are healers of consciousness & thought.
	5th dimensional civilization. There is no sickness.
	One of the most advanced civilization in our galaxy.
	The fleets from Arcturus protect the planet Earth with thousands of ships.
	On this planet there is semi physical density.
	→ Arcturians.
	→ Ela, Mishar, Shaari.
ARCTURUS 2	Arcturus 2 is one of the 3 populated worlds in the system (out of 12 planets).
	One of the most advanced civilizations in this galaxy.
	Gravity is almost 3 times Earth's.
	Spiritual population number in the billions (it is a transitional planet).
	This 5th-dimension civilization is a prototype of Earth's future.
	2,5 times larger than Earth. Water makes up about 3 quarters of the planet. There is no salt. The atmosphere is about 6 times denser than Earth's. Purple is a predominant color.
ARES	They have huge motherships in the Ares Constellation.
ARIAN	Planet in the Pleiades.
ARIEL	Moon of Uranus.

	Orbit:	190,930 km,
	Diameter:	1158 km,
	Radius:	579 km,
	Discovered:	1851,
	Composition:	40 – 50% water ice, the rest is rock,
	Surface:	interconnected valleys, hundreds of kilometers long, more than 10 km deep.

ASEFETAS	The Belt of Orion.
Asteroids	There are probably at least 1000 asteroids larger than 1 km in diameter that cross the orbit of Earth.
	The largest are: Ceres(1), Pallas(2), Vesta(4), Hygieia(10).
ATARMUNK	3rd planet of the Sirius B solar system Akonowai.

ATLAS   Moon of Saturn.
                              Orbit: 137,670 km,
                              Diameter: 30 km (40 x 20),
                              Radius: 14 km,
                              Discovered: 1980.

ATLAS   Red planet of origin.

ATTASIC UNIVERSE

                              The unified field of all consciousness where there is no
                              separation.

AURIGA CONSTELLATION
                              Stars: Capella.
                              Home of the Dracos.
                              There are benevolent and malevolent races of Dracos.

AVYON   Planet of the Felines located in the Vega star system of Lyra, was
                              the original home of the Humans.
                              Blue paradise planet with mountains, lakes, streams, oceans.
                              First planet Avyon (1st Earth) was destroyed in the
                              Great Galactic War.
                              (2nd Earth) this planet in the Pleiades was destroyed when the
                              humans used their advanced technology to destroy the invading
                              forces of reptilian hybrids that in turn destroyed their own
                              planet.
                              3rd Earth is our Earth.

BARNARD I   Other name of Planet X.

BARNARD 33   Also known as Horsehead Nebula, located in the Orion
                              constellation.
                              → Horsehead Nebula.

BELINDA   One of the ten innermost moons of Uranus.
                              Orbit: 75,255 km,
                              Diameter: 68 km,
                              Radius: 34 km,
                              Discovered: 1986.

BELLACHIA   In the 12th universe.
                              Other name Betelgeuse in the Orion Constellation.
                              Inhabitants are humanoid in appearance & many have Lyran
                              linage.

BELLATON   Planet in the Sirius-B star system.
                              Home planet of humanoids and Insectoids.
                              It seems they are in a civil war, some are for the Federation,
                              others are for the Alpha Draconians and Orions.

BELLATRIX	Blue giant star in the Orion constellation.

Distance: from Earth 112.5 (243) light-years,
Diameter: about 5.7 times the Sun,
Brightness: about 1,000 times the Sun.
Also known as Amazon Star.

Home of the short Greys, about 3.5 ft tall.
Home of a mean Reptiloid race that is genetically engineered.
Also harbors many of the original egg-laying Reptilians.
The security levels there are one of the highest in this galaxy.
A Dinoid race approached Earth 26,000,000 years ago.
→ Lyra.
→ Bellatricians, Greys, Orange.
→ Draconian Empire.

BELLONA

Former 5th planet of the Solar System.
Other name of Maldek.

BERNARD'S STAR

Home world of the Orange.
→ Corporate Collective.
→ Bernarians.

BETA CENTAURI

→ Aris.

BETEIGUEX

Other name of Betelgeuse.

BETELGEUSE

Red super giant star in the Orion constellation.
One of the largest known stars.
Betelgeuse is a dying star.
Distance: 427 light-years from Earth.
Also known as: Al Mankib, Betelgeuze, Beteiguex, Betelguex, Betelgeuze.

There is a purple colored planet from which many UFOs come from. They use vehicles like space ships to enter the Earth's atmosphere.
Jointly occupied by Greys and giant humans that are about 9 to 12 ft tall.
→ Betelgeusians.
→ Bellachia, Lyra.

BETELGEUZE

Other name of Betelgeuse.

BETELGUEX

Other name of Betelgeuse.

BIANCA

One of the ten innermost moons of Uranus.
Orbit: 59,165 km,
Diameter: 44 km,
Radius: 22 km,
Discovered: 1986.

BIAVEH   Planet where the Biaviians originate. Located in the Tarian constellation, about 450 light-years from Earth.

BILA   Planet in Lyra, destroyed by the Alpha Draconians.

Black Hole   Some 38 black holes have been discovered in the universe.
                        You cannot have a galaxy without a black hole.
                        Super massive black holes are one million to one billion times the mass of the sun and are found at the centers of galaxies. They are invisible.
                        The energy output of a massive black hole is comparable to the energy of the galaxy over it's entire lifetime.

BLAZAR   A blazar is a special type of quasar that beams an intense jet of radiation in our direction.
                        All radio-loud quasars may be blazars.
                        Blazars are much brighter types of quasars.

BOOTES CONSTELLATION
                        Planets: Adalia, Arcturus 2.
                        Stars: Arcturus, Izar, Muphrid, Seginus.
                        → Alana, Dextra, Samaza, Zoltar.
                        → Corporate Collective.

CALIBAN   Moon of Uranus.
                        Orbit: 7,200,000 km,
                        Diameter: 80 km,
                        Radius: 40km,
                        Discovered: 1997.
                        Retrograde and highly inclined orbit.
                        Unusually red in color.

CALLISTO   Moon of Jupiter.
                        Orbit: 1,883,000 km (1,170,000 miles),
                        Diameter: 4800 km,
                        Radius: 2400 km,
                        Discovered: 1610,
                        Atmosphere: very tenuous, composed of carbon dioxide.
                        Surface is covered entirely with craters and is rich in ice.
                        There is no evidence of a magnetic field.
                        Larger than Pluto.
                        3 times darker than Europa.

CALYPSO   Moon of Saturn.
                        Orbit: 295,000 km,
                        Radius: 13 km,
                        Discovered: 1980.

CANIS MAJOR   Star system.
Stars: Sirius.
→ Venaticians.

CANIS MINORIS CONSTELLATION
→ Procyon, Procyon-A, Procyon-B.
→ Procyonans.

CANOPUS   2nd brightest star in the sky.

CAPELLA   Yellow-white and brightest star in the Auriga constellation.
Means „she-goat".
42 light-years from Earth.

Home of benevolent Dracos.
→ Draconian Empire.
→ Capellans.

CAPH   White star at 2.4 magnitudes in Cassiopeia.

CAPPELLA   → Capella.

CARME   One of the eight outer moons of Jupiter.
Orbit: 22,600,000 km,
Diameter: 40 km,
Radius: 20 km,
Discovered: 1938.
Retrograde, unusual orbit.

CASSIOPEIA   (M52).
Planets: Aray, Zel.
Stars: Achid, Caph, Gamma Cass, Marfak, Ruchbah,
Schedar, Segin.
→ Antonni, Santon.

CENTAUR   Star system.
There is plant, animal, human life form that is equivalent to our
Middle Ages.

CENTAURS   A class of small icy bodies that orbit the Sun between Saturn and
Uranus.

CENTAURUS   Star constellation.
Stars: Alpha Centauri, Beta Centauri.

CENTRAL SUN   The central sun with it's mass intelligence is in a neutral state.
Also known as Celestial Home.

CENTURUS   Planet in the Alpha Centauri system.
Belongs to the Universal Confederation.

CERES   Largest main-belt asteroid.
                     Diameter: 932 km,
                     Radius: 466 km,
                     Discovered: 1801.

CERPICAN   Morella is a city on this planet.
                     People: Oxmalc, Yenon.

CETUS CONSTELLATION
                     (Whale).
                     Pre Cetacean refugees from planet Earth arrived there approx.
                     8,000,000 B.C.E.
                     → Tau Ceti.
                     → TauCetians.

CETUS STAR SYSTEM
                     Composed of 6 planets.
                     Distance from Earth 800 light-years.
                     There lives a civilization of advanced land Cetaceans.

CHARON   Moon of Pluto.
                     Orbit: 19,640 km,
                     Diameter: 1172 km,
                     Discovered: 1978.
                     Charon and Pluto keep the same face (rotate synchronously).
                     Charon's surface seems to be covered with water ice, quite
                     different from Pluto.

                     Artificially planetoid built as an orbiting space-docking center.
                             Also has large warehouses like Pluto.
                     The cargos of visiting starships are unloaded here and then
                     ferried to Pluto by more conventional craft.

CHOWTA   Name of Ursa Minor in the Orion tongue.
                     → Ursa Minor.

CLARION   Star & planetary system in Orion that is of a positive nature.
                     Member: Aura Rhanes.

COMA BERENICES
                     Galaxy.

COMA CLUSTER   Contains thousands of galaxies.
                     Diameter: 1,500,000 light-years.

CORDELIA   One of the ten innermost moons of Uranus.
                     Orbit: 49,752 km,
                     Diameter: 26 km,
                     Radius: 13 km,
                     Discovered: 1986.
                     Is the smallest moon of Uranus.

CRESSIDA	One of the ten innermost moons of Uranus.
	Orbit: 61,767 km,
	Diameter: 66 km,
	Radius: 33 km,
	Discovered: 1986.

DAAL
Universe.
Origin of dolphins.

DAL
Universe.
→ Asket, Nera.
→ DAL's.

DARK SHAN
→ SHAN.

DARNAT
Planet in the Sirius system.

DEIMOS
The smaller and outermost of Mars' two moons.
Orbit: 23,549 km,
Diameter: 12.6 km (15 x 12.2 x 11),
Discovered: 1877.
Composed of carbon-rich rock and ice, like C-type asteroids.
Is the smallest moon in the Solar System.

Artificial moon, placed some 3000 years ago.
→ Mars.
→ Stanton Friedman.

DEMONICOUS
Planet out of Solar System, the people "Demons" are bad.

DENEB
Other names for this star are Deneb el Adige, Arided, Aridif, Gallina, or Arrioph.
White Super giant star, 1600 light-years from earth, estimated 60,000 times the luminosity of the Sun, mass about 20 times the Sun's mass.

DEPOINA
Moon of Neptune.

DERN
Is our universe.

DESDEMONA
One of the ten innermost moons of Uranus.
Orbit: 62,659 km,
Diameter: 58 km,
Radius: 29 km,
Discovered: 1986.

DESPINA
Irregularly shaped moon of Neptune.
Orbit: 52,600 km,
Diameter: 148 km,
Radius: 74 km,
Discovered: 1989.

DEXTON   Planet in the Orion Constellation.
                    They can live up to 3000 years.

DEXTRAS   Comet in the way to Earth.

DIONE   Moon of Saturn.
                    Orbit: 377,400 km,
                    Diameter: 1118 km (695 miles),
                    Radius: 560 km,
                    Discovered: 1684.
                    Is composed primarily of water ice but must have denser material
                    like silicate rock.
                    Rotates synchronously.

DIONE-B   Moon of Saturn.
                    Official name is Helene.
                    → Helene.

DOG STAR   Is Sirius.
                    → Sirius

DRUAN   Lies in the Nol System.

EARTH   Orbit: 149,600,000 km,
                    Diameter: 12,756.3 km (8,000 miles),
                    Radius: 6378 km,
                    Crust: 40 km,
                    Velocity: 21 km/sec, 1260 km/h, 75,600 km/h,
                                        1,815,156 km/day,
                    Age: 4,000,000,000 years old (estimated).
                    Densest planet in the Solar System.
                    Mean density is 5.245 times that of water.
                    Has a negative magnetic field, because Earth rotates clockwise.
                    Earth, Io, Triton and Venus are the only bodies in the Solar
                    System that are known to be volcanically active.
                    The planet could hold a population of 11 billion.
                    Harvard studies have put Earth's population capacity at 44
                    billion.

                    Created: 4,500,000,000 B.C.E.
                    Has the Grand Universe number 5,342,482,337,666.
                    Great Cycle Orbit: 206,000,000 years around the Great Central
                    Sun of the Milky Way Galaxy.
                    Here live 3rd and 4th dimensional beings.
                    Name of the Stella people is "The Garden".
                    The waiting list for incarnations is about 11,000,000,000 souls.
                    Earth lies along a galactic trade route into the Andromedan
                    galaxy.
                    First existed in the galactic core. The galactic Elohim thrust
                    planet Earth into her present position to balance the galaxy and
                    change its shape to spiral. Originally, the Earth was an ice planet
                    in a different orbit, closer to Mars, and nothing but ice.

Had at least 8 complete reversals of her poles.

"Our" planet is a cosmic laboratory, and we are but Guinea Pigs to those who have kept us prisoners on Earth.

100,000 humans reporting missing every year!

There are leaving about 100,000 children per year from all over the world.

Ancestors came from the Pleiades.

The original races were green-skinned, blood color was green.

The 12 tribes came from 12 different galaxies.

Black people are the only original race of this planet.

The rest came from other planets. Some say the Blacks came from Sirius.

The Chinese came from the civilization Ashan and Hoova.

The Japanese were taken from Mars. It is said that the Chinese also came from Mars.

The Cherokee Indians came from the Pleiades. First they wend underground before they decided to come up to the surface.

Densest physical planet in the local universe.

The only planet with free will in the universe.

Each being in the universe has to incarnate on planet Earth, at least 1 time.

The only place in the universe where beings can transmute negativity into positivity is on planet Earth.

Crop Circles are made by extraterrestrials.

There are many Zeta-Reticulis and entities who origin from Orion constellation who are embodied in human-bodies.

The reptiles were brought from Jupiter, Neptune contributed mermaids & mermen, Venus brought unicorns & fairies, Uranus brought the Sasquatch.

Unicorns mutated into deer, reptiles mutated into birds, mermaids & fairies have withdrawn to Earth's etheric dimension.

All of the languages of the planet have their origins within the structures of extraterrestrial languages, the letters and their numerical values.

There are some 1,800 reptilians inside: have been responsible for some 37,000 human children disappearing. They drain fluids from the brains of children while they are in fear, it is like a narcotic.

100 to 200 miles under the surface are 1,837 reptilians, 17 Humans from Sirius-B, 18,000 Grey clones inside Earth and the Moon, 141 Orion beings from 9 different races.

The flood of Noah was as a result of the movement of Earth from one orbit to another around the sun, magnetic poles of the Earth rotated 180 degrees.

The native American races are the remnants of the ancient Babylonians, they were brought there and hidden underground just prior to the flood of Noah.

There is a tremendous amount of extraterrestrial technology buried in Nigeria.

It is also said that planet Earth is hollow and has an inner sun. The hollow Earth is inhabited by humans.

Also known as: Eridu, "Garden", "Great Tomb", Hollow Earth, Maldek, Saras, Shan, Tara, Terra, Urantia, "World of the Cross").
→ Arcturians, Seeders.
→ 196,000 B.C.E., 225,000 b.C, 1,000,000 B.C.E., 8,000,000 B.C.E.
→ Agam Des.

EDENTIA   Planet, headquarters of Norlatiadek.

EL NATH   Star in the Taurus constellation.

ELARA   One of the eight outer moons of Jupiter.
Orbit: 11,737,000 km,
Diameter: 76 km,
Radius: 38 km,
Discovered: 1905.

ENCELADUS   Moon of Saturn.
Orbit: 238,020 km (147,948 miles),
Diameter: 505 km (314 miles),
Radius: 260 km,
Discovered: 1789.
Composed mostly of water ice and silicate rock. Most reflective object in the Solar System. Surface is dominated by water ice. Has a significant atmosphere. Surface temperature -200C (-330 Fahrenheit).

ENSA   Minor sector of Universes, consists of 100 local universes. Capitol is Uminor the Third.

EPIMETHEUS   Moon of Saturn.
Orbit: 151,422 km,
Diameter: 115 km (144 x 108 x 98), (72 miles),
Radius: 57 km,
Discovered: 1980.
→ Janus.

EPSILON BOOTES
Home of the Dows.
→ Draconian Empire.
→ Dows.

EPSILON ERIDANI
There live the Ataien, Ummites.
Human colony, work closely with the Tau Cetians.
→ Andromedan Federation, Galactic Federation.
→ Ataien, Ummites.

ERIDU   Sirian name for Earth.
→ An.

ERITERA   Planet in the Andromeda galaxy.

EROS	Asteroid.
ERRA	Planet in Taygeta in the Pleiades/Plejaren. Erra is 10% smaller than Earth. There are 5th dimensional beings. About 400,000 people live there. Following Errans are/were in contact with Billy Meier: Elektra, Enjana, Florena, Isados, Pleja, Ptaah, Quetzal, Rala, Samjang, Semjase, Tauron, Zafenatpaneach. Their voyage to Earth takes about 7 hours.
ERRA-TAYGETA	(Pleiades), member of the Galactic Federation.
ESSASSANI	Planet in the Orion constellation, about 500 light-years from Earth. This planet was chosen as one of the homes for the hybrids. Essassani means "Place of Living Light". Channel: Walter D. Pullen. → Bashar.

EUROPA

Moon of Jupiter.

Orbit:	670,900 km (416,000 miles), 600,000 km (370,000 miles) above Jupiter's cloud tops,
Diameter:	3138 km,
Radius:	1569 km (972 miles),
Discovered:	1610,
Atmosphere:	very tenuous, composed of oxygen.

Europa has hydrated salt minerals.
A little bit smaller than Earth's moon.
Larger than Pluto.
Has one of the brightest surfaces in the Solar System (rich in ice).
Has a thin outer layer of ice.
Europa's surface is exceedingly smooth.
Composed primarily of molten silicate rock.
There are only 3 craters found that are larger than 5 km, indicating that recent or geologic activity has removed the traces of older impacts.
Europa's most striking aspect is a series of dark streaks crisscrossing the entire globe, thousands of kilometers long, which are caused by the tides raised by Jupiter's gravitational pull.
Of the moons in the Solar system only Europa, Ganymede, Io, Titan and Triton have an atmosphere.
The evidence is now strong for a subsurface ocean of liquid water.
Europa has a weak magnetic field.

There is a place for hybrids.

EXXON	Galaxy. Planets: Owander.

FLOREIDA   Galaxy.
                       Planets: Osiran.

FOMALHAUT   Brightest star in the Piscus Austrinus Constellation.

                       Beings: Eia.

GALATEA   Irregular shaped moon of Neptune.
                       Orbit: 62,000 km,
                       Diameter: 158 km,
                       Radius: 79 km,
                       Discovered: 1989.

GALAXY   The Local Cluster of Galaxies contains at least 28 separate
                       galaxies, including Andromeda, Milky Way.
                       An estimated 125 billions of galaxies exist in this universe.

                       Each galaxy, depending on it's origin, goes through a phase of
                       ascension every 26,000 years.
                       There is a galactic federation in each of the inhabited galaxies of
                       our universe.
                       → Black Hole, Milky Way.

GALAXY CLUSTER   Galaxy cluster are the largest gravitationally bound structures in
                       the universe, typically contains a few hundred to thousands of
                       galaxies, each of which in turn contains many billions of stars.
                       There are known over 100 galaxy clusters.

GALILEAN MOONS
                       Galileo discovered 1610 the Jovian moons Callisto, Europa,
                       Ganymede & Io.

GAMMA CASS   Middle star in Cassiopeia.
                       White binary star, magnitudes 2 & 11.

GANYMEDE   Largest moon of Jupiter.
                       Orbit: 1,070,000 km,
                       Diameter: 5262 km,
                       Radius: 2631 km (1637 miles),
                       Discovered: 1610,
                       Atmosphere: thin, composed of oxygen, very similar
                                       to Europa.
                       Largest moon in the Solar System.
                       Larger in diameter than Mercury, much larger than Pluto.
                       Of the moons in the Solar System only Ganymede, Callisto,
                       Europa, Io, Titan and Triton have an atmosphere.
                       Has it's own internally generated magnetic field.
                       Hidden salt-water ocean believed.
                       Has a very old surface, highly cratered, dark regions, extensive
                       array of grooves & ridges.
                       Ganymede is covered with lots of ice.

Also known as Morlen.

People: Antar, Lertrad, Oesceve, Olea, Oletamo, Olmex, Omen, Omuni, Ordelat, Ossim, Oxalc, Oxiram, Oxlam, Oxmalc.

GARDEN → Earth.

GAROUCHE Water-bound planet populated by an intelligent fish form.

GLAY Galaxy in Pacifica.

GRAND UNIVERSE

Consists of Superuniverses like the Grand Universe.

Urantia's (Earth's) registry number in the catalogue of inhabited worlds on Uversa and Paradise is 5,342,482,337,666.

GREAT CENTRAL SUN

At the core of the Milky Way galaxy.

→ Earth.

GREAT TOMB → Earth.

GREATER MAGELLANIC CLOUD

Neighbor galaxy of the Milky Way.

HALE BOPP Distance from Sun: 2,000,000,000 km (March 2001).

The tail measures at least 2,000,000 km.

It is not a comet.

HATONA Planet in the Andromeda galaxy.

HELENE Moon of Saturn.

Orbit: 377,400 km,
Diameter: 33 km (36 x 32 x 30).
Radius: 16 km,
Discovered: 1980.

Sometimes referred to as Dione-B.

HELIOS Other name for our Sun.

HERCOLUBUS Other name for Planet X.

HERCULES CLUSTER

Several humanoid colonies are there.

HIDDEN UNIVERSE

God's playground.

HIMALIA   Brightest of the eight outer moons of Jupiter.
                        Orbit: 11,480,000 km,
                        Diameter: 186 km,
                        Radius: 93 km,
                        Discovered: 1904.

HOBUS   Moon of Mars (Russian name).

HOLLOW EARTH   In Northern Canada close to the North Pole there is a 78 miles
                        diameter opening into the planet.
                        → Earth.

HOOVA   → Twelve Civilizations (Hoova).

HORSEHEAD NEBULA
                        Also known as Barnard 33, located in the Orion constellation.
                        Lies just south of the bright star Zeta Orionis.
                        Is a cold, dark cloud of gas and dust.

HUT-RON   3rd planet of Sirius B.

HYADES   Open cluster in the Taurus Constellation.
                        Contains about 200 stars.
                        Diameter: central group is about 10 light-years, outlying
                                         members until about 80 light-years.
                        Distance: 150 (151?) light-years from Earth.

                        Various colonies are member of the Galactic Federation.
                        Ancestors came from Lyra.
                        → Taurus Constellation.
                        → Hyadeans.

HYDRA   Star cluster.
                        → Solemine.

HYGIEIA   Asteroid.
                        Radius: 215 km,
                        Discovered: 1849.

HYPERION   Moon of Saturn.
                        Orbit: 1,481,000 km,
                        Diameter: 266-286 km (410 x 260 x 220) (165 miles),
                        Radius: 143 km,
                        Discovered: 1848.
                        Hyperion is the largest highly irregular (non-spherical) body in
                        the Solar System.
                        Composed of water ice with only a small amount of rock.
                        Hyperion is the only known body in the Solar System that rotates
                        chaotically.

IAPETUS

Moon of Saturn.
Orbit: 3,561,300 km,
Diameter: 1436 km (892 miles),
Radius: 730 km,
Discovered: 1672.
Iapetus must be composed almost entirely of water ice.

IARGA

Planet approx. 10 light-years from Earth.
It is almost completely a water world, greater than Earth, much denser (greenish) atmosphere than Earth, has a slow rotation.
→ Iargans.

INNER EARTH

→ Earth.

IO

Closest moon of Jupiter.
Orbit: 421,000 km (262,000 miles),
Diameter: 3630 km,
Radius: 1815 km,
Discovered: 1610,
Atmosphere: thin, composed of sulfur dioxide and
                perhaps other gases, space-cold,
Temperature: -150 (surface),
Volcanoes: Loki (the most powerful volcano in the
                Solar System), Tvashtar.
About the size of the Earth moon.
Larger than Pluto.
Hottest body outside the Sun, up to 1610 Celsius (2910 Fahrenheit).
The most volcanically active body in the Solar System.
Has more than 100 active and large volcanoes that emit sulfur and sulfur dioxide, a small part of this material escapes in space.
The Amirani lava flow is the largest active field lava flow in the Solar System, more than 300 km (190 miles), over 620 square kilometers (240 square miles).
Primarily composed of molten silicate rock.
Io has little or no water.
Io, Earth, Triton & Venus are the only bodies in the Solar System that are known to be volcanically active.
It is indicated that Io has an iron core with a radius of at least 900 km.
Io faces always the same side toward Jupiter.
Of the moons in the Solar System only Io, Callisto, Europa, Ganymede, Titan & Triton have an atmosphere.

ISHNA

Planet in the Sirius system where the Crystal People live. Has a large blur white star.

IUMMA

Also known as Wolf 424.
→ Andromedan Federation.

IUMMO

→ Ummo.

JANOS   Radioactive polluted planet after an asteroid/meteor shower that
                    destroyed the surface and underground cities.
                    → Janosian.

JANUS   Moon of Saturn.
                    Orbit: 151,472 km,
                    Diameter: 181 km (196 x 192 x 150) (113 miles),
                    Radius: 89 km,
                    Discovered: 1966.
                    Janus and Epimetheus are co-orbital, differ by only 50 km.

JERUSEM   Planet, headquarters of Satania.

JULIET   One of the ten innermost moons of Jupiter.
                    Orbit: 64,358 km,
                    Diameter: 84 km,
                    Radius: 42 km,
                    Discovered: 1986.

JUPITER   Orbit: 778,330,000 km,
                    Diameter: 142,984 km,
                    Radius: 71,492 km,
                    Atmosphere: 60,000 km thick.
                    Has 61 known moons (2003/06/06), 21 distant moons have
                    been discovered (2003), most of them are about 1 – 5 km in size.
                    Inner moons: Callisto, Europa, Ganymede, Io.
                    Outer moons: Adrastea, Amalthea, Ananke, Carme,
                                    Elara, Himalia, Leda, Lysithea, Metis,
                                    Pasiphae, Sinope, Thebe.
                    The outer satellites are all tiny, less than 100 km (62 miles).
                    Largest of the 9 "known" planets.
                    More than 10 times the diameter of Earth, more than 300 times
                    Earth's mass.
                    Jupiter's mass is almost 2.5 times the mass of all other planets
                    combined.
                    2nd brightest planet in the Solar System, 4th brightest object in the
                    sky.
                    Composed largely of hydrogen and helium.
                    Mean density is 1.314 times that of water.
                    Clouds are of ammonia crystals, made up of 89% hydrogen, 11%
                    helium (75%/25% by mass) with traces of methane, water,
                    ammonia and rocky material.
                    Winds reach more than 400 miles per hour.
                    Jupiter radiates more energy into space than it receives from the
                    Sun.
                    Jupiter has a huge magnetic field, much stronger than Earth's.
                    Jupiter's magnetic field has more than doubled.
                    Its magnetosphere extends more than 650,000,000 km, past the
                    orbit of Saturn.
                    Jupiter has rings like Saturn's but much fainter and smaller, they
                    seem to contain no ice.
                    The Great Red Spot is larger than Earth.

Some of the moons are artificial, some are used as recreational areas.

The Great Red Spot is the location for Jupiter's main city.

A gigantic force field around Jupiter causes light to be reflected in a strange way.

Jupiter has a beautiful surface, golden sky, warm air.

The planet's environment is altered and controlled in occupied areas.

Is a light blue sun on the 5th density.

Jupiter has the oldest native race and civilization in the Solar System.

It was the only planet that was inhabited when the other planets were colonized.

Beings invisible, space ships more developed than Uranus ships.

Entities that are living there inside the planet are of the gaseous state.

The Jupiterians are reptiles.

J.W., Fleets for evacuation.

Is the home of the black race.

→ Jupiterians.
→ El-Tar, Elexar, Esola, J.W., Jehoshaphat, Jove, Orbido, Zorb.

KAHRONA   Planet in Orion.

KANTARIA   Planet in the binary Sirius star system.

KHAN MAYOR   Second sun of Sirius.

KHOOM   Planet in the binary Sirius star system.

KOLDAS   → Koldasian System.
                     → Koldasians.
                     → Valdar.

KOLDASIAN SYSTEM
                     Member of the Galactic Federation.

KOMESSO   Planet.
                     → Amassia, Desmaorah.

KONDOR   Planet.

KORENDER   Colonized human planet.

KRUGERKO   The planets in this system are full of minerals, platinum, plutonium, silver.

KUIPER BELT   There are about 600 known Kuiper Belt Objects, most of which are only about 100 km in diameter, and all of which were discovered since 1992 by different scientists who have been looking for them. It is similar to the asteroid belt, but beyond Neptune and contains maybe 100 times more material.

The Kuiper Belt region of the solar system, which stretches from just past Neptune to beyond the farthest reaches of Pluto's orbit, was only discovered in 1992, but continues to reveal new knowledge into the formation processes of the planets.

New objects discovered in the year 2001 - 2004, called: 2001 KX76, Varuna, 2002 AW197, 2002 LM60 (Quaoar), 2004 DW.

→ Quaoar.

LARGE MAGELLANIC CLOUD (LMC)
160,000 – 170,000 light-years from Earth. Closest galaxy to Milky Way.

LARISSA   Moon of Neptune.
Orbit: 73,600 km,
Diameter: 193 km,
Radius: 96 km,
Discovered: 1989.
Irregular shaped (non-spherical), heavily cratered.

LASMUR   Planet in the Orion constellation.

LATANIA   Galaxy.
→ Thor.

LEDA   One of the eight outer moons of Jupiter.
Orbit: 11,094,000 km,
Diameter: 16 km,
Radius   8 km,
Discovered: 1974.
One of the smallest moons in the Solar System.
The smallest moon of Jupiter.

LEMURIA   Planet.
→ 156,000 B.C.E.

LEO CONSTELLATION
→ Mistris.

LOCAL CLUSTER of GALAXIES
There are at least 28 separate galaxies including Andromeda, Milky Way.

LYRA	There were 14 planets, 3 were destroyed by the Alpha Draconians. There were 3 inhabited planets: >> Mu, >> Shapeshifter race (Changelings), >> Reptilians. There was a war between this 3 races in which planet Mu was destroyed by a brown dwarf star that was steered by the Shapeshifters. The planet of the Reptilians was thrown in a different orbit and the inhabitants evacuated their planet. The Shapeshifters also left for Orion (Bellatrix and Betelgeuse). 14,000,000,000 habitants. Have more than one race type on their planet. Work closely with the DAL's & Pleiadians. After the war they fled to the Pleiades, Hyades and Vega. The human race lived there for approx. 40,000,000 years in peace. The Lyrans began evacuating their planet over 22,000,000 years ago. All of the human race comes from Lyra, although the human race did not originally exist in Lyra, it came from an other galaxy. Stars: Vega. Planets: Bila, Merck, Mu, Teka. → Lyrans. → Mu.

LYRA CONSTELLATION

Lyra is Arabic and means „swooping eagle".
→ Pegasians.

LYSITHEA	One of the eight outer moons of Jupiter. Orbit: 11,720,000 km, Diameter: 36 km, Radius: 18 km, Discovered: 1938.
M31	Is the Andromeda galaxy. → Andromeda Galaxy.
M45	Are the Pleiades.
M51	Also called NGC 5194, Whirlpool galaxy.
M52	→ Cassiopeia.
M82	10,000,000 light-years from Earth.
MAKIER	→ Maldek.
MALADEC	→ Maldek.

MALDEC   Planet dominated by female warriors.
                        → Maldek.

MALDEK   Diameter: 46,920 km (29,000 miles).
                        Was Earth-like, contained many oceans, continents, lakes. It
                        became a planet on which reptiles and various dinosaur species
                        became high levels of sentiency, but they became exploited by
                        dark forces.
                        A planet once orbiting between Mars & Jupiter was destroyed by
                        Nibiru, also destroyed the colonies on Mars, Venus and Earth.
                        There was an interplanetary war between the Lemurian
                        descendants from planet Mu in the Lyra star system who had
                        settled on Maldek and the Atlantean descendants who had settled
                        on Earth.
                        The Aryans, Reptilians, Shapeshifter were also involved in this
                        war.
                        The Aryans, Ashtar and the Shapeshifter decided to sacrify the
                        entire planet rather than to let take over the Reptilians this
                        planet. A couple billion people died in that explosion.
                        A group of Maldek evacuated before to the planet Earth in the
                        year 186,500 B.C.E. Some of them traveled back in time to the
                        year 387,000 B.C.E.
                        Maldek had two or three moons:
                        >>   the largest chutes became Earth and our moon,
                        >>   an other one is the moon Phobos.
                        Served for over 1,000,000 years as the dark Anchara Alliance's
                        headquarters, Galactic Federation forces destroyed Maldek.
                        (*100,000 B.C.E., 1,000,000 B.C.E., 2,400,000 B.C.E.*) destroyed in
                        a war by the Galactic Federation, against the Dinoid/Reptoid
                        forces. Fugitives came to Earth from this bad planet.
                        The Rockefeller family & those close to it, are souls of the
                        leaders of the former planet Maldek, most of them are in the
                        United States.
                        Remains are the asteroid/planetoid belt.
                        Destroyed with atomic energy by the locals with some cousins of
                        the Pleiades and various renegades.
                        Was destroyed in the war of Forces of Light and Forces of the
                        Dark.
                        Had been ruled by women, like the Greek Amazons.
                        Inhabitants were called Abbenaki, Abernache.
                        Other names: Bellona, Maladec, Maldec, Mallona, Malona,
                        Mardek, Marduk, Nemesis, Phaeton, Tinmet.
                        Is in process of being reconstructed.
                        → Mars, Moon of Earth, Pluto, Saturn, Senayaga.
                        → 8.000.000 B.C.E., 705,000 B.C.E., 500,000 B.C.E.
                        → Athena, K-L-Lia, Ranya.

MALLONA   → Maldek.

MALONA   → Maldek.

MARDEK   → Maldek.

MARDUK   Other name of Maldek.

MARFAK   Star in Cassiopeia.

MARIACA   Planet in the first universe. Was one of the planets
                     destroyed in the Galactic Wars.
                     Inhabitants of Mariaca are the architects of the universe.

MARS   Orbit: 227,940,000 km,
                     Closest distance to Earth: 35 to 63 million miles.
                     Diameter: 6794 km (4,200 miles),
                                       (when in fact it is 11,421 miles),
                     Radius: 3398 km (3397 km),
                     Day: 24h 37 min (24.623 hours),
                     Year: 687 Earth days, 668.61 Mars days,
                     Mass: 11 % of Earth,
                     Gravity: 38 % of Earth,
                     Atmosphere: very thin, composed of
                                       95.3 % carbon dioxide, 2.7 % nitrogen,
                                       1.6 % argon, 0.15 % oxygen,   0.03 %
                                       water.
                                       The Martian atmosphere is getting sizably
                                       thicker, in 1997 the atmosphere was twice as
                                       dense as calculated,
                     Temperature: -140 to +20 Celsius (-133C to +27C),
                                       average – 55C,
                                       (when in fact it's average temp. is 59
                                       degrees at the equator).
                     Has only two moons: Deimos, Phobos (Hobus).
                     Has the largest mountain in the Solar System, rising 24 km
                     (78,000 ft).
                     There are some volcanoes.
                     Has a system of canyons 4000 km long, 2 to 7 km deep.
                     Has an impact crater that is over 6 km deep, 2000 km in
                     diameter.
                     Mars has very strong winds and dust storms.
                     Has permanent ice caps at both poles composed mostly of solid
                     carbon dioxide (dry ice).
                     Has water ice clouds.
                     Has large, weak magnetic fields.

                     Babylonian's name was Nergal.
                     Colonized 2,000,000 B.C.E., destroyed 1,000,000 B.C.E. by the
                     Dinoid/Reptoids from Maldek.
                     Beings are visible.
                     Inhabited in the 5th dimension.
                     There were two intelligent races competing: an ant-like race and a
                     praying mantis-like race. The "praying mantis" race ascended,
                     "Mars Face" is a relict of the praying mantis race, the ant race
                     was very warlike. After they destroyed themselves, larger
                     numbers incarnated on Earth.

The Martians are mostly scientific. The Martians have
a totalitarian system.

The average height goes from 2,70 to 3,60 m. They live in a
much denser environment.

Mars had a very high state of consciousness until it was attacked
by great forces of control.

It is the home of the yellow race.

There exist a U.S base!

The Germans were there.

Mars has a huge (ancient) underground facility built by the
Sirians.

KOR is located in the Utopia area on the North Regio Plateau.

Mars is a link between the Solar System and the outer galaxies.

45% of all spacecraft in this sector of space is produced on Mars.

The moons Deimos and Phobos act as dynamic stabilizers of
Mars' orbit around the Sun.

They were placed there as a result of the planet Maldek
destruction.

The blast of the destroyed planet Maldek (Mallona) almost
damaged completely Mars, transforming it into an arid desert.
The nations there migrated to Earth. To keep Mars in orbit, they
constructed two artificial moons around it.

There are 16 bases of the Galactic Federation and it's planned to
add another 6 bases.

There is a galactic base of the Starfleet underground with the
central of communications, the station KOR, directed by Cmdr.
Korton.

There is an old (1,000,000 B.C.E.) Orion Group base that has
been reactivated and is completely underground:

64 square miles, 5 levels, extends to 8,500 ft below surface, fully
operational since June 1994, contains 2,111 scout craft, over
100,000 Orion & Draconian troops.

Mars has been inhabited for 3.8 billion years.

In the old buried Lyran city (113,000,000 B.C.E.) there is now an
Earth base called Eve, reactivated with the help of the Greys. It
stretches over an area of 118 miles. it houses approx. 300,000
human beings.

Much of the hardware taken to Mars came from the Moon first,
via Russia & Diego Garcia in the Indian Ocean.

There is an other Earth base called Adam, which stretches 2.6
miles in diameter.

→ 1959, 77,000 B.C.E., 1,000,000 B.C.E.

→ Alalu, Efi, Kor.

→ Arianiva, Firkon, Glenzia, Ilmuth, Ithacar, Korton, Lotan,
Malacandra, Masar, Meck-Tau, Merku, Myl-La N-Trok, Nur El,
Winka, Zo.

→ Arcathians.

MAWUVIA   Destroyed planet, prototype of Earth.
                         → Nirih.

MERCK   Planet in Lyra, destroyed by the Alpha Draconians.

MERCURY

Orbit: 57,910,000 km (46,000,000 to 70,000,000 km),
Radius: 2439 km,
Atmosphere: very thin,
Surface: very large cratered.
Used to be a moon of Saturn.
Mercury's orbit is highly eccentric.
Mercury rotates 3 times in 2 of its years.
Has a large iron core, about 1800 to 1900 km in radius.
The silicate outer shell is only 500 to 600 km thick.
Mercury's north pole shows evidence of water ice in the protected shadows of some craters.
Has a small magnetic field.
Mercury has no known satellites.

Used as a research station.
Was originally a moon of another planet.
Once had a small sister planet called Vulcan.
→ El Morya, Veritilbia.

MEROPE

Star located in the Pleiades.

Meteorites

Hoba, the largest found meteorite weighs 60 tons and was found in Namibia.
About 120 impact crater have been identified on Earth.
Meteor craters:
>> Arizona, near Winslow: diameter: 1200m, deep 200m,
>> Tunguska: this meteor destroyed about 50 km2, the sound of the explosion was heard in London,
>> Yucatan, near Chicxulub: diameter 180 km.

METHARIA

Home planet of the Santinians.
Earth-like, one big continent and many islands.
Population 3.5 billion.

METIS

One of the four inner moons of Jupiter.
Orbit: 128,000 km,
Diameter: 40 km,
Radius: 20 km (12 miles),
Discovered: 1979.

METON

Planet, visited by Elizabeth Klarer.
Inhabitants: Akon.

MILKY WAY   About 100,000 light-years across, 100 billion stars.
                          The center of the galaxy is about 26,000 light-years from Earth.

                          50,000,000,000 B.C.E. birth of Milky Way galaxy.
                          This galaxy consists of nine spiral arms connected to a central
                          core.
                          There are 77 other galaxies around this one.
                          There are over 135 billion human beings in the 8 galaxies closest
                          to ours.
                          There are 3 major players in this galaxy:
                          >>   Galactic Federation,
                          >>   Orion Empire,
                          >>   Reptoid Federation.
                          There are only 2 pure races in this galaxy:
                          >>   Alpha Draconians,
                          >>   Elohim.

MIMAS   Moon of Saturn.
                          Orbit: 185,200 km,
                          Diameter: 398 km (247 miles),
                          Radius: 196 km,
                          Discovered: 1789.
                          Mimas' surface is dominated by an impact crater 130 km (80
                          miles) across and 10 km (6 miles) deep, known as Herschel.
                          Composed mostly of water ice with only a small amount of rock.

MINTAKA   One of the bright stars in the Belt of Orion.
                          Hot blue bright giant star.
                          Distance: 233 (920 (+/- 210)) light-years from
                                            Earth,
                          Brightness: about 3,000 times the Sun's.
                          Means „Belt".

MIRACH   Distance: 199.4 (+/- 9.3) light-years from Earth.
                          Also known as:
                          >>   Merach,
                          >>   Mirac,
                          >>   Mirak,
                          >>   Mizar.

                          Central sun in the Andromeda system.
                          There are 919 stars revolving around Mirach.
                          Approx. 130 stars have inhabited planets, some of them have
                          been on Earth before.

MIRANDA

Innermost of Uranus' large moons.

Orbit: 129,850 km,
Diameter: 472 km,
Radius: 236 km,
Sun distance: about 3 billion km.

Miranda is about half water ice and half rocky material.

Miranda's surface is all mixed up, heavily cratered terrain intermixed with weird grooves, valleys and cliffs (one over 5 km high).

MOON (of Earth)

Orbit: 384,000 km,
Radius: 1738 km (2100 miles),
Atmosphere: none, but now is growing an atmosphere, made up of a 6000 km deep natrium compound layer,
Age: 6.2 billion years.

Larger than Pluto.

The Moon is older than Earth.

It faces always the same side toward Earth.

The Moon rotates synchronously.

There is ice on the poles in some deep craters.

Moon's largest crater – on the far side – is 2250 km in diameter and 12 km deep (the largest impact basis in the Solar System).

The Moon has no global magnetic field.

The natrium atmosphere is about 6,000 km deep (June 2002). In the year 1969 there was <u>no</u> atmosphere on the moon.

The Earth had two moons at the time of Lemuria, one was destroyed by the Atlantean upheaval to Lemuria about 25,000 B.C.E. with the intention to destroy Lemuria.

Was a huge Reptilian ship that invaded Earth many thousands of years ago. They were driven off the Earth by the Lyran Empire, there they remain until they are to be reactivated by an huge incoming Reptilian ship of the same kind. These reptilians also maintain bases on Venus and some of the moons of the outer planets.

There live about 18,000 Greys (on and under the surface).

Human beings have been there for about 50 years, it started with the Germans which moved on to Mars.

There are bases of the U.S., Russia & Great Britain.

There are approx. 36,719 human beings from Earth, only Aryans by birth.

It was a natural moon that was brought to Earth (9,000 B.C.E.) (by the Starfleet?) from deep space.

The present moon was one of two Maldek moons.

Our moon has an atmosphere on the hidden side.

The Moon has several man-made lakes upon its surface, it possesses a gravity field.

Apollo 15 took pictures of water vapor clouds that appeared from the hidden side which has many large underground lakes.

Parts of the surface soil are radioactive.

Has been inhabited periodically for 1.8 million years.
It is hollow and contains huge underground facilities built by ETs and later by humans from Earth.
Many of the great craters were 9 domed cities destroyed during a war about 111,000 B.C.E.
The Moon is in fact an artificial satellite and there are many bases on it.
It was one of 4 moons around the 17th planet of the Chowta system (Ursa Minor).
It was an outpost for members of the Orion Group and was inhabited by 5,000,000 Orion militaries.
→ Year 2003, 111,000 B.C.E.
→ Black Monks, NWO.
→ Chowta, Maldek, Ursa Minor.

MORLEN   Other name of Jupiter's moon Ganymede.

MU   Planet in the Lyra star system.
Origin of the Lemurian and Atlantean civilizations.
Many of the inhabitants evacuated to a planet in the Orion star system before planet Mu was destroyed by a brown dwarf star in an interplanetary war.
Almost 2,000,000,000 people died in that catastrophe.
→ Lyra.

MUKTARIN   4th planet of the Sirius B solar system. This planet resembles Earth, there live whales and dolphins.

Multiverse   All universes together.

MUSHABA   Planet in the Alcyone Star System in the Pleiades. This planet was transferred from the Andromeda Galaxy.

MYTON   Planet in the Pleiades.

NAIAD   Irregularly shaped moon of Neptune.
Orbit: 48,200 km,
Diameter: 58 km,
Radius: 29 km,
Discovered: 1989.

NEBADON   Our local universe, capital is Salvington.

NEBIRU   Other name of Nibiru.

NEJALCAN   Planet, star gate station.

NEMESIS   Other name of Maldek.

NEPTUNE   Orbit: 4,504,300,000 km,
                     Diameter: 49,532 km,
                     Radius: 24,764 km,
                     Discovered: 1846,
                     Surface temp.:   -240 C,
                     Atmosphere: 86 % hydrogen,
                                       19 % helium,
                                       1 % methane,
                     Spin: 16 h 7 min,
                     Year: 163 years 9 months.
                     Has 8 moons: Despina, Galatea, Larissa, Naiad, Nereid, Proteus, Thalassa, Triton.

4th largest planet (by diameter), Neptune is smaller in diameter but larger in mass than Uranus.
Neptune's atmosphere is more active than Uranus's.
The Great Dark Spot in the southern hemisphere has the size of Earth, but now has disappeared.
Storms with wind speeds more than 1100 miles (2000 km) per hour at the equator.
Atmosphere is 17 times as massive as the Earth.
For a few years Neptune is the most distant planet because of Pluto's eccentric orbit.
Neptune is of blue color.
It radiates more than twice as much energy as it receives from the Sun.
Neptune has very dark rings.
Neptune's magnetic field is oddly oriented and now is increasing.

Higher evolved than Earth, but until yet no space travel.
Very beautiful planet, has an electric-blue atmosphere.
The vegetation has returned to a state of natural wilderness, as the native race is living in the atmosphere.
→ Lalur.
→ Neptunians.

NEREID   Moon of Jupiter.
                     Orbit: 5,513,400 km (1,353,600 km to 9,623,700 km),
                     Diameter: 340 km,
                     Radius: 170 km,
                     Discovered: 1949.

Nereid's orbit is the most highly eccentric of any body in the Solar System.

NERGAL   Babylonian name of Mars.

NGC 5194   Is M51.

NGC 7479   100,000,000 light-years from Earth.

NIBIRU

12th planet of our solar system.

There was a marriage between a royal female being from Orion and a royal male being from Sirius B.

Their offspring was called "Nibiru".

Inhabited by immortals.

Is now part of the Galactic Federation.

Nibiru comes along every 3,600 years, traveling between the Sirius System and the Solar System.

Nibiru did not have to do anything with Atlantis.

Also known as:

>>   Nebiru,

>>   Niburu,

>>   Nubiru.

→ Alalu.

→ 10th Planet.

→ starship Nibiru.

→ Nibirians.

NIBURN

Planet of the gods.

This planet will reach the solar system in the year 1997.

NIBURU

→ Nibiru.

NOL SYSTEM

Following are contact people with Billy Meier:

Ektol, Lumia, Sana, Ters.

NORLATIADEK

Constellation, consists of 100 local systems. Headquarters is Edentia.

NUBIRU

→ Nibiru.

OBERON

The outermost of Uranus' moons.

Orbit: 583,420 km,

Diameter: 1523 km,

Radius: 761 km,

Discovered: 1787.

Mixture of about 40 to 50 % water ice, the rest is rock.

Oberon's surface is heavily cratered, large faults across the entire southern hemisphere.

OBRAIDON

New planet supposed to being manifested now in our solar system.

OMNIVERSE

The Omniverse consists of our Matter Universe as well as its Anti-Matter Twin/DAL counterpart Universe, and also the 12 densities.

Oort Cloud

A circle of frozen debris just outside the Solar System.

OPHELIA   One of the ten innermost moons of Uranus.
Orbit: 53,764 km,
Diameter: 32 km,
Radius: 16 km,
Discovered: 1986.

ORION   There exists only one Reptilian race, all the others are from different constellations.
Started the Galactic War. There are also light people.
They could have a base in the Aleutian Islands.
Planets/stars: Bellachia, Betelgeuse, Clarion, Dexton, Pacifica, Rigel, Styx, Turellian, Zelia.
→ Ari-An, Ciakar, D'Naar, Greys, Nordics.
→ Atna, Melia, Orvon, Roann, Thoth-Mus-Zurud.

ORION CONSTELLATION
Means „the Hunter".
The three Belt Stars are aligned in exactly the same way as the three pyramids.
Distance: 243 – 1500 light-years from Earth.
Stars: Alnilam, Alnitak, Bellatrix, Betelgeuse,
Mintaka, Rigel, Saiph.
Star systems: Alpha Draconi, Barnard 33, Horsehead Nebula.
Planets: Essassani, Lasmur, Rizq.

ORION NEBULA   Has 4 bright stars called Trapezium.
Distance: 1500 light-years from Earth,
Diameter: 6 light-years.

ORLOFF   Planet. Ambassador is Baldor.

ORVONTON   Superuniverse that consists of major sectors of universes, like Splandon, …
Seventh segment of the Grand Universe.

OSIRAN   Planet in the galaxy Floreida.
→ God Thoth.

OWANDER   Planet in the galaxy of Exxon.

PALLAS   Asteroid.
Radius: 261 km,
Discovered: 1802.

PAN   Innermost moon of Saturn.
Orbit: 133,583 km,
Diameter: 25 km (16 miles),
Radius: 10 km,
Discovered: 1990.
Saturn's smallest moon.

PANDORA   Moon of Saturn.
                       Orbit: 141,700 km,
                       Diameter: 84 km (114 x 84 x 62) (52 miles),
                       Radius: 46 km,
                       Discovered: 1980.
                       Has an unpredictable orbit.
                       Has at least 2 large craters 30 km in diameter.

parsec   3,26 light-years.

PASAKA   "Indigo Planet" in the 12th universe.
                       Most are young souls, most of the Indigo Children born
                       on Urantia were born up from 1976.

PASIPHAE   One of the eight outer moons of Jupiter.
                       Orbit: 23,500,000 km,
                       Diameter: 50 km,
                       Radius: 25 km,
                       Discovered: 1908.
                       Pasiphae's orbit is retrograde and unusual.

PEGASUS CONSTELLATION
                       Vast cluster of over 1,000 stars.
                       Distance from Earth 200 – 3,000 light-years.
                       Stars: Pegasus.

                       There are many star nations and they have huge motherships.
                       Pre Cetacean refugees from planet Earth arrived there approx.
                       8,000,000 B.C.E.
                       → Pegasians.

PHAETON   Russian name of Maldek.

PHOBOS   Larger and innermost of the two moons of Mars.
                       Orbit: 9378 km,
                       Diameter: 22.2 km (27 x 21.6 x 18.8) (12 miles),
                       Length: 17 miles,
                       Orbit: 7 h 40 min,
                       Discovered: 1877.
                       This is an unusual orbit velocity (too close to the planet Mars to
                       have such a velocity).
                       Phobos is heavily cratered.
                       May be covered with a layer of fine dust about a meter thick.
                       The most prominent feature on Phobos is the large crater named
                       Stickney.
                       Composed of carbon-rich rock and ice, like C-type asteroids.

                       It has ruins on it.
                       Artificial satellite of Mars that was placed 3000 years ago.
                       There live 2,000 Greys.
                       Inhabited by miners from Maldek, inside the moon.
                       The Greys are doing genetic engineering there.

→ Maldek, Mars.
→ Stanton Friedman.

PHOEBE   Moon of Saturn.
                   Orbit: 12,952,000 km,
                   Diameter: 220 km,
                   Radius: 110 km,
                   Discovered: 1898.
                   Phoebe does not rotate synchronously and its orbit is retrograde.

PHOENIX   10th planet in the Solar System.
                   Orbit: > 3000 years,
                   Perihelion: asteroid belt between Mars & Jupiter.
                   Has a powerful magnetic force field.
                   When visible from Earth it can be observed in the Southern
                   Hemisphere in the Phoenix Constellation.
                   Planet dominated by female warriors.
                   Granted the refugees Charon, Cronos, Demeter, Kore and others
                   from planet Styx in Orion permission to land.
                   Athena (Greek Goddess) represents this planet on the Planetary
                   Council.

PHOTON BELT   The photon belt is the cosmic trigger force to shift humanity
                   from 3rd to 4th dimension, from separation into oneness.
                   → Alcyone.

PISCUS AUSTRINUS CONSTELLATION
                   Distance from Earth 23 light-years.
                   Stars: Fomalhaut.
                   → Fomalhautans.

PLANET of the THREE SPIRES
                   Planet that seems to be a storehouse of all knowledge.
                   → Dolores Cannon.

PLANET X   Brown dwarf star that orbits both Solar System's suns (our Sun
                   and its dark twin sun). 5 to 6 times bigger than Jupiter.
                   First spotted in the year 1983.
                   Should pass our solar system again in the year 2003 after approx.
                   3,660 years.
                   Also known as:
                   >>   10th Planet,
                   >>   Barnard I,
                   >>   Hercóbulus,
                   >>   Red Planet,
                   >>   The Destroyer.
                   → 10th Planet.
                   → Year 1983.

PLEIADES   Most famous star cluster on the sky.
The Pleiades star cluster contains over 3000 (400 – 500) stars.
Also known as M45, the Seven Sisters.
Distance from Earth 434 - 446 light-years, 13 light-years across.

Human Colony approx. 25,000 B.C.E.
They are in the 5th (7th) interdimension.
Erra-Taygeta is part of the Pleiades.
Ancestors came from Lyra, some of the Pleiadians of Lyran ancestry settled briefly in later Lemuria and early Atlantis, some mixing with Earth creatures.
The Pleiadians are the fathers of Earth people.
They have 3 bases on Earth: Russia, Switzerland and South America.
Part of the Galactic Confederation.
Seat of government for our local Vega galaxy.
Not all Pleiadians are positive.
"elado" = "hello", "tomu bel" = "good-bye".
Planets: Aarmon, Acitares, Aldebaran, Alderon, Aryan, Avyon (destroyed), Myton, Xinon.
Stars: Alcyone, Merope, Taygeta.
Races: Amphibians, Aryan Humans, Reptilians.
→ Altair.
→ Nordics.
→ Asket, Athar Ismar, Blaji, Candor, Nera, Paulson, P'taah, Sananda, Semjase, Spartan.

PLEIADIAN SECTOR
Includes the Solar System.

PLUTEROUS   Destroyed home planet of the Greys.

PLUTO   Orbit: 5,913,520,000 km (strongly elliptical),
                         (2,800,000,000 to 4,600,000,000 km)
Diameter: 2274 km (1400 miles),
Radius: 1137 km (1160 km, +/- 1%),
Year: 247.7 Earth years
Day: 6.4 Earth days
Discovered: 1930,
Temperature: -235 to –210 C (-238 to –228 C),
Atmosphere: methane, extremely tenuous, during the time of
                its perihelion,
Moons: Charon.
Smallest planet of the Solar System.
Smaller than Earth's Moon, Callisto, Europa, Ganymede, Io, Titan, Triton.
The density is lesser than Mars, hardly has any light.
Pluto rotates synchronously but in the opposite direction from most of the other planets and at times is close to the Sun than Neptune.
Probably is a mixture of 70 % rock and 30 % water ice.

Pluto is undergoing global warming, as evidenced by a three-fold increase in the planet's atmospheric pressure during the past 14 years.

Pluto's orbit is much more elliptical than that of the other planets, and its rotational axis is tipped by a large angle relative to its orbit. Both factors could contribute to drastic seasonal changes.

Pluto's atmospheric temperature varies between around minus 235 and minus 170 degrees Celsius, depending on the altitude above the surface. The main gas in Pluto's atmosphere is nitrogen, and Pluto has nitrogen ice on its surface that can evaporate into the atmosphere when it gets warmer, causing an increase in surface pressure.

Has a predominantly nitrogen atmosphere (with a surface pressure 100,000 times less than that on Earth).

Is a former satellite of Neptune.

Pluto is an arid desert world of white sand.

Pluto is used as storage warehouses and has spaceports which are visited by starships of various Solar System planets and from many galaxies.

A journey by spacecraft from any of the Solar System planets is only a matter of minutes.

It is used – because of its proximity to the edge of the Milky Way galaxy – as a stop to our neighbor galaxy, the Great Magellanic Cloud.

Was taken from the Oort Cloud by Cronos.

Was created as a penal colony for the survivors of Maldek.

The Plutonians are from 0,90 to 1,20 m tall.

Venus supplies the light to Pluto.

The Plutonians have a great influence because they are governed by outer space entities from Arcturia.

→ Charon.

POLARIS   World of Reptiloids and Greys.

Very similar to Earth, but younger & higher developed.

Extremely technological advanced; buildings with 1000 stores & more.

Red-orange sky, deserts are blue.

→ Draconian Empire.

PORTIA   One of the ten innermost moons of Jupiter.

Orbit:	66,097 km,
Diameter:	110 km,
Radius:	55 km,
Discovered:	1986.

PROCYON   Binary star.
                          Brightest star in the Canis Minoris Constellation.
                          Distance from Earth 11.4 light-years.

                          Home of the Nordics.
                          Was subdued by Rigelian Greys in recent centuries, but has been
                          liberated recently with the help of other Federation worlds.
                          The planets are occupied by 23 billion human beings in 5 solar
                          systems.
                          → Andromedan Federation.

PROCYON-A   Six relatively small planets.
                          The Human colony occupies the fourth planet, the Amphitoid-
                          Reptoid colonies are on the 2nd & 3rd planet.

PROCYON-B   There are no planets.

PROMETHEUS   Moon of Saturn.
                          Orbit: 139,350 km,
                          Diameter: 102 km (145 x 85 x 62) (63 miles),
                          Radius: 46 km,
                          Discovered: 1980.
                          Prometheus has a number of ridges and valleys and several
                          craters about 20 km in diameter.

PROSPERO   Moon of Uranus.
                          Orbit: 10,000,000 to 25,000,000 km,
                          Diameter: 30 to 40 km,
                          Radius: 20 km,
                          Discovered: 1999.

PROTEUS   Moon of Neptune.
                          Orbit: 117,600 km,
                          Diameter: 418 km (436 x 416 x 402),
                          Radius: 209 km,
                          Discovered: 1989.
                          Irregular (non-spherical) in shape.

PROXIMI CENTAURI
                          Distance from Earth 4.3 light-years.
                          Is the closest known star to Earth.

PUCK   One of the ten innermost moons of Uranus.
                          Orbit: 86,006 km,
                          Diameter: 154 km,
                          Radius: 77 km,
                          Discovered: 1985.
                          Puck is very dark.

QUAOAR	Orbit:	a billion kilometers beyond Pluto km,
	Diameter:	1250 km (800 miles),
	Distance	6,500,000,000 km,
	Year:	288 Earth years.

(Also known as 2002 LM60) has not been officially named yet. New planet? Discovered in the year 2002 (2002LM60) and appears to be the largest object in the Kuiper Belt.

Quaoar is greater in volume than all known asteroids combined.

"Quaoar" moves around the Sun every 288 years in a near perfect circle. Like the planet Pluto, Quaoar dwells in the Kuiper Belt, an icy debris field of comet-like bodies extending 5 billion kilometers beyond Neptune's orbit.

Over the past decade more than 500 icy bodies - Kuiper-Belt Objects or "KBOs" for short - have been found there. With a few exceptions all have been significantly smaller than Pluto.

Quasar

Quasars are extremely powerful bright objects capable of generating the luminosity of one trillion suns within a region size of Mars' orbit.

Quasars are star-like objects that emit more energy than 100 giant galaxies combined and are among the most distant objects found so far in the universe.

→ Blazar.

RED PLANET   Other name of Planet X.

RETIKULUM   Dangerous.

RHEA	Saturn's second largest moon.	
	Orbit:	527,040 km,
	Diameter:	1528 km (949 miles),
	Radius:	765 km,
	Discovered:	1672.

Composed primarily of water ice with rock (less than 1/3 of its mass).

Rotates synchronously.

Very similar to Dione.

RIGEL   Blue-white super giant star in the Orion constellation.
                            7th brightest star in the sky.
                            Brightest star in the Orion constellation.
                            Diameter: 65 times the size of the Sun
                            Distance: about 1,050 – 1,400 (770) light-years from
                                             Earth.
                            Rigel is actually a triple star system (Rigel, Rigel B, Rigel C).

                            There is a race of Reptilians that is different from the Dracos.
                            Once home of the Nordics.
                            Attacked by the Draconians and their Grey mercenaries.
                            Refugees fled to the Jovian moons, Procyon and Sirius.
                            People (Greys)have no freedom of thought.
                            → Thoth.
                            → Ciakar, Greys.
                            → Draconian Empire.
                            → Earth.

RIGEL B   Smaller blue star which orbits Rigel.
                            Distance between Rigel and Rigel B is about 23 light days.

RIGEL C   Extremely close to Rigel B, about the diameter of the Sun
                            system.

RIGEL KENTAURUS
                            Other name is Alpha Centauri.
                            → Alpha Centauri.

RIZQ   Planet in the Orion Constellation.

ROSALIND   One of the ten innermost moons of Uranus.
                            Orbit: 69,927 km,
                            Diameter: 54 km,
                            Radius: 27 km,
                            Discovered: 1986.

RUCHBAH   Star in Cassiopeia.
                            Arabic for "knee".

S1981/S14   Moon of Saturn.

S1986/U10   Inner moon of Uranus.
                            Distance from Belinda: 1,200 km (750 miles).

S2001/U1   Moon of Uranus.

S2003/U1   Inner moon of Uranus.
                            Diameter: 16 km (10 miles),
                            Distance from Earth: 2,800,000,000 km
                                             (1,700,000,000 miles),
                            Distance from Uranus: 97,700 km (60,600 miles),
                            Day: 22h 09 min.

S2003/U2	Inner moon of Uranus.
	Diameter: 12 km (8 miles),
	Distance from Earth: 2,800,000,000 km (1,700,000,000 miles),
	Distance from Uranus: 74,800 km (46,400 miles),
	Distance from Belinda: 300 – 700 km (200 – 450 miles),
	Day: 14h 50 min.

S2004/S1   Moon of Saturn.
Diameter: 3km (2 miles),
Distance from Saturn: 194,000 km (120,000 miles),
Could be same moon as S1981/S14.

S2004/S2   Moon of Saturn.
Diameter: 4km (2.5 miles),
Distance from Saturn: 211,000 km (131,000 miles).

S2004/S3   Moon of Saturn.
Distance from Saturn: 141,000 km (86,420 miles).

S2005/S1   Moon of Saturn.
Diameter: 6.5 km (4 miles),
Distance from Saturn: 136,500 km (84,200 miles).

SAGITTARIUS CONSTELLATION
A Reptilian race approached Earth 26,000,000 B.C.E.

SAIPH   Blue super giant star in the Orion constellation.
Diameter: 11 Suns,
Distance: 720 (+/- 120)light-years from Earth,
Brightness: about 6000 times the Sun.

SAKASIA   Planet in the 1st universe.
→ Mikael Ashtar.

SARAS   Other name of planet Earth.

SATANIA   Headquarters is Jerusem.

SATURN   Orbit: 1,429,000,000 km,
Diameter: 120,536 km (equatorial),
108,728 km (polar),
Radius: 60,268 km,
Rings: 250,000 km (diameter),
1.5 km (thickness).
The rings are made of nearly 100 % water ice, somewhat contaminated by meteoric dust. The origin of the rings is unknown.
Currently has 35 or 36 known moons, 18 are named.
Moons: Atlas, Calypso, Dione, Enceladus, Epimetheus, Helene (Dione-B), Hyperion, Iapetus, Janus, Mimas, Pan, Pandora,

Phoebe, Prometheus, Rhea, Telesto, Tethys, Titan, S1981/S14, S2004/S1, S2004/S2, S2004/S3, S2005/S1.
Saturn is the least dense of the planets.
Gravity (0.7) is less than that of water.
About 75% hydrogen, 25% helium, with traces of ammonium, methane, water and Rocky material.
Saturn radiates more energy into space than it receives from the Sun.
Saturn has a significant magnetic field.

The rings is a force field that was built at the time of Maldeks destruction.
There is a physical native race.
Mercury used to be a moon of Saturn.
Saturn is the great administrative center in our solar system also called the Saturn Tribunal.
Solarian Tribunal on the moons of Saturn, member of the Galactic Federation.
Transition planet, beings are visible,
Space ships bigger than Uranus ships, but more dense.
Is the home of the red race.
There are many beautiful cities on Saturn, marble is used in the construction of many of the buildings.
The environment is controlled, wide variety of colors, extraordinary beautiful parks.
Inhabited in the 5th dimension.
There is the laboratory of the 6 dimensional genetics engineers for Earth.
→ Anachiel, Ankhiel, Balin, Cassiel, Ishra, Kadar-Monka, Lurga, Philip, Ramu, Rigel, Soltec, Zelna, Zuhl.
→ Saturnians, Telosians.
→ Saturn Tribunal.

SCHEDAR   Multiple star in Cassiopeia.
                     Pale rose colored.
                     2.2 to 2.8 magnitudes.

SCOBISA   Planet in the Swan star system.

SEDNA   Second reddish planet in the Solar System. 10th planet?
                     Kuiper-Belt object.
                     Also known as 2003 VB12.
                     Orbit: 8,000,000,000 miles,
                     Diameter: 1,770 km (1100 miles) estimated,
                     Discovered: 2004.

SEGIN   Star in Cassiopeia.

SENAYAGA	Planet of Sirian Humanoids in the Sirius B star system. There was a war between the Sirian Humanoids and the Red Drac Reptilians. The Reptilians won and took over the planet, the Sirian Humanoids fled to Maldek.
SERPENS	Star constellation.
SETEBOS	Moon of Uranus. Orbit: 10,000,000 to 25,000,000 km, Diameter: 30 to 40 km, Radius: 20 km, Discovered: 1999.
SEVEN SISTERS	Are the Pleiades.
SHAN	The only planet, that rejected the Radiant One. Other name of the planet Earth.
SIGNUS ALPHA	Star system, some of those are here on Earth.
SILOX	Planet. One of its inhabitants is Mardox.
SINOPE	One of the eight outer moons of Jupiter. Orbit: 23,700,000 km, Diameter: 36 km, Radius: 18 km, Discovered: 1914. Sinope is the outermost of Jupiter's satellites. One of the smallest moons in the Solar System. Sinope's orbit is retrograde and unusual.
SIRIUS	Known as "Dog Star". Double star system (possibly triple star) in the Canis Major Constellation. Elliptical orbital period of 50 years. 8.6 light-years from Earth. Great place of light in this galaxy. They possess the most advanced technology in the universe. Sirian names ending in „tron" indicate a galactic title such as Lord or Teacher. Home of the sacred Blue Lodge of Creation. The Jerusalem Command is in charge there. Settled Venus (4D), then Egypt. Egyptians are interbreeding of Sirians and Pleiadians. → Aumtron, Beth, Marcia, Metatron, Sheatzo, Sirai, Teletron, Washta. → Kanus Empire. → Kantarians, Telosians.

SIRIUS MULTI STAR SYSTEM
> → Sirius Star System.

SIRIUS STAR SYSTEM
> 8.6 light-years from Earth.
> Multiple-star system containing 9 stars.
> Sirius A, B, C, D and E possess solar systems.
> It's symbol is the "Ummac Dan".
> Planets: Bellaton, Darnat, Kantaria, Khoom.
> → Council of Nine.
> → Nommos.

SIRIUS A
> Brightest star in the northern sky, over 20 times brighter than the Sun, 8.7 light-years from Earth, mass of more than 2 suns.
>
> Has 3 inhabited planets.
> Federation world of a race of humanoids, Sasquatch and genetic human-feline hybrids.
> They are in a civil war with a planet in the Sirius-B system that is controlled by Reptilian and Amphibian humanoids.
> Home of the brave, most wise Pshaat.
> There lived a Lion race on 2 planets.
> There lived originally non-humans.
> The humans are called Katayy.
> They are considered benevolent.
> There are red-skinned races.
> Their ancestors are Lyrans that escaped during the war.
> The whales & dolphins were brought from there.
> → Joysia.
> → Pshaat, Sirians.

SIRIUS B
> About 8.3 light-years from Earth.
> Blue-white dwarf, invisible to the naked eye, 10,000 times dimmer than Sirius A, 4 times as large as the Earth, surface is 300 times harder than diamonds & has a temperature of about 25,000 degrees Celsius, its interior has a density 3000 times that of diamonds, has a mass equal to the mass of the sun, diameter is 90% that of Earth, gravity is 400,000 times that of Earth.
>
> Inhabited by a human race called in Sirian language Akonowai.
> There are 6 planets, the 3rd and 4th are inhabited by more than 600,000,000 people that live in subterranean communities:
> >> 3rd planet:
> Has a red-orange sky with a rare bluish cloud.
> Has less water than the 4th planet.
> There live many creatures in one interconnected sea.
> Most of vegetation is purple-blue, lush forests, huge very high mountains, enormous prairies.
> Their main cities are located some 80 to 320 km (50 – 200 miles) in the inner earth.
> On the surface there are 144 main temple sites.
> >> 4th planet(Muktarin):

Inhabited by Humans.

Similar to Earth, approx. 1.25 times the size of Earth.

A year has 440 days (11 months of 40 days).

A day has about 24 hours (similar to the home worlds in the Lyran constellation).

Semi tropical type of climate without high variances, many trees with purple bark.

There is one huge ocean about the size of the Pacific Ocean.

A few huge mountain systems that leave the seacoast with very small compact beaches. Very little white sand, predominantly reddish brown colored sand.

Most of the planet are broad hilly plains, vast river systems and lakes. Soils have orange and purple tones with orange-like browns.

First colonized planet in the Sirius B star system, about 4,300,000 years ago.

They live in cavern-like systems (huge underground cities) and have small colonies and temple sites on the surface.

Until now has its original pristine state.

Home of the regional council of the Galactic Federation.

Home of the Great Blue Lodge of Creation.

One planet imploded.

The planets around Sirius B are very arid and are generally occupied by Red Drac Reptilians.

contains the galactic human home worlds, colonized by a Lyran/Sirian civilization.

One planet is inhabited by Reptilian-Amphibian humanoids who have established a treaty with the Alpha Draconians and Rigelians.

This triple alliance is determined to bring planet Earth under their control. Several underground armies are already on Earth.

Skin color is red, beige, black.

Meeting Point of the Galactic Federation Council.

There is a terrible civil war going on right now.

A large armada is on its way to the Solar System and allegedly arrive around 2004.

3 large alliance ships entered the Sol System hiding in the comet Hale Bopp's tail and are now in an orbit around Mercury.

Planets: Bellaton, Hut-Ron, Senayaga.

→ Corporate Collective.

→ Pegasians, Sirians.

→ 4,300,000 B.C.E.

SIRIUS C

It's now just being terra-formed.

Inhabited by a human race.

There are only very small colonies.

Used for storage and administration tasks for the large trade and commerce with other planetary systems in this sector of the Milky Way.

SIRIUS D

Same function as Sirius C.

Inhabited by a human race.

SIRIUS (White sun)

Has a planet called Ishna.

SIRIUS (Yellow sun)

Collapsed. There lived four races on a planet: Eata, Karidel, Orotheta, Paetri. Together they are called Paschats.
→ Paschats.

SIRIUS 1

Planet of pure thought. Directs the 10th interdimension.

SIRIUS 2

Planet of pure thought. Directs the 11th interdimension.
Here they are training the masters.

SIRIUS 3

Planet of pure thought. Directs the 12th interdimension.
Original source of the Christ Consciousness.

SIRIUS 4

Planet of pure thought.

SOL SYSTEM   → Solar System.

SOLAR SYSTEM   Distance: 29076.5 light-years from the Central Sun (Black Hole),
Velocity: 86,400 km/h.
26,000 light-years from Milky Way's center, rotates once every 240 million years.
9 "known" planets.

There will be discovered all of the 16 planets in the Solar System until the year 6,000. All planets have spiritual entities on them.
12 planets, all populated (inside the planets), hide in an other time segment.
13 planets, in 5th density there are 27 planets.
There is biological life on 7 planets and 15 moons.
President of the delegation for all planets is Ra.
→ Interplanetary Federation of Planets.
→ 206,000,000 B.C.E., 317,000 B.C.E.
→ Year-2040, Year-3000, Year-6000.
→ Abu Kash Kar.

SOLENIUM   Solenium & Zoleinium were once 1 planet. after time the planet split into 2.

SORXERMA   Planet of the Pleiades.

SPLANDON   Major sector of local universes, consists of 100 minor sectors of universes, headquarters is Umayor the Fifth.
It is the 5th major sector of the super universe of Orvonton.

STELLA   → VENUS, people live with sun inside this planet,
Diamonte, El Thonn, James, Marine, Moff, Thonn, Tuleo

STEPHAN'S QUINTET

A group of 5 galaxies (NGC7317, 7318A, 7318B, 7319, 7320).
Lies about 270,000,000 light-years from Earth (in the constellation of Pegasus).
NGC7320 is only 35,000,000 light-years from Earth.

STEPHANO

Moon of Uranus.

Orbit:	10,000,000 to 25,000,000 km,
Diameter:	30 to 40 km,
Radius:	15 km,
Discovered:	1999.

STYX

Planet in Orion.
Charon, Cronos, Demeter, Kore.

SUN (of Earth)

Diameter:	1,390,000 km,
Radius:	697,000 km,
Temperature:	core: 15,600,000 K,
	corona: >1,000,000 K,
	surface: 5,800 K (photosphere),
Rotation:	equator: 25.4 days,
	poles: 36 days,
Age:	4,600,000,000 years (estimated),
Color:	yellow-white.

Brightest object in the sky.
The sun contains more than 99.8% of the total mass of the Solar System, Jupiter contains most of the rest.
About 75% hydrogen, 25% helium (by mass).
The Sun is not a solid body like Earth.
Our sun is a violent star and is capable of producing explosive flares and hurling clouds of matter toward Earth.
Sunspots can be as much as 50,000 km in diameter.
The Sun's magnetic field is very strong, its magnetosphere extends well beyond Pluto.
The Sun's magnetic field increased by 230 % since 1901.
The solar wind is about 450 to 750 km/sec.

The Sun itself is not hot. There are beings who live inside the Sun.
20,000,000,000 B.C.E. the Sun appeared and created a proto-solar system.
Our Sun is hollow, as all the planets are.
The Sun is really a planet who has civilizations.
There is a second sun behind the Sun, it is visible from Mars.
The second sun is denser, heavier and not as hollow as the sun we see.
Archangel Michael Essence.
Also known as Helios.
→ Awaana, Michael.
→ Year 2011.

Superuniverse

Orvonton.

SUTARUS   Star system in the Andromeda galaxy.
                       Planets: Vedra.
                       → 2,500,000 B.C.E.

SWAN   Star system.
                       Planets: Scobisa.

SYCORAX   Moon of Uranus.
                       Orbit: 12,200,000 km,
                       Diameter: 160 km,
                       Radius: 80 km,
                       Discovered: 1997.
                       Sycorax's orbit is retrograde and highly inclined.
                       Unusual red in color.

TARA   Future name of Earth.

TAU CETI   In the Cetus (Whale) Constellation.
                       Distance from Earth 11.8 light-years.

                       There lives a completely different Reptilian race.
                       Home world of the Tau Cetian Humans.
                       Member of the Galactic Federation.
                       → Andromedan Federation.
                       → Tau Cetians.

TAU CETI III   Only powers of the mind, no technology,
                       For visit only Astral Travel is possibly.
                       Blue sun, oceans have no salt, trees are high as mountains.

TAURUS CONSTELLATION
                       About 150 light-years from Earth.
                       Stars: Aldebaran, El Nath.

                       They have huge motherships.
                       → Hyadeans.

TAYGETA   Star in the Pleiades.
                       Race: Pleiadians.
                       Home of Nordic like refugees from the ancient Draconian attack
                       on Lyra.
                       Peaceful Lyrans landed on planet Erra in the year 228,000 B.C.E.
                       → Andromedan Federation.

TEKA   Planet in Lyra, destroyed by the Alpha Draconians.

TELESTO   Moon of Saturn.
                       Orbit: 295,000 km,
                       Radius: 15 km,
                       Discovered: 1980.

TERMINOUS   Home planet of Lord Hatonn in the Vela System.

TERMINUS HATONN
                       Other name of Terminous.

TERRA   Called Terra by the Arcturians.
                       → Earth.

TETHYS   Moon of Saturn.
                       Orbit: 294,660 km,
                       Diameter: 1060 km (659 miles),
                       Radius: 530 km,
                       Length: 750 km (470 miles),
                       Discovered: 1684.
                       It is almost completely composed of water ice, similar to Dione
                       and Rhea.
                       There is a huge impact crater, called Odysseus, 400 km in
                       diameter.
                       There is also a huge valley, called Ithaca Chasma, 2000 km long,
                       100 km wide, 3 to 5 km deep.

THALASSA   Irregularly shaped moon of Neptune.
                       Orbit: 50,000 km,
                       Diameter: 80 km,
                       Radius: 40 km,
                       Discovered: 1989.

THEBE   One of the four inner moons of Jupiter.
                       Orbit: 222,000 km,
                       Diameter: 100 km (100 x 90),
                       Radius: 50 km (31 miles),
                       Discovered: 1979.
                       Has 3 or 4 large craters.

THUBAN   Other name of Alpha Draconis.

TINMET   → Maldek.

TIPHON   Planet in Alpha Draconis, inhabited by Reptiloids.
                       Home star of the political representative from Draco.
                       → Khoach.

TISHTAE   Star in the Andromeda constellation (Galaxy).
                       Has 9 planets, all of them are equal or greater than Jupiter.

TITAN   Largest moon of Saturn.
                   Orbit: 1,221,830 km (759,000 miles), 16 days,
                   Diameter: 5150 km (3200 miles),
                   Radius: 2575 km,
                   Discovered: 1655,
                   Temperature: +178 C (95 Kelvin),
                   Atmosphere: thick, opaque (nitrogen, methane & oily
                   hydrocarbons), pressure 1.6 Earth's.
                   Titan is surrounded by a globular cloud of gas, some 70,000 km
                   (43,496 miles).
                   Larger in diameter than Mercury, larger and more massive than
                   Pluto.
                   A cold, dark, smog-shrouded world, nearly half the size of Earth,
                   Titan is the only moon in the solar system with a thick
                   atmosphere.
                   Titan is about half water ice and half rocky material.
                   Has no magnetic field.
                   Rotation is synchronous.
                   Of the moons in the Solar System only Titan, Callisto, Europa,
                   Ganymede, Io and Triton have an atmosphere.

TITANIA   Largest moon of Uranus.
                   Orbit: 436,270 km,
                   Diameter: 1578 km,
                   Radius: 789 km,
                   Discovered: 1787.
                   Mixture of about 40 to 50 % water ice, the rest is rock.
                   Has cratered terrain and systems of interconnected valleys
                   (hundreds of km long).

TOUCAN   Star cluster.
                   → Ibhaka.

TRANTOR   Home planet of the Universal Confederation headquarters of the
                   Solar Cross. The city covers the whole planet.
                   Was the headquarters for 20,000,000 star systems.
                   Beings: Elan, Erisa, Sig-Mar.

TRAPEZIUM   The four bright stars in the Orion Nebula.

TRITON   Largest moon of Neptune.
                   Orbit: 354,760 km,
                   Diameter: 2700 km,
                   Radius: 1353 km,
                   Discovered: 1846,
                   Temperature: -235 C (-391F).
                   Atmosphere: very tenuous, composed mostly of nitrogen with
                                     small amount of methane, extends up 5 to 10
                                     km (with a surface pressure 100,000 times less
                                     than that on Earth).
                   Probably about 25 % water ice, 75 % rocky material.

Almost the entire southern hemisphere is covered with an ice cap of frozen nitrogen and methane.
Has extensive valleys and ridges.
Triton has ice volcanoes.
Of the moons in the Solar System only Triton, Callisto, Europa, Ganymede, Io and Titan have an atmosphere.
Triton, Earth, Io and Venus are the only known bodies in the Solar System to be volcanically active.
Larger than Pluto.
Triton's orbit is retrograde.

TUITHANIA   Planet that is Venus on another dimension. Home planet of Omnec Onec.

TURELLIAN   Located in a remote part of the constellation Orion.
The inhabitants are chiefly reptilian & extremely peaceable, the planet remains neutral.

TYPON   Typon was the "soul-eating" god of the Egyptians.
→ Tiphon.

TYRANTOR   Planet.

TYRANTUS   Planet.

TYTHAN   Planet.
Prince Neosam and princess Negonna allegedly came from there to planet Earth.

UHR   Planet.

UMBRIEL   One of the large moons of Uranus.
Orbit: 265,980 km,
Diameter: 1170 km,
Radius: 585 km,
Discovered: 1851,
Surface: heavily cratered.
Mixture of about 40 to 50 % water ice, the rest is rocky material.
Umbriel is very dark.

UMMO

14 light-years from Earth.

Planet in the Wolf 424 system, inhabited by the Ummites. They need 8 to 9 months to get here.
Quite similar to Earth.
Has oceans, a single continental landmass, considerable volcanic activity.
Alleged hoax, that was invented by Spanish parapsychologist José Luis Jordan Peña with help of occultist Trinidad Pastrana from Madrid, Spain, having played the role of the mysterious Marisol who served as a mediator between the aliens and their human contacts.
→ Ummites.

UNIVERSE

It exists one major universe with seven surrounding universes, each sub universe contains billions (150,000,000,000) of other universes. Only 5 to 10 % are inhabited.
This is the 6th of 10 universes.
There exist 100 Billion galaxies.
Our universe is a 21 trillion year old hologram.
There are 9 million life forms in the universe at this particular time.
A universe is constantly changing in shape.
There are hundred of thousands of races and sub races in the universe.

Original races in this universe: Felines, Carians.
Primary races in this universe: Felines, Carians,
                                    Reptilians, Humans.

The Felines and Carians created the Reptilians and Humans in their image, and thus became the first parent races in this universe.
The Humans are the youngest of the 4 primary races. They were first created by the Felines on a planet in the Vega Star System of the Lyra Constellation.

Universal Game:
Having evolved to the level of integration and completing the Universal Game in their original universe, a group of 90 were invaded to this universe to set up and oversee the Universal Game here.
About 40% are Humans, 60% are Reptoids, Greys, Insectoids and about 300 or more civilizations who have visited our Earth.
Now the majority of the Universe is at peace.
There remain a few troubled areas, one of the most troubled is Earth.
The physical universe has 6 sub planes (subdivisions), all below the astral plane.
The astral plane itself has 150 sub planes, usually referred to as dimensions or densities.
→ Grand Universe, Nebadon, Orvonton, Splandon, Superuniverse.
→ Ashtar (Space) Command.

UR   Planet.
                          There is developing a primitive life form.

URANTIA   Planet in our local universe Nebadon, other name of Earth.
                          → Earth, Nebadon.

URANUS   Has 24 moons: Ariel, Belinda, Bianca, Caliban, Cordelia,
                          Cressida, Desdemona, Juliet, Miranda, Oberon, Ophelia, Portia,
                          Prospero, Puck, Rosalind, S1986/U10, S2001/U1, S2003/U1,
                          S2003/U2, Setebos, Stephano, Sycorax, Titania, Umbriel.
                          Orbit: 2,870,990,000 km (1,700,000,000 miles),
                          Diameter: 51,118 km (equatorial),
                          Radius: 25,559 km,
                          Discovered: on March 13, 1781,
                          Uranus year: 84 Earth years,
                          Atmosphere: 83% hydrogen, 15% helium, 2% methane.
                          Third largest planet (by diameter) in the Solar System. Uranus is
                          larger in diameter but smaller in mass than Neptune.
                          Composed primarily of rock and various ices, about 15%
                          hydrogen and a little helium.
                          Uranus' blue color is the result of absorption of red light by
                          methane in the upper atmosphere.
                          Has 11 faint rings.
                          Uranus' magnetic field is not centered. Uranus' magnetic field is
                          changing.
                          Wind speeds are roughly half those found on Neptune.

                          Venus was a moon of Uranus.
                          Beautiful planet, artificially maintained climate, similar to Earth,
                          forests, lush vegetation, one large ocean, relaxed and peaceful
                          atmosphere.
                          Uranus is abundant with plant & mammal life.
                          Transition planet, planet of equalization, higher than Mercury,
                          Venus, Earth, Mars, Saturn.
                          Saturn is renowned for its learning institutions.
                          Decents of an extraterrestrial race who landed on Uranus
                          (refugees from space wars).
                          The Sasquatch come from Uranus.
                          Beings invisible, color light-green, size x 1.5 earth-size, weight
                          approx. 21 kg, clothes like old-Egyptian.
                          Space ships have ball form, radius 10 - 15m.
                          Voyage to Earth 2 month (16 Uranus days).
                          There is a plant & animal life on the planet, but it exists at a
                          different frequency.
                          → Affa, Conderius, Homogenius, Jemetiem, Katonis, Ro,
                                 Sagamemnon, Sandius, Uxtaal.
                          → S2003/U1, S2003/U2.
                          → Venus.
                          → Uranians.

URSA MINOR   In Orion language called Chowta.
                     Is a very large system, holding 21 planets and 47 moons.
                     Our moon is said to have been made around the 17th planet.

VAN ALLEN BELT   Rests of planet Maldek.

VARUNA   Object in the Kuiper Belt.
                     Diameter: about 900 km (540 miles).

VEDRA   Planet in the Sutarus star system in the Andromeda galaxy.
                     → Vedrians.

VEGA   Hot white star in the Lyra Constellation, magnitude zero, 5th
                     brightest star, 3rd brightest in the Northern Hemisphere,
                     brightest in the Summer sky.
                     Brightest star in Lyra. 25 light-years from Earth.
                     Diameter: 3 times bigger than Sun.
                     58 times brighter than the Sun.
                     Surface temperature approx. 9,500 degrees Kelvin.

                     Solar system with 6 planets.
                     True origin for humans.
                     Ancestors came from Lyra.
                     Main headquarters of the Galactic Federation of Light.
                     → Vink.
                     → Andromedan Federation, Galactic Federation.
                     → Sirians.

VELA SYSTEM   About 1500 light-years from Earth.
                     → Hatonn.

Veldor Sector

VENUS   Orbit: 108,200,000 km,
                     Diameter: 12,103.6 km,
                     Radius: 6,052 km,
                     Venus day: 243 Earth days,
                     Venus year: 224.7 Earth days,
                     Atmosphere: carbon dioxide 96% (thick & steamy),
                     Temperature: 460 C (860 F).
                     Atmosphere pressure is 92 times that of the Earth's at sea-level,
                     surface temperature is about 482°C, rotates from east to west,
                     there are more than 100,000 volcanoes.
                     Much of the surface is covered by lava flows.
                     Venus, Earth, Io and Triton are the only bodies in the Solar
                     System that are known to be volcanically active.
                     Brightest planet in the Solar System.
                     Venus' rotation is retrograde (counter-clockwise, which produces
                     a positive magnetic field.
                     Venus is slightly smaller than Earth, 95% of Earth's diameter,
                     80% of Earth's mass.
                     Density and chemical composition is similar to Earth.

has few craters.

Slow winds at the surface (only a few km/hour), at the cloud tops about 350 km/hour. Clouds made of sulphuric acid.

Venus has no magnetic field.

Venus is hotter than Mercury.

Venus was a moon of Uranus.

There are more than 39 Venus planets.

Leader of the "chain of Venus planets" are Sanat Kumara and Lady Venus.

Planet is in the 5th dimension inhabited.

Has several large oceans, much rainfall.

In controlled locations, the atmosphere is mild and balm, outside the controlled climate of selected locations the planet is exactly as current science says.

Settled by Sirians (4D).

Colonized 2,000,000 B.C.E., destroyed 1,000,000 B.C.E. by the Dinoid/Reptoids from Maldek.

Venus had 3 moons.

Most advanced spiritual planet in the universe.

Base of the Christos Beings, head is Sanat Kumara.

The intelligences of Venus are very highly involved. Venus is one entire period of evolution in advance of earth. About 5,000 years in advance of Earth.

Two different life forms, one is physical, the other is etheric. All is created by thought.

Mixed planet, beings are visible.

Venus supplies the light to Pluto.

Incidentally, the Santinians maintain bases there.

Is the home of the white race.

Ashtar's home planet.

There are reptilian bases.

Sunflowers were brought to Earth by Venusians.

→ 1,000,000 B.C.E.

→ George Adamski.

→ Retz (Rits, Teutonia).

→ Amaru, Anahuac, Anitac, Ashtar Sheran, Atunez, Bellarion, Borealis, Ceres, Delron, Donn Thor, Dracel, Elys, Etel, Izhar, Jill Thor, Kalna, Lady Venus, Merelle, Mora, Oesceve, Omnec Onec, Oniac, Orthon, Perelandria, Rampiac, Rosinac, Rumilac, Sampiac, Sanat Kumara, Savitri, Semun-Iac, Serapis Bey, Serionac, Soloviac, Teel, Terec, Titinac, Valiant Thor, Venajoa, Venosia, Voltra, Xenialac, Xozian.

VERDANT

14,000,000 light-years from Earth.

Their home planet is about 2,5 times the Earth size.

Member of the Intergalactic Federation of Sovereign Planets.

→ Verdants.

VESTA

Asteroid.

Radius: 265 km,

Discovered: 1807.

VIXALL   Planet.
                        2,500 light-years from Earth.
                        There is an advanced spiritual and technological civilization.
                        → Alta.

VULCAN   Innermost planet in the Solar System.
                        Former sister planet of Mercury.
                        Was lost between a small Galactic Federation battle and a dark
                        Ancharan fleet in the end of the 19th century.

WHIRLPOOL GALAXY
                        Other name of M51.

WIRTANEN   Comet.

WOLF 424   About 14 light-years from Earth.

                        Iumma is the name of the Ummites for Wolf 424.
                        Planet with a magnetic field much more intensive than that of
                        Earth.
                        Ummites are an Scandinavian appearance race.
                        Their insignia resembles an "H" with an extra vertical bar in the
                        middle and the four corners of the "H" tapered into an outward
                        curve.
                        Planets: Ummo.
                        → Andromedan Federation, Galactic Federation.
                        → Ummites.

XINON   Planet in the Pleiades.

YORE   Planet in the galaxy of Glay in Pacifica.
                        → Osanta.

ZEL   Planet in Cassiopeia in the 11th interdimensionality.

ZELIA   Planet in the Orion constellation.
                        → Orvon.

ZENATAE   Star in the Andromeda constellation (galaxy?).
                        Has 27 planets around the binary stars.
                        They have light blue skin.
                        → Morenae, Vissaeus.
                        → Zenetaens.

ZENETAE   → Zenatae.

ZETA 1, 2, 3   Star system.
                        Little grey people. They have great technology.
                        They are in the lower form of energy, they are not helpful.

ZETA RETICULI   Star system neighboring the Orion constellation.
Is not the original star system of the "Grays", they brought themselves there by a time/space catastrophe on their original planet.
Most of the Greys are servants or mercenaries of the reptilian race.
1954 landed in Holloman Air Force Base. They stated their planet was dying and they needed quarters on Earth to conduct genetic experiments that might allow their race to survive, this in exchange for certain technology.
President Eisenhower signed a treaty with them, they could abduct humans on a limited basis.
→ Oris.
→ Greys.

ZETA I RETICULI
37 light-years from Earth.
→ Corporate Collective.
→ Zetas.

ZETA II RETICULI
37 light-years from Earth.
→ Draconian Empire.
→ Zetas.

ZICONA   Planet in Orion.
Lifespan 3500 years and more.

ZICONIA   City on the planet Yore.

ZOLEINIUM   → Solenium.

4. SPHERES, DIMENSIONS, LIGHT CITIES, ALIEN BASES

4.1 Dimensions

1st DIMENSION   Slowest dimension: Atoms, molecules, minerals.
Iron crystal core at the centre of the planet, the centre of gravity, this place holds all physical beings in form.

2nd DIMENSION   Plane of plants, animals.
Home of telluric powers and elemental beings.

3rd DIMENSION   Physical Creation Realm.
Plane of thought or mind.
Physical is reality.
Linear space and time.
Color spectrum of 72 (73?) frequencies.

4th DIMENSION   Transition Realm (astral plane).
Plane of the ego, will of life-spirit.
Zone of dreams and feelings.
Is a state of consciousness, awareness and being, everybody becoming psychic.
There are the fairy kingdoms.
Physical is not quite reality.
Is a gray, polarized plane, housing the forces of Light & Darkness.
The battle between good & evil starts here.
Extreme mutability of form.
Is a place where all records of the karmic patterns and past lives are kept. Soul's place between incarnations.

5th DIMENSION   Etheric Form Realm.
Plane of Light (Heaven).
Luminous light bodies.
Living in a light body enables eternally living.
5th dimension beings have no body. Negative beings are unable to enter the 5th and upper dimensions.
You can create & manifest anything you want directly.
There are still men, women, children.
They still make love.
There are the fairy kingdoms.
Form's purpose is defined.
No physical pain, no fear, immortality.
We incarnate here as androgynous stellar beings.
We live on stars.
Travel through the doorway at the center of the star.
It is beyond the polarity of light & dark.
Color spectrum of 223 (214?) frequencies.
The Solar System will have 27 planets.
Jupiter will be a light-blue sun.

6th DIMENSION

Etheric Realm.
Plane of Teaching, Creation, Sacred Geometry.
Place of languages and patterns.
Ascended Masters.
It houses the Akashic records.
We find astronomical & genetic codes.
There are still men, women, children.
They still make love.
Form develops a purpose.

7th DIMENSION

Free Form Realm / Guidance Realm.
Spirit has form.
Living vortexes.
Androgynous, archetype of the state which is usually reached between the 7th & 8th dimension, by the merging of Twin Souls.
7th dim. beings come in many forms.
Frequency of the Ascended Masters.

8th DIMENSION

Spiritual Light Realm.
Light becomes spirit.
Cosmic light, which links all galaxies to each other and creates the universe.
Group Souls (collection of entities that work together as one).
Every cell is a conscious entity.
The place where entities create morphogenetic fields that are used to organize the information that travels along the photonic highways.
Home of the Galactic Federation.

9th DIMENSION

Dimension of integration.
Creation of Form & Hierarchies.
Pure darkness.
Black holes, includes gateways to other universes.
Transition from formless to form.
The place of return to the Universal Self.

10th DIMENSION

Is like the outer shell of the universe, beyond it is the void.
The place of Soul Family.
There are billions of them, within this shell are progressively smaller shells, each representing a dimension-unified field of consciousness known as the Holy Spirit, also called Christ Consciousness.

11th DIMENSION

Plane of Passion and Desire.
The Seed & Soil of Universes.
Black Hole.
Where the Grand Masters train the Masters.
Sirius 2: one of the 4 planets of pure thought.
Also referred as the Palace of Pronunciation or the Golden Gates.

12ᵗʰ DIMENSION   The less dense.
                           Merging of all existing realities.
                           The place from which all reality comes from, the origin of all that
                           is.

... DIMENSIONS   Innumerable higher dimensions and planes of reality.

4.2 Spheres, Places, Planes

26,000 YEAR CYCLE	The whole of each planet's structure will be rebirthed again every 26,000 years (Earth-time).
Anunna	Angels, terrestrial spirits.
Archons	Primordial planetary spirits.
Astral plane	The astral is the buffer zone between understanding & misunderstanding. You have always to project above.
Atlan	Capital of Atlantis.
Bandolier	In Santa Fe is a very powerful site. Sacred spot that integrates the star & the planet energy.
BARDO	The state of consciousness between lives.
Benad Hasche	Female angels. Means „Daughters of God".
Chaldkydri	Archangels with 12 wings.
CHRIST ENERGY	It comes along with a sense of self-realization. → Buddha, Jesus, Maitreya, Moses, Sananda.
COLLECTIVE SUBCONSCIOUS	→ Akashic Records.
COLLECTIVE UNCONSCIOUS	→ Akashic Records.
CORN CIRCLES	→ Crop Circles.
COSMIC MIND	→ Akashic Records.

Crop Circles	They are not new.
	Historical documents show that in the past they were thought to be made by the Devil.
	They were hiding the truth from the people.
	Eyewitnesses report from light balls, which are seen flying with high velocity over cornfields.
	In the summer 2002 there are about 20 Crop Circles around of Avebury on cornfields in a range of about 30 km (20 miles).
	Known Crop Circles are in England, Australia, California, Canada, Germany, Japan, Norway and recently also in Switzerland.
	They are especially frequent in South West England and oftentimes completely perfect.
Devas	Physical Elementals.
EASTER ISLAND	The giant statues are remnants of Lemuria, about 20,000 years ago.
	Place of natural force, place of the apostles?
ELEMENTALS	Lower type of benevolent nature spirits.
	They are ruled by higher spirits, such as archangels or devas.
Elohim	Chief inter-dimensional Creator Beings.
	→ Elohim.
GOHBAR	In the highlands of Abyssinia, place of natural force.
Gondwanaland	→ Antarctica.
Grant Teton Mountain Range	
	Location of one of the two major ascended masters retreats in America, the other one is Mt. Shasta.
Guidance Realm	7th dimension.
	→ Kirael.
HABURU	General galactic language.
Halls of Amenti	Our local star gates.
Holy Mountains	Australia: Mount Kosciusko, New South Wales.
	Mount Ramshead, Thredbo, New South Wales.
	California: Mound Baldy, Mount Baldy Village, Southern California, about 50 miles east of Los Angeles.
	Mount Tallac, South Lake Tahoe,

	Northern California.
Colorado:	Castle Peak, Aspen.
England:	Brown Willy, Bodmin, Cornwall.
	Holdstone Down, Combe Martin, North Devonshire.
	Kinderscout, Hayfield, Derbyshire.
	Old Man, Coniston, Cumbria.
	Yes Tor, Oakhampton, Devonshire.
France:	Le Nid D'Aigle, Les Houches.
New Hampshire:	
	Mount Adams, Gorham.
New Zealand:	Mount Wakefield, Southern Alps.
Scotland:	Ben Hope, Tongue, Sutherland.
	Creag-An-Leth-Chain, Aviemore, Strathspey.
Switzerland:	Mount Madrigerfluh, Davos.
Tanzania:	Kilimanjaro, Oloitokitok.
Wales:	Carnedd Llewelyn, Bethesda, Gwynedd, North Wales.
	Pen-Y-Fan, Brecon, South Wales.

Hyperachii	Archangels that guide the universe.
JINNISTAN	Imaginary country, which was home to the Genies (Jinns) who served king Solomon.
KA LUA	Is Lemuria (Hawaiian name).
KAMALOKA	The nearest Astral Plane surrounding Earth.
Keres	Malignant spirits, also considered as souls of the dead.
Kosovo	It was planned to settle there 12 million aliens (from Hale-Bopp Comet?).
Lake Manosowar	In Tibet, → Nagas.
Light year	About 5.88 trillion miles (9,460,500,000,000 kilometers).
Merkaba	Another name for one's Light Body. Allows self to shrink to baseball size and to travel anywhere, instantly.
Mayan Calendar	3113 B.C.E. until 2012 C.E.
Mount Kurama	In Japan, is a very powerful site. Sacred spot that integrates the star & the planet energy.
New Jerusalem	The New Jerusalem will be made up of the following states: Illinois, Iowa, Kansas, Missouri, Nebraska. → Year 2005.

Novensiles	Angels: Cupra, Ercle, Mantus, Mars, Menrva, Sethlans, Summanus, Tina, Vejovis.
Orb	Round object, conscious energy form.
Osirian Civilization	The Mediterranean Sea was a large and fertile valley. The people there built huge megalithic structures and they had electricity. Some of the blocks weigh between 1,200 and 1,500 tons!
Patala	Located in India. A subterranean serpent race dwells there. → Agartha, Bhogavati.
Photon Belt	Also called: >> Golden Nebula, >> Golden Radiance, >> Manasic Vibration.
Porthologos	Living Library.
Poseid	Real name of Atlantis.
Posid	Other name of Posiedos.
Retz	Spiritual capital of Venus. Also known as Rits.
Rits	→ Retz.
Roswell	The UFO that crashed on July 1947 was doughnut shaped, approx. 35 ft. in diameter.
Salazere	Sacred temple complex in South America.
Salvington	Capital of our local universe Nebadon.
Sedim	Guardian Spirits.
SHALMALI	Lemuria was called "Land of Shalmali", at the time it existed. → Lemuria.
SHAMBALLA	Ascended Masters.

Silbury Hill	Artificial conical multilayer hill, strikingly regularly formed. Each of its segments is from another Britain region. Biggest prehistoric man-made construction of Europe, about 2500 B.C.E. Basis diameter: 168 m, Diameter on top: 30 m, Height: 38 m.
Snakeworld	Multileveled cavern system under the southwestern slopes of the Himalaya mountain range where the Nagas dwell. There a serpent cult of humans and reptilians dwell, which is said to have had contact with the Thule Society during World War II. → Nagas.
Soul Group	A Soul Group contains 144,000 Monads. A Monad contains 144 individuals. A Monad contains 12 Oversoul Souls. A Oversoul contains 6 sets of Twin Flames (Twin Souls, one female & one male). A Primary Soulmate Group is a set of Twin Flames, which is separated into a male and a female Twin Soul. "Near Twins" are the other 5 sets of Twin Flames. "Secondary Soulmates" are the other 132 individuals of a Monad.
Spectra 4	Is the astral communications belt.
St. Martin's Land	Subterranean caverns beneath Europe. → Greens.
Star of Bethlehem	Was a spaceship:
Stone Mountain	One of the two Record-Keeper Crystals in the world. in Atlanta GA.
Stonehenge	Most famous place of worship in Europe.
Tiahuanaco	Megalithic constructions which were built to last for thousands of years. Sacred temple complex in Bolivia, has a pyramid in his center.
UIGER CIVILIZATION	Gobi desert, the cities were ocean ports.
Uluru	One of the two Record-Keeper Crystals in the world, in Australia.
Umayor the 5th	Capital of the major sector of local universes.

Uminor the 3rd   Capital of the minor sector of local universes (Ensa).

UNIVERSAL MIND   → Akashic Records.

Urantia Book   Channeled material from extraterrestrial in the 1930's and was released 1956.
                             Also known as the Urantia Papers, 2097 pages.
                             Similar to the Holy Bible.
                             Urantia Foundation, 533 Diversey Parkway, Chicago, IL 60614.

Violet City   Home of St. Germain in the 5th dimension.

VORTEX   Energies that arise from a point along a grid where light strands crisscross.
                             Also known as power spots, sacred sites.

Walk-In   Is a Soul transference.
                             This is where 2 souls have agreed to switch places. Not all Walk-Ins are extraterrestrial.
                             They have come from many dimensions and universes.
                             There are about one million Walk-Ins on this planet at this time, said Djwhal Khul.

YaPool   Galactic Temple of Sanat Kumara.
                             Last temple of the mythical Thule.
                             It is well known as the home of the Gods.
                             Subterranean city, about 100 km in diameter, gigantic oceanic Galactic Federation Base, galactic home of the ancients, last outpost of Thule.
                             Located in the Gulf of Biscay, nearly 30 km from the coast of Northern Spain, between the cities of San Sebastian and Santander, 5000 m (8 to 9 km?) below sea level.
                             It consists of a subterranean territory made up by various caves.
                             The entire area corresponds to the Basque provinces in Spain and France.
                             Directly connected through tunnels to the coast.
                             YaPool has a number of dimensional portals on the surface.
                             In the base live and operate many star breeds.
                             → Agartha Network.

4.3 Light Cities, Underground Cities

Acambaro

Strange archaeological site in Mexico, about 4500 B.C.E., discovered 1944 by Waldemar Julsrud, a local German merchant.

Adocentyn

Sacred City, was located in the east of Egypt, 12 miles long on each of its four sides, built by the Egyptian god Thoth.

AGAM DES

Secret spiritual city on Earth.
Headquarter of the Galactic Federation.

AGARTHA

In Agartha there are many people of many races.
The Agarthian people originate from the ancient master ShaYa and his feminine expression WooPaa.
There are allegedly several entrances:

Egypt, Pyramid of Gizeh

Himalaya, Tibet
The entrance to the underground city of Shonshe is allegedly guarded by Hindu monks. The opening is located beneath the Potala in Lhasa.

Iguaçú Falls, border of Brazil and Argentina

Kentucky Monmoth Cave, south-central Kentucky

Manaus, Brazil

Mato Grosso, Brazil
The city of Posid supposedly lies beneath this plain.

Mongolia
The underground city of Shingwa allegedly exists beneath the border of Mongolia and China.

Morona-Santiago, Ecuador
Discovered by Juan Moricz.

Mount Epomeo, Italy

Mount Shasta, California
The Agarthian city of Telos allegedly exists within and beneath this mountain.

North Pole

Rama, India
Beneath this surface city is a long lost subterranean city, also named Rama.

South Pole

→ ShaYa, WooPaa, YaPool.
→ Agartha Network, 25,000 B.C.E.

AGARTHI   → Agartha.

Akahim   Gigantic stone city at the border of Brazil and Venezuela.

Akakis   First ancient stone city, lies in Mexico, built about 12,000 B.C.E.

Akakor   Ancient stone city, lies on the foothills of the Andes in the mountains between Brazil and Peru, built about 12,000 B.C.E.
There were another 26 stone cities around Akakor:
>>   Cadira, Venezuela
>>   Emin, Brazil
>>   Humbaya, Bolivia
>>   Ofir, Brazil
>>   Paititi, Bolivia
>>   ...

AKASHIA   The big room of all memory.
→ Akashic Records.

AKASHIC CHRONICLE Reader: Johnnie Prochaska.
→ Akashic Records.

AKASHIC Records Universal filing system. It has all knowledge.
Life records of all souls that have spent lifetime in physical Creation. Records document in great detail each event that occurred during all moments of every lifetime.
Also called:
>>   Akashia,
>>   Akashic Chronicle
>>   Cosmic Mind,
>>   Library,
>>   the collective subconscious,
>>   the collective unconscious,
>>   Universal Mind.

AKASIA   Central Computer of Earth.

Ancient Underground Cities

Exist below:
>> Andes,
>> Brazil,
>> Himalaya,
>> Iraq,
>> Maui,
>> Mt. Shasta,
>> ...

ARCHAIC CHRONICLES → Akashia, Akashic Records.

BHOGAVATI

A subterranean serpent race, called Nagas, dwells there. The entrance is somewhere in the Himalayas.
→ Agartha, Patala.
→ Nagas.

Cadira Ancient stone city in Venezuela.

Catharia Underground city.

CAVERN There live about 50 billion (descendants of Atlantean people).

CIUDAD SUBTERRÁNEO de los ANDES

In a crater in South Venezuela (jungle).
Populated by the Secret Society of Scientists.

Emerald Cities Hurqalya, Jabalqa, Jabarsa, Oz.

Emin Ancient stone city in Brazil.

FOURTEEN ETHERIC CITIES OF THE EARTH

7 are located over deserts or continents, the other 7 are located over large bodies of water.
>> Brazil,
>> Glastonbury, England,
>> Golden City, over Sahara Desert,
>> Shamballa, over Gobi Desert,
>> Tucson, Arizona.

Giza

There is a vast megalithic metropolis, reaching several levels below the Gizeh plateau, 15,000 years old, complete with hydraulic underground waterways.
One of several entrances to Agartha.
→ Agartha.

Gobi Desert

Beneath Gobi Desert there is an inner city called Aghopa (Agapa, Agartha).

Himalaya   There is the underground city Shonshe located.
                        One of the several entrances to Agartha.
                        → Agartha, Shonshe.

Humbaya   Ancient stone city in Brazil.

Hurqalya   Emerald City, square-shaped, 40,000 miles on each side.

Iguacu Falls   Lies between Brazil and Argentina.
                        One of the several entrances to Agartha.
                        → Agartha.

Jabalqa   Emerald City, square-shaped, 40,000 miles on each side.

Jabarsa   Emerald City, square-shaped, 40,000 miles on each side.

KALAMU   40,000-year-old city near Malibu, California.

Kalnigor   City was built by our forefathers, the Lyrans.

Library   → Akashia, Akashic records.

Manaus   One of several entrances to Agartha is in Manaus, Brazil.
                        → Agartha.

Manoa   Sacred temple complex in South America.

Mato Grosso   One of several entrances to Agartha is in Mato Grosso,
                        Brazil. Beneath there lies the underground city of Posid.
                        → Agartha.

Monmouth Caverns   One of several entrances to Agartha is in south central
                        Kentucky.
                        → Agartha.

Morella   City in the planet Cerpican.

Morona Santiago   One of several entrances to Agartha is about 150 km
                        south of Quito in Morona Santiago, discovered by
                                the Argentine archaeologist Juan Moricz.
                        → Agartha.

Mount Epomeo   One of several entrances to Agartha is in Italy.
                        → Agartha.

Mount Shasta   → Mt. Shasta.

Mt. Arunachala	Sacred mountain in Tiruvannamalai, South India. Most sacred holy place of all there is supposed to be a city inside the mountain. The adepts from inside Mt. Arunachala can change their shape to any human or animal form and travel incognito in the outside world. Is one of the major spiritual power spots on Earth.
Mt. Shasta	4,300 m (14,162/14,380 ft)high. Mt Shasta is the cone of an extinct volcano (the largest in the continental U.S.A), part of the Cascade chain of volcanoes extending south from Washington. Located at the northern extremity of the Sierra Nevada Mountain range located in Siskiyou County in Northern California. On a clear day you can see it from at least 100 miles away. Mt Shasta is a magnetic mountain, so much that some planes cannot fly over it. Shastina is a slightly smaller volcanic cone close to Shasta's summit. Beneath/in the mountain is one of several entrances to Agartha. There live over 1 million. They can live thousands of years in the same body. They came there before a thermonuclear war destroyed the Earth's surface, only 25,000 were saved. It is a focus for angels, Lemurians, spaceships and spirits. Is one of the major spiritual power spots on Earth. It is the seat of understanding. Location of one of the two major ascended masters' retreats in America, the other one is Grand Teton Mountain Range. The masters meet here, working for the upliftment of humanity on Earth. Some Lemurian people migrated to Mt. Shasta when Lemuria began to sink. → Agartha Network, Telos. → Adama, Sharula Dux. → Lemurians. → Nola Van Valer.
New Mexico	There is a Light City over New Mexico.
North Pole	One of several entrances to Agartha. → Agartha.
Ofir	Ancient stone city, powerful seaport, at the mouth of the Amazon river in Brazil, built by Samon. → Samon. → 3056 B.C.E.

Oz   Emerald City, known by the Rosicrucians.

Paititi   Ancient stone city in Bolivia.
                            Lost kingdom that lies between Brazil and Peru.
                            Average age of the inhabitants is about 900 to 1100
                            years.
                            Member: Alcir.

Posiedos   Underground city supposedly lying underground the
                            Mato Grosso region in Brazil.
                            → Agartha.

Rama   Beneath this city in India is the long lost city (also called)
                            Rama. This is one of the entrances to Agartha.
                            → Agartha.

SHAMBALA   Secret City, known as "Hidden Kingdom".
                            Shambala is also a state of mind according to the
                            Tibetan Lama Chögyam Trungpa Rinpoche.

Shamballah   → 25,000 B.C.E.

Shambhala   → Shambala.

Shangri-La   Secret city.

Shingwa   Underground city beneath the border of China and
                            Mongolia.
                            → Agartha.

Shonshe   Underground city in the Himalayas (Tibet). Entrance
                            allegedly guarded by Hindu monks. The opening is
                            located beneath the Potala in Lhasa.
                            → Agartha, Himalaya.

South Pole   One of several entrances to Agartha.
                            → Agartha.

TELOS   Ancient Lemurian City of Light below Mt. Shasta,
                            California.
                            Located approx. 1 mile below ground level, multi-leveled
                            city built within a vast cavern, some 5 miles wide and 20
                            miles long.
                            There live over 1,000,000 in peace and prosperity.
                            they can live thousands of years.
                            They came there 10,000 B.C.E.
                            The main residents are said to be descended from the
                            Quetzals and the Naga-Mayas.
                            → Agartha Network.
                            → Adama.
                            → Atlans, Telosians.

TEUTONIA   City on planet Tuithania (Venus on another dimension). Hometown of Omnec Onec.

Trantor   Capital City of the Confederation on planet Trantor.

4.4 Alien Bases

Acqualium

Confederation underwater base which is entirely Venusian, located 35o northwest of Chancay, Peru.
Member: Titinac.

ANU TEA

Extraterrestrial base in the Japanese Sea.

AREA51

→ Colonel William Woodward .

AZLANTA

A huge submarine base of the Ashtar Starfleet in the Atlantic Ocean.

Blue Base

Extraterrestrial operational base, in responsibility of Venusian Masters.
From there leave spaceships to Venus and Ganymede.
Close to Paititi, South America.

Cerilum

Base of the Confederation. Also known as Rumi-Suyo in Huanuco, Peru.
Commander is Sordaz from Apu.

Clipper Mountains

Near Danby, California.
There were seen motherships going into the mountains.

Columo

Medical orbiting base.
Chief is Erjabel from Apu.

Crystal City

Base on Jupiter's moon Ganymede.

DEIMOS

The Starfleet base on one of the artificial moons of Mars.

ELDORADO

Largest physical starfleet base on Earth, located underneath parts of Bolivia, Brazil, Peru.

KEIRA

Oldest Starfleet base in the Solar System.

Ladakh

Underground UFO landing base in India.

Panamint Mountains

Adjacent to Death Valley in California.
There is the major base of the Federation.

Peenemünde

Planned space city by the VRIL Company.

Peralta Gold Mines, Mexico

There is a Draco base camp.

Pine Grap, Australia	Near Alice Springs, Central Australia. There is a Illuminati-Grey Alien base under Pine Grap.
Ravenrock	Underground city of the NSA located south of Blue Ridge summit in Pennsylvania.
Rumi Suyo	Other name of the Confederation base in Hanuco, Peru.
Solomon Islands	In Malaita there is a subterranean UFO base.

Alien Bases and Alien Underground Bases

Alabama.

Algeria:	Tahot mountains.
Amarillo, Texas:	(East of Amarillo).

Andes:

Antarctica, New Berlin:	A massive joint humanoid-reptilian underground system called "New Berlin" lies below the Neu Schwabenland mountains.
Area 51, Nevada:	A government installation where daily UFOs and Alien contact was (and is) a normal event of the day. Facility was closed in 1998, probably because of too much public interest. Commonly referred to as S-4 at Groom Lake. There were 150,000 personnel in this facility, About 85% military personnel, 15% civilians. Levels 1 to 15 are manmade, levels 16 to 27 were built by an other race, they are just facilitating them. They are cloning there human beings.
Atlantic Ocean:	Benevolent Alien facility.
Belconnen, Australia:	Secret underground base in the Australian Capital Territory (ACT) near Canberra. There are at least 3 stories underground.
Bishop, CA:	There are landing ports.
Botswana:	Kamahak.
Boulder, Colorado:	Under Table Mountain.
Braxton, Missouri:	East of Braxton.

Brazil: Moto Brava Cuinva.
                                     Base of the Venusian.

Burley, Idaho.

Butte, Montana   Near Pipestone Pass, south of Butte.

Canada: Alberta, near Calgary.
                                     Banff, Benevolent Alien facility.
                                     British Columbia, near Dawson Creek.
                                     Grand Tetons,   Benevolent Alien facility.
                                     Ontario, in North Bay, there is a large NORAD facility.

Cheyenne Mountain (Space Command), Colorado.
                                     A government installation where daily UFOs and Alien
                                     contact was (and is) a normal event of the day.

Chile: North of Calama.

China Lake Naval Air Stations, California:
                                     A government installation where UFOs and Alien
                                     contact was (and is) not a normal daily activity.

Corsham, Wiltshire, UK: Huge underground base, known as Corsham Computer
                                     Centre (CCC).
                                     One tunnel links Corsham with the nearby village of
                                     Hawthorn, also the RAF base at Rudloe Manor.

Creed, Colorado.

Datil, New Mexico.

Death Valley, California.

Deep Springs, CA.

Denver International Airport   Transportation & human containment.

Dougway Proving Grounds, Utah.
                                     A government installation where daily UFOs and Alien
                                     contact was (and is) a normal event of the day.

Dulce – 4 Corners Area, New Mexico:
                                     Base of the Alpha Draconians.
                                     Was started in 1937/38 by the army engineers,
                                     completed in 1965/66, to connect tunnels to Page,
                                     Arizona.
                                     Multi-level base (over 4000 ft long).
                                     The underground mega-complex is nearly the size of
                                     Manhattan.

There are over 100 secret exits near and around Dulce, many around Archuleta Mesa other around Dulce Lake and even as far as Lindrich.

There are over 18,000 of the short Greys at the Dulce Facility.

Most of the aliens are on levels 5, 6 and 7.

LEVEL 1:   contains   the   garage   for   street maintenance.

LEVEL 2:   contains the garage for trains, shuttles, tunnel-boring machines and disc maintenance.

LEVEL 4:   human-aura   research,   telepathy, hypnosis, dreams.

LEVEL 6:   "Nightmare Hall". it holds the genetic labs.

LEVEL 7:   there are humans in cages, usually dazed or drugged.

They are taking humanoid embryos out of this base to somewhere else.

In 1975 in a demonstration one Grey alien was killed and several dozen human scientists & security officers.

In 1979 were the Dulce wars. The resistance was led by Thomas Edwin Castello (head of security) with 9 other workers, others joined, also a few tall Reptilians (there were apparently traitors in the midst of this resistance). The White Dracos held several thousand abductees in cages or cryogenic containment, so that their body parts could be used for various biogenetic experiments, or worse.

In a rescue operation died over 200 aliens and 66 special forces. Later almost all of the resistance were slaughtered.

Edwards AFB, California:	A government installation where UFOs and Alien contact was (and is) not a normal daily activity.
Eglin AFB, Florida:	A government installation where UFOs and Alien contact was (and is) not a normal daily activity.
Egypt:	Close to the Libyan border, as big as the state of Maryland. Cairo: underneath the Gizeh plateau. Base of Lyrans and Sirians. Base of the Aldebaran human militarists.
Four Corners:	U.S Government Star Visitor Reception Area.
Fort Meade, Maryland:	They are cloning duplicates like Jimmy Carter, Walter Mondale, ...
France, Mount Blanc:	Benevolent Alien facility that is shared by 7 races.
Ft. Belvoir, Virginia:	Home of the Army Corps of Engineers.

Ft. Lewis – Madigan, Washington State
                                 Bio-medical & bio replication.

Furnace Creek, California: Massive base of Vegans from Lyra.
                                 Galactic Federation base.

Groom Lake, Nevada: → Area 51.

Himalaya.

Idaho.

Iran: In a desert in the middle of the country.

Iraq: Base of the Orions.

Lancaster – Tehachapi, California
                                 Aerospace & computing.

Lawrence Livermore Laboratories, California
                                 A government installation where UFOs and Alien contact was (and is) not a normal daily activity.

Little Cottonwood Canyon – Dougway, Utah
                                 Cloning & cybernetics.

Loring AFB, Maine: A government installation where UFOs and Alien contact was (and is) not a normal daily activity.

Los Angeles County, California

                                 Created in the 1950's and enlarged in the 1990's.

MacDill AF Base, Florida   A government installation where UFOs and Alien contact was (and is) not a normal daily activity.

Madagascar: In the mountains there is a base of the Ciakars.

Madigan, Seattle, WA.

Maledive Islands: Base of the Centaurians.

Massachusetts: Large underground facility of the Korendians.

Masurine Islands: Underwater base.

Maxwell AF Base, Florida

                                 A government installation where UFOs and Alien contact was (and is) not a normal daily activity.

Menwith Hill, GB:	Britain's Area 51. 8 miles from Ilkley Moor, contains over 1,800 personnel, contains a maximum of 20 Greys. It's part of a global network of 28 "spy bases" belonging to the US National Security Agency (NSA). The base has 6 underground levels and extends outwards for several miles.
Mercury – Area 51, Nevada:	Nuclear & antigravity.
Mojave Desert, California.	
Mongolia:	Xining.
Montana.	
Montauk – Camp Hero, Long Island:	Quantum-hyperspace mechanics & microwave mind-control.
Mount Blackmore, Southwestern Montana	
Mount Hood, Oregon:	The military is cloning human beings there like: Carter, Mondale, Astronauts Crippen & Young, ...
Narragansett Bay, Newport Rhode Island:	War College. From here access to an underground facility.
Narvik.	
Nevada:	Base of the Venusians. Base of the Zetas.
New Mexico:	Holloman AFB. Altairians landed there in the 1960's. → Altairians.
New Mexico:	Los Alamos Laboratories. A government installation where UFOs and Alien contact was (and is) not a normal daily activity.
New Mexico:	Sandia Base. The military is cloning human beings there like: Carter, Mondale, Astronauts Crippen & Young, ... Base of the Zetas. A government installation where UFOs and Alien contact was (and is) not a normal daily activity.
Pacific Ocean:	Underwater base.
Page, Arizona.	

Palmdale Area, California: There are clear pictures of the entrance to the underground facility.

Panamint Mountains: Huge Galactic Federation underground facility.
                                    → Suvians.

Paradox, Nevada.

Pine Gap, Australia: In the center of Australia.
                                    Many of the things that are being taken to the Moon are leaving from here.

Point Pleasant, West Virginia

                                    → Mothmen.

Russia: Karaga.
                                    Monchegorsk Airbase,
                                        crashed extraterrestrial spaceships.
                                    Odinstovo (Moscow),
                                        crashed extraterrestrial spaceships and a lien bodies.
                                    Sakaueen.
                                    Semipalatinsk,
                                        they are cloning there human beings.
                                    Serov: Ural Mountains.
                                    Zhitkur,
                                        crashed extraterrestrial spaceships and alien bodies.

Salt Lake, Utah.

Snowny Mountains, Australia

                                    Base like Pine Gap.

Solomon Islands, Malaita: Subterranean UFO base.

South Africa: Base of the Koldasians.

South Sandwich Islands.

St. Paul, Minnesota   (South of St. Paul).

Sudan: Nyala Range.

Sunspot, Nevada.

Superstitious Mountains, Arizona.

Sweden: Under Gotland Island.
                                    Private island.

<u>Tehachapi Mts:</u>	There is supposed to be an underground facility.
<u>Tibet:</u>	Benevolent Alien facility. Base of the Venusians.

<u>Twenty-Nine Palms Marine Corps Base, Southern California.</u>

<u>Ucrania:</u>	Herson Base.
<u>Washington:</u>	2 bases.
<u>West Point, New York:</u>	Army's officer training academy.
<u>White Mountains, Arizona:</u>	A government installation where daily UFOs and Alien contact was (and is) a normal event of the day.

<u>White Sands Army Missile Range, New Mexico.</u>

<u>Wyoming</u>.

<u>Yucca Mountains, Nevada:</u>	19 miles of caverns & tunnels used for the construction of gravity craft.
<u>Zaire:</u>	Kindi (West of Kindi).
Wasatch Mountains	The CIA is involved there.

5. SPACESHIPS

5.1 Ezekiel's Encounter

It always was so clear to me,
I hope you'll take it well
As right as rain in black and white
Those words by Ezekiel.

He witnessed All with his own eyes
Described the best he could,
At first he didn't realize
If they were bad or good.

The heavens opened from the north
The Fire filled the sky,
Ezekiel was really shocked
And wondered "How and Why"

The rings with eyes were high above
Held up by the magic force.
He was confused and terrified
By a bunch of UFO'.

The Amazing spacecrafts touched the ground
Reflecting the neon light
The rotating wheels as lightning
Were radiant and bright

Ezekiel was blinded… Yet…
He could see better still
He'd seen the Light! Oh lucky man!
What an ecstatic thrill.

The creatures landed on the Earth
On the strangest wheels he'd seen
They were not animals, not men
But something in between

They had four wings on their four sides
Which wrapped the bodies tight
Perhaps they wore fine long robes
Flowing in the windy night.

Their hands were under their wings
The hands of a human being
It's possible, that two or four of them
Were flying each machine

The creatures had four faces too.
The Man-Lion on the right
But on the left the face of an Ox
And Eagle by its side

Their feet were straight and their soles
Were just as calves or moose
Or maybe the man described at best
The golden platform shoes

The creatures radiated light
From their heads to their feet
They moved without looking back
Oh what a weird breed

Their heads were covered all around
But He still could see them through
What were their helmets made, of glass?
Here's some home work for you

Above their heads was hovering
Another strange machine
With the eldest captain on its board
Who looked like a human being

The Loud voice came from the craft
Instructions followed… and then…
Ezekiel was lifted up
For a little ride with them

Imagine what he must have felt
That scared and simple man
The first man from the Earth to fly?!
It must've been some fun

The hissing noise of the space-machine
Confused his tired brain
Remember, that he'd never seen
A light bulb, a car or a plane

In fact he even didn't know
That the world was round as ball
So Really He did very well
By describing IT at all

As strange as it may sound to you
The "God's" sapphire throne
Could have been a blue plastic chair
Where the eldest sat alone

Of course he had to teach us Life
The Boss of the advanced race
So don't forget, that our God
Came down from outer space

He did predict a lot of things
Because he moved with speed of light
If we could get that quick to stars
We'd see Christ get crucified

Sophisticated Being as God
Supreme in every way
"Created" Adam and then Eve
you've heard of DNA…

Remember what the bible said
God put Adam into a deep sleep
That anesthetic must've been strong
To remove his spare rib

When those two multiply in full
Experiment went wrong
Human beings played out of tune
And they didn't sing the song

The modern man got as far as the moon
But there's endless space
One day he'll fly and will discover
The world of a simple race

The world as One we used to know
With no technology
Where even radio or matches
The gifts from Gods would be

Mr. Smith will come and go or stay
But stories will be told
The legends of "Deity" mr. Smith
Will be read by young and old:

"That strange sophisticated race
Who look so much like us
Who taught us in so many ways
And helped us in the past"

We resembled them, but help us God
We use $^1/_{10}$ of our brain
If we use the rest or even half
Then more we would explain

If we use the brain, the good old world
Would be a better place
And All the warnings from above
We would digest with grace

Because They know, but we don't
Please notice every sign
Crop circles… one of them to read
And some will blow your mind

They're trying to tell us many things
And Yet… they let us Be,
The day might come, when they'll get fed up
And "throw away the key"

The human being with all it knows…
And that's not much at all
I hope that man will learn somehow
And will reach that highest goal

I am not trying to change your mind
I'm just opening the door
The prehistoric art in caves
Will tell you so much more

Just look at the paintings done by men
Thousands of years ago
Gods in helmets and space-suits
And crafts with magic glow

I should have written this in stone
So it will live forever... well...
I've done a few stranger things
That's all, my name is Yeva.

Thank you.

Relevant Old Testament texts
[book of Ezekiel is between Jeremiah & Daniel]:

Encounter 1 1:1 -28 2: 2, 9&10 3: 1-3, 12 -15

Encounter 2 3:22-24

Encounter 3 8:1-4 9:1 - 11 10:1-22 11: 1-2, 22-25

Encounter 4 40:1-4 43:1-7

5.2 Starships by races

Andromedan starships:

Scout Ships:	Sombrero-shaped, 15 to 20 m.
Command Ships:	Lens-shaped, up to 805m long.
Motherships:	Shape is oblong, 4800 km long (3000 miles).
	Presently (May 2004) there are 2 motherships around planet Earth.

Arcturian starships:

Are the finest in the entire universe, they are propelled by crystals.   The crystals conduct light energy from the Great Central Sun.

Scout Ships:	Bell-shaped, 12.2 to 22.9 m.
Command Motherships:	Lens-shaped, > 22.5 km long.
Motherships:	Almost cigar-shaped, 16,000 km (10,000 miles).

Bellatrician starships:

Scout Ships:	Dewdrop shaped and beetle-shaped, 30.5 to 122m.
Motherships:	Like large tadpoles, 1.6 to 640 km.

Biaviian starships:

Motherships:	Egg-shaped, diameter 40 kilometer.
	They have hybrids there. They have domed gardens inside.

Centaurian starships:

Scout Ships:	Bell-shaped, with a large circular wing attached to the underside, 14 m in diameter, 9.1 m high.
Command Ships:	Cigar formed, with a small bulge in the middle, longer than 6o m.

Earth starships:

There are bases in Archuleta Mesa, Dulce, Durango Co, Taos N.M. and the main fleet is stored at Los Alamos.

Fomalhautan starships:

Human Scout Ships: Ovoid like water drops, 18.3 to 26 m in diameter.
Human Motherships: Multi-layered cigars, 3.2 to 1,920 km.
Dinoid-Reptoid Scout Ships: Beetle-shaped, 30.5 m in diameter.
Dinoid-Reptoid Motherships: Amoeba-shaped, 13 to 14,400 km.

Human spaceships:

                                        Traditionally saucer shaped, metallic, powered by thought energy.

Korendian spaceships:

                                        Disc-shaped.

Lyran beamships:

                                        Diameter: 7 m, crew: 3 members.

Martian starships:

                                        Similar to a robot but have intelligence with awareness. These crafts are under the direct control of various tribunals throughout the universe. After these crafts are built they are placed in an orbit beyond Pluto. Then they disappear, after a certain time they reappear now possessing awareness, which was given to them in an other dimension.
                                        These Chronomonitor starships are the most remarkable intelligences in the physical universe.

Mintakan starships:

Spaceships: Mushroom-shaped, 15.2 to 46 m in diameter.
Motherships: 160 to 1,000 km. Usually kept in deep space.

Nors starships:

                                        They use 7 different types of space Crafts, 5 are manned.
Cigar Shaped Ships: 100 ft long, 25 ft wide.
Disc Shaped Ships:
Doughnut Shaped Ships:
Spherical Shaped Ships:
Ball Shaped Ships:

Pegasian starships:

Defense Ships:	Rounded equilateral triangle, each side is approx. 22.56 m long.
Scout ships:	Oblong, 25.9 m in diameter.
Command Ships:	Double lens atmospheric command ship, 402 m long.

Pleiadian beam ships:

Beam ship type 1:	Diameter: 7 m, crew: 3 members. Reddish bottom, emits humming sound.
Beam ship type 2:	Like type 1, but white top dome, reddish/orange ports.
Beam ship type 3:	Diameter: 7 m, gold/silver finish, dimensional travel.
Drone:	Diameter: 3,5 m, crew: pilot less, robotic.
Large spaceship:	Diameter: 20 m, 18 ports around rim, red/orange bottom.
Miniscout ship:	Diameter: 5 m, crew: 1 member. Dark grey metallic, atmospheric only.

Procyonan starships:

	Represent technologies of a most advanced form, over 50 billion years old.
Scout ships:	Teardrop shaped or beetle shaped, 13.72 to 61 m.
Motherhips:	Snowflake shaped or jellyfish shaped, 161 to 6,440 km long.

Reptilian spaceships:

Cylinder shaped, but also have egg or globe shaped ships. The craft are organic, solar/star energy powered.

Sirian Motherships:

Have the size of a small planet.

Tall Whites spaceships:

Scout ships:	Ellipsoid or egg-shaped, row of large windows on each side. Color: white. Travel to Mars possible.
Spaceships:	*500 ft long, 300 ft wide, 70 ft high.* Color: black.

Tau Cetian starships:

Scout ships: Diamond shaped plasma craft, 61 to 76.2 m long.
Motherships: Look like a series of multi-layered blood cells in stacks
                        of 20 to 50 cells, 6.44 to 70.84 km in diameter.
                        Are usually the command ships of Galactic Federation
                        exploration fleets.

Ummo spaceships:

                        Diameter: 50 m.

Vegan beam ships:

                        Diameter: 8 m.

Venusian spaceships:

                        Diameter: about 700 ft, height: about 300 ft.
                        No visible controls, they run the ship through thought
                        control. Can travel through time.

Verdant starships:

                        → Goodwill.

5.3 Starships by names

ALAHOY

Mothership of Excalabar, approx. 400km long.
2000 scout ships in that mothership.
Excalabar is the Commander of all the scout ships.

ALIGNMENT

Medical ship of the First Fleet.
Work together with the Ascended Masters, the Arcturian medical teams, the Emerald Star people.
Cmdrs.: Alisha, Galimai-A.

ALPHA

One of the seven main motherships.
Direct representative of the Life Bearers, the council Alpha-Omega.
The ship is composed by cosmic plasma and is not at all comparable to any other type of extraterrestrial ship.
Alpha is more a Merkaba than a technological manifestation.

ANDRENA 72

Spacecraft of Zel, they have 72 occupants.
Diameter approx. 910m, height about 135m.

ASTRA

Ancient Indian spaceship.

ASTRANDA 17

Experimental craft from the Orion galaxy from the Planet Pacifica.

ASTRONA

Spacecraft of Grand Space Commander Petron.

ATHENA

Starship of the Arcturians.
Mothership of Ashtar, about 24,000 occupants, about 250 doctors.
→ Dextra.

ATLA

Medical ship.

AZELDA

Spacecraft of Candor. 21 occupants.

BABYLON

Starship.

CAPRICORN

Helena is Captain of this starship of the Galactic Federation.
→ Lavar.

CENTRALIA

Mothership of Glasstaria.

COLLINESTA

Starship. Member: Eleanor.

CRYSTAL BELL

Starship of Woodok.
Ship has landed many times on the volcano Etna in Sicily.
→ Ithacar, Woodok.

DOVE   Mothership of Sananda, 100 miles long.

GOODWILL   Star cruiser of the Verdants.
                         Diameter: 8,000 ft by 300 ft (1,5 mile).
                         Center: 3,000 ft high.
                         Height: 1,365 ft.
                         Crew: 22,000 most of them scientist.
                         Was built 200,000 years ago.

HATONN   Starship of Cmdr. Hatonn from planet Terminus Hatonn.

IANKA   Space ship.

INTREPID   Spaceship of Lord Adolphius.

JANUS   Starship.
                         → Venajoa.

LIGHT   Starship of Commander Awaana has 300 or more crewmembers.
                         → Awaana.

MARIGOLD   Mothership from the Intergalactic Brotherhood. Close to Earth
                         positioned.
                         Also known as: City of Lights, Crystal City, Jeweled City, New
                         Jerusalem.

METHARIA   Spaceship, diameter 31 meter.

NIBIRU   Is not a planet with one civilization, instead it is a starship of the
                         United Stars Nations.
                         Nibiru is a Cosmic living being.
                         Nibiru is also a planet and a battle star and is a little over 3 times
                         the size of Earth.
                         Nibiru was originally a planet that was thrown out of orbit with
                         the implosion of Sirius B.
                         Nibiru is a red planet with a gold hue that travels the galaxy.
                         It's atmosphere produces a red-brown light frequency.
                         Nibiru is not a brown dwarf, the brightness comes from the gold
                         suspended in its atmosphere.
                         Four-dimensional flagship of the Milky Way Galaxy's Galactic
                         Federation.
                         Many species live inside the hollowed out planet.
                         On the Nibiru there are representatives of many different
                         civilizations that live aboard it: (Carians, Felines, Froglike beings,
                         Greys, Humans, Insectillians, Liquidians, Reptilians).
                         From 2000 B.C.E. until recently , Nibiru only had access to
                         stargates in the 4th dimension.
                         Is in orbit around our sun (Dec. 1999).

ODIN   The huge VRIL-7 spaceship Odin left in the year 1945 for a visit
                         in the Aldebaran star system.

PEGASUS	English for Pelegai. ***Pegasus Fleet:*** There are over 1,000 Lightships in the Pegasus Fleet. → Mothership Pelegai.
PELEGAI	Flagship of the 9D Nibiruan Council. Last remaining flagship of the Galactic Federation Council from Lyra. Part of a fleet of Lightships. The ship is propelled by thought, navigator Janus. It was built on the planet Avyon (First Earth) in the Vega Star System of the Lyra Constellation. Pelegai is the higher dimensional version of Nibiru. Members of the House of Aln and the House of Avyon live and work on Pelegai at this time (Carians, Felines, Humans, Reptilians). Its symbol is a winged horse flying through a triangle surrounded by a circle. Has access to all star gates up to the 9th dimension of our universe, given by the founders. → Janus.
PELLA 3	Spaceship.
PHOENIX	Mothership, great starship of Cmdr. Soltec. Is a refurbished dead planet. Also known as Tetros. 16.1 miles long. → Richard Miller. → Soltec.
PLEYA III	Exploring evacuation ship. Length: 1,5 km. Crew: 600. Floors: 7.
SHAN CHEA	An Ashtar Command mothership. It is a city in itself. Diameter over 100 miles, has many Scout Ships on board.
SHARE	Space carrier ship, multidimensional existence. Ashtar Squadron headquarters. Size: 42 x 13 x 8 km, length: 600 m, room height: 12 m, 12 basic decks.
TETROS	Other name of starship Phoenix.
TIPUS	Venusian spaceship. Crewmember: Rosinac, Rumilac, Sampiac (Cmdr.), Titinac (female).
TRANSVAAL	Mothership, 16.1 miles long.

VAILIXI   Atlantean spaceship which could maneuver in space, air and underwater.
Types: cigar shaped, saucer shaped.
Used about 22,000 B.C.E.

VICTOR ONE   Starship of Valiant Thor, 300 feet in diameter,
current position: Lake Mead, Nevada.
Commander: Valiant Thor.
Crew: about 200.
Member: Donn Thor, Jill Thor, Teel, Uniah, Valiant Thor, Yo.

VIMANA   Ancient Indian spaceship.
There were at least 4 different types of Vimanas:
>>   cigar shaped,
>>   circular with portholes and a dome, double-deck.

VRIL-7   Spaceship built by the VRIL Company in the year 1944/1945.

WEST STAR   Mothership, starship of the Star Command under the command of Commander Veyares.
Houses several hundred thousand intergalactic representatives.
Member: Mishar, Shaari, Veyares.

ZELLA 17   Spacecraft of Atna.

5.4 UFO Crashes and Forced Landings

Year 1561	Nuremberg, Germany.
Year 1909.12.22	Chicago, Illinois. West of Chicago, never found.
Year 1938.Summer	Czernica, Poland. Near Jelenia Gora, seized by Germany.
Year 1941	San Diego, California. In the ocean west of San Diego. The UFO was retrieved by the Navy. Some dead Zeta Reticulians (Greys).
Year 1941.04	Cape Girardeau, Missouri. Three alien victims.
Year 1941.06	Byelorussia. Near Goszevo & Dubrovki. Wreckage salvaged by NKVD troops and taken to Omsk. Later taken to Zhitkur (1945).
Year 1945	Bulgaria. Wreckage taken to Zhitkur.
Year 1945	Romania. Wreckage taken to Zhitkur.
Year 1947.07.04	Roswell, New Mexico: 5 aliens, one living. This most known crash was not on July 2, but July 4. Two crafts crashed after colliding in the air during an electrical storm. One was manned with Greys, the other with Orange from the Andromeda Star System.
Year 1947.07.07	Bozeman, Montana. This is an open case.
Year 1947.07.07	Shreveport, Louisiana. Hoax.
Year 1948.03	Socorro, New Mexico.

Year 1948.03.25   Aztec (Hart Canyon, 12 miles east of Aztec), NM.
Ship diameter: about 100 ft., 18 ft across, 72 inches high. Almost completely undamaged, 14 to 16 dead small humanoid aliens, probably from Venus, found inside this craft. Take to Muroc Air Force Base, later taken to Wright-Patterson Air Force Base, Ohio.
This incident was also dated 1948-02-03, 1948-02-13 and 1948-04-25.
Possible hoax.

Year 1948.07   Mexico (South of Laredo).
Possible interception by American Military aircraft, 1 alien body.

Year 1948.10.02   Phoenix, Arizona (Paradise Valley, Cave Creek).
Allegedly crashed in the Dreamy Draw area, but actually crashed near Cave Creek (10 miles away).
2 aliens, about 4.5 ft. tall.

Year 1950   Mexico, close to the border of Texas (Del Rio).

Year 1950.10.09   Albuquerque, New Mexico.
3 alien bodies.

Year 1950.12   Del Rio, Texas.

Year 1952   New Mexico.

Year 1952.02.14   Ely, Nevada.
16 alien bodies.

Year 1952.09.12   Spitzbergen, Norway.
Also dated June 1952, 2 alien bodies.
Possible fake.

Year 1953   White Sands, New Mexico.

Year 1953.04.18   S.W.) Arizona.

Year 1953.05.20/21   Kingman, Arizona.
1 alien body, 4 ft. tall, dark brown complexion, silvery metal suit without helmet.

Year 1953.06.19   Laredo, Texas.
4 alien bodies.

Year 1953.07.10   Johannesburg, South Africa.
5 alien bodies.

Year 1953.10   Grachevka, Orenburg, Russia.
Disc-shaped, approx. diameter 5 meters, band of multi-colored lights. Wreckage taken to Zhitkur.

Year 1953.10.13   Dutton, Montana.
                             4 alien bodies.

Year 1955   Eucla, SA, Australia.
                             Alleged crash, alien photo.

Year 1955   Nowra, NSW, Australia.
                             UFO saga.

Year 1955   Kazakhstan.
                             Allegedly taken intact UFO to Zhitkur.

Year 1955.05   Brighton, England.
                             4 alien bodies.

Year 1956   Nevada desert.
                             Zeta Reticulan hybrid Raechel crash-landed in the Nevada desert.

Year 1957   Semipalatinsk, Kazakhstan.
                             Crash on the nuclear test site, taken to Zhitkur.

Year 1957.07.18   Carlsbad, New Mexico.

Year 1957.09.15   Ubatuba, Brazil.
                             Possible fake.

Year 1958   Utah (desert).
                             UFO intact, 4 alien bodies.

Year 1958.09   (N.E.) Kazakhstan.
                             UFO about 15 meter in diameter, taken to Zhitkur.

Year 1959.01.21   Gdynia, Poland.
                             Crashed into the Gdynian harbor basin. About 3 meters in
                             diameter, hemispherical shaped. 1 or 2 alien bodies allegedly
                             taken to Moscow.

Year 1960.03   New Paltz, New York.
                             A small humanoid was captured by authorities and taken by the
                             CIA, where the alien died 28 days later, 2 escaped.

Year 1961.04.28   Leningrad, Russia.
                             Near Korb Lake.

Year 1962.04.18   Las Vegas, Nevada.

Year 1962   Semipalatinsk, Kazakhstan.
                             Allegedly crashed near the nuclear test site, taken to Zhitkur.

Year 1962   Northern Russia.
                             Disc-shaped, taken to the Odintsovo air base near Moscow.
                             Alleged crash.

Year 1962.06.12   Holloman AFB, New Mexico.
                             2 alien bodies.

Year 1964   ?
                             2 intact UFOs allegedly taken to the U.S. Military by
                             extraterrestrials.

Year 1964.10.11   Ft. Riley, Kansas.
                             9 alien bodies.

Year 1965.12.09   Kecksburg, Pennsylvania.
                             Open case.

Year 1966.06.17   Elista, (North) Caucasus, Russia.
                             Exploding UFO.

Year 1966   Topolevka, Tomsk, Russia.
                             A UFO crashed into the taiga, near Topolevka.

Year 1966/1968   Kentucky/Ohio area.
                             UFO intact, 3 alien bodies.

Year 1966.10.27   (N.W.) Arizona.

Year 1967.10.04   Shag Harbour, Nova Scotia, Canada.
                             Ship's diameter about 60 ft.

Year 1968   Arhangelsk, Russia.
                             Kolguev Island, north of Arhangelsk, taken to the Odintsovo
                             base.

Year 1968.02.12   Orocuré, Columbia.
                             Open case.

Year 1969   Pennsylvania.
                             UFO recovered.

Year 1972.07.18   Morocco.
                             Sahara desert, 3 alien bodies.

Year 1973.07.10   (N.W.) Arizona.
                             5 alien bodies.

Year 1974   Donetsk, (Northern) Rostov, Russia.
                             Globe shaped UFO exploded. Debris examined by many people.

Year 1974.05   Chili, New Mexico.
                             Allegedly taken 60 ft. wide metallic craft to the Kirtland AFB.

Year 1974.07.15   Spain.
                             Open case.

Year 1976.05.12	Australia. Crash in the desert, 4 alien bodies.
Year 1976.08	Nowra, Robertson, NSW, Australia.
Year 1976.08.08	Presidente Prudente, Sao Paulo, Brazil. Open case.
Year 1977.04.05	(S.W.) Ohio. 11 alien bodies.
Year 1977.06.22	(N.W.) Arizona. 5 alien bodies.
Year 1977.08.17	Tobasco, New Mexico. 2 alien bodies.
Year 1978	(Western) Kazakhstan. Allegedly a UFO, looking like a fighter aircraft, was shot down by Soviet military, UFO and aliens were taken to Zhitkur.
Year 1978	? Landed UFO, cylinder shaped, about 35 meters long, allegedly taken to Zhitkur.
Year 1978.05.06	Bolivia. Open case.
Year 1979	Rinburg, Ural, Russia. Crash into the Ural region near the village of Rinburg, wreckage taken to the Odintsovo air base.
Year 1979.02.17	Zhigansk, Yakutiya, Russia. A disc shaped UFO with a mirror-like surface crashed into the banks of the Lena river. Alien bodies allegedly autopsied at the Moscow State University.
Year 1979.09	Banka Banka, Northern Territory, Australia. Remains of burnt area and ash found.
Year 1980	Lismore, NSW, Australia. Possible newspaper fake.
Year 1981.05	Murmansk, Russia. Exploded on the Kolsky peninsula, debris taken to the Monchegorsk air base.
Year 1981.08.22	Argentina. Maybe 2 dead aliens. Open case.

Year 1983   Kazakhstan.
                          Allegedly shot down with an experimental laser weapon.

Year 1983.05.15   Ordzhonikidse, (Northern) Caucasus.
                          Cone shaped UFO allegedly tracked on military radar and shot
                          down by ground air defense, wreckage taken to the Odintsovo
                          base.

Year 1984   Murmansk, Russia.
                          Alleged crash, wreckage taken to the Monchegorsk military base.

Year 1984   Siberia, Russia.
                          Taymyrian area, dolphin shaped UFO recovered from river and
                          taken to Zhitkur base.

Year 1984.07.20   Baku, Azerbaijan.
                          Crash in the Baku mountains.

Year 1986.01.29   Dalnegorsk, Russia.
                          Globe shaped, steel-colored UFO crashed on the Isvestkovaya
                          mountain near Dalnegorsk, debris examined. Levitated 6 times
                          until finally burned out. It is assumed that it rather was a bad
                          landing than a crash.

Year 1987.08   Leningrad, Russia.
                          Rocket shaped, about 14 meters long, taken to the Monchegorsk
                          air base.

Year 1987.09   Tutaev, Yaroslawl, Russia.
                          UFO dogfight over the town of Tutaev, eventually crashed into a
                          bog in the Darvinskiy reserve, wreckage taken to Zhitkur.

Year 1987.11.02   Krasnovodsk, Turkmeniya.
                          A UFO landed (about 80 kilometers from Krasnovodsk) on the
                          Caspian Sea and exploded, only debris was an oily slick in the
                          sea. The UFO's diameter was about 290 meters.

Year 1988.11   Afghanistan.
                          7 alien bodies.

Year 1988.11.22   Tomsk, Siberia, Russia.
                          Near Al'myakovo, Western Siberia. It was said it was a bolide
                          meteor.

Year 1989   Siberia, Russia.
                          A large UFO, just outside of the city of Omsk in Western
                          Siberia, taken to the Odintsovo base.

Year 1989.05   South Africa.
                          2 alien bodies.

Year 1989.06	Siberia, Russia. North of the Tumen region, Western Siberia. Alleged live aliens were taken to the Odintsovo base near Moscow.
Year 1989.07	South Africa. 9 live aliens taken in 2 galaxy transports to Wright AFB.
Year 1989.09.16	Zaostrovka, Ural, Russia. Fight between 6 grey UFOs and a golden UFO over the town of Zaostrovka, Perm, golden one shot down by the others, wreckage taken to Zhitkur.
Year 1989.09.25	Moriches Bay, Long Island, New York. South shore off of Moriches Bay. Shot down by U.S. Military. Also dated September 28, 1989. Definitely no hoax.
Year 1989.Autumn	Dushanbe, Tajikistan, Russia. Explosion of a small globe shaped UFO.
Year 1990.09.26	Uzbekistan. Traces of a possible UFO crash found in the Kyzylkumy desert.
Year 1991.11	Kazakhstan. UFO dogfight over the town of Ezibastuz, Pavlodar. Allegedly one of them crashed.
Year 1991.11	(North) Kabardino Balkar Republic. UFO shot down by Russian fighter crashed near Prohladnyi. UFO and aliens taken to Zhitkur.
Year 1991.11.24	Shirley, New York. Remote area of Southhaven Park.
Year 1992	South Haven Park. Alleged crash.
Year 1992.04.15	Buffalo, New York. 10 miles north of Buffalo, diameter about 100 ft.
Year 1992.06.25	Moldova, Ucrania. Soviet MIG fighter allegedly collided with a UFO, both crashed.
Year 1992.11-24	Long Island, New York. Possible crash near South Haven Park.
Year 1993.08.09	Nikolaev, Ucrania. UFO allegedly shot down by military and crashed.

Year 1994.05.15   Kharkov, Ucrania.
                             About 40 kilometers south/south-west of Kharkov, near the
                             village of Ohochee. Debris examined by civilian UFO
                             researchers and revealed as extraterrestrial.

Year 1994.06   Kiev, Ucrania.
                             UFO shot down by Ukrainian military, about 100 km northeast
                             of Kiev and taken to the military base at Herson, there they
                             discovered alien bodies.

Year 1995.05   Carpathian Mountains, Ucrania.
                             UFO shot down near the Rumanian border, wreckage taken to
                             the Herson military base.

Year 1995.11   Chechnya Republic.
                             Explosion of an UFO near the small town of Itum-Kale.
                             Wreckage taken by Chechnyan forces. All records of the event
                             destroyed during the Chechnyan war.

Year 1996   Varghina, Brazil.
                             UFO debris and alien bodies were brought to the U.S.A.

Year 1996.06.23   Pinedale, Arizona.

Year 1996.08   Zaporozhe, Ucrania.
                             A huge UFO exploded near the village of Shirokee.
                             Wreckage recovered by the Security Bureau of Ucrania and taken
                             to the Herson military base.

Year 1997.03.15   Wegorzewo, Suwalki Province, Poland.
                             Site cleaned up by Polish army, no survivors.

Year 1997.08   North Caucasus, Russia.
                             Elliptical shaped UFO crashed into the forest near Mezmay,
                             Krasnodarsky Kray.

Year 1999,04,15   Guam.
                             UFO beaches in Uranas Reef.

6. LIGHTWORKER, RESEARCHERS, INVESTIGATORS, EXPERIENCERS

6.1 Lightworker and Channels

Aleuti, Francesca   Channel to Voltra.

Alla-An, Jyoti   Channel to Mellora, Pelghi.
Reiki Master, Teacher of Magnified Healing.
The Light Expansion Center, P.O.Box 2135,
Boulder, CO 80306-2135.
3250 O'Neil Circle-D13, Boulder, CO 80301.
Voice Mail: (720) 406-1894.
lightexpansion@angelfire.com
lightexp@bouldernews.infi.net
http://www.geocities.com/HotSprings/Spa/3365/Ninth.html

Allingham, Tim   Psychic, teacher, healer.
Phone: 404-252-4540.

Altea, Rosemary   Internationally spiritual renowned medium.
Lives in England and Vermont.
http://www.rosemaryaltea.com
http://www.soultospirit.com

Aluna Joy Yaxk'in   Internationally known speaker, author, clairvoyant.
P.O.Box 1988, Sedona Az 86339.
Phone: 928-282-6292.
http://www.1spirit.com/alunajoy
alunajoy@kachina.net

Amassia   Is Danielle Leclerc.

Ammachi   Present incarnation of Divine Mother in India and the United
States.
P.O.Box 613, San Ramon, CA 94583.
Phone: (510) 537-9417.
http://www.amilight.com/masters/masters.html

Anand, Margot   Sacred Sexuality teacher. Putnam, NY.

André   Channel from Portugal.
Channel to the Council of Nine.

Angel, Karen   Channel to the Time Lords.
http://www.midcan.co.nz/newage.htm

Anka, Darryl

Contactee. Channel to Bashar.
Bashar Communications, Inc., 1920 North Lake Avenue, Suite 108 (PMB-178), Altadena, CA 91001.
1-8776-BASHAR   (Toll Free),
1-877-622-7427 (Toll Free),
1-888-590-2649 (Toll Free).
1-888-590-2650.
info@Bashar.org
http://www.Bashar.org/

Armitage, John

Channel to Merlin, Vywamus.
Flat 1, Ash Lodge, Patier Road, St. Saviour,
Jersey, Channel Islands JE2 7LN
0044 (0) 1534 67655, mobile: 0044 (0) 468 132977.
drdas@globalnet.co.uk
shamball@itl.net

Asari A

Light worker, channel to Ashtar, channel to the Council on Universal Understanding & other ascended masters.
P.O.Box 621, Westcliffe CO, 81252.
719-783-2504.

Azizova, Lenura

Russian psychic.

Babarazakov, Ungar Turmatovich

Uzbekian healer.

Bailey, Alice

Channel to Djwhal Khul.

Bainbridge, John

Incarnation of Edgar Cayce.

Baker, Robert

Trance channel to Archangel Gabriel.

Baker Eddy, Mary

Is Ascended Lady Master Theosophia.
http://www.ascension-research.org/messenger.html

Balducci, Corrado

Catholic theologian, leading exorcist.
Member of the Curia of the Roman Catholic Church.

Balhesteros, Carmen

Psychic, healer, head of Pax Universal, Sao Paulo, Brazil.

Ballard, Edna

Is Ascended Lady Master Lotus.
http://www.ascension-research.org/messenger.html
→ Lotus.

Ballard, Guy W.   Founder of the I AM Activity.
Is Ascended Master Godfre.
Claimed to have had an encounter with St. Germain on the
slopes of Mt. Shasta in 1930.
http://www.ascension-research.org/messenger.html
→ Godfre.

Ballas-Beeson, Joy Rev.
Channel to Bartholomew.
Wirral Light Circle, Wirral England.
davidp@globalnet.co.uk
http://www.users.globalnet.co.uk/~davidp/wlcinfo.htm

Banks, Mary-Jane   Channel.
MaryJaneBanks@netscape.net.

Barnard, George   Channel to Machiventa, Moronson.
Urantia Book.
http://www.1111publishers.com

Bartholic, Barbara   Hypnotherapist & abductions researcher for 25 years.

Beaconsfield, Hannah
Channel to the Pleiadians.

Bearse, Christine   Channel to Metatron, the Brotherhood of Light.
cbearse@ct1.nai.net
cbearse@mail1.nai.net
http://w3.nai.net/~Ibearse/Rainbow.htm

Belsey, Ashian   Channel to El Morya.
ashian@lightkeys.com
www.lightkeys.com/ashian/

Bender, Hans Prof.   German parapsychologist.

Bennet, Ingrid   Channel.
P.O.Box 101-566, North Shore Mail Centre,
Auckland, New Zealand.
http://www.newage.com.au
ingrid@ihug.co.nz

Berg, Charlene   She's specialist in herbs & their uses.
Liberty KY.

Billings, Helen   ACCET therapist.
Helenb415@aol.com

Birnes, William J.   Writer, book publisher.

Blackburn, Meg

Reverend Dr.
Internationally recognized Master Healer, channeler, speaker, writer, and graphic artist.
She is an Ordained Minister in both Spiritual Science and Metaphysics.
http://spiritlite.com
spiritlite1@aol.com
inquiries@spiritlite.com
Mail: Rev. Dr. Meg Blackburn, P.O. Box 331, Richland, WA 99352.

Blavatski, Helena Petrovna, Madame

Channel to the Ascended Masters.
The woman behind the Myth.
Was born of Russian nobility in 1831 and died on May 8, 1891.
In July 1878, became the first Russian woman to acquire the U.S. citizenship.
→ Mahatmas.

Boltwood, Geoffrey

Healer from England.

Boros, Attila

Hungarian UFO Artist.

Brother Philip

Channel to Sanat Kumara.
He is of the Abbey of the Brotherhood of the Seven Rays in the Peruvian Andes, near Lake Titicaca.

Brown, David

Channel to Kryon of the Magnetic Service.
http://kryon.org.za/

Brownell, Winfried

Channel to Kadar-Monka.

Browning, Leslie Dru

Astral Traveler.
http://www.onelight.com/les/zyne/zyne.htm

Bryce, Sheradon

Channeler.

Buergin, Luc

Swiss PSI expert, journalist.

Burns, Barbara

Channel to Vywamus.

Cali, John

Channel to Chief Joseph.

Cannon, Dolores

Past Life Regressionist, psychic researcher.
Channel to Nostradamus.
P.O.Box 754, Huntsville, AR 72740-0754.

Carey, Ken

Channel.

Carrasco, Mercedes

Ummo messenger.
→ Ummo.

Carroll, Lee   Channel to Kryon.

Cartwright, Dawn   Licensed Sky Dancing Tantra instructor.
                                    Dakini Moon Tantra Studio, P.O.Box 14758,
                                    Long Beach, CA 90803.
                                    (562) 495-0127.

Cayce, Edgar   Late American mystic (1877 – 1945).
                                    Gave between 1901 and 1945 thousands of trance readings.
                                    Channel to the Arcturians.
                                    Trance reader of the Akashic Records.
                                    Was incarnated as John Bainbridge.
                                    Is now incarnated as David Wilcox.

Centara, Channie Cha
                                    Incarnated extraterrestrial.

Chapman, Kari Rev.   Astara Mystery School, 792 W. Arrow Hwy,
                                    P.O.Box 5003, Upland, CA 91785-5003.
                                    Phone: 909-981-4941.
                                    Channel to Archangel Michael, Mother Teresa, Zoser.
                                    http://www.namaste-wi.com/
                                    http://www.astara.org
                                    mail@astara.org

Chora, Larissa V.   Russian clairvoyant, psychic.

Christianne, Maia   Wings of Light, Church of the Holy Flame.
                                    krystos@Spiritheart.org
                                    Maia@spiritheart.org

Christina   Walk-in from Venus. She came in a 25-hour trip in a mothership.
                                    Then she was brought by a scout ship to Tibetan monks. She
                                    was brought up in the body of an adapted child. She has healing
                                    powers.
                    http://world-famous.com/Alternate-Venus/Alien-Life -On-Venus-2.html

Clark, Libby   Spiritualistic medium from Gt. Britain.

Cleeland, June   Clairvoyant, medium from Sidney, Australia.

Clemente, Kasandra   Channel.
                                    → Forenna.

Coffey, Chip   Channeler, psychic, medium, tarot reader.
                                    Atlanta, Georgia.
                                    Phone: 770-806-0369.
                                    Chipcoffey@aol.com
                                    http://www.chipcoffey.com

Cole, Yvonne
Channel to the Ashtar Command.
P.O.Box 218, Scaly Mountain, NC 28775.

Collingwood, Anne
Channels portraits.
The Sanctuary of Enlightenment,
6, Hunters Way, Croydon, Surrey, CR0 5JJ, UK.
Anne@angelic.com

Colson, Lucy
Channel to Andromeda Rex, Joshua, Kadar-Monka.

Cook, Maurice B.
Channel to Master Hilarion of Earth's Spiritual Hierarchy.

Cooper, Diana
Ascension Teacher, channel for angels.

Cori, Patricia
Channel to the Sirian High Council.
http://www.sirianrevelations.net/messenger.shtml
http://www.iuniverse.com

Cota-Robles, Patricia Dianne
Is a counselor at the Swan Clinic of Natural Healing in Tucson, AZ.
http://1spirit.com/eraofpeace/
eraofpeace@aol.com
The New Age Study of Humanity's Purpose Inc.,
P.O.Box 41883, Tucson AZ 85717.

Courtenay, Edwyn
Channel to Djwal Khul.

Craig, Ruth A.
Channel to Kuthumi.
twchurch@kuthumi.com
ruthacraig@kuthumi.com

Creme, Benjamin
Channel to Maitreya.

Cristina
→ Christina.

D'Montford, Dr. S.
Shambhallah Awareness Centre, P.O.Box 537,
Burleigh Heads, Gold Coast Qld.4220,
Phone/fax: 61+ 7 55 338 448.
she@shambhallah.com.au
http://www.shambhallah.com.au

Dames, Ed
Remote Viewer.

Danrich, Karen
Channel to Lady Athena.
http://www.calltoascend.org/ALCryform.html

Davidson, Christine
Channel to El Morya.
Phone: (540) 988-4042.
114 Watts Street, No Tazewell, VA 24630-9406.

De Paoli, Ornesha
Channel.

Diandra   Channel to Archangels, Ascended Masters, Jesus,
                               Salem, Space Command.
                               inwardinc@aol.com
                               http://www.inwardjourney.com
                               Phone: 1-888-980-5780, 1-630-527-0123 outside USA, Canada.

Dombrowski, Bev(Dranda)
                               Dranda is her spiritual name.
                               The Light Messenger, c/o Bev Dombrowski,
                               218 E. Hinckley St., Mt. Shasta, CA 96067.
                               Phone/fax: 530-926-1411.
                               http://www.lightmessenger.com
                               pegasusiam@snowcrest.net
                               Channel to Gabriel, Janus, Kuthumi, Great White Brotherhood.

Donahue, Aaron C.   Remote Viewer.
                               http://perdurabo10.tripod.com/themind ofjamesdonahue/id218.html

Donnelly, Sheilagh   info@bzzzz.co.uk

Donner, Valerie   Spiritual Counselor, intuitive healer, writer, poet. Founder of the
                               Ground Crew website.
                               Channel to Djwhal Khul, Kuthumi, Mira, Mother Mary, St.
                               Germain, the Intergalactic Council, the Pleiadian High Council.
                               P-O.Box 5705, Walnut Creek, CA 94596-5705.
                               Phone: 925-287-8976.
                               Phone: toll free 866-281-2402.
                               valeriedonner@sbcglobal.net
                               http://www.thegroundcrew.com
                               valeriedonner@earthlink.net

Dor Dempriey, Louis

                               Trance channel.
                               http://www.newage.com

Duby, Ralph   Channel.

Dudde, Bertha   (1891-1965). Jesus medium, prophet.

Duval, Maria   Clairvoyant.

Dux, Sharula   Channel.
                               Also called: Bonnie Condey, Bonnie Godoyo.
                               Was born in 1725 in Telos, currently living in Santa Fe, New
                               Mexico with her husband Shield. She has falsely used a social
                               security number which was assigned to a man called Craig W.
                               Ball who lives in Willard, UT.
                               World Ascension Network, 369 Montezuma St,
                               Suite 221, Santa Fe, NM 87501-2626.
                               Phone: 505-438-8679.
                               → Sharula.

Dvir, Adrian

Israeli medium, psychic and healer.

Eaton, Jan

Channel to Isis, Sananda.
→ Lilian Whalley.

Ederveen, Helena

Healer, helps people to empower themselves.
c/o Spiritual Science Institute, P.O.Box 22714, Santa Barbara CA, 93105.
Phone: 805-564-1956.
Contact: Susan Swern, 1410 Big Valley Dr.,
Colorado Springs CO, 80919.
Phone: 719-539-7393, 800-775-0712 ext. 778.

ElectRa Ahn

Light worker, she offers the Ahn Wand with the TACHION Energy.
Channel to Saint Germain, Sananda-Jesus.
P.O.Box 927, Westcliffe CO, 81252.
Phone: 719-783-2504.

Eppich, Ron

Channel to Ash-Kar.
http://www.uforia-research.com

Essene, Virginia

Fanning, Arthur

Fickes, Bob

Channel to the Ascended Masters.

Fisher, Lexi

He is a Sky Dancing Tantra teacher.
→ Kip Moore.

Fitzgerald, Caroline

Also known as Radha.
Channel to El Morya, Elohim, Mother Mary, Quan Yin, Sananda, Archangel Sandalphon, Vywamus.
Wirral Light Centre, Flat 1, Ash Lodge,
Patier Road, St Saviour, Jersey, JE2 7LN Channel Islands, UK.
Phone: +44 (0) 1534 67655,
Mobile: +44 (0) 979 711089.
shamball@itl.net
http://www.users.globalnet.co.uk/~davidp
http://www.spiritweb.org/Spirit/caroline-fitzgerald.html
http://www.greatdreams.com/walkin.htm

Forenna

Her real name is Kasandra Clemente.
Channel/Messenger of Lord Saint Germain.
Circle One Center for Healing Light, Media & Communications.
Phone: (505) 982-8001.
vision@newmexico.com

Forster, Gery   gforster@tlccomputers.com.au
                             http://www.onelight.com/forster/

Francis, Liz   Channel.
                             lizart@southcom.com.au
                             http://www.newage.com.au

Freder, Sara   Clairvoyant.

Furphy, Phyllis   Artist and starseed.
                             She draws the most exquisite realistic portraits of Guides, Angels,
                             Starseed Fathers and beings on other dimensions.
                             2811 F Street #18, Sacramento CA, 95816.
                             Phone: (916) 441-4412.
                             phyllisfurphy@hotmail.com

Gabbitas, Alec Christos
                             Channel to Sananda.

Galante, Josi   Artist, experiencer.

George, Isaac   Channel to Archangel Ariel, Archangel Michael, Jesus, St.
                             Germain, Ascended Masters.
                             Spirit life, 360 West 27th Place, Eugene, OR 97405.
                             Phone: (541) 683-3692, 1-800-891-8044 (Toll Free).
                             spiritlife@444.hotmail.com
                             isaac@archangelariel.com
                             archariel@hotmail.com
                             angels_lynn@yahoo.co.uk
                             http://www.newage.com.au
                             http://www.archangelariel.com

Gibson, Sheila   Earth name of Omnec Onec from Venus.
                             http://www.almaranea.net/stars/venus.html

Gilmore, Laurie   Channel to Metatron.
                             http://www.worldlightcenter.com/

Green, Santari   Channel to Metatron.
                             2 Durston Close, STREET, Somerset BA16 OJU UK.
                             Phone: 01458 448567.

Green, Soleira   Channel to Metatron.
                             → Santari Green.

Griffin, Allan

Gudnason, Lauri   Full trance channel.
                             Phone: (435) 723 0605.
                             Channel to Metatron.
                             http://www.newage.com.au

Hale-Watson, Beverly, Rev.
Affiliated with the ministry of the Seven Fold Peace Foundation.
4704 Quail Ridge Drive, Charlotte, NC 28227.
Phone: 704-545-8042.

Haley, Leah A.   Alien experiencer, abductee, abduction researcher.

Hall, Sue   Channel to Kuthumi, Mother Mary, Lord Sananda, Saint Germain, Tara.

Hammons, Mark   m-hamm@vm1.spcs.umn.edu

Hand Clow, Barbara   Claims that the Nibiruans found a way to incarnate in human bodies and infiltrate our government directly.

Hardisheck, Lyuri   → Lyara.

Hart, Carrie   Spiritual healer. Channel to Quado.
http://www.quado.com
http://www.carriehart.com
carriehart@msn.com

Hartwick, Lois   Channel to Hilarion, Sananda, St. Germain, Thoth.
http://www.planetlightworker.com
hilo@bcn.net

Hayakawa, Norio

Haydon, Abbey Channel.
P.O.Box 1137, Sedona, AZ 86339.
Phone: (928) 204 – 5617.
http://www.spiritualguidance.com
abby@spiritualguidance.com

Hazlewood, Mark

Heartwood, Zaralya   She is a psychic reader.
Reminds people how to heal themselves.
Phone: 719-539-3700, 719-395-2088.

Herman, Ronna   Ronna is a spiritual astrologer, counselor and teacher.
Channel to Archangel Michael.
StarQuest, 6005 Clear Creek Drive, Reno,
NV 89052.
Phone/fax: 775 856-3654.
ronnastar@earthlink.net
http://ronnastar.com
http://www.spiritweb.org/Spirit/ronna-herman.html

Herzog, Roberta S. Rev. Dr.

Reader of the Akashic Records. She has more than 30 years of experience.
Roberta S. Herzog Enterprises, Inc.
P.O.Box 20188, Greenville, North Carolina 27858
Fax: 252-756-3182.
http://www.robertaherzog.com/akashic_record.htm
iamlux@aol.com

Hill, Ethel P.   Channel.

Hoagland, Richard   Ex NASA employee, scientist, space archaeologist.

Holeman, Daniel B.   Artist.
http://www.awakenvisions.com/

Holloway, Lisa   Channel to Hilarion.

Holmes, Jean Rev.   She is a medium and healer.
Phone: (970) 874-0290, fax (970) 874-1258.
http://www.higherwisdom.com
revjean@acsol.net
lbeckman@coyotenet.net

Home, Daniel Dunglas

Scottish spiritualist (1833-1886). The most celebrated physical medium of the 19th century.

Hoodwin, Shepard   Channel to Archangel Michael.

Hoppe, Geoff   Channel to Tobias.

Howard, Frank   Channel to Space Commander Alizantil.

Huayta, Willaru   Spiritual Messenger, Cuzco, Peru.

Hubbard, Ron L.   Founder of Scientology.

Huckfield, Nikki   She is an author, facilitator, healer, psychic and channel.
Her spirit name is Alloya Ye Ra Har.

Innocente, Geraldine Channel to Astrea, Archangel Chamuel, Cyclopea, Gaia,   El
Morya, Maitreya, Mother Mary, Paul the Venetian, Virgo.

Isis-Astarte (Ruth)   ruth@aloha.net

Jackman, Jan   She is from UK.
She is a natural psychic, full-body trance Contactee.
Channel to the Greys.

Jacob, Daniel   Channel.
http://www.lightworker.com

Jankananda, Swami   Founder of the Scandinavian Yoga & Meditation School. Haa Course Center, 34013 Hamneda, Sweden. Phone: +46 372 55063, fax: +46 372 55036. bindu@inet.uni-c.dk

Jarett, Kingsley   Channeler.

Jasmuheen   Australian spiritual teacher.

Jennings, Hanneke ND

Spiritual Healer, Teacher, poet, channeler. Universal Light Co., P.O.Box 374, Mt Evelyn 3796 Vic, (Melbourne), Australia. Phone (03) 9735 4662, fax (03) 9735 4656. Channel to the Cosmic & Planetary Hierarchies. http://www.newage.com.au

Jones, Aurelia Louise

She has telepathical contact to the Lemurians underneath Mt. Shasta. Channel to Adama. Mt. Shasta Light Publishing, The Lemurian Connection, P.O.Box 1509, Mt. Shasta, CA 96067-1509. Phone: 530-926-4599, fax: 530-926-4159. http://www.mslpublishing.com http://www.onelight.com/telos/wintonellis.htm aurelia@mslpublishing.com

Jordan Pena, Jose Luis

Spanish parapsychologist who supposedly invented the Ummo affair. → Ummo. http://www.strangemag.com/ummo.html

Jordan-Kauble, Debbie

http://www.debshome.com

Jung, Carl Gustav   Psychiatrist.

Kaly, Hagai   Healer and trance medium.

Karnaze, Coral   Galactic counselor.

Karta Purkh Singh Khalsa

He's herbal medicine specialist. Phone: 303-665-6170.

Kay, Wendy   Metaphysical teacher.
                         http://www.oralin.com
                         info@oralin.com

Kennedy, Suzanna   Metaphysical teacher, healer.
                         Lives in Sedona, Arizona.
                         http://www.realitycrafting.com/
                         suzanna_k@hotmail.com

Kincannon, Kara   Channel to Mother Sekhmet.
                         kara-kincannon@iwon.com

King, George Sir   Channel to Aetherius, Jesus, Cosmic Masters.
                         Founder of the Aetherius Society in 1954/1955.

King, Jani   Channel to P'taah, St. Germain.
                         Raised in Putararu, New Zealand.
                         At present resides in Queensland, Australia.
                         First contact with P'taah in 1947, second in 1961.
                         Light Source P'taah, P.O.Box 1251,
                         Joshua Tree, CA 92251.
                         Phone: 888-803-1777 (toll free).
                         Phone: 760-366-0375, fax: 760-366-0385.
                         ptaah@earthlink.net

Kinniburgh, Donna   Deep Trance Medium.
                         Channel to a large group of spiritual entities who call themselves
                         "Reflection".
                         www.rainbow-lady.com
                         source@rainbow-lady.com
                         donna@rainbow-lady.com
                         http://www.newage.com.au

Kirkwood, Annie   Channel to Mother Mary.

Kirkwood, Guy

Klein, Birgit   Channel to Archos.

Klein, Eric   Channel to Saint Germain, Sananda.
                         Phone/fax: 408-459-7791.
                         P.O.Box 498, Santa Cruz CA 95061-0498.

Kore, Rebecca   Galactic Counselor.

Korsholm, Celeste   P.O.Box 4044, Sedona AZ 86340-4044.
                         Phone: (602) 282-1294.
                         jananda@sedona.net

Kramer, Bettina   Channel.

Kristina   → Christina.

Kumar, Vijay — http://www.godrealized.com

Lady Cassandra — Channel to Lady Gaia.

Lady Isis — Walk-in, came in June 14, 1971.
ladyisis@gte.net

Lailel — Is Dianne Robbins.

Lamb, Barbara — Psychotherapist, Crop Circle investigator.
Star Seed therapist.
Claremont.

Langman, Jim — Channel to the Emissaries of the Light.

Larkins, Lisette — Contactee, experiencer, born in Southern
California, first contact in 1987.
c/o Hampton Roads Publishing Company,
1125 Stoney Ridge Road,
Charlottesville, Virginia 22902
http://www.talkingtoets.com
lisette@talkingtoets.com

Lavar — Channel to Capt. Helena of the starship Capricorn of the
Galactic Federation.
wizzard9@earthlink.net

Lazar, Robert — Quantum physicist-engineer in Los Alamos.

LeBreton, Robert Paul —
Cmdr.
Ashtar Space Command Communications,
2901 State Hwy 6, HC 77 Box 42,
Laguna, New Mexico 87026.
Phone: (505)-836-7534.
http://www.topica.com/lists/Wizzard9
wizzard9@earthlink.net

LeClerc, Danielle — Is Amassia.

Lee, Gloria — Channel.

Leigh, Amber — Trance channel to the OHERA Group of Guardian Beings.
Phone: 303-414-2727, 303-4-5-2727.

Leir, Roger Dr.M.D. — Alien Implant Removal Surgeon.

Leland, Susan — Channel to Lord Ashtar and Mother Sekhmet.

Leopold, P. — Channel to Homogenius, Ro.
Vienna, Austria.

Lewis, Pepper   Channel to Lady Gaia.
                                    The Peaceful Planet, P.O.Box 4135,
                                    West Hills, CA 91308.
                                    Phone: (818) 713-1966.
                                    http://www.ThePeacefulPlanet.com
                                    http://home1.gte.net/ladyisis/MotherEarth.htm
                                    PepLewis@aol.com

Lieder, Nancy   Channel to Zeta Reticuli.

Liljenquist, Victoria   UFO contactee, visionary, angel contactee.
                                    Contacted at age 5.
                                    Clinical Certified Hypnotherapist, Healer, Lecturer.
                                    Phone: (602) 955-7222.
                                    victoria@victoriaslight.com
                                    http://www.victoriaslight.com

Lindsey, Barbara   Psychic.

Long, Kathleen

Lorgen, Eve Frances   Abductee, abductions researcher of 15 years, counselor.
                                    Spiritual warrior that rose in the San Francisco Bay.
                                    http://alienlovebite.com/main.htm
                                    eve@alienlovebite.com
                                    eve@nightsearch.net
                                    Bookings@alienlovebite.com

Loucadou, Walter von Dr. Dr.
                                    Leading German parapsychologist and ghost researcher.

Luppi, Diana   Channel.

Lyara   Estes, Sara   Other name of Lyuri Hardisheck.
                                    Spiritual messenger.
                                    Of the Golden Ray Center, Phoenix.
                                    Channel to Alphon, Cassion, Cetti, Hilarion, Jycondria, Lytton,
                                    St. Germain.
                                    Lyara c/o Celestial Cooperative, P.O.Box 2231,
                                    Oroville, WA 98844.
                                    http://www.operation-terra.com
                                    http://www.operationterra.com
                                    lyara@operationterra.com

MA'al   She is a Reiki Master, Spiritual Teacher.
                                    Channel to Saint Germain, Sanat Kumara, Vywamus.

MacBeth-Louton, Gillian

Channel to Mary Magdalene, Sophia, the Council of Sol, the Pleiadian Council of Light.
http://www.star-knowledge.com/
http://www.thequantumawakening.com/

MacNeil, Marian

Channel to star visitor Neuman.

Mack, John

Harvard psychiatrist.

Maharshi, Ramana

Hindu sage.

Maia

Channel to Tahuti.

Malone, Sue Ellen

Channel.

Marciniak, Barbara J.

Internationally acknowledged trance channel to the Pleiadians. The Pleiadians have been speaking through Barbara Marciniak since May 18, 1988.
Bold Connections Unlimited,
P.O.Box 782, Apex, NC 27502

Marie, Nancy

Author, gifted psychic.
c/o Mt Shasta Magazine, P.O.Box 1289,
Mt Shasta, CA 96067.
msmag@bestweb.net
http://www.innereyepublishing.com
http://mountshastamagazine.com

Marss, Jim

Free-lance writer.

Matthews, Anne

Channel to Djwhal Khul.
deeana@javanet.com

Matthews, Arthur

Scientist, contactee to Venusians.

Matthews, Maureen

Channel.

Mayi Ma, Ananda

Incarnation of Divine Mother (1896-1982), born in Bangladesh.
http://amilight.com(masters/masters.html

Mc Cannon, Tricia

American clairvoyant.

McMoneagle, Joseph

Remote Viewer for more than 25 years.

Meier, Billy   Semjase-Silver-Star-Center, Schmidrüti, Switzerland.
                           Contactee.
                           Was contacted over 130 times between 1976 and 1986 by
                           Pleiadians.
                           On January 28, 1986, the planned 11-year period for the official
                           contacts had ended.
                           Billy has contact to Asket, Florena, Menara, Nera, Pleja, P'taah,
                           Quetzal, Semjase, Taljda, etc.

Meyer, Kay Eileen   Is actively involved in the transformation of human will into
                           Divine Will.
                           The New Age Study of Humanity's Purpose, Inc.,
                           P.O.Box 41883 Tucson, AZ 85717.
                           Phone: 520-885-7909 (Margy Vaughan),
                           Fax: 520-749-6643.
                           eraofpeace@aol.com

Michel, Jean   Cmdr. Lyur,
                           P.O.Box 3106, Marion, NC 28752, USA.
                           wolfheart8@hotmail.com
                           cptnlyur@hotmail.com
                           http://www.starshiplight.com/

Milanovich, Norma Dr.
                           Channel to Athena, El Morya, Kuthumi, Sananda and the
                           Arcturians.

Miller, David K.   Channel to Archangels, Arcturians, Helio-ah,
                           Juliano, Sananda, Tomar, Vywamus.
                           Arcturian Groups of Forty,
                           P.O.Box 4074, Prescott, AZ 86302.
                           http://cybertrails.com/index.html
                           http://cybertrails.com/groupofforty/
                           zoloft@cybertrails.com

Miller, Florence Jeannette
                           Is now Ascended Master Kristine.
                           (Feb. 27, 1936 – Sept. 19, 1979).

Miller, Richard   Contactee. First contact in 1954 at Ann Arbor in Michigan where
                           he met Soltec.
                           Founder of the organization "Star Cross" in San Jose, California.
                           → Soltec.

MirRa   Channel to Morvica of the Galactic Confederation.

Moen, Bruce   Afterlife explorer, book author.
                           Resides in Denver, Colorado.
                           http://www.nexusmagazine.com/bmoen.html
                           http://www.afterlife-knowledge.com

Montgomery, Ruth | Died in June 2001.
Pam Lawniczak, 215 Parkview Street,
Walbridge, OH 43465.
http://www.greatdreams.com/walkin.htm
http://www.junecleeland.com

Moody, Raymond | NDE researcher.

Mooney, Tom | Channel.

Moore, Chester | Bigfoot researcher.

Moore, Judith K. | Channel to Laiolin, the Arcturian Council and the Council of Aboraha.
Santa Fe, New Mexico.
Phone: (505) 351-4730.
redclay@newmecico.com

Moore, Kip | She is a Sky Dancing Tantra teacher.

Moore, Mary Margaret

Channel to Bartholomew.

Morehouse, David A., PhD.

Former CIA psycho spy (remote viewer).

Mt Shasta, Peter | Health consultant.
Began working with the Ascended Masters in 1972 when St. Germain materialized before him.
http://www.mountshastamagazine.com/ms_mystique/

Moulton Howe, Linda

Investigative reporter, author and TV producer.
P.O.Box 21483, Albuquerque, NM 87154.
Fax   505-797-7908.
http://www.earthfiles.com
earthfile@earthfiles.com

Müller, Andreas | Crop Circle researcher from Saarbrücken, Germany.

Muth, Saemmi | Channel to Lenduce, Vywamus.

NADA-Yolanda | Channel to Sananda.

Nartoomid, Christianne & Simeon

Spirit Heart Sanctuary, P.O.Box 1357,
Kapa'a, Kaua'I, HI 96746
Phone: 808-822-7176
http://www.spirtheart.org
http://www.spiritmythos.org
krystos@spiritheart.org
→ Shamayyim.

Neill, Steve

Neruda, Jamisson

Alias Dr. Anderson.
Son of an electrical engineer from Sorota, Bolivia.
In 1956 Neruda's father discovered a crashed UFO.

Nesbitt, Kathryn L.

Channel to Mikiah.
Yellow.rose@gte.net

Newlon, Terri

Channel to Djwhal Khul.
Holistic Consulting,
110E. Cortez Dr # 203, Sedona, AZ 86351.
Phone (home/office): 928-284-5505,
Phone mobile: 602-391-6239.
terri@onepost.net
www.DjwhalKhul.com

Newton, Isaac Sir

Was one of the most influential scientists who ever lived (1642-1727). Predicted the end of the world for 2060.

Nidle, Sheldan

Channel to the Galactic Federation of Light.
Changed his name from Sheldon to Sheldan.
Planetary Activation Organization
P.O.Box 880151,
Pukalani, Maui, HI 96788-0151, U.S.A.
Voice mail (808)243-0728, fax (808)572-4751.
paorg@hawaii.rr.com
http://www.paoweb.com

O Riley, Carolyn Ann

Channel to Archangel Michael, writer, drawer.
4316 Sarasota Lane, Mckinney, Texas 75070-4450.
Phone: 972-540-1557, fax 972-540-1612.
caoriley@carolynannoriley.com
http://www.carolynannoriley.com/

Oberth, Herman Prof.

German rocket expert, considered the father of the space age.

Oliver, John J.

Channel to Jerhoam.

Orsitsch, Maria

Medium.

Osborn, Maurice
Crop Circle researcher.
http://www.uforia-research.com

Pastrana, Trinidad
Ummo messenger.
Occultist from Madrid, Spain.
→ Ummo.

Pati, Carlo
Tantra instructor.
Kreative World,
732 Montecillo Rd., San Rafael, CA 94903,
Phone: (415) 507-0752.
info@kreativeworld.com

Payne, John
Channel to Spirit Guide Ommi.

Pecci, Ernie
Psychiatrist in California,
Founder of the Association for Past Live and Therapies (APRT).

Percival, John
Channel to Excalibur, Vartar.
http://www.newage.com.au

Pereira, Patricia L.
Medical transcriptionist, multidimensional telepath from Boise, Idaho.
Founder of the Wolf Foundation in 1984.
Channel to the Arcturians.

Plato
Told the original story of Atlantis (335 B.C.E.)

Presson, Julie
Channel.
http://www.newage.com.au
earthlink@cyberport.com

Prochaska, Johnnie
Reader of the Akashic Records.

Prophet, Elizabeth Clare
Channel to Babaji, Gaia, Hilarion, Kali, Lady Venus, Maitreya, Mother Mary, Omri-Tas, Paul the Venetian, Raphael, Sanat Kumara, Shiva, Uriel, Virgo.

Prophet, Marc
Ascended Master Lanello.
Channel to Chamuel, Djwhal Khul, El Morya, Jophiel, Maitreya.
http://www.ascension-research.org/messenger.html
→ Lanello.

Prout, Susan
Angel drawing artist, angelic portraits.
http://www.angelicreflections.com/susan/void/morninglight.gif
Phone: (816) 220-7761.

Pullen, Walter D.
Channel to Bashar.
Astara@msn.com

Pulos, Lee Dr.   Paranormal researcher.
                              http://www.manari.com/experts.htm

Quinsey, Mike   Channel to Atmos, Diane, Ela, Sa Lu Sa.
                              michael@quinsey.wanadoo.co.uk
                              → Galactic Federation.

Radha   Is Caroline Fitzgerald.
                              → Caroline Fitzgerald.

Ramtha   Ramtha's School of Enlightenment,
                              P.O.Box 1210, Yelm, Wa 98597.
                              Phone 800-347-0439, 360-458-5201.

Regehr, Ron

Robbins, Dianne   Also known as Lailel.
                              Channel to Adama of Telos.
                              P.O.Box 10945, Rochester, NY 14610.
                              Phone 585-442-4437, fax 585-244-9060.
                              HollowEarth@photon.net
                              TELOS11@msn.com
                              http://www.onelight.com
                              http://www.DianneRobbins.com

Roberts, Jane   Seth.

Robinson, David   Channel.
                              10 Mount Edge, Hopton, Stafford, ST1B OTG UK.
                              Phone: (01785) 212293.

Rodehaver, Gladys   Channel to Ashtar.

Rodgers, Robin   Healer from Invercargill, New Zealand.

Rodwell, Mary   Australian counselor, hypnotherapist.

Roeder, Dorothy   Channel to Ranoash.

Rolfe, Brian   Channel to Vajrapani.
                              → Lilian Whalley.

Rother, Steve   Channel to The Group.
                              http://www.lightworker.com/beacons/

Royal Holt, Lyssa   American psychologist who travels worldwide.
                              Contactee.
                              Royal Priest Research, P.O.Box 12626,
                              Scottsdale, Arizona 85267.
                              Channel to Akbar, Bashar, Germane, Saint Germain.
                              http://www.worldtrans.org/lyssa/tape104.html

Rundell, Fernella   Channel to the Brotherhood of Light.

Ruppelt, Edward J.   Former director of project "Blue Book", 1951.

Ruppert, Michael C.   http://www.copvcia.com

Salazar, Christine   Galactic Counselor.

Sanders, Alexander   Was born in Manchester in 1929 and died in 1988.
Proclaimed himself as King of Witches. At age of 9 he copied his
grandmother's Book of Shadows.
http://www.themystica.com/mystica/articles/s/sanders_alexander.html

Saunders, Jessica   Tarot Reader & Reiki Master.
Channel to Raphael, Teseshuan & other Ascended Masters for
more than 30 years.
P.O.Box 34, Ordway CO, 81063.

Scallion, Gordon Michael
      Prophet.

Serenia, Qala   Channel from Phoenix.

Shaffer, George   Prophet.
http://www.bright.net/~gshaffer/earthchange.htm
gshaffer@bright.net

Shaari   Female Walk-In of a female Pleiadian/Arcturian hybrid in 1989.
Is about 750 years old.
Commander in the Star Command who works as a holographic
healer and a interdimensional teacher.
Channel to Abraham, Malaya and the Intergalactic Council of
Twelve.
Shaari & Trilite Seminars, P.O.Box 22040,
Brentwood Bay B.C., Canada, V0S IR0.
Phone: 604-360-8708.
→ Veyares.

Shalie   Channel to Commander Aleva of the Ashtar Space Command.

Shamayyim, Maya   Holistic healer & channel.
P.O.Box 235, Crestone CO, 81131,
Phone: 719-256-4057, 719-256-4499.

Shandera, Jaime   Agent of the Secret Government.

Shapiro, Lia   Channel to the Pleiadians.

Shearer, Carolyn   Channel to El Morya, Lady Venus, Maitreya, Mother Mary.

Shepherd, Jennifer   Channel to the Council of Light.
P.O.Box 1433, Princeton, NJ 08542.

Sheppard, Sandi   Channel to Ashtar, Sananda.

Sheran, Ariana   Channel to Ashtar, Portia.
                             Cloverleaf Connection, 138 Sturgeon Drive,
                             Saskatoon, SK S7K 4B3.
                             http://cloverleafconnection.ca
                             info@cloverleafconnection.ca

Sherwood, Jilaen   Artworker.
                             http://www.alienalley.com/jilaen.html
                             http://www.jilaensherwood.com
                             jilaen@jilaensherwood.com

Simelunas, Donna   Channel to Saint Germain.
                             hialchemy@hotmail.com

Simmons, Kay   Channel to Lady Kadjina.

Sims, Darrel   UFO investigator & researcher, certified Hypnotherapist,
                             abductee, former CIA operative.
                             Houston UFO Network (HUFON).
                             http://chelsea.ios.com/~dalemv19/hufon/

Siragusa, Eugenio   Contactee.

Sister Thedra   Channel to Efi, Sananda.

Sitchin, Zacharia   Archaeologist and historian in the Middle East.
                             Researcher of ancient (Sumerian) civilizations.
                             → Nibiru.

Smith, Gary   Founder of the Sacred Merkaba Techniques.

Smith, Helene   Pseudonym of Catherine Elise Müller, a late 19th century medium
                             from Geneva, Switzerland. Born about 1863.

Smith, Lisa J.   Warriors of Peace Incorporated.
                             Channel to: Elijah, Michael, Sananda, Sanat Kumara.
                             Lisajsmith@juno.com
                             warriorsofpeace@aol.com
                             http://members.aol.com/warriorsofpeace/index.html
                             http://www.warriorsofpeace.com/sanandachannels.html

Smith, Tom H.   Channel to Ashtar. Louisville, Ky.

Sohini, Genevieve   Sky Dancing Tantra instructor.
                             → Carlo Pati.

Solomon, Paul   Trance reader of the Akashic Records.

Spivey, Dan   Channel.

Sprinkle, R. Leo, Prof. Dr.Ph.D.
Psychologist, hypnotherapist, abduction & UFO researcher. University of Wyoming.

Squin de Flexian Templar.

Starcrystal Channel to Benoch.
http://msn.communities.com/InTouchGalacticFederation

Starr, Jelaila Walked-in June 23, 1992, in January 1997 Jelaila completed her initial training as a Galactic Messenger and founded the Nibiruan Council.
5987 Peacock Ridge Road, Ste. 105,
Rancho Palos Verdes, CA 90275.
Phone: 310-541-7179,
Fax: 310-541-0379.
432 E.Gregory Bld., Kansas City, MO 64131.
Phone: 816 – 444 4364, fax 816 – 444 4365.
http://www.NibiruanCouncil.com/html/body_contactus.html
jelaila@nibiruancouncil.com
info@NibiruanCouncil.com
jelaila@gte.net

Sterling, Fred Rev. Channel to Kirael.

Stevenson, Sandy Channel to Kuthumi.

Stites, David Channel to Korton Toltec.
http://free.prohosting.com/11star11

Stocks, Glenda Channel to Yeorgos.

Stone, Dr.Joshua David
Channel to Djwhal Khul.
Dr. Joshua David & Wistancia Stone,
28951 Malibu Rancho Rd., Agoura Hills, CA 91301.
Phone: 818 706-8458, 818 769-1181,
Fax: 818 706-8540.
drstone@best.com
http://www.drjoshuadavidstone.com

Stone, Wistancia Telepathic voice channel, spiritual teacher.
Channel to angels, archangels, masters.
28951 Malibu Rancho Road,
Agoura Hills, CA 91301.
Phone: 818-706-8533.
wistancia@charter.net
wistancia@drjoshuadavidstone.com
http://www.wistancia.com
http://www.drjoshuadavidstone.com/wistmain.htm
→ Dr. Joshua David Stone.

Stranges, Frank, Ph.D.

Contactee to the Venusians.
Interspace Link, P.O.Box 73,
Van Nuys, CA 91408-0073.
Phone/fax: (818) 989-5954.
http://www.nicufo.com
→ Valiant Thor.

Surmely, Jean Michel

P.O.Box 71, Mt Ida, AR 71957.
cptlyur@earthlink.net

Swann, Ingo

Gifted natural psychic.
Parapsychology researcher.
He worked at the United Nations for 12 years.

Sweet, Juliette

Personal friend of Sharula Dux.

Takes, Steve

Artist.

Talbot, Nancy

American Crop Circle researcher.

Tate, Nancy

Channel to Lord Adolphius, Avenda, Bachari, Baldor,Lord Enki,
Lotar.
http://www.treeofthegoldenlight.com

Teller, Edward

Weapons Scientist, "Father" of the Star Wars Program, warned
President Reagan about possible alien invasion.

Tessman, Diana

Channel to Tibus, Space Brotherhood.

Thyme, Lauren O.

She is a psychic & spiritual counselor, healer, channeler, book
author.
http://www.SacredTravel.com

Toye, Lori Adaile

Channel to El Morya, Kuthumi, Mother Mary, Saint Germain,
Sananda, Sanat Kumara.

Tuella

Channel to Andromeda Rex, Hatonn, Korton.
Medium for Ashtar, channel since the early 70's.
She lives now on the mothership of Ashtar.

Van Valer, Nola

Has seen St. Germain.
She visited a temple inside a cavern beneath Mt. Shasta. Inside
she met Phylos, a Tibetan Ascended Master and many other
Ascended Masters like Jesus.
The Radiant School of Seekers and Servers,
P.O.Box 378, Mount Shasta, CA 96067.
Phone: 530-926-5373.
http://www.mountshastamagazine.com/ms_mystique/

Villas Boas, Antonio First known UFO abductee from Brazil, had a sexual relationship with an extraterrestrial female in Oct. 1957.

Vintner, Anne → Anne Collingwood.

Ward, Suzy Channel to Matthew.

Weber, Connie Other name of Marla.
→ Marla.

Westover, Jeff Artist.
http://www.alienalley.com
frequentflyer66@yahoo.com

Weyrick, Jeannie Channel to Raphael.

Whalley, Andrew Channel to Ascended Masters, Ashtar, Kuthumi, Mother Mary, Sananda.
Son of Lilian Whalley.
Knutsford Ascension Group,
6 Sharston Crescent, Knutsford, Cheshire, WA16 8AF, UK.
Phone: ++44 (0) 1565 653644.
101456.3432@compuserve.com
→ Lilian Whalley.

Whalley, Helen Channel to Mother Mary, Lady Quan Yin, Tara.
Knutsford Ascension Group.
→ Lilian Whalley.

Whalley, Lilian Channel to Archangel Michael, Mother Mary, Lady Quan Yin, Sananda, Sanat Kumara, St. Germain.
Mother of Andrew Whalley.
Knutsford Ascension Group.
101456.3432@compuserve.com
http://www.users.globalnet.co.uk/~davidp

Wheeler-Ballard, Edna
1886-1971, messenger for Saint Germain and the Ascended Masters of the Great White Brotherhood from the late 1920's until Feb. 10, 1971.
Was the co-founder of the „I Am" Activity with her husband Guy W. Ballard.
http://ascendedmaster.ac/lotus.html
→ Lotus.

Whitaker Clifton, Maureen
Channel to Proctor 51 of the Akashic Records.
For Info about Proctor 51:
P.O.Box 756, Delta CO, 81416-0756.
Phone: 970-835-8481.

White, Marion L. Channel to Mother Kumara, Sananda.

Whitfield, Joseph   Channel to Kuthumi.

Withrow, Carol   Channel to Semjase.
http://www.JaSe1.com
carol@Jase1.com
carolwithrow@yahoo.com

Wilcox, David   His former incarnation was Edgar Cayce.

Wilkinson-Izatt, Dorothy
Contactee, psychic.
Had first contact on November 9th, 1974.
She has about 350 films about UFOs.
She lives in Canada.
http://www.manari.com/dorothy.html

Williamson, Marianne
Spiritual channelings.

Winston, John F.   johnf@mlode.com

Wiseman, Richard Dr.
British ghost researcher.

Withrow, Carol   Channel to Semjase.
The Church of JaSé Spiritual Connections, Orlando, Florida.
Phone: (407) 944-4121, (407) 944-4120.
http://www.jase1.com/
Carol@JaSe1.com

Woodard, Billie Faye
Colonel, Inner Earth experiencer.
At her age of 12 lived 6 months among the Hollow Earth
residents, she was adopted, her true parents live in the Inner
Earth. She has an unknown blood type.

Woodward, William
Colonel of the United States Air Force. He was first stationed at
Area 51, Nevada, January 28, 1971 through 1982. In that period
of service he visited the Hollow Interior of the Earth six times,
800 miles deep.

Worcester, David   Channel.

Worley, Donald   Alien Abduction researcher.
http://www.abduct.com/worley/worley17.htm

Wright, Debbie   Full Trance channel to Ashtar, Metatron, Michael, Sananda.
revdeb@wildapache.net
janisel@wildapache.net

Yandeau, Paul   Channel to St. Germain.

Yeva   Poet, artist, philosopher.
                           http://www.yevasuniverse.com
                           http://www.alienalley.com/Yeva.html
                           yevalien@charter.net

Young, Bob   Showlow, Arizona.
                           Channel to Soltec.

6.2 Contactees, Abductees and Experiencers

A better expression for abductee is experiencer or contactee. The implants normally serve to locate or protect the experiencers, not to control them.

Adamski, George   Contactee to:
>> Firkon (Martian),
>> Ilmuth (female Martian),
>> Kalna (female Venusian),
>> Orthon (Venusian),
>> Ramu (Saturnian),
>> Zuhl (Saturnian).
The man who took the first picture of a flying saucer.

Anders, Carla   Abductee.

Anderson, Simon   UFO witness on September 4, 2004 and September 5, 2003 at the UK Air Show in Goodwood, West Sussex, Great Britain.
http://www.rense.com/general57/uufo.htm

Andreasson, Betty   Abductee.

Angelucci, Orfeo   Contactee.

Anka, Darryl   Contactee.
Bashar Communications, Inc., 1920 North Lake Avenue, Suite 108 (PMB-178), Altadena, CA 91001.
1-8776-BASHAR   (Toll Free),
1-877-622-7427 (Toll Free),
1-888-590-2649 (Toll Free).
1-888-590-2650 .
info@Bashar.org
Channel to Bashar.

Archer, Barbara   Abductee.

Arnold, Kenneth   First known UFO witness.

Begay, Will   UFO witness, Nov. 2, 1967, Idaho.

Bethurum, Truman   (1898-1969). Contactee to female spaceship captain Aura Rhanes from July 27, 1952 and 1954.
He encountered 9 aliens in the Nevada desert, 8 men, one woman. Complete tripulation of the spaceship 32 men, all with obscure eyes and hair.
→ Aura Rhanes.
http://www.ufoinfo.com/roundup/v05/rnd05_45.shtml

Boirayon, Marius   UFO witness.
P.O.Box 148, Eudlo, Qld4554, Australia.
http://www.nexusmagazine.com//dragonsnake.html
solomongiants@optusnet.com.au

Boylan, Richard J. , Ph.D.,
Abductee, Director Star Kids Project.
Researcher into extraterrestrial-human encounters, Clinical hypnotherapist, scientist, university instructor.
LLC 2826 O Street, Ste. 2,
P.O.Box 22310, Sacramento, CA 95822 (95816).
Phone/fax/voice-mail: (916)422-7400, (916)422-7479.
drboylan@sbcglobal.net
drboylan@jps.net
http://www.drboylan.net
http://www.drboylan.com
http://www.jps.net/drboylan/

Brown, Charlotte   Abductee.

Bucknell, Melissa   Abductee.

Carlsberg, Kim   Abductee.
P.O.Box 8307, Calabasas CA 92302.
http://www.abduct.com/aaer/q50.htm

Carlsson, Gustav (Gösta)
He is a contactee in the year 1946 in Sweden with people from another planet (This beautiful Scandinavian looking people have a lifespan of about 1000 years).

Carter, Michael Experiencer.

Collier, Alex   Contactee.

Constable, Trevor James
Contactee from New Zealand.

Cortile, Linda   False name of Linda Napolitano.
→ Linda Napolitano.

Craspedon, Dino   Contactee.

Croonquist, Linda   Abductee.

Dagenais, Betty   Abductee.

Dixon, Phylis   Contactee, she was attacked by negative small human type aliens in 1977 and rescued by Venusians.

Doreal, Maurice   Contactee.
http://www.think-aboutit.com/aliens/cosmology_101.htm

Eberle, Wolfgang   German UFO contactee.

Enders, Carla   Abductee, abducted 1965 with 25 other children.

Forestal, James   Abductee.
                              Former Secretary of Defense.

Fry, Daniel   Contactee.

Galante, Josi   Artist, experiencer.

Garcia, Stan   Abductee.

Gilliland, James   Contactee to Blaji (Sept. 1999 at Mt. Adams), Melia.
                              Thousands of sightings are documented from there.
                              Director ECETI,
                              Trout Lake, Washington.
                              http://psi-app.com/gillrep.html
                              http://www.eceti.org/contact.htm
                              http://www.cazekiel.org
                              → Blaji, Melia.

Goldman, Lydia   Abductee.

Green, Gabriel   Contactee, died September 11, 2001 in the WTC crash. Was
                              president of AFSCA, the former largest UFO investigative
                              agency in the world.

Haley, Leah A.   Alien experiencer, abductee, abduction researcher.
                              Abducted by extraterrestrials and the U.S. military.

Hamilton, Pamela   Pamela is an abductee.

Hermann, Bill (William)
                              Abductee, abducted, March 18, 1978 in Charleston, South
                              Carolina.

Hickson, Charles   Abductee, abducted, Oct. 11, 1973 in Pascaguola, Mississippi
                              together with Calvin Parker.

Hill, Barney & Betty (Eunice)
                              Abductees (Experiencers).
                              953 State St., Portsmouth, NH 03801-4554.

Holland, Ralph   Contactee. Real name is Rolf Telano.
                              → Rolf Telano.

Howard, Dana   Contactee.

Howard, Jason   Abductee.

Hunter Gray, John   Abductee.

Ivanoff, Aino   Abductee, she was abducted Apr. 2, 1980 in Pudasjarvi, Finland.

Jackman, Jan   She is from UK.
She is a natural psychic, full-body trance Contactee.
Channel to the Greys.

Jakobsen, Edith   UFO and alien witness together with Asta Solvang on August 20, 1954 at Mosjoen, Northern Norway.

Johnston, Meisha   Contactee.

Johnstone, Colleen   Abductee.

Jones, Aurelia Louise

She has telepathical contact to the Lemurians underneath Mt. Shasta.
Channel to Adama.
Mt. Shasta Light Publishing,
The Lemurian Connection, P.O.Box 1509,
Mt. Shasta, CA 96067.
Phone: 530-926-4599, fax: 530-926-4159.
http://www.onelight.com/telos/wintonellis.htm
aurelia@mslpublishing.com

Jordan, Debbie   Abductee, sister of Kathy Mitchell.

Jordan-Kauble, Debbie

http://www.debshome.com

Kane, Gloria   Abductee.

Kennedy, Christine   Abductee.

Kerr, Roger   Contactee.
rakerr@orci.com
http://www.zayra.de/soulcom/orionlizards/

Klarer, Elizabeth   Contactee in the year 1956 who fell in love with Akon from planet Meton. Had contact with humanoids from the Alpha Centauri System. She died in 1994 in South Africa. Her highly intelligent son was called Ayling.

Krapf, Phillip H.   Former newspaperman of the Los Angeles Times.
Contactee to the Verdants.
→ Verdants.

Lake, Gina   Contactee.

Larkins, Lisette   Contactee, experiencer, born in Southern California, first contact
                              in 1987.
                              c/o Hampton Roads Publishing Company,
                              1125 Stoney Ridge Road,
                              Charlottesville, Virginia 22902
                              http://www.talkingtoets.com
                              lisette@talkingtoets.com

Layne, Patti   Abductee.

Leslie, Melinda   UFO abductee.

Liljenquist, Victoria

                              UFO contactee, visionary, angel contactee.
                              Contacted at age 5.
                              Clinical Certified Hypnotherapist, Healer, Lecturer.
                              Phone: (602) 955-7222.
                              victoria@victoriaslight.com
                              http://www.victoriaslight.com

Lindgren, Sten   Physical contactee from Sweden to a female space captain.

Lorgen, Eve Frances

                              Abductee, abductions researcher of 15 years, counselor.
                              Spiritual warrior that rose in the San Francisco Bay.
                              http://alienlovebite.com/main.htm
                              eve@alienlovebite.com
                              eve@nightsearch.net
                              Bookings@alienlovebite.com

Lowery, Garry   Contactee.
                              Bakersfield, California.

Maguire, Marian   Abductee.

Markley, Dhyana   Contactee to Eeon (a being of Inner Earth).
                              Planetary Activation Organization,
                              P.O.Box 880151, Pukalani, Maui, HI 96788-0151.
                              Voicemail: (808) 243-0728,
                              fax: (808) 573-2867.
                              paorg@hawaii.rr.com
                              http://www.paoweb.com

Martin, Pam   Abductee.

Matthews, Terry   Abductee.

Meier, „Billy"   Eduard Albert
Semjase-Silver-Star-Center, Schmidrüti, Switzerland.
Contactee, first contact at age of 5.
Was contacted over 130 times between 1976 and 1986 by Pleiadians. On January 28, 1986, the planned 11-year period for the official contacts had ended.
Billy has contact to Asket, Florena, Menara, Nera, Pleja, P'taah, Quetzal, Semjase, Talida, etc.
http://www.theyfly.com/
http://www.nexusmagazine.com/articles/Henoch%20Prophecies.html
michael@theyfly.com
→ Erra.

Mellas, Landi   Experiencer.

Menger, Howard   Contactee. First contact in 1932 in High Bridge, New Jersey when he was about 10 years old. Married in the year 1956 the Venusian woman Marla (Connie Weber).
→ Marla.

Michalak, Stephen   Canadian UFO witness at the Falcon Lake, Winnipeg.

Michel, Jean   Cmdr. Lyur,
P.O.Box 3106, Marion, NC 28752, USA.
wolfheart8@hotmail.com
cptnlyur@hotmail.com
http://www.starshiplight.com/

Miller, Richard   Contactee in the 50's.
Had his initial close encounter in 1954 with Soltec. Was aboard the starship Phoenix.
→ Soltec.

Mills, Laura   Abductee.

Mitchell, Kathy   Abductee, sister of Debbie Jordan.

Moody, Charles   Abductee, abducted Aug. 13, 1975 in Alamogordo, New Mexico.

Morgan, Beth, Janet & Karen
Abductees.

Morningsky, Robert   Contactee, Hopi/Apache dancer.

Morrison, Kathleen   Abductee.

Napolitano, Linda   Abductee, abducted Nov. 30, 1989 in Manhattan, N.Y.
Famous as Linda Cortile.

Negrón, Claudia   Abductee.

Nelson, Buck   Contactee.
                             Lived (1894-1982) in Ozark Mountains, Missouri. In 1955 he met
                             extraterrestrials and was cured by the aliens. Had visited Mars,
                             the Moon, Venus.

Norkin, Israel   Contactee.

Norman, Ruth   Contactee to Satan.

Odell, Michael   Contactee to the Morontia being.

Oswald, Luli   Brazilian UFO contactee in the 1980.

Owens, Pam & Chris   Abductees, abducted Nov. 1978 in Trier, Germany.

Owens, Ted   Contactee.

Parker, Calvin   Abductee, abducted Oct. 11, 1973 in Pascaguola, Mississippi
                             together with Charles Hickson.

Paz Wells, Sixto   Contactee from Puerto Rico, had contact on February 7, 1974 in
                             the Chilca desert, Peru.

Peters, Michelle   Abductee.

Petersen, Kelly   Abductee.

Polones, Victor   Brazilian UFO witness.

Popovich, Marina, Dr.
                             Russian UFO witness and investigator.
                             Famous ex Soviet military test pilot.
                             She also has paranormal psychic ability.
          http://www.world-famous.com/Marina-Popovich/Marina-Popovitch-1.html

Reed, Allison   Abductee.

Reilly, Doris   Abductee from Harrisburg, Pennsylvania.

Reis, Herminio & Bianca
                             Abductees, abducted Jan. 21, 1976 in Matles-Barbosa, Brazil.

Renaud, Bob   Contactee.
                             Had physical contact with the Korendians.
                             Produced photos of Korendian starships.
                             http://www.think-aboutit.com/aliens/seventy.htm

Reshma, Kamal   Abductee.

Rice, Ted   Abductee.

Riddle, George   Contactee.

Riley, Martin

Contactee.
Was abducted in 1953 at the age of seven by the Biaviians and kept for three days on a huge mothership near planet Saturn. Since then was visited by the same extraterrestrials every eleven years.
Was in contact with different extraterrestrial races:
>> Biaviians,
>> Dorians,
>> Nyptonians,
>> Skreeds,
>> Stagyians.
Met different aliens:
Nela, O-Nee-Sayer-Wann Nela, O-Qua Tangin Wann Tan, Skreed, Tan.
http://www.thecomingoftan.com
curtis@tradenet.net
Histority Productions, 91 River Rd.,
Stockton New Jersey 08559.
Phone: 609-397-8446, fax: 609-397-1860.

Royal Holt, Lyssa

American psychologist who travels worldwide.
Contactee.
Royal Priest Research, P.O.Box 12626,
Scottsdale, Arizona 85267.
Channel to Akbar, Bashar, Germane, Saint Germain.
http://www.worldtrans.org/lyssa/tape104.html

Samuelson, Joel

Abductee.

Sanders, Lucy

Abductee.

Shapiro, Robert

Contactee.

Simpson, Belinda

Abductee.

Simpson, Lucy

Abductee.

Siragusa, Eugenio

Contactee from Italy, has contact with Adoniesis.

Solem, Paul

Contactee in 1948.

Solvang, Asta

UFO and alien witness together with Edith Jacobsen on August 20, 1954 at Mosjoen, Northern Norway.

Starr, Jelaila   Walked-in June 23, 1992, in January 1997 Jelaila completed her initial training as a Galactic Messenger and founded the Nibiruan Council.
5987 Peacock Ridge Road, Ste. 105,
Rancho Palos Verdes, CA 90275.
Phone: 310-541-7179,
Fax: 310-541-0379.
432 E.Gregory Bld., Kansas City, MO 64131.
Phone: 816 – 444 4364, fax 816 – 444 4365,
http://www.NibiruanCouncil.com/html/body_contactus.html
jelaila@nibiruancouncil.com
info@NibiruanCouncil.com
jelaila@gte.net

Steckling, Fred   UFO witness, father of Glen Steckling.

Steckling, Glen   UFO witness, son of Fred Steckling.

Steiner, Susan   Abductee.

Steinhauser, Anton   German UFO witness.

Stevenson, Sarah   Abductee.

Stonebrooke, Pamela
                          Contactee. She has had numerous encounters with reptilian beings.
P.O. Box 1552, L.A., CA 90078-1552.
http://www.laweekly.com/ink/printme.php?eid=10209
http://www.greatdreams.com/reptlan/reps.htm
galactic_diva@telis.org

Stranges, Frank, Ph.D.
                          Contactee to the Venusians.
Interspace Link, P.O.Box 73, Van Nuys, CA 91408-0073.
Phone/fax: (818) 989-5954.
http://www.nicufo.com
→ Valiant Thor.

Strieber, Whitley & Anne
                          World's best known close encounter witness.

Summers, Kay   Abductee.

Telano, Rolf   Contactee to Borealis from Venus from the race of the Nors, in 1950.
Also known as Ralph Holland.
      http://www.beyond-the-illusion-com/files/New-Files/951130/venussptxt
                          → Nors.

Thernstrom, Jack   Abductee.

Thomson, Steve   Abductee.

Tossie, Guy   UFO witness, Nov. 2, 1967 in Idaho.

Valdez, Armando   Chili contactee (April 25,1977).

Valentich, Frederick

Abductee.

Van Tassel, George   Contactee. (1910-1978).
Was said to be the first American who had direct contact with
Ashtar.

Van Valer, Nola   Has seen St. Germain.
She visited a temple inside a cavern beneath Mt. Shasta. Inside
she met Phylos, a Tibetan Ascended Master and many other
Ascended Masters like Jesus.
The Radiant School of Seekers and Servers,
P.O.Box 378, Mount Shasta, CA 96067.
Phone: 530-926-5373.
http://www.mountshastamagazine.com/ms_mystique/

Villa, (Apolinar)Paul

Contactee in June 1963.

Villas Boas, Antonio

First known UFO abductee from Brazil, had a sexual relationship
with an extraterrestrial female in October 16, 1957.

Vlierden, Card   Contactee.
Produced photos of Koldasian spaceships.
http://www.think-aboutit.com/aliens/seventy.htm

Vorilhon, Claude   Contactee.
http://www.rael.org

Walden, Dr. James L.

Abductee.

Walsh, Courtney   Abductee.

Walton, Travis   Abductee, abducted in Heber in the mountains of Arizona, Nov.
5, 1975. He disappeared for 5 days.

Weiking, Knud   Contactee.

West, Channie   Contactee from Sweden.
Contacted at the age of 5. She works with angels,
extraterrestrials, Light Beings. She speaks 35 extraterrestrial
languages.

Wilkinson-Izatt, Dorothy

Contactee, psychic.
Had first contact on November 9th, 1974.
She has about 350 films about UFOs.
She lives in Canada.
http://www.manari.com/dorothy.html

Williamson, George Hunt

Early UFO contactee.
Alias Brother Philip.

Wilson, Katharina   Abductee.
Puzzle Publishing, P.O.Box 230023,
Portland, OR 97281-0023.
http://www.abduct.com/

Wilson, Steve Col.   UFO experiencer, Star Seed.
Head of Project Pounce.

Wolf, Michael, Dr.   Contactee to Kolta, a Grey from Zeta Reticuli.
Member of the NSC SSG Committee that was earlier called MJ-
12.
http://www.jps.net/drboylan/
http://www.swa-home.de/wolf2b.htm

Woodard, Billie Faye

Colonel, Inner Earth experiencer.
At her age of 12 lived 6 months among the Hollow Earth
residents, she was adopted, her true parents live in the Inner
Earth. She has an unknown blood type.

Woodward, William   Colonel of the United States Air Force. He was first stationed at
Area 51, Nevada, January 28, 1971 through 1982. In that period
of service he visited the Hollow Interior of the Earth six times,
800 miles deep.

Yanca, Dionisio   Abductee, abducted Oct. 28, 1973 in Bahia Blanca, Brazil.

Zeigler, Roxanne   Abductee from New York.

6.3 UFO Researchers, Investigators

Adair, David   Space technology expert.

Akdogan, Haktan   UFO researcher and founder of the International UFO museum
in Istanbul, Turkey.
Sirius UFO Space Sciences Research Center,
Istanbul, Turkey.
Buyuk Parmakkapi Sk: No: 14 Kat: 1-2, Beyoglu,
Istanbul, Turkey.
http://www.siriusufo.org
info@siriusufo.org
Phone: 90-212-252 86 46, 90-212-252 86 82.
Fax: 90-212-252 87 07.

Alford, Alan F.   Independent researcher and author who is widely recognized as
one of the world's leading authorities on ancient mythology,
mysticism and the origin of world religions.
Walsall, England.
http://www.eridu.co.uk

Anderson, Dr.   Member of the ACIO (level 12).
It might be a pseudonym of Dr. Jamisson Neruda from Bolivia.

Andrus, Walt   UFO investigator.

Anfalov, Anton A. Head of the Ukrainian UFO Research.

Athayde, Reginaldo de Brazilian UFO researcher.

Atlanti, Shawn   UFO investigator, hypnotherapist.
He resides in San Diego.

Bachurin, Emil   Russian UFO researcher.

Back, Roberto Affonso Brazilian UFO researcher.

Barker, Gray   UFO investigator.

Barski, Stanislav   Polish UFO researcher.

Basterfield, Keith   Australian UFO researcher.

Bayliff, Ann   UFO researcher.

Bedell, Susan   UFO researcher.

Bender, Al   American UFO research pioneer, contactee.
                                  http://www.nexusmagazine.com//meninblack.html

Berliner, Don   UFO researcher.

Bigelow, Robert   UFO researcher.

Black, Jerry   UFO researcher.

Bletchman, Robert   UFO investigator.

Bonenfant, Rick   UFO researcher.

Boros, Attila   Hungarian UFO Artist.

Boylan, Richard J. , Ph.D.,
                                  Abductee, Director Star Kids Project.
                                  Researcher into extraterrestrial-human encounters, Clinical
                                  hypnotherapist, scientist, university   instructor.
                                  LLC 2826 O Street, Ste. 2,
                                  P.O.Box 22310, Sacramento, CA 95822 (95816).
                                  Phone/fax/voice-mail: (916)422-7400, (916)422-7479.
                                  drboylan@sbcglobal.net
                                  drboylan@jps.net
                                  http://www.drboylan.net
                                  http://www.drboylan.com
                                  http://www.jps.net/drboylan/

Brookesmith, Peter   British ufologist.

Cannon, Dolores   Past Life Regressionist. UFO investigator.
                                  Channel to Nostradamus.

Carlson, Dan   UFO researcher.

Chalker, Bill   One of the leading Australian UFO researchers.

Clark, Larry   New York MUFON researcher.
                                  http://www.nymufon.org/reportform.htm

Clear, Constance   UFO researcher.

Convey, Graham   UFO researcher, president of UFO-BC.
                                  http://www.manari.com/experts.htm

Cooper, Timothy   California UFO researcher.

Cooper, WilliamWilliam Cooper Foundation, P.O.Box 3299,
                                  Camp Verde, CA 86322.

Courant, James   UFO investigator.

Covo, Claudeir	Brazilian UFO researcher.
Cury, Rafael	Brazilian UFO researcher.
Davenport, Peter	UFO investigator and Director of the National UFO Reporting Center (NUFORC) in Seattle. UFO-Hotline: 206-722-3000. http://www.ufocenter.com http://www.abduct.com/aaer/
Davis, Isabel	UFO researcher.
Dean, Robert & Cecillia	UFO researcher.
Dennett, Preston	UFO investigator.
Dickson, George	UFO researcher of the Long Island UFO network, N.Y.
Dodd, Anthony	British UFO and abduction researcher.
Dolan, Richard M.	Historian, UFO researcher.
Doyle, Patricia , PhD	UFO investigator. http://ww.rense.com/general28/truths.htm dr_p_doyle@hotmail.com
Durant, Bob	Ufologist for MUFON. http://www.abduct.com/aaer/
Dusenberry, Lisa	UFO researcher.
Dvuzhilny, Valeri	Russian UFO investigator.
Escamilla, José	UFO investigator. http://RoswellRods.com
Fairfax, Bob	UFO investigator.
Farish, Lou	UFO researcher.
Fawcett, George	Former UFO researcher from Massachusetts. MUFON State Director of North Carolina.

Filer, George A.   UFO investigator.
                           MUFON Eastern Director,
                           MUFON Sky watch Investigations,
                           MUFON UFO JOURNAL,
                           103 Oldtowne Road, Sequin TX 78155-4099.
                           Phone: 609 654-0020, 1-800 UFO-2166.
                           http://www.abduct.com/aaer/
                           http://www.abduct.com/aaer2/
                           http://ufoinfo.com/filer/index.html
                           http://mufon.com
                           Majorstar@aol.com
                           Mufon@aol.com

Fiore, Dr.   Abduction researcher.

Flores, Geronimo   Mexican UFO investigator.

Ford, John   UFO investigator, New York.
                           Founder of Long Island UFO Network in 1985.
                           Incarcerated in jail for conspiracy on   June 12, 1996.

Forster, Gery   gforster@tlccomputers.com.au
                           http://www.onelight.com/forster/

Fowler, Raymond E.
                           UFO researcher, Wenham. Director of MUFON.

Friedman, Stanton D.
                           Canadian UFO researcher, famous nuclear physicist.
                           Says that the Martian moons are metallic, hollow, artificial
                           satellites that have orbits, densities and speeds impossible by all
                           known laws of physics!
                           Agent of the Secret Government.
                           http://www.think-aboutit.com/aliens/seventy.htm

Garza, Yturria   Mexican UFO investigator.

Geigenthaler, Adolf   German UFO researcher.

Gersten, Peter   Executive Director of CAUS.

Gevaerd, Ademar José, Prof.
                           Brazilian UFO researcher.
                           Head of the Committee of the Brazilian UFO Researchers.
                           http://www.ufo.com.br
                           gevaerd@ufo.com.br

Goldner, Jay   Crop Circle expert.

Good, Timothy

UFO researcher.
39307 Lark Road, P.O.Box 1206,
Big Bear Lake, CA 92315.
http://www.majesticdocuments.com/sources/timcooper.html

Gordon, Stan

UFO researcher, investigator.

Gottschall, Sheryl

UFO researcher, hypnotherapist for 16 years.
Phone: (07) 3376 1780.
http://www.acufos.asn.au
http://www.uforc.as.au
gottscha@bigpond.net.au

Greer, Steven, M.D.

UFO investigator.
Director of the Center for Study of Extraterrestrial Intelligence
(CSETI).
Director, Disclosure Project, P.O.Box 2365,
Charlottesville, VA 22902.
http://www.disclosureproject.org
updates@disclosureproject.org

Grief, Avi

Head of Israeli UFO Research Center.

Haley, Leah A.

Alien experiencer, abductee, abduction researcher.
Greenleaf Publications, P.O.Box 331416,
Murfreesboro, TN 37133-1416.
Phone: 615-896-1549.
Fax: 615-896-1356.
office@greenleafpublications.com

Hall, Richard

UFO researcher.
Former president of NICAP.
Brentwood, Maryland.

Hallet, Marc

Some people say that he is a UFO debunker.

Hamilton, Bill (William)

UFO investigator.

Hastings, Robert

40 Evergreen Circle, Caropines,
Myrtle Beach, South Carolina 29575.

Hendry, Allan

Former UFO investigator for CUFOS.

Hesemann, Michael

UFO investigator.

Hickman, Jim

Alien abduction researcher, Oklahoma.

Hoagland, Richard

Ex NASA employee, scientist, space archaeologist.

Honey, Chop A.

UFO investigator for the Government.

Hopkins, Budd   Abduction and UFO researcher, New York.

Hynek, J. Allen   UFO researcher, astronomer.

Iskiovet, Farida   (Former?) U.N. UFO investigator.

Jacobs, David M., Ph.Dr.
                              Abduction researcher, UFO researcher, historian.
                              Theory of Alien Invasion.
                              Department of History, Temple University,
                              Philadelphia, PA 19122.
                              DJacobs@VM.Temple.edu

Jordan, Harry Allen
                              UFO investigator.

Jordan, Peter   UFO investigator.

Kasher, John Dr.   UFO investigator, physics professor.
                              Director of MUFON Nebraska.

Keel, Jordan   Ufologist, leading UFO writer and researcher in America.

Keyhoe, Daniel   UFO researcher.

Kitchur, Randy   Canadian UFO researcher.

Klass, Philip Julian
                              Abduction researcher, CIA agent. It is said he is a debunker of
                              UFO sightings.

Knell, Bill   Abduction investigator, researcher.
                              Director of Island Skywatch, New York.
                              Phone: (718) 591-1854.

Lamb, Barbara   Psychotherapist, Crop Circle specialist.
                              Star Seed therapist.
                              Claremont.

LeBreton, Robert Paul
                              Cmdr.
                              Ashtar Space Command Communications,
                              2901 State Hwy 6, HC 77 Box 42,
                              Laguna, New Mexico 87026.
                              Phone: (505)-836-7534.
                              http://www.topica.com/lists/Wizzard9
                              wizzard9@earthlink.net

Leir, Roger K. Dr.M.D.
                              Alien Implant Removal Surgeon.

Leopizzi Harris, Paola
UFO investigator.

Levens, Brian
UFO researcher, writer, poet.
http://www.alienlovebite.com

Lindemann, Michael
German UFO researcher.

Lorgen, Eve Frances
Abductee, abductions researcher of 15 years, counselor.
Spiritual warrior that rose in the San Francisco Bay.
http://alienlovebite.com/main.htm
eve@alienlovebite.com
eve@nightsearch.net
Bookings@alienlovebite.com

Lyster, Karen
UFO researcher.
http://www.karenlyster.com/Directory.html

Maccabee, Bruce
UFO investigator.
MUFON's Maryland Director.
http://www.abduct.com/aaer/

Mack, John E.
UFO and abduction researcher, psychiatrist.
Harvard University.

Marss, Jim
UFO investigator, reporter, author.
http://www.harpercollins.com

Martin, Jorge
UFO investigator and journalist from Puerto Rico.

Matthews, Arthur
Scientist, contactee to Venusians.

Maussan, Jaime
Mexican UFO researcher and investigator, tv journalist.
http://www.ovnis.com.mx
web@ovnis.com.mx
http://www.rense.com/general52/deff.htm

McLean, Hamish
UFO investigator from APRG, Gisborne, New Zealand.

Mesnard, Joël
French UFO researcher.

Michel, Aimé
French UFO researcher.

Michel, Jean
Cmdr. Lyur,
P.O.Box 3106, Marion, NC 28752, USA.
wolfheart8@hotmail.com
cptnlyur@hotmail.com
http://www.starshiplight.com/

Moore, Chester
Bigfoot researcher.

Moore, William   Ufologist who is CIA backed.
                            Agent of the Secret Government.
                            He had released disinformation to researchers.

Mosely, Jim   UFO investigator.

Moulton-Howe, Linda
                            UFO investigator.
                            http://www.earthfiles.com

Müller, Andreas   Crop Circle Researcher from Saarbrücken, Germany.

Nyman, Joseph   Abduction researcher, UFO investigator, Massachusetts.

Osborn, Maurice   Crop Circle researcher.
                            http://www.uforia-research.com

Parrish, Doug   UFO investigator.

Petit, Marco   Brazilian UFO researcher.

Popovich, Marina, Dr.
                            Russian UFO witness and investigator.
                            Famous ex Soviet military test pilot.
                            She also has paranormal psychic ability.
        http://www.world-famous.com/Marina-Popovich/Marina-Popovitch-1.html

Ramalho, Fernando   Brazilian UFO researcher.

Randi, James   Some people say he is a debunker.

Randle, Kevin   UFO researcher.
                            http://www.abduct.com/aaer/b15.htm

Randles, Jenny   Abduction researcher.

Roberts, Augie   .   Ufologist and UFO witness.

Rogerson, Peter   UFO researcher from Gt. Britain.

Ruben, Marilyn   UFO investigator.
                            http://www.abduct.com/

Ruppelt, Edward J.   Former director of project "Blue Book", 1951.

Salisbury, Frank   UFO researcher, biologist.

Salla, Michael E. PhD

It is said he is a UFO disinformant.
Researcher in Residence Center for Global Peace,
American University.
http://www.exopolitics.org
http://www.galacticdiplomacy.com
drmsalla@exopolitics.org

Schmitt, Don UFO researcher. CUFOS Director.

Schneider, Phil UFO researcher, possible disinformant.

Shandera, Jaime Agent of the Secret Government.

Sims, Darrel UFO investigator & researcher, certified Hypnotherapist,
abduction researcher, abductee, former CIA operative.
Houston UFO Network (HUFON).
http://chelsea.ios.com/~dalemv19/hufon/

Smirnov, Yuriy A. Russian UFO researcher, Yaroslavl.

Smith, Wilbert Canadian UFO researcher.

Spaulding, William UFO researcher.
Ground Saucer Watch (GSW), Phoenix, Arizona.

Spencer, John Abduction researcher.

Sprinkle, R. Leo, Prof. Dr.Ph.D.

Psychologist, hypnotherapist, abduction & UFO researcher.
University of Wyoming.

Stone, Clifford UFO researcher.

Stonehill, Paul UFO investigator.

Story, Ronald UFO investigator.

Strainic, Michael Canadian National Director of MUFON Canada.

Stringfield, Leonard H.

Expert UFO crash retrieval and abductions researcher. Pioneer
of American Ufology.
4412 Grove Avenue, Cincinnati 45227, Ohio.

Subbotin, Nickolay Russian UFO researcher of RUFORS.

Svahn, Clas Swedish UFO investigator of UFO Sweden.

Swiatek, Rob UFO researcher.

Taff, Barry E., Dr.Ph.D.
                        UFO investigator.

Talbot, Nancy   American Crop Circle researcher.

Taylor, Barry   UFO researcher, Australia.

Taylor, Lynn   UFO researcher/investigator.
                        http://www.abduct.com/aaer/lt72.htm

Teller, Edward   Weapons Scientist, "Father" of the Star Wars Program, warned
                        President Reagan about possible alien invasion.

Terziski, Vladimir   UFO & Alien researcher.

Thompson, John C.   UFO investigator.
                        Former MUFON State Director of Georgia.
                        http://www.abduct.com/aaer/

Turner, Karla   Abduction researcher.

Vallee, Jacques   American/French UFO researcher.

Velasco, Jean-Jacques
                        French UFO investigator.

Vincel, Carla   UFO researcher.

Von Keviczky, Colman S.
                        Ufologist and Hungarian military scientist. 1909 – 1998.
                        http://www.abduct.com/aaer/

Waeber, Rolf   UFO researcher, Zurich, Switzerland.

Walter, Werner   UFO researcher, Mannheim, Germany.

Watson, Nigel   UFO investigator from Gt. Britain.

Webb, David F.   Scientist and UFO investigator from Boston.
                        Regional Director of MUFON.

Webb, Walter N.   UFO investigator.

Wingfield, George   British UFO researcher, Crop Circle reporter.

Winston, John F.   johnf@mlode.com

Woodard, Billie Faye
                        Colonel, Inner Earth experiencer.
                        At her age of 12 lived 6 months among the Hollow Earth
                        residents, she was adopted, her true parents live in the Inner
                        Earth. She has an unknown blood type.

Woodward, William — Colonel of the United States Air Force. He was first stationed at Area 51, Nevada, January 28, 1971 through 1982. In that period of service he visited the Hollow Interior of the Earth six times, 800 miles deep.

Worley, Donald — Alien Abduction researcher.
http://www.abduct.com/worley/worley17.htm

Young, Kenny — One of the most important UFO investigators, died January 31, 2005.

Young, Robert — UFO investigator.

Zagorski, Janusz — Polish UFO researcher and Crop Circle specialist.

Zechel, Todd — UFO investigator.

7. BEINGS

7.1 Space People, Masters, Angels, Light Beings, Spiritual Guides

A'ALBIEL	Angel in service of archangel Michael.
AARAH	Councilor.
AARON	
ABAN	Angel.
ABARIEL	Angel used for invocations.
ABASDARHON	Supreme ruling angel.
ABDIEL	Seraph.
ABEKO	Other name of Lilith.
ABEL	8300 B.C.E., his spiritual guides: Venus & Capella, was born in Gandes (cavern in Syria), moved to Lake Evana (Iraq), at the age of 18 he knew all his past lives, was murdered at the age of 33 in Nairi (Kurdistan) in order of Cain, with a stab with a dagger.
ABEL	Judging angel. He is one of the 12 Powers with this task.
ABIGRAEL	Recording angel.
ABITO	Other name of Lilith.
ABRAHAM	Patriarch. Earlier incarnation of Ascended Master El Morya. Channel: Shaari.
ABRID	Angel.
ABU KASH KAR	Keeper of the Akashic Libraries of the Solar System.
ABUDAMIR	Intraterrestrial master from the Andean Magnetic Center in Chile.
ABUZOHAR	One of the angels of the Moon. Responsive to invocations in ritual magic.
ACHAIAH	He is a Seraphim, Angel of Patience.
ACHAMOTH	Daughter of Pistis Sophia, mother of the evil god Ildabaoth.
ACHELIAH	Angel.

ACKMAN   Space Commander.

ADAGA   Wife of Upasu Arasatha.

ADAM/ADAMU   Father of Abel, from Atlantis, real name: Adamu de Ethea, 8300
                        B.C.E. His first wife was Lilith.
                        Incarnation of Lord Sananda.
                        → Lilith.

ADAMA   Ascended Master & High Priest of Telos (city below Mt. Shasta).
                        Master of Love and Compassion.
                        Lives in his body for over 600 years.
                        Spiritual leader of the Melchizedek lodge.
                        Channel: Aurelia Louise Jones, Lailel.

ADAMU DE ETHEA
                        → Adam.

ADELLA   Space Commander, is a psychologist from the 9th dimension.
                        The spaceship is 15m in diameter, in height from 3,60m to
                        4,20m.

ADNACHIEL   Angel that holds dominion over the sun sign Sagittarius.

ADNAI   Angel.

ADOLPHIUS   Of the spaceship Intrepid.
                        Channel: Nancy Tate.

ADONIESIS   Interdimensional being.
                        Chief Coordinator of the Ashtar Command.
                        Head of the largest physical base of Ashtar's Starfleet on Earth
                        (named Eldorado) and located underground on parts of Bolivia,
                        Brazil and Peru.
                        He also carries the Christ energy.
                        Incarnations: Akhenaton.
                        Contactee: Eugenio Siragusa, Italy.

ADONIS   Member of the Planetary Council.

ADUACHIEL   He alternates with Phaleg as a ruling angel of the order of angels.

AEB   A guide from Apu, communicating with contact groups in Tacna,
                        Peru.

AELOHIN/AHELOIN
                        Spirit guide of Jhasua, Juno, Krishna, Moses.

AEOLUS   Ascended Master.

AESCAPULUS	Lord, Leader of the Council of Nine, leader of the Great Blue Lodge of Creation.
AETHERIUS	Venusian Cosmic Master. 3456 years old (in 1954). His seat of Government is Saturn. Channel: George King.
AF BRI	Angel that controls the rain.
AFFA	From planet Uranus.
AFRIEL	Angel that is believed to grant vigor, vitality, youth.
AFSI-KHOF	Angel.
AFTIEL	Angel of twilight.
AG-AGRIA	A guide and teacer.
AGIEL	Angel who is the presiding intelligence of Saturn.
AGRAT BAT MAHLAT	Angel of Prostitution. One of the 4 mates of Samael. Also known as Iggereth.
AHA	Angel of the order of dominations, a spirit of fire used in cabalistic magical operations.
AHADIEL	Angelic enforcer of the law.
AHURA MAZDA	Was Sanat Kumara. → Sanat Kumara.
AKATRIEL	Angel of Prayer, Proclamation. Revealer of the divine mysteries. Also called Akrasiel.
AKBAR	Mogul emperor from India, incarnation of El Morya. Lives on a desert planet in Orion. They have four very thick layers of skin to protect them from the harsh environment, olive-colored skin (brown with a greenish tinge). Channel: Lyssa Royal.
AKIBEEL	Manifesting Angel, fallen angel.
AKON	Scientist from planet Meton.
AKRASIEL	Other name of Akatriel.
AL USSA	Female angel.

ALALU   Former ruler on Nibiru. Vanquished from Earth and exiled to Mars. The only king of Nibiru ever to be buried on another planet, 430,000 B.C.E.
The face on Mars is the image of Alalu.

ALANA   Female Space Commander from the planet Adalia in the Bootes Constellation. She is about 2,40m tall, her body looks greenish, slanted eyes, very large nose, small mouth and chin & short hair.

ALCIR   Intraterrestrial master, regent and record keeper from the lost kingdom of Paititi.

ALCYONE   Lord, Twin Flame of (Mother) Sekhmet.

ALDELAN   Cmdr. of the Ashtar Command.
From the small planet Aarmon in the Pleiades.

ALDIS   Father of Adam, from Atlantis, (8350 B.C.E., later reincarnated as Lucas the Evangelist.

ALDRIX   A guide from Apu, assigned to contact groups in La Coruña, Spain.

ALEATHIN   Extraterrestrial in contact with Dolores Cannon.

ALENA   From Lyra.

ALEPH   Other name of Archangel Uriel.

ALEVA   Commander of the Ashtar Command.
Channel is Shalie.

ALIMIEL   Angel.

ALIMON   Angel.

ALISHA   Cmdr. of the Ashtar Command.
She is on the medical ship "Alignment" with her sister Cmdr. Galimai-A.

ALISHA SHERAN
                     → Alisha.

ALIZANTIL   Space Commander.
Channel is Frank Howard.

ALMORA BABA   Present form of the immortal Master Babji.

ALOHA   Elohim of the 6th (purple/gold) Ray of Brotherhood, Peace. Twin Flame of Peace.

ALPHA-HUARI   Minor brother of Anfion, later incarnated as Cain.

ALPHON	Commander of the Intergalactic Fleet. Member of the Ashtar Command.
ALTA	Space scientist from planet Vixall.
ALTA-ZAR	Telepathic Liaison working with KOR. Member of the Solar Cross. → KOR.
ALTARIB	Angel.
ALTEA	From civilization Altea. Also known as. >> Altima, >> Atlas, >> Zeus.
ALTIMA	→ Altea.
ALUE	Guardian Spirit of planet Earth. Other name of Archangel Sandalphon. Channel: Caroline Fitzgerald. → Sandalphon.
ALYSTAR	Keeper of the Records for the Galactic Federation.
AMABAEL	Angel.
AMAEL	Ruling angel prince of the order of Principalities.
AMALIEL	Angel of Punishment, Weakness.
AMARU	A guide from Venus, assigned to contact groups in Spain.
AMASSIA	Female from planet Komesso.
AMATIEL	Renewing angel.
AMAZARAC	Fallen angel that gave instructions in all secrets of sorcerers.
AMAZON	Other name of Amazonia.
AMAZONIA	Elohim of the 1st (blue) Ray of Faith, God's Will, Power. Twin Flame of Hercules. 14 to 15 ft tall. Also known as Amazon.
AMBHAMSI	→ Sujata.
AMBRIEL	Angel of general protection.

AMERISSIS   Goddess of Light. Twin Flame of El Morya.
                       Incarnations:
                       >> Lady of the Lake (King Arthur was El Morya).

AMILIUS   First incarnation of Jesus (Lord Sananda) in Atlantis.

AMINAEL   Intraterrestrial master of the grotto of Huagapo, Peru.

AMITIEL   Angel that grants equality, love, peace, truth, understanding.

AMIZO   Other name of Lilith.

AMMACHI   Present incarnation of Divine Mother in India and United States.
                       → Ammachi.

AMOR   Telepathic supervisor from Aldebaran, working with KOR.
                       Member of the Solar Cross.
                       → KOR, Solar Cross.

AMORA   Elohim of the 3rd (pink) Ray. Twin Flame of Heros.
                       → Heros.

AMRAM   Father of Moses, of the race of Levi, 1500 B.C.E.

AN   Dark Lord, a Sun God, he is not Anu.
                       Former Supreme Commander of an Annunaki Reptilian race.
                       Sirian king who destroyed in a war entire worlds, including their
                       moons and colonies.
                       King An sent his son Ea and his daughter Ninhursag to rebuild
                       the destroyed world of Eridu (Earth).

ANACHIEL   Angel who helps deal with people & shyness.
                       Other name of Rigel from Saturn.
                       → Rigel.

ANAEL   One of the 7 angels of creation. Prince of the archangels.
                       Angel of Learning, Students & Teachers. Exercises dominion
                       over the Moon and Venus.
                       Other name of Archangel Haniel.

ANAFIEL   Chief of the crown judgment angels of the Merkabah.

ANAHITA   Female angel of high rank.

ANAHUAC   A guide from Venus.

ANAKHANDA MUSHABA
                       Grandmaster. Incarnated extraterrestrial.

ANAMELECH   Obscure demon.

ANANE   Angel.

ANANEA	Lord, one of the six major Seraphims.
ANANIEL	Angel.
ANAUEL	Protecting angel of bankers & commerce.
ANDROMEDA REX	
	Of the Intergalactic Council of the Space Confederation. Ambassador and Commander of the Ashtar Command. Member of the Ashtar Command. Channel: Lucy Colson, Tuella.
ANFIAL	Angel.
ANFION	White prophet of Atlantis, last king of the race of Tolsteka, his spiritual guides: Isis & Orfeo, 22300 B.C.E.
Angel	The Angelic Kingdom expresses the joy of just being. Angels are a single consciousness with individual expressions. They will only appear briefly at the level of the 3rd dimension. Angels really do not have a need for wings. Many of the so called angels are in truth extraterrestrials.
ANGERECTON	Angel.
ANIEL	Said to be an archangel.
ANITAC	Female guide from Venus. Commander and technician assigned to interdimensional investigation. Works together with the Confederation's underwater base "Acqualium", North West of Chancay, Peru. This base's population is entirely Venusian. → Acqualium.
ANITOR	High holy angel.
ANIXIEL	Angel of the Moon.
ANKHIEL	Angel, other name of Rigel from Saturn. → Rigel.
ANRAR	A guide from Apu.
ANON SA RA	Prince, star visitor from the Altair system.
ANTAR	Commander and spaceship technician from the base in Crystal City, Morlen (Ganymede, the moon of Jupiter). He was born in Morlen and also functions as a coordinator for other extraterrestrial guides.
ANTAREL	A guide from Apu.

ANTHRIEL   Angel of Balance & Harmony.
                       Said to be an archangel.

ANTON   Fleet Cmdr. from the Silver Fleet.
                       Member of the Ashtar Command.

ANTONNI   Space Commander from the planet Aray in Cassiopeia.
                       He is a philosopher.

ANTU   Wife & sister of Anu, mother of Enlil.

ANTULIO   From Atlantis, king Ateneas, language Tolsteka.
                       His father: Haman-Arasat, mother: Wilkiria.
                       His origin: Central Sun of Sirius.
                       Author of the Antulion Chronicles (base for the temples of
                       Memphis, Luxor, Thebes, On [thousands of years later], also for
                       Krishna, Persia, Socrates, Platon, Aristotle, Ptolemy), 16700
                       B.C.E.

ANU   Commander of the starship Nibiru until 2000 B.C.E. and from
                       1999 C.E. until now.
                       His son Enlil is carrying the majority of the responsibilities on
                       the job.
                       From the race of the Humans.
                       Father of Enki & Enlil, grandfather of Marduk.
                       Reigning patriarch of the 5 dimensional House of Avyon.
                       Head of the 5D Nibiruan Council.
                       Leader of the Annunaki.
                       Is not the same as An.
                       → An.

ANZU   Enki's original pilot.

APOLLO   God, avatar, really existed.
                       Member of the Planetary Council.
                       Elohim of the 2nd (yellow) Ray of Illumination, Omniscience,
                       Understanding, Wisdom.
                       Guardian of the Cosmic Christ Consciousness.
                       Twin Flame of Lumina.
                       Is considered by some to be the Solar Logos.
                       Millions of angels serve under Apollo & Lumina.

APOLLONIUS   Grand Master, born 2 C.E.

APOLLONIUS of Tyana
                       Incarnation of Sananda. Was real.

APRAGSIN   Divine messenger.

APSU   Female angel.

AQUARIEL   Angel of Grace & Divine Protection.
Said to be an archangel.

ARALIM   Angel.

ARAMAITI   Other name of Armaita.

ARATHIEL   Angel.

ARAUCHIA   Angel.

ARBATEL   Revealing angel.

ARCHOS   Spiritual being.
Member of the Interplanetary Federation.
Channel: Birgit Klein.

ARCTURUS   Lord, from planet Arcturus.
Chief of the Space Armada from Arcturus.
Connected to the Alliance & Brotherhood of Interplanetary Fellowship.

ARCTURUS   Elohim of the 7th (violet) Ray of Freedom, Invocation, Mercy, Transcendence, Transmutation.
Twin Flame of Victoria.

ARDAREL   Angel of Fire.

ARDOUISUR   Female Cherub.

ARDOUSIUS   Female angel.

AREHANAH   Angel.

ARIANIVA   She is from Mars.

AREL   Angel of Fire.

ARELLA   Angel, messenger.

ARIAL   Angel.

ARIAS   Angel of sweet smelling herbs.

ARIEL   Archangel, feminine counterpart of Uriel.
Ariel means: „ Lion(ess) of God".
Angel of Money, New Beginnings.
Angel of the order of Thrones.
Spirit guide of Jhasua, Juno, Krishna, Moses.
Rebel-angel who is overcome by the seraph Abdiel on the first day of the great war in Heaven.
Assisted Archangel Raphael in the curing of disease.

Ariel is the angel who controls the demons.
Air or water spirit.
Member of the Council of Ain Soph.
Channel: Isaac George.

ARIELLA   Other name of Ariel.

ARIMANIUS   A Drac leader (Satan) who can inhabit a physical body.
                         Chief of the Fallen Angels.

ARIS   Grandfather of Jehovah.
                         From Beta Centauri.

ARISTIEL RA EL
                         Name of Cmdr. Alisha.
                         → Alisha.

ARIZIAL   Angel.

ARMAITA   Female archangel.
                         Spirit of Goodness, Truth, Wisdom.
                         Also known as:
                         >>   Aramaiti,
                         >>   Armaiti.

ARMAITI   Other name of Armaita.

ARMENDEUS   Sirian Ambassador General.
                         Bearer of the Blue Flame.

ARMERS   Angelic leader, fallen angel.

ARMISAEL   Angel of the Womb.

ARURU   Mother of Gilgamesh.

ARZAL   Angel.

ASAEL   Angelic leader, fallen angel.

ASAPH   Angel.

ASARU   Former Lord of the Ciakar.

ASASIEL   Angel.

ASH-KAR   Channel is Ron Eppich.

ASHA   Virtue.

ASHIDA Cmdr. of the Ashtar Command.
Other name of Cmdr. Galimai-A.
→ Galimai-A.

ASHRIEL Angel of the Earth.

ASKET An extraterrestrial woman from Timar in the DAL Universe.

ASTAR (not Ashtar)
A guide from Apu.

ASHTAR → Ashtar Sheran.

ASHTAR-ATHENA Wife of Ashtar Sheran.

ASHTAR SHERAN Great Coordinator of space fleet.
Highly evolved being of strict and upright military bearing.
Well-known commander throughout our universe.
Former Commander of the Ashtar Galactic Command.
He is an important member of many Galactic, Intergalactic and Universal Councils.
Is one of the Seven Rays of the Christ Word.
Ambassador from the Great Central Sun Hierarchy.
High Council of Melchizedek.
Ascended Master. 6th to 8th dimension being.
Has a talent to flush out negativity.
Etheric being that has not been physically embodied on planet Shan (Earth).
Ashtar's home planet is Venus.
In summer 1998 he was relieved of his duties.
His mothership Shan Chea measures 1000 miles.
His base is in Alpha Centauri.
He is not Mikael Ashtar!
He is not the head of the Ashtar Command.
He was the channel for Mikael Ashtar.
It is said he had direct contact with George Van Tassel.
His wife is Ashtar-Athena.
His daughter is Cmdr. Galimai-A.
Also known as:
>>   Gabri-An,
>>   Nirih,
>>   Sher-An,
>>   Sherna.
Channel: AsariA, Susan Leland, Gladys Rodehaver, Sandi Sheppard, Ariana Sheran, Tom H. Smith, Tuella, Andrew Whalley, Debbie Wright.
→ Maldek.
→ Mikael Ashtar.

ASHTEROTH Other name of Astarte.

ASHTORETH Other name of Astarte.

ASIEL   Angel.

ASRON   Angel.   Asron means: „Vow of God".

ASSIEL   Angel of Healing.

ASSYRIA   Lady.

ASTARIBO   Other name of Lilith.

ASTARTE   Also known as:
                     >>   Ashteroth,
                     >>   Ashtoreth,
                     >>   Ishtar.

ASTOR   Grand Space Commander.

ASTRA   Grand Space Commander.

ASTREA   Lady Master.
                     Elohim of the 4th (white) Ray of Hope, Perfection, Purity and
                     Wholeness.
                     Personifies the Human Concept of Kali.
                     Twin Flame (feminine complement) of Purity.
                     Channel: Geraldine Innocente.

ATABBA   Name of Adam.

ATAPHIEL   Angel.

ATAR   Angel of Fire.

ATEL   Angel.

ATHAR ISMAR   She is from the Pleiades.

ATHENA   Lady Commander. Master.
                     Space Command. Ashtar Command.
                     She is on mothership of Ashtar.
                     She comes in the ray of the Divine Mother.
                     She is tall & blonde.
                     Incarnated on planet Maldek.
                     Her daughter is Cmdr. Galimai-A.
                     Member of the Planetary Council.
                     Channel: Karen Danrich, Dr. Norma Milanovich.
                     → Ashtar-Athena, Pallas Athena.

ATIA   She is the head of a universal order of Cosmic Virgins.
                     Her coming at Fatima in 1947 was with a spaceship.
                     Other name of Mother Mary.

ATHAR ISMAR She is from the Pleiades.

ATLAS King of Atlantis at the time of Atlantis' destruction, approx. 9,500 B.C.E. Wanted to reestablish the Lemurian Empire.
Father of Isis, Osiris, Seth. Husband of queen Mu.
→ Altea.

ATMOS Pleiadian Representative of the Galactic Federation.
Channel Mike Quinsey.

ATNA Space Commander from planet Dexton in the constellation of Orion.
Name of the spacecraft is Zella 17. Height about 2m, short light brown hair, slanted grey eyes, small nose, rounded face, small mouth, larger ears, very small neck, very large shoulders, muscular metallic body, they have an interesting sex life, no more than 2 offspring.

ATON.MOSES → Moses, 1500 B.C.E.

ATRICA Extraterrestrial working with KOR.
Member of the Solar Cross.
→ KOR, Solar Cross.

ATTARIS Angel of Winter.

ATUESUEL Angel of Omnipotence.

ATUNEZ A guide from Venus.

ATUNIEL Angel of Fire.

AUEL Angel of the Sun.

AUMTRON Representative on the Central Sun Council.
Sirian expert on science.

AUPHONIM Angel.

AURA RHANES Female Captain of a spaceship from planet Clarion. Was in contact with Truman Bethurum in 1954.

AURIEL Other name of Archangel Uriel.

AURORA Twin Flame of Archangel Uriel.

AUSIUL Angel.

AV.ISIS.THIMETIS
  Daughter of pharaoh Seti Ramses I. Mother of Moses.
Reincarnation of Wilkiria (16700 B.C.E.), 1500 B.C.E.

AVA   Name of Eve.

AVALON   Captain of the Floridian Mountains Communications Center for
                          the Southwest.
                          Member of the Ashtar Command.

AVENDA   Channel is Nancy Tate.

AVERRAN   From the Galactic Center.
                          Overseers for the evolution & progress on Earth.

AVITUE   Other name of Lilith.

AWAANA   5th dimensional being from the Sun.
                          Member of the Ashtar Command.
                          She is the Commander of the starship Light.

AYIB   Spirit of planet Venus.

AYMELEK   Angel of the Moon.

AYSCHER   Angel.

AZACACHIA   Angel.

AZAEL   Angel. Azael means "Whom God Strengthens".

AZARADEL   Angel that taught the motions of the Moon, fallen angel.

AZARAEL   Angel of Earth.

AZAZAEL   Negative angel, Prince of Darkness.
                          The highest of the Jinns (Genies).
                          He taught (and is still doing) all the hidden knowledge, occult
                          sciences and warring methods to humans.
                          Also known as:
                          >>   Azazel,
                          >>   Baphomet (by the Babylonian Brotherhood),
                          >>   the Devil,
                          >>   Iblis.

AZAZEL   → Azazael.

AZBUGA   One of the 8 great Throne Angels.

AZBUGAH   Other name of Azbuga.

AZIBEEL   Angelic leader, fallen angel.

AZKEEL   Angelic leader, fallen angel.

AZLIEL   Angel of Invocation.

AZRA'IL   Other name of Azrael.

AZRAEL   Archangel, Angel of Death.
                     Also known as Azra'Il.

AZUR-MAH   Intraterrestrial master and regent of the Door of Hayumarca,
                     Peru.

AZURIEL   Lord, one of the six major Seraphim.

BAAL   Other name of Bael.

BABAJI   Immortal Master of the Himalayas in India, his other name is
                     Goraknath.
                     Babaji is an Avatar who had retained his physical form for
                     centuries, is about 5,000 years old.
                     Guru of the 19th Century Indian Master Lahiri Mahasaya.
                     Now incarnated as Almora Baba.
                     He travels by thought, manifests anything needed from the air,
                     dwells mostly in Almora, India.
                     Channel: Elizabeth Clare Prophet.

BABALON   Goddess. Mother of all creation.
                     Avatar of the Eleventh Hour.

BABIEL   Angel of Courage and Motivation.

BACHARI   Was incarnated in Sumeria.
                     Channel is Nancy Tate.

BAEL   Spirit.
                     Also known as:
                     >>   Baal,
                     >>   Marduk.

BAGDIAL   A corpulent angel.

BAHMAN   Other name of Archangel Gabriel.

BAHRAM   Angel of Victory.

BALDOR   Ambassador of the planet Orloff.
                     Channel is Nancy Tate.

BALIDET   Angel of the Air.

BALIN   Galactic Being from Saturn.

BALLATON   Angel.

BALLERIAN   Member of the Ashtar Command.

BALTHAZAR	→ Kuthumi.
BALTHIAL	Angel.
BAPHOMET	Name of Azazael by the Babylonian Brotherhood.
BAR ABBAS	Not Barrabas. He went to France with the rest of the family. → Jesus.
BARACHIEL	Archangel.
BARADI'EL	Ruling angel of the order of Dominions.
BARAKAIAL	Angel of the Stars, fallen angel.
BARAKIEL	Ruling angel prince of the order of Archangels. Ruling angel prince of the order of Virtues. Barakiel means „Lightning of God". Also known as: Barbiel or Barkiel.
BARBELO	Daughter of Pistis Sophia.
BARBIEL	Other name of Barakiel.
BARCHIEL	Angel.
BARDIEL	Angel of Hail.
BARESCHAS	Angel.
BARIEL	Angel of Jupiter.
BARKAIAL	Angel.
BARKIEL	Other name of Barakiel.
BARPHARANGES	Angel.
BARRABAS	→ Bar Abbas.
BARTHOLOMEW	Ascended Master. Channel: Joy Ballas-Beeson, Mary Margaret Moore.
BARTZACHIAH	Angel.
BARUCH	Chief Guardian Angel of the Tree of Life.

BASHAR	Benevolent multidimensional being from the year 2863, he is a hybrid. He is from the lush planet Essassani in the Orion constellation. Representative of the Galactic Association of Worlds. Bashar is Arabic and means "Messenger". Channel: Darryl Anka, Walter D. Pullen.
BAT ZUGE	Other name of Lilith.
BATNA	Other name of Lilith.
BATRAAL	Angelic leader, fallen angel.
BEA	Captain, spacewoman.
BEBUROS	Angel.
BEDALIEL	Angel.
BEHEMIEL	Angel.
BEK'TI	A being who crashed 1947 in Roswell, survived and was rescued by the Hopi.
BELLARION	Scientist from planet Venus. Member of the Solar Cross.
BELSAZAR	Powerful Reptilian Lord. Supreme Ruler over the 6 most powerful Reptilian races who had formed a huge intergalactic empire.
BEN NEZ	Angel. → Ruchiel.
BENAD HASCHE	Female angels.
BENOCH	From the Galactic Federation.
BETEA	Lord, one of the six major Seraphim.
BETH	Messiah from Sirius.
BETHEUEL	Angel.
BI-LA	Tibetan guide. → Council of Four.
BILAIR	Other name of Satan.
BILAR	Other name of Satan.
BILID	Other name of Satan.

BLAEF   Angel.

BLAJI   Pleiadian Isrish (Master-teacher). Interdimensional traveler from
                       the future. She has been a great teacher to many.
                       She is in telepathic contact with James Gilliland.

BOB SOLOMON   Extraterrestrial, 200 years old (1955).
                       → Buck Nelson.

BOEL   Throne Angel.

BOHINDRA   Grandfather of Eve, patriarch of the Kobdas.
                       Magician of love, 8400 B.C.E.

BOREALIS   High Priestess of the Mother Temple from Venus, but not born
                       on Venus. Extraterrestrial from Venus.
                       → Rolf Telano.

BUALU   Angel of Omnipotence.

BUDDHA   Lord of the World. Ascended Master, teacher of light.
                       His spirit guides: Isis & Orfeo.
                       His mother: Maya (Mayadevi). His father Suddhodana, born in
                       Kapilavastu, Nepal, 600 B.C.E., (550 – 479 B.C.E.).
                       Messenger of Sanat Kumara.
                       Founded Buddhism in the 6th century B.C.E.
                       Carries the Christ Energy.
                       Also known as:
                       >> Gautama,
                       >> Gautama Buddha.

BURCHAT   Angel.

BUTATOR   Angel of Calculations.

CABRIEL   Angel.

CADMIEL   Angel.

CADMUS   Of Phoenicia, other name of Enoch.
                       → Enoch.

CAHETEL   Seraphim.

CAIN   Was not the son of Adam, was the son of Enki.
                       Was married to his half-sister Luluwa (Annunaki princess).

CALUEL   Angel.

CAMAEL

Archangel, Angel Chief of the order of Powers, one of the holy Sefiroth.
Ruling angel of the order of Seraphim.

CAMBIEL

Angel.

CAMBILL

Angel.

CANDOR

Female Space Commander from the 3rd star of the Pleiades from the spacecraft Azelda.   Her age is about 700 years, they can live up to 2000 years or more.
On her planet are about 150 million people, they have physical bodies.

CAPABILE

Angel messenger of the Sun.

CAPHRIEL

Angel.

CARACASA

Angel of Spring.

CASSIEL

Archangel, Governor of Saturn.
He is one of the Seven Rays of the Christ Word.

CASSION

Member of the Ashtar Command and the Great White Brotherhood.
Channel: Lyara.

CASTIEL

Angel.

CATHETEL

Angel.

CAZEKIEL

God of Eternal Bliss. Ascended Master.
He has long golden hair and a golden beard.

CECEA

Female intraterrestrial master and regent of the inner retreats in South America.

CEDAR

Angel.

CEILIARA

Being of Gaia.

CEPHETAS

Lord, one of the six major Seraphim.

CERES

A guide from Venus.

CERVIHEL

Ruling angel prince of the order of Principalities.

CETTI

Member of the Ashtar Command and the Great White Brotherhood.
Channel: Lyara.

CHABALYM

Cherub, Seraph.

CHAIOTH	Angel.
CHAMAEL	Said to be an archangel.
CHAMUEL	Lord, Archangel of the 3rd (pink) Ray. Archangel of Love, Angel of Adoration. Chamuel means „He who sees God". Channel: Geraldine Innocente, Mark Prophet.
CHAMYEL	Throne Angel.
CHARBIEL	Angel.
CHARMAN	Angel.
CHARMS	Angel.
CHARON	Refugee from planet Styx in Orion. → Phoenix.
CHAROUM	Angel.
CHASAN	Angel.
CHASCHMALIM	Angel of Invention.
CHASMALI	Angel.
CHASSAN	Angel.
CHASSIEL	Angel.
CHAYLON	Cherub, Seraph, invoked in ritual magic.
CHAYO	Throne Angel.
CHAYYIEL	Cherubim.
CHERATIEL	Angel.
CHERIOUR	Angel.
CHERMES	Angel.
CHIRON	Master Chiron is another who is returning from the Alpha Centaurian complex.
CHISMAEL	Spirit of planet Jupiter.
CHOCKMAHEL	Angel.

CHOSNIEL Angel.

CHRONOS King of Atlantis.

CHUPACABRA A chupacabra is an ugly, hairy creature about 4 ft tall, large standup ears on top of it's head, huge eyes of varying colors, long skinny arms and legs with claws, and a tail.

CHURCARA Reptilian, contacted Meisha Johnston.

CLARION Lady Clarion.

CLAYMORE, RONALD
Grand Space Commander. 9th interdimensionality.
Ronald in Glay at the University of San Tam.

COBAZAR Father of the Draconian Jehovah.

COLARION Grand Master.
The wise councilor from the "Council of Nine".

COLOPATIRON Angel.

COLUMBUS Incarnation of Saint Germain.

COMATO Angel.

COMMISSOROS Angel of Spring.

COMTE DE SAINT-GERMAIN
→ St. Germain.

CONDERIUS From Uranus, lived before in the Peruvian Andes, three lives on Venus.

CONFUCIUS Lord, Ascended Master.
Was born in a poor family in the year 551 B.C.E. in the state of Lu.
His Twin Flame is Lady Cassandra.
Incarnation of Djwhal Khul.

CORABAEL Angel.

CORAT Angel of the Air.

COSIMA Space being from another universe.

COUNT OF SAINT GERMAIN
→ St. Germain.

COUNT ST. GERMAIN
→ St. Germain.

CROESUS   Of the "Praying Mantis" race on Mars.
Incarnations:
>> Croesus, king of Lydia (Western Turkey),
>> Suleiman II.
Member of the Planetary Council.

CRONOS   Came with his family group from planet Styx in Orion.
The refugees landed on planet Phoenix in the Solar System.
He is responsible for creating planet Pluto.
→ Pluto.

CRUCIEL   Angel.

CUPRA   Personification of Light. One of the Novesiles.

CYCLOPEA   Member of the Karmic Board, Lord of Karma for the Earth.
Elohim of the 5th (green) Ray of Concentration, Healing, Music,
Truth.
Cyclopea means „All-Seeing Eye of God".
Twin Flame of Virginia. 14 to 15 ft tall.
Channel: Geraldine Innocente, Mark Prophet.

DAGIEL   Angel.

DAMABIAH   Angel.

DAMEAL   Angel.

DAMSOWZULVITZ
Former Lord of the Alcyones.

DANEL   Angelic leader, fallen angel.

DANIEL   Angel of the order of Principalities.
High holy angel who bears the name of Shemhamphorae.

DAR-NELL   Female extraterrestrial .
Member of the Solar Cross.

DAREL   Angel.

DEGALIEL   Angel.

DELAKA   Grand Space Commander.

DELL   Extraterrestrial entity.

DELRON   From Venus.

DEMETER   Refugee from planet Styx in Orion.
Mother of Cronos.

DERDEKEA	Female angel. Referred to as the Supreme Mother.
DESMORAH	Female from planet Komesso.
DEVAINE	Real name of Devin.
DEVANAGUY	Mother of Krishna, 3000 B.C.E.
DEVECIA	Angel.
DEVIL	Also called Diabolos.
DEVIN	(Devaine) from the race of the Felines lives on the flagship Pelegai. Reigning patriarch of the 9 dimensional Royal House of Avyon. Head of the 9 dimensional Galactic Federation's Nibiruan Council. Son of Shimbala, brother of Jelaila, half-brother of Jehowah.
DEXTRA	Space Commander of a scout ship of the Athena. From the Booth Constellation.
DIABOLOS	Other name of the Devil.
DIAMONTE	She is from starship of Thonn (1948).
DIANA	Lady Master, goddess, really lived. Twin Flame of prince Oromasis.
DIANA	Twin Flame of Elohim Arcturus. Other name of Victoria.
DIANE	Representative of the Galactic Federation. Channel is Mike Quinsey.
DILAKA	Grand Space Commander.
DINA	Angel.
DINIEL	Angel.
DIVAI	Mother of Jehovah, Jelaila.
DIVINE MOTHER	→ Mother Mary, Mother Meera.
DJIBRIL	Spirit.
DJIN	Elemental King. Helper of Archangel Gabriel.

DJWAL KUL   → Djwhal Khul.

DJWHAL KHUL   Master of the 2ⁿᵈ Ray of Love & Wisdom.
                         Tibetan Master who was known as Gai Ben-Jamin.
                         Is able to materialize, dematerialize, bilocate.
                         Also known as:
                         >>   Djwal Kool,
                         >>   Djwal Kul,
                         >>   Master D.K.,
                         >>   The Messenger of the Masters,
                         >>   The Tibetan.
                         Incarnations:
                         >>   Lemuria, with Lord Himalaya,
                         >>   many lives in the mountains of Asia,
                         >>   Kleinias (favorite pupil of Pythagoras),
                         >>   first Chela of Lord Gautama Buddha,
                         >>   Confucius
                         >>   Aryasanga (who translated the Sutras of Patajali).
                         Worked with El Morya, Kuthumi & St. Germain in bringing
                         forth Theosophy.
                         His teacher is Master Kuthumi.
                         Ascended in the 19ᵗʰ century.
                         Channel: Alice Bailey, Edwyn Courtenay, Valerie Donner, Anne
                         Matthews, Terri Newlon, Marc Prophet, Joshua David Stone.

DON JUAN   → Kachora.

DONACHIEL   Angel.

DONEL   Angelic guard.

DONN THOR   Vice Commander of Victor One from Venus.

DONQUEL   Angel of Love.

DOUMA   Other name of Doumah.

DOUMAH   Angel.
                         Also known as: Douma, Duma.

DRACEL   A guide from Venus.

DRACON   Angel.

DRAKKAR   Was a Draconian dark lord. He is gone into the light.

DUCHIEL   Angel.

DUMA   Other name of Doumah.

DUMUZI   First husband of Inanna, son of Enki.

EA   Is Ioannes of Ur, other name of Enki. Son of king An.
                          Genetic scientist.

EEON   Inner Earth guide.
                          Being of a subterranean city 400 miles below Denver,
                          Colorado.

EFI   Martian Master.
                          Channel is Sister Thedra.

EGALMIEL   Angel.

EHERES   Angel.

EIA   Female starship commander from the Fomalhaut System.
                          Member of the Solar Cross.

EIAEL   Angel.

EILO   Other name of Lilith.

EIRNILUS   Angel.

EISHETH ZENUNIM

                          Angel of Prostitution.   One of the 4 mates of Samael.
                          Also known as Isheth Zenunim.

EISTIBUS   Angel of Divination.

EKTOL   From Druan in the Nol System.

EL ADREL   Angel.

EL AURIA   Angel of Flame.

EL EL   Angelic guard.

EL MORYA   Lord (Chohan) of the 1st Ray (Blue Flame).
                          Tibetan Master.
                          Ascended Master from Mercury, friend of Lord Kuthumi,
                          ascended 1898.
                          Has dark brown hair, piercing brown eyes.
                          Came from planet Mercury.
                          Was on planet Lasmur in the Orion constellation.
                          Working for the Brotherhood of Light.
                          His teachers were Hercules and Maha Chohan.
                          Master Kuthumi is a long time friend of him.
                          Works together with Ascended Master Vogoda.
                          His Twin Flame is Amerissis.
                          Founder of the Summit Lighthouse.
                          Founder of the Theosophical Society together with Khutumi.
                          Incarnation on Earth:

>>   Almo, a Priest Scientist in Atlantis,
>>   Abraham from Ur (the Hebrew patriarch), progenitor of
      the twelve tribes,
>>   Melchior (one of the Three Wise Men),
>>   King Akbar the Great (1542 – 1605),
>>   King Arthur, 5th/6th century,
>>   (Saint) Thomas Becket (Archbishop of Canterbury)
      (1118 – 1170), (martyred),
>>   (Saint) Thomas More (1478 – 1535), (martyred),
>>   Thomas Moore, Irish poet, 19th century,
>>   El Morya Khan (Unascended Master), Tibetan Mahatma,
      King of India, retained his body for 325 years before he
      made his ascension (????-1898).
Channel: Ashian Belsey, Christine Davidson, Caroline Fitzgerald
(Radha), Godfre, Dr. Norma Milanovich, Mark Prophet, Carolyn
Shearer, Lori Adaile Toye.
→ Chohans.

EL-TAR   Telepathic Liaison from planet Jupiter working with KOR.
                     Member of the Solar Cross.
                     → KOR, Solar Cross.

EL THONN   Father of Thonn.

ELA   From Arcturus.
                     Channel is Mike Quinsey.

ELAMIZ   Angel.

ELAN   Tribunal Interpreter from Trantor.
                     Member of the Solar Cross.

ELEANOR   She is from the starship Collinesta.

ELEKTRA   Pleiadian from Erra.

ELEXAR   Telepathic Liaison from planet Jupiter working with KOR.
                     Member of the Solar Cross.
                     → KOR, Solar Cross.

ELIHU   Celestial name of Saint Germain.

ELIJAH   Ascended Master, prophet.
                     Incarnation: John the Baptist.
                     Channel: Lisa J. Smith.

ELIMIEL   Angel of the Moon.

ELISHA   Earlier incarnation of Jesus.

ELOA   Female angel.

ELOHIM   Archangel, Hebrew god of the Old Testament. Is the chief manipulator behind the angelic war. He is not Lucifer.

ELOMEEL   Angel.

ELOMNIA   Angel.

ELOUAI   High Angelic Being.

ELRON   Grand Commander. Commander of the Athena.

ELYS   Cosmic Being, mainly 5th or 6th dimensional.
Member of the Ashtar Command.
Officer from Venus, 9 ft tall.

ENECHIE   Angel.

ENEDIEL   Angel of the Moon.

ENJANA   Pleiadian from Erra.

ENKI   Is human and reptilian.
Reigning patriarch of the 4 dimensional House of Aln at this time. Enki has become patriarch of the 5 dimensional House of Aln and also the Head of the 5 dimensional Nibiruan Council representing the Dark.
Father of Cain, Dumuzi, Luluwa, Marduk, Nergal, ...,
Brother of Enlil, son of Id.
Was betrayed and killed by his brother Enlil & his body is buried inside the "Face" tomb on Mars.
In Egypt was called P'taah.
Also known as:
>>   Ea,
>>   P'taah.
Channel is Nancy Tate.

ENLIL   Brother of Enki, son of Anu & Antu, father of Nannar, Ninurta.
Legitimate heir of Nibiru.
Is Jehovah.

ENOCH   Patriarch, real name is Thoth.
Eldest son of Cain, Noah's grandfather.
He lived 385 years and did not die.
Represents Earth on the Planetary Council.
Was the Messenger of Sanat Kumara.
Full member of the Galactic Councils aboard the admiral ships of Ashtar & Sananda.
Incarnation of Lord Sananda.
"The man who walked with God".
Influenced prophets such as Nostradamus, Edgar Cayce.
Also known as:
>> Cadmus (of the Phoenicians),

>> Edris (in the Koran),
>> Henoch,
>> Henok,
>> Nokodemion,
>> Palamedes (of the Greeks),
>> Thoth (god of the Egyptians),
>> Ziasandra (in Sumeria).
Channel: J.J.Hurtak.
→ Thoth.

EOLUTH   Cherub, Seraphim.

ERESHKIGAL   Half-sister of Inanna, daughter of Nannar, wife of Nergal.

ERISA   Telepathic Liaison from Trantor working with KOR.
                        Member of the Solar Cross.
                        → KOR, Solar Cross.

ERJABEL   A guide from Apu, in charge of the medical orbiting base
                        Columo.

ERNON   Rai of Suern. Prophet, 11,000 B.C.E.
                        A Messenger of God at the time of Atlantis.

EROSOTI   Planetary genius of Mars.

ERTRAEL   Angel.

ESCHIEL   Angel.

ESOLA   Lord of planet Jupiter.
                        Member of the Spiritual Hierarchy.

ESPIACENT   Angel.

ESTRELLIA SHERAN
                        It is not her real name up there. She has no biological relation to
                        the Sheran's. Her job: do any kind of mapping or astronomical
                        information.

ESU   Lord of planet Earth. Jesus name on celestial level. Sananda, his
                        real name.
                        Member of the Spiritual Hierarchy.

ETEL   A guide from Venus.

ETH   Angelic Power.

ETNAKIEL   Intraterrestrial master from Mt. Sinai, Egypt.

EUCHEY   Angel.

EURABATRES	Angel of planet Venus.
EVA/EVANA	Mother of Abel, real name: Evana de Ethea, 300 B.C.E.
EXCALABAR	Grand Space Commander of the White robes.
EXCALIBUR	Is a force from the advanced civilization of Arcturian.
EZEKEAL	Lord, one of the six major Seraphim.
EZEKIEL	Archangel, Angel of Death & Transformation. Was in Sananda's craft.
EZGADI	Angel.
EZRIELI	Angel.
FAITH	Archangel.
"Falcon"	32,000 B.C.E., 11,000 B.C.E.
FAMIEL	Angel of the Air.
FANUEL	Throne Angel.
FAVARDIN	Cherubim.
FILON	From Alexandria, (reincarnation as Kobda Babel, Prophet Nathan of Salomon, Joseph (son of Jacob & Esen)), adoptive son of Moses, founder of the Essener School.
FIRKON	Extraterrestrial, Martian friend of George Adamski in 1953 and 1954.
FLORENA	Pleiadian from Erra.
FRACIEL	Angel.
FROMZON	Angel.
FURLAC	Angel of the Earth.
FUTINIEL	Angel.
GABRIEL	God's messenger, Throne Angel. Archangel of Annunciation. Ruling angel prince of the order of Archangels. Ruling angel prince of the order of Cherubim. Angel of Death, Dreams, Fire, Life, Mercy, Mysteries, Prayer, Resurrection, Revelation, Vengeance. Works on the 4th (white) Ray of Ascension with Master Serapis Bey.

Gabriel dictated the Koran to Mohammed.

Gibril is the Islamic name of Gabriel.

Gabriel means „God is my Strength", „Hero of God", „Man of God".

He is in charge of soldier-angels and is responsible for the extinction of nations. Is said to be the angel that destroyed Sodom.

Subordinate of Metatron. Boss of Uzziel.

Also known as:

>>   Bahman,

>>   Gibril

>>   Lord of the Astral Plane.

Channel: Robert Baker, Bev (Dranda) Dombrowski.

GABRIELLA   Angel.

GABUTHELON   Angel.

GAIA   Also known as:

>>   Goddess of Earth,

>>   Lady Earth,

>>   Lady Gaia,

>>   Mother Earth,

>>   Mother Gaia,

>>   Virgo.

→ Virgo.

GALGALIEL   Angel.

GALIMAI-A   Cmdr. of the Ashtar Command.

Also known as Cmdr. Ashida, Ray-ella Le El.

Daughter of Ashtar & Athena.

→ Starship Alignment.

GALIZUR   Other name of Archangel Raziel.

GALMON   Angelic guard.

GAMIEL   Angel.

GANESH   Ascended Master.

GARGATEL   One of the 3 Angels of Summer.

GAUTAMA   Lord of the World.

→ Buddha.

GAUTAMA BUDDHA

→ Buddha.

GAVIEL   Angel of summer.

GAZARDIEL Angel.

GEDARIAH Angel.

GELIEL Angel of the Moon.

GENO Angel of the order of Powers.

GERMAEL Angel.

GERMAIN → Germaine.

GERMAINE Ascended Master. Lord of the Violet Ray.
Member of the Ashtar Command.
Also known as Germain, Germane, St.Germaine, St.Germain,
Saint Germaine.
Incarnations:
>> Leonardo da Vinci.
>> William Shakespeare.
>> Lived in France in the 18th century.
Channel: Lilian Whalley.

GERMANE A group consciousness energy. Germane therefore chose this
term to somewhat personify his energy.
Channel: Lyssa Royal Holt.
→ Germaine.

GETHEL Angel.

GIBRIL → Gabriel.

GIEL Angel.

GILGAMESH Illegitimate grandson of Utu, his mother was Aruru.

GLASSTARIA From the mothership Centralia.

GLAURA Other name of Glauron.

GLAURON Spirit of the air.
Also known as Glaura.

GLENZIA She is from Mars.

GLMARIJ Angel.

GLON From the Galactic Command.

GLUND-OYARSA Lord of the Solar System.
Member of the Spiritual Hierarchy.

GOD

Exist of 12 single "spirits".

Also known as: Abba, Abhir, Abonsam, Absolute, Ada, Adelphia, Adibuddha, Adonai, Afra, Aglibol, Agni, Ahriman, Ahura Mazda, Ahuramazd, Akongo, Aksobhya, Ala, Alatangana, Alfalfa, All Light All Darkness, All Soul, Allah, Allmächtiger, Almighty, Alochem, Amaterasu, Amaterasu-Ohmikami, Amerissis, Amitabha, Amma, Amoghasiddhi, Amon, Amora, Anat, Ancient of Days, Anuket, Aondo, Apap, Arebati, Arion, Asase Yaa, Ash, Asherah, Ashtoreth, Astrea, Ataa Naa Nyongmo, Atete, Atum, Aum, Aum-En-Ra, Bes, Bhaga, Brama, Branch, Brother, Bumba, Cagu, Cghene, Cha Ara, Cosmic Consciousness, Creation, Creator, Creator of The Universe, Deidad, Déu, Deus, Deva, Devi, Dios, Divine, Durba, Duty, Edeke, Ehyeh Asher Ehyeh, Ekanetra, Eknath, El, El Elyon, El Hai, El Olam, El Roi, Eloah, Elohim, Elohim El Elyon, Elohim El Olam, Elohim El Roi, Elohim El Shaddai, Enundu, Eurynome, Father, Father of Lights, Father of my Father, Fidi Mukullu, Gaunab, Gauri Matta, Gayatri, Gibini, God Almighty, God Most High, God-the-Father, Gott, Govinda, Grand-father, Grand-mother, Great Life, Great Mother, Great Spirit, Ha Shem, HaShem, Hadad, Hanuman, Hao, Hari, Ha'shem, He Who Has No Name, Heh, Hehet, Hemantadevi, Hiranyagarbha, Holy Spirit, Holy Trinity, Hu, Huang Ti, I Am, Imana, Io mataaho, Io matangaro, Io matanui, Io matua, Io matua te kore, Io nui, Io roa, Io take take, Io te pukenga, Io te toi o nga rangi, Io te wananga, Io te whiwhia, Ishi, Ishvara, Ishwara, Itonde, Jah, Jahmanjah, Jave, Jehovah, Jehovah Elohim, Jehovah-Jireh, Jehovah-M'Kaddesh, Jehovah-Nissi, Jehovah-Rohi, Jehovah-Rophe, Jehovah-Sabaoth, Jehovah-Shalom, Jehova-Shammah, Jehovah-Tsidkenu, Judge, Ka Tyeleo, Kadosh, Kalisia, Kalunga, Kartikeya, Kek, Keket, Khnum, King of All Kings, King of Heaven, Kotisri, Kuladevata, Kurios, Kwoth, Kyumbe, Legba, Lesa, Libanza, Loki, Lord, Lord God, Lord of Hosts, Lord of the Universe, Lord our Master, Love, Ma Kiela, Maat, Mahaveera, Maiterya, Manjushri, Masri, Mbomba, Mbongo, Mbotumbo, Meresger, Mizu-Ha-No-Me, Mukulumncandi, Mungu, My Creator, Na Ngutu, Naunet, Ndaula, Ngai, Niamye, Nyame, Nzambi, Oduduwa, Ogiuwu, Oi, Omichle, Omsa, One, Onuris, Ophion, Orunmila, Osanobua, Our Father, Oversoul, Padma Sambhava, Pain, Paramatama, Parvati, Patar, Pavan-Suta, Pemba, Phyi-sGrub, Prajapati, Primordial Consciousness, Radha-Swami, Raluvimbha, Ram, Rastafari, Ratnasamhava, Ratri, Rubanga, Sa, Saphat, Satyanarayana, Shaddai, Shankpana, Shekin, Shekinah, Shepherd, Shu, Sia, Source, Source of All, Suchinito, Suku, Supreme Being, Supreme Creative Force, Supreme Creator, Svarog, Takkiraja, Tao, Tar, Tara, Te Kore, Tefenet, The Creator, Theos, Thunor, Thy Maker, Torout, Tsunigoab, Tzevaot, Umvelinkwangi, Universal Dreamer, Universal Mind, Unkulunkulu, Unumbote, Vairochana, Vaivasvata Manu, Vajrasattva, Vayu, Venilateshwer, Venkatachalapath, Venkateshwara, Vighneshwer, Vinayail, Virat, Vishwa, Waka, Weri Kumbamba, Woden, Ya 'Aahad, Ya 'Aakhir, Ya 'Aazalee,

Ya 'Aallah, Ya 'Aawwal, Ya 'Aadil, Ya 'Azeez, Ya 'Azeem, Ya 'Alim, Ya 'Ali, Ya Ba'eeth, Ya Baaqiy, Ya Baari, Ya Barr, Ya Baseet, Ya Basir, Ya Batin, Ya Fatih, Ya Ghaffaar, Ya Ghanee, Ya Ha'iy, Ya Hadi, Ya Hafiz, Ya Hakim, Ya Hakim-al-Mutlaq, Ya Halim, Ya Hameed, Ya Haqq, Ya Hasib, Ya Hatim, Ya Jaami, Ya Jabbar, Ya Jaleel, Ya Jameel, Ya Kabeer, Ya Kareem, Ya Khabeer, Ya Khafeez, Ya Khalaaq, Ya Lateef, Ya Majid, Ya Malik, Ya Malik-al-Mulk, Ya Manee', Ya Mannaan, Ya Mateen, Ya Mu'akhherr, Ya Mu'idd, Ya Mubdee, Ya Mughnee, Ya Muhayim, Ya Muhyee, Ya Mujeeb, Ya , Mukeed, Ya Mukhbeer, Ya Mumeed, Ya Mumeen, Ya Muntaqim, Ya Muqaddeem, Ya Muqsit, Ya Muqtadir, Ya Musawwir, Ya Muta'alee, Ya Mutakabbeer, Ya Nafi', Ya Noor, Ya Qadeer, Ya Qawee, Ya Qayyoom, Ya Quahhar, Ya Quddos, Ya Ra'oof, Ya Rabb, Ya Raffee, Ya Raheem, Ya Rahmaan, Ya Raqeeb, Ya Rasheed, Ya Razzaaq, Ya Saboor, Ya Salaam, Ya Samee', Ya Sammad, Ya Shaakir, Ya Shahid, Ya Shakoor, Ya Tawwab, Ya Waahid, Ya Waarith, Ya Wadood, Ya Wahhab, Ya Wajeed, Ya Wakeel, Ya Walee, Ya Walee al-Ahsan, Ya Waliy, Ya Wasi', Yah, Yahweh, Yahweh Adonai, Yahweh Elohim, Yahweh Jireh, Yahweh Maccaddeshcem, Yahweh Nissi, Yahweh Ropheka, Yahweh Sabbaoth, Yahweh Shalom, Yahweh Shammah, Yahweh Tsidkenu, Yaro, Yemekonji, Yezdan, YHWH, Zurvan.
→ Supreme Creative Force.

GODAR A guide from Apu.

GODFRE Ascended Master.
Divine Complement, Twin Flame of Ascended Lady Master Lotus.
Incarnations: Guy Ballard.

GOO-LING Ascended Master, Saint.
Member of the Great White Brotherhood.

GOR-ED Telepathic Liaison working with KOR.
Member of the Solar Cross.
→ KOR, Solar Cross.

GORAKNATH → Babaji.

GOTZONE Angel, messenger.

GRADIEL Angel of Mars.
Gradiel means: „Might of God".

GRAMAHA From the Ashtar Galactic Command.

GRETCHEENYAL Female Verdant, also called Gina.

GUABAREL Angel of autumn.

GURID   Angel.

GUTRIX   Angel of the Air.

HA-TONN   Other name of Hatonn.

HAATAN   Genius.

HABBIEL   Angel.

HAHAEL   Other name of Hahahel.

HAHAHEL   Virtue. Also called Hahael.

HAHAIAH   Cherubim.

HAKAMIAH   Cherubim. Guardian of France.

HAKEM   Angelic guard.

HALACHO   Genius.

HALLIZA   Angel.

HALUDIEL   Angel.

HAM MEYUCHAD   Cherubim.

HAMAL   Angel.

HAMATIEL   Angel.

HAMIED   Angel of Miracles.

HANANIEL   Archangel.

HANIEL   Archangel, Virtue. Ruling angel prince of the orders of Principalities & Virtues.
Also known as Anael.

HANNUEL   Angel.

HANTIEL   Angel.

HARABAEL   Angel of the Earth.

HARIEL   Angel of Animals.

HARONE   Zeta Reticuli consciousness.

HARSHIEL   Angel.

HARUDHA   Angel of Water.

HARVIEL   Angelic guard.

HASHMAL   Ruling angel of the order of Dominions (Dominations).

HASHMED   Angel of Annihilation.

HASMODIA   Spirit of the Moon.

HATHOR   Goddess, wife of all gods, sister of Sekmeth.
                       She is also known as Shiva.
                       Represents an ascended civilization of the 4th / 5th dimension.

HATIPHAS   Genius.

HATONN   Lord, Grand Chief Commander of the 7th Fleet.
                       Reptilian being, 9 ½ ft tall.
                       There is also a Reptilian faker with this name.
                       He is from the planet Termin(o)us Hatonn in the Vela System.
                       Teacher & Master of the Higher Worlds.
                       A Keeper of the Akashic Records, Record Keeper for the Space
                       Confederation.   He is assigned to starship Hatonn.
                       Chief Councilor for the Council of 48.
                       Of the Space Council.
                       Speaker of the Great Solar Tribunal of the Space Federation.
                       From the Galactic Federation of Planets.
                       Member of the Ashtar Command. Member of the Solar Cross.
                       Was the instructor of Pharaoh Cheops in Egypt.
                       Friend of Soltec.
                       Also known as Ha-Tonn.
                       Channel is Tuella.

HAVEN   Genius of Dignity.

HAYYEL   Angel of Animals.

HEIGLOT   Angel of Snow Storms.

HELEMMELEK   Angel.

HELENA   Captain of the starship Capricorn of the Galatic Federation.
                       Channel is Lavar.

HELIO-AH   Arcturian.

HELIOS   Cosmic Being.
                       Divine Complement of Vesta.

HELISON   Angel.

HENOCH   Other name of Enoch.

HENOK			Other name of Enoch.

HERAKHAN BABA

A master of great love and power.
Manifested his adult body from the ethers in a cave near
Herakhan, India in 1970. There he sat for 45 days in motionless
meditation, not eating, drinking or sleeping. He took over his
ashram of previous incarnations in Herakhan and left his body in
1984.

HERCULES			Elohim of the 1st (blue) Ray of Faith, God's Will, Power.
Hercules means „Glory of the Air".
Twin Flame of Amazonia. Teacher of El Morya.

HERMES			Teacher of Light, Master & Teacher of Universal Wisdom.
Member of the Planetary Council.
Ancient Egyptian sage.
Was called „the Scribe of the Gods".
Incarnation of Ascended Master God Mercury.
→ Tehuti, Thoth (Hermes Trismegistus).

HERMES TRISMEGISTUS
Means "Thrice Great".
→ Hermes, Thoth.

HEROS			Elohim of the 3rd (pink) Ray of Charity, Compassion, Divine
Love, Omnipresence.
Twin Flame of Amora.

HILARION			Ascended Master of Mount Nebo.
Lord (Great Chohan) of the 5th Ray (Emerald Ray, Green
Flame), he lives in Emerald City.
Born at Tabatha, near Gaza, Palestine, about 290 – 372.
Has golden hair, blue eyes.
Member of Earth's Spiritual Hierarchy. Member of the Ashtar
Command.
Incarnations:
>> A priest in the Temple of Truth, Atlantis,
>> Saint Hilarion,
>> Saint Paul the Apostle (Saul of Tarsus),
>> Iamblichus, born in Coele, Syria.
Channel: B. Cooke, Lois Hartwick, Lisa Holloway, Lyara,
Elizabeth Clare Prophet.
→ Chohans.

HILKAR			Wise man from Atlantis, 16700 B.C.E.
First notary of Antulio.

HIMALAYA			Lord.

HISMAEL			Spirit of Jupiter.

HIZARBIN	Genius of the Sea.
HNGEL	Angel.
HODNIEL	Angel.
HOLY MARY	Mother Mary.
HOMOGENIUS	Scientist of Uranus landed 1973 close to Vienna, Austria. Lived in Theosapia, Middle Greece 371 B.C.E., moved 335 B.C.E. to Venus. Channel: P. Leopold.
HORMUZ	Angel.
HORUS	Came from civilization Altea by space ship. Member of the Planetary Council. Eldest son of Osiris.
HUMASTRAV	Angel.
HURMIZ	Daughter of Lilith.
HUSAEL	Angel.
IACOAJUL	Angel.
IADARA	Angel.
IAHMEL	Angel of the Air.
IAX	Angel.
IBHAKU	Space Commander from the Toucan star cluster.
IBLIS	Other name of Azazael.
ICIRIEL	Angel of the Moon.
ICU	A guide from Apu.
ID	Mother of Enki. Princess of the Dragon People.
IDRAEL	Angelic guard.
IEDIMIEL	Angel.
IEHUIAH	Angel.
IEIAIEL	Angel of the Future.

IELAHIAH	Angel.
IETUQIEL	Angel.
IGGERETH	Other name of Agrat Bat Mahlat.
IKKAR SOF	Angel.
ILLURU	Reptilian being.
ILMUTH	Female Martian who was in contact with George Adamski in 1953.
IMMANUEL	Lord, one of the six major Seraphim.
IMRIEL	Angel. Imriel means „Eloquence of God".
IN HII	Angel of the North Star.
INA	First leader of the Ughu Mongulala.
INANNA	Cousin of Marduk, daughter of Nannar & Ningal, wife of Dumuzi, Sargon, ... → Ishtar, Thel Dar.
INDRIEL	Angel.
INGETHAL	Angel.
IOANNES	Also known as Ea in Ur.
IOELET	Angel.
IOFIEL	Archangel. Also known as: Yofiel, Zophiel. → Zophiel.
IONEL	Archangel of Healing & Health.
IREL	Angel.
ISADOS	Pleiadian from Erra.
ISDA	Angel of Food.
ISHETH ZENUNIM	Other name of Eisheth Zenunim.
ISHLIAH	Angel.
ISHRA	Woman officer from Saturn.

ISHTAR	Other name of: >> Astarte, >> Inanna.
ISIS	Name of Ninhursag in ancient Egypt, also called Ninti. Represents divine recreative power. Member of the Council of 12. (Ur) Spirit guide for: Anfion, Buddha, Numu. Wife of Ra. Came from civilization Altea by space ship. Daughter of king Atlas of Atlantis. Channel: Jan Eaton. → Ninti.
ISLANDA	She is from the Andromeda Galaxy.
ISMA'IL	Guardian angel.
ISMOLI	Angel of the Air.
ISRAEL	Throne Angel.
ISRAFEL	Archangel, Angel of Music, Resurrection. Israfel means „the Burning One". Also known as Israfil.
ISRAFIL	Other name of Israfel.
ISROSS	Grand Space Commander from the planet Arcturia from Sirius.
ITA	Other name of Lilith.
ITHACAR	→ Ithakar.
ITHAKAR	Interdimensional being from Mars. Member of the Ashtar Command. Works on starship Crystal Bell under Captain Woodok.
ITHURIEL	Angel.
ITKAL	Angel.
ITQAL	Angel.
IZHAR	Venusian in charge of initiation temples on Venus planets.
IZORPO	Other name of Lilith.
J. W.	From Jupiter. Member of the Ashtar Command. Channel: Gloria Lee.

JAHOEL   Ruling angel of the order of Seraphim.

JAHOVAH   → Jehovah.

JAMES   Apostle.

JAMES   Second officer on starship of Thonn (1948).

JANIEL   Angel.

JANUS   Light Being.
                       He is a navigator on the mothership Pegasus that is propelled by
                       thought.
                       Combination of humanoid & positive loving & positive loving
                       reptilian characteristics. Very large eyes, nostrils (does not use
                       oxygen to breathe) and an opening for nourishment, smooth
                       body with an appendage at the hips.

JAOEL   Other name of Jehoel.

JAPHKIEL   Ruling angel prince of the order of Thrones.

JARIEL   Angel.

JAZAR   Genius.

JEDUTHUM   Other name of Jeduthun.

JEDUTHUN   Angel that leads 1550 other angels.

JEHIEL   Angel of Animals.

JEHOEL   Angel of Fire.

JEHOSHAPHAT   From Jupiter.
                       Head wedge-shaped and broad at the back and narrowing to a
                       pointing nose in front, the ears are holes partly covered with a
                       flexible fold of skin, scaly tough skin in a wide variety of green
                       tones, rows and rows of small   teeth, has a tail, hands are long,
                       thin and claw-like, three slender fingers.

JEHOSHUA   He became the favorite of the Egyptian Pharaoh.
                       Incarnation of Lord Sananda.

JEHOVAH   Is Enlil.
                       Jehovah is the reigning patriarch of the 9 dimensional House of
                       Aln.
                       Head of the 9D Nibiruan Council.
                       Son of Divai & the Draconian Cobazar, half-brother of Devin.

JEHOWAH   → Jehovah.

JEHUDIEL   Ruling angel prince of the order of Archangels.

JEHUEL   Prince of Fire.

JELAILA   → Jelaila Starr.
Sister of Devin, daughter of Divai.

JELIEL   Seraph.

JEMETIEM   From Uranus, lived before in the Peruvian Andes, after that one
life on Venus.

JENIS   Telepathic Liaison working with KOR.
Member of the Solar Cross.
→ KOR, Solar Cross.

JERAZOL   Angel of Power.

JERHOAM   Master.
Channel John J. Oliver.

JESUS   Lord of the 6th Ray.
10th dimensional being, Hybrid.
World Teacher jointly with Kuthumi since Jan. 1, 1956.
Held the 6th Ray for 2,000 years.
Ascended Master, Twin Flame of Lady Master Magda.
Is a son of the Elohim.
Member of the Great White Brotherhood.
Was one of the greatest Spiritual Healers.
Studied in Egypt, Greece, Persia, Syria, and Tibet.
Traveled around the globe, at the age of 14 with Joseph in
Glastonbury.
Was born Feb. 16, 2 C.E. It is said he was born 7 B.C.E., but
true birthday is on April 24.
Did not die at the cross but died at Massanda in 64 B.C.E.
It was Lord Maitreya, who ascended after the crucifixion, not
Jesus. 9 years after the crucifixion Jesus incarnated as Apollonius
of Tyana, who was a great teacher and philosopher.
Chief of Hoova.
Is not a member of the Ashtar Command.
Initiated by Lord Maitreya and the Pleiadians.
First incarnation was Amilius.
Also known as Orthon, Sananda.
Jesus is Greek, means Joshua or Jehoshua.
It is said that Jesus Christ never existed, it was a complement of 3 persons:
>>   *Yeshua Ben Joseph,*
>>   *Yeshua Malathiel,*
>>   *his son Bar Abbas.*
Channel: Isaac George, George King.
→ Adam, Amilius, Bar Abbas, Elisha, Enoch, Jehoshua,
Jmmanuel, Joshua, Maitreya, Melchizedek, Sananda, Yeshua
Malathiel, Zend.

JEU   Angel, Overseer of Light, Power.

JHASUA   → Sananda, highest commander of Earth for all inhabitants. His spirit guides are: Aelohin, Ariel.
                          Father: Joseph of Nazareth, mother: Myriam of Jericho.

JHUDIEL   Angel.

JIBRIL   Archangel.

JILL THOR   She is from Venus.

JMMANUEL   Spiritual leader, who later was known as Jesus.
                          His father was Gabriel of the Pleiades, his mother was Mary of Lyran descent.

JOEVAN   Father of Eve from Atlantis (country: Otlana), (8350 B.C.E.).

JOHN the APOSTLE
                          → Kuthumi.

JOHN the BAPTIST
                          Incarnation of Elijah.

JOMIAEL   Angel.

JON-TON   Commander.

JOPHIEL   Archangel of Illumination of the 2nd (yellow/golden)Ray.
                          Ruling angel prince of the order of Thrones.
                          Was the first World Teacher for our world.
                          Jophiel means "Beauty of God".
                          Channel: Mark Prophet.

JOR-EL   He is a walk-in.

JOSEPH of Aramaea
                          Traveled with Jesus around the world,
                          Came from civilization Altea.

JOSEPH   Chief of civilization Aragon.

JOSHUA   Prophet.
                          Joshua is Hebrew, means Jesus {Greek}.
                          Of the Spiritual Hierarchy.
                          Incarnation of Lord Sananda (Jesus).
                          Assisted Moses to lead the Jews to the Promised Land.
                          Member of the Ashtar Command.
                          Channel: Lucy Colson.
                          → Sananda.

JOUSTRIEL	Angel.
JOVE	Other name Jupiter (Roman god). Member of the Planetary Council for Jupiter. He is almost 9 ft tall and completely bald, sparkling green eyes.
JOYSIA	Feline from the 9D House of Avyon. Chief Genetics Engineer from the Galactic Federation's Sirian A Council. Head of Earth's accelerated DNA Recoding Program from the Sirian A Alliance.
JULIANO	Is Arcturian. Channel: David K. Miller.
JULLIANO	→Juliano.
JUNO	Avatar, Magician of thunder & storm, from Lemuria, his spiritual guides: Aheloin, Ariel. 45800 - 45755 B.C.E.
JUPITER	→ Jove.
JYCONDRIA	Commander from the Ashtar Space Command, Assistant to Ashtar. Member of the Ashtar Command. Channel: Lyara.
KA-L-LIA	Telepathic Liaison from Maldek, works with KOR. Member of the Solar Cross. → KOR, Solar Cross.
KABNIEL	Angel.
KABSHIEL	Angel.
KACHORA	Grandfather Kachora is the real „Don Juan" of the Carlos Castaneda books.
KADAR	→ Kadar-Monka.
KADAR-MONKA	Protector of the Earth, Space Master. Ashtar Command. Father of Soltec. Representative of Earth on the Great Tribunal of the Saturn-Tribunal & Space Federation. Member of the Solar Cross. Channel: Winfield Brownell.
KADI	Angel. Also known as Kadiel.
KADIEL	Other name of Kadi.
KADJINA	→ Lady Kadjina.

KADRU   Naga goddess.

KAHLNA   → Kalna.

KAIEL SHERAN   Eldest son of Mikael Ashtar.
                       A representative of the Galactic Federation Council.

KAIN   Adoptive brother of Abel, 8300 B.C.E.
                       His symbol: RING OF THE RED SERPENT, founder of the
                       black magician (later of Sumer), he took his mother Eve as
                       hostage in Nairi, Kurdistan.

KAKABEL   Angel.

KALI   Hindu Goddess.
                       Kali is represented as a black woman with 4 arms; in one hand
                       she has a sword, in another hand the head of a slain demon. For
                       earrings she has 2 dead bodies and wears a necklace of skulls. She
                       has 3 red eyes, her face and breasts are besmeared with blood.
                       Her tongue protrudes from her mouth, she has white teeth.
                       Her only clothing is a girdle of 50 dead men's hands that
                       represents one of the 50 letters of the Sanskrit alphabet. With
                       one foot she stands on the breast of her husband Shiva.
                       Is said to be Kalimath, the sister of Cain's wife Luluwa.
                       Also known as:
                       >>   Dark Mother,
                       >>   Demon Slayer,
                       >>   Kali Ma,
                       >>   Kali the Destroyer,
                       >>   Kalika,
                       >>   Kalimath,
                       >>   Lady of Life,
                       >>   Lilith,
                       >>   Maha Kali,
                       >>   The Black Goddess,
                       >>   The Dark Goddess.
                       Channel: Elizabeth Clare Prophet.

KALIEB   Grand Chief Commander.
                       Interdimensional being from the planet of Kahrona in Orion.
                       Approx. 994 years old, 7 to 9 ft tall, brown hair and eyes, almond
                       shaped eyes.
                       Member of the Orion Command.
                       His scout ship is approx. 30 ft in diameter, 21 ft in height, he has
                       2 assistants.

KALNA   Female Venusian who was in contact with George Adamski in
                       1953. Also known as Kahlna.

KAMAEL   Other name of Camael.

KANDILE   Angel.

KANSAS   Brother of king Ugrasena, 3000 B.C.E.
                       Member of the Red Serpent.

KAOS   God from the authority of the kingdom of God.

KAPELLA   Spirit guide of: Abel.

KAPILA   Also known as Kapila-Kumara.
                       One of the Seven Holy Kumaras.
                       One of the Seven Sons of Brahma.
                       → Seven Holy Kumaras.

KAPILA-KUMARA
                       → Kapila.

KARTTIKEYA   → Sanat Kumara.

KATONIS   Psychologist of planet Uranus.
                       Member of the Solar Cross.

KAY-NEE   Being from the future of the race of the Karidel Paschats.
                       → Karidel, Paschats, Sirius(Yellow Sun).

KATZFIEL   Angel Prince of the Sword.

KEA   Other name of Lilith.

KELEMARIAH   Female.

KEMIEL   Angel.

KEMUEL   Other name of Camael.

KEPHAREL   Angel.

KERUB   Angel.

KERUBIEL   Ruling angel prince of the order of Cherubim.

KERUBIM   Angel.

KFIAL   Angel.

KHOACH   Reptilian being from Tiphon (Draco).

KHRISNA

Avatar. Is considered the perfect example of the Divine.

Prince of justice & peace, born in the island of Bombay (49 towers like these in Lemuria (Numu)), 3000 B.C.E. Traveled to Tibet & Ceylon.

Complete white hair at the age of 25.

Wrote: Bhagavad-Gita & Uphanishad.

His disciples wrote: Vedas, Puranas, Mahabharata, Righveda & Zenda Avesta of the Persians.

Took his knowledge in Golconda from copies of the Antulion Chronicles.

Was killed by an arrow directly into his heart.

His disciples: Arjuna, Zenda & Paricien fled to Nepal & Tibet.

Incarnation of Sai Baba, Sananda, Vishnu.

KHUFU

6257 B.C.E.

KI, Dr.

→ Ontein.

KINICH AHAU

Ascended Master.

KIRA

Master of Transmutation.

Only one incarnation on Earth as a dog.

KIRAEL

Master, Light Being of the 7th dimension of the Guidance Realm.

Channel: Fred Sterling.

KIRTABUS

Genius of Languages.

KLA-LA

Space Commander & Master of Dynamics of energy and force.

Head of the Galactic Tribunal on Aldebaran-3.

Member of the Alliance of the Galaxies. Member of the Solar Cross.

KLEINIAS

Incarnation of Djwhal Khul.

KLYCON

Space Commander made 1 phone call from outer space.

KMIEL

Angel.

KOKAVIEL

Angel.

KOKOS

Other name of Lilith.

KOLTA

A Grey in contact with Dr. Michael Wolf.

KOOT HOOMI

Other name of Kuthumi.

KOOT HOOMI LAL SINGH

Other name of Kuthumi.

KORE

Refugee from planet Styx in Orion.

KORNIEL	Angelic guard.
KORTON	6th dimensional being from the Alcor System. Commander of the Ashtar Command. Master of all Space Communications & Coordinator of messages. Head of the Galactic Center of Communications (KOR) on the planet Mars, he is not a Martian. Member of the Ashtar Command and the Solar Cross. Channel: Susanna Thorpe-Clark, Tuella. http://www.hotkey.net.au/~korton/index.html → Ashtar Command.
KORTON TOLTEC	Cmdr. Channel is David Stites.
KOTECHA	Angel of the Seal.
KOTHUMI	Other name of Kuthumi.
KRILL	Ambassador of Greys from Zeta on Earth.
KRISHNA	→ Krishna.
KRISTINE	Ascended Lady Master. Incarnations: >> Florence Jeannette Birnie-Visscher Miller (Feb 27, 1936 – Sept 19, 1979). >> Saint Teresa of Avila (16th century).
KRYON	Cosmic Being, Master of Magnetic Service. Channel: Lee Caroll, David Brown.
KUAN YIN	Goddess of Mercy. Also known as Quan Yin. Member of the Karmic Board. Channel: Janna Shelley Parker. → Quan Yin.
KUKULKAN	→ Quetzalcoatl.
KULBA	A guide from Apu.
KUMAD	Cosmic Being.
KURMA	Avatar.
KUT HUMI	Other name of Kuthumi.

KUTHUMI   Lord, Ascended Master, World Teacher jointly with Jesus-
                      Sananda since Jan. 1, 1956.
                      Formerly Chohan of the 2nd (yellow) Ray of Divine Illumination.
                      Teacher of Djwhal Khul. Kuthumi's teacher was Maitreya.
                      Lived during the 19th century as Mahatma Kuthumi, he worked
                      with Madame Blavatsky.
                      Founded 1875 the Theosophical Society together with El Morya.
                      Member of Earth's Spiritual Hierarchy and the Ashtar
                      Command.
                      Incarnations as:
                      >>   Thutmose III, 1460 B.C.E.,
                              Pharaoh, prophet, high priest.
                      >>   Pythagoras, (582 B.C.E.-507B.C.E.),
                              Greek philosopher.
                      >>   Aristotle.
                      >>   Lao-Tze (6th century B.C.E.).
                      >>   Balthazar, one of the 3 Magi (Three Wise Men).
                      >>   John the Beloved (Apostle).
                      >>   Theodosius, Roman Emperor (4th century).
                      >>   Sir Percival, 5th century (Parzifal of King
                              Arthur's Camelot).
                      >>   St. Columa, Apostle of Caldonia (5th century).
                      >>   Saint Francis of Assisi, (1181/82-1226).
                      >>   Erasmus of Rotterdam, (1469-1536).
                      >>   Leonardo da Vinci (15th/16th century).
                      >>   Shah Jahan, Mogul emperor of India
                              (1592-1666),
                              the Taj Mahal was built for his beloved wife
                              Mumtaz Mahal, who died in 1631.
                      >>   Koot Hoomi Lal Singh, Shigatse, Tibet.
                      Also known as: Koot Hoomi, Koot Hoomi Lal Singh,
                      Koothumi, Kut Humi.
                      Channel: Ruth A. Craig, Bev (Dranda) Dombrowski, Sue Hall,
                      Dr. Norma Milanovich, Sandy Stevenson, Lori Adaile Toye,
                      Andrew Whalley, Joseph Whitfield.
                      → Maitreya.

KUTIEL   Angel.

KUWAYA   Lord, represents the essence of Divine Will.
                      Oversees primary energies of Creation that are needed to carry
                      out Divine Plan. Works with Lord Siraya.
                      „Ku" means divine fire or spirit, „Wea" means the divine
                      thought upon which it is embodied.
                      → Supreme Creative Force.

KUWEA   Other name of Kuwaya.

KWAN YIN   → Quan Yin.

KYRIEL   Angel of the Moon.

KYRON	KRYON? Channel Lee Carroll.
LABUSI	Angel.
LACTU	Contact specialist on planet Earth. Member of the Solar Cross.
LAD	Other name of Metatron.
LADY ATHENA	→ Athena.
LADY CASSANDRA	Her Twin Flame is Lord Confucius.
LADY CLARION	Ascended Master.
LADY EARTH	→ Lady Gaia, Virgo.
LADY GAIA	Ensouls planet Earth. Also known as Mother Gaia. Channel: Lady Cassandra, Pepper Lewis.
LADY GUADALUPE	Avatar and Star Visitor.
LADY ISIS	→ Isis.
LADY KADJINA	Channel: Kay Simmons.
LADY LETO	Ascended Lady Master, ascended 400 years ago. She has golden hair. Incarnations: >> 11th century in Scotland.
LADY MAGDA	Ascended Lady Master. Twin Flame of Jesus. Ascended 1944. Incarnations: >> Mary Magdalene, >> Aimee Semple McPherson (1890-1944).

LADY NADA   Lord of Karma.
                         Chohan of the 6th Ray (Ruby Flame) of Devotion, Freedom,
                         Justice, Ministry, Peace.
                         „Nada" means „nothing", which refers to her great humility.
                         It's said to be the Twin Flame of Jesus.
                         Took over the position of Jesus/Sananda on the 6th Ray.
                         Works also on the 3rd (pink) Ray of Divine Love.
                         Ascended Lady Master (Love & Understanding).
                         She has served on many Light Councils.
                         Last incarnation as a Priestess in the Temple of Divine Love in
                         Atlantis.
                         Member of the Karmic Board.
                         → Chohans.

LADY POMONA   Ascended Lady Master.
                         Also known as:
                         >> Goddess of Fruit.

LADY PORTIA   Lord, Lady Master of Karma.
                         Goddess of Freedom, Justice and Opportunity.
                         Twin Flame of Saint Germain.
                         Member of the Karmic Board.
                         Is not her name on the Council of Twelve.
                         Channel is Ariana Sheran.
                         → Council of Twelve.

LADY QUAN YIN   → Quan Yin.

LADY ROWENA   Master of astrology.
                         Ascended Master.
                         Wears a Celtic Cross on her medieval headdress.
                         Has deep dark eyes.
                         Captain of a ship and leader of a large fleet that works for higher
                         dimensions.
                         Earth name: Evangeline Adams.

LADY SALENA   Light Being who has never incarnated upon planet Earth and
                         never will.

LADY VENUS   Leader of the "chain of Venus planets" with Sanat Kumara.
                         Divine Complement of Sanat Kumara.
                         → Venus.

LAE   Grand Chief Commander. Grand Space Commander.
                         Visited 199,000,000 cultures.

LAHARIEL   Angel.
                         Assistant of Archangel Michael.

LAHIRI MAHASAYA
                         19th Century Indian Master, disciple of Babaji.

LAIOLIN	11th dimensional energy. Channel: Judith K. Moore.
LAKSHMI	Goddess of beauty, good fortune and wealth.
LALUR	Medical specialist from planet Neptune. Member of the Solar Cross.
LAMACH	Angel of Mars.
LAMED	Other name of Archangel Uriel.
LAMEDIEL	Angel.
LANELLO	Ascended Master. Incarnations: >> Mark L. Prophet, >> Pericles, >> Lancelot, >> Origen, >> Ikhnaton, >> Noah (prophet).
LANTO	Lord, Chohan of the 2nd Ray (Yellow Flame). Ancient Chinese master who lived about 400 B.C.E. He is said to have accomplished more than any other master of Earth. → Chohans.
LAO TSE	Teacher of light.
LAO-TZU	Member of the Planetary Council. Incarnations: >> Maldek >> Pluto >> China, around 650 B.C.E. Was not the founder of Taoism.
LAQUIDO	Starship commander of the Galactic Federation.
LARZOD	Angel.
LAZAI	Angel.
LE-AR	Extraterrestrial working with KOR. Member of the Solar Cross. → KOR, Solar Cross.
LEBES	Angel.
LECABEL	Angel.

LEICH   From Spectrola.

LELAHEL   Angel.

LELIEL   Angel.

LENDUCE   Teacher.
                          Channel Saemmi Muth.

LEPHA   Angel of the Seal.

LERTRAD   A guide from Morlen (Ganymede).

LETO   → Lady Leto.

LEXON   Space Commander made 1 phone call from outer space.

LHASA   Extraterrestrial (?). Lived for 300 years and was the king of the
                          Ugha Mongulala tribe in South America.

LILITH   Lilith is another great energy, along with Vulcan. These are all
                          beings from old Atlantis and prior to that Pangaea and Lemuria.
                          The first created female, the first of all succubi, forerunner of
                          Eve.
                          Mother of Hurmiz, Luluwa.
                          One of the 4 mates of Samael.
                          Female demon, first wife of Adam.
                          Also known as:
                          >>   Abeko, Abito, Amizo, Astaribo, Avitue, Bat Zuge,
                          >>   Batna, Eilo, Ita, Izorpo, Kali, Kea, Kokos,
                          >>   Odam, Partasah, Patrota, Podo, Satrina, Talto.

LING   Lord, Ascended Master.
                          Incarnations: Moses.

LITTLE IAO   Other name of Metatron.

LIWET   Angel.

LO CHI   Avatar at a pre-Lemurian time.
                          He was fond of wearing a silver robe.
                          At the end of his reign a mass ascension took place.

LOGOS   The oldest angel.

LONIEL   Angel.

LOTAN   Liaison supervisor, KOR, Mars.
                          Member of the Solar Cross.
                          → KOR, Solar Cross.

LOTAR   Channel is Nancy Tate.

LOTUS

Ascended Lady Master.
Divine Complement, Twin Flame of Ascended Master Godfre.
Incarnations:
>> Edna Ballard Wheeler (1886 – 1971),
>> Benjamin Franklin,
>> Joan of Arc,
>> Adina on the Island of Britain.

LOVE-STAR

LUANDA

A benign Grey.

LUCIFER

Is not the fallen angel Satan. Former Lord of the Draco.
Lucifer means „Light Giver".
Incarnated as a Reptilian being.
Also known as Nephilim.
→ Elohim.

LUEL

Angel.

LULUWA

Annunaki princess. Is said to be Kali's sister.
Wife of Cain, daughter of Enki, Lilith.

LUMA'IL

Guardian angel.

LUMIA

From Druan in the Nol System.

LUMINA

Elohim of the 2nd (yellow) Ray of Illumination, Omniscience,
Understanding, Wisdom.
Guardian of the Cosmic Christ Consciousness.
Twin Flame of Apollo.

LURGA

Lord of planet Saturn.
Member of the Spiritual Hierarchy.

LYRIA

Other name of Archangel Ariel.

LYTTON

Commander, Intergalactic Fleet.
Cosmic Being, Light Being.
Member of the Ashtar Command.
Channel: Lyara.

MACH

Angel.

MACHIDIEL

Angel. Means „Fullness of God".
Also known as: Malchidiel, Melkejal.

MACHIVENTA

Channel: George Bernard.

MADAN

Angel of Mercury.

MADIMEL

Angel.

MADOR   Angel.

MAEL   Archangel of the Water.

MAGDA   → Lady Magda.

MAHA CHOHAN   Ascended Being. Maha means Lord.
                       Also known as Lord of Civilization.
                       Teacher of El Morya.

MAHADEO   Angel.

MAHARIEL   Angel.

MAHATMA   Cosmic Being.

MAION   Angel of Saturn.

MAITREYA   Lord, from the Great Central Sun & Sovereignty of Great
                       Cosmic Government.
                       Master of the 6th Ray.
                       Oftentimes called Master of Masters and has served in this
                       position for 2,500 years.
                       Voice of the Great Cosmic Government.
                       He is an aspect of Jesus/Sananda.
                       Incarnation of Sananda.
                       It was Lord Maitreya, who ascended after the crucifixion, not
                       Jesus.
                       Carries the Christ Energy.
                       Usually wears a white robe, has golden hair, violet eyes.
                       Maitreya means "Lord of Love", „Universal Love", derived from
                       the Sanskrit word „maitri".
                       Maitreya embodied upon Earth millions of years ago as a
                       volunteer (guardian) from the planet Venus.
                       World Teacher until Jan. 1, 1956 when this office in Hierarchy
                       was passed jointly to Jesus & Kuthumi.
                       Great initiator of Jesus. Kuthumi's teacher.
                       He is on the planet now.
                       Said to be the next Buddha and also the next Christ.
                       Is believed to rebirth in 30,000 years.
                       Some believe he was Krishna, and that he inspired the life of
                       Jesus.
                       Also known as:
                       >>   Cosmic Christ,
                       >>   Planetary Buddha.
                       Works under Gautama Buddha as Planetary Buddha.
                       Member of the Council of Nine.
                       Channel: Benjamin Creme, Geraldine Innocente, Elizabeth Clare
                       Prophet, Mark Prophet, Carolyn Shearer.

MAKTIEL   Angel.

MALACANDRA	Lord of Massar on planet Mars. Member of the Spiritual Hierarchy.
MALACHIM	Angel.
MALAIKA	Angel.
MALANTOR	A 5th and 6th dimensional Arcturian being. Intergalactic counselor.
MALAYA	A consciousness of the Goddess.
MALCHIDIEL	Other name of Machidiel.
MALKIEL	Angel.
MALKUT	Holy Sephira.
MALLONA	Spirit of planet Maldek.
MALWA	Daughter of the king of Golkonda, India. Wife of Krishna.
MALTIEL	Angel.
MANAKEL	Angel of Aquatic Animals.
MANU	Angel of Fate.
MARDERO	Demon of disease.
MARDOX	Is from Planet Silox.
MARDUK	Current ruler of Earth & Nibiru. Directs the Secret Government on Earth. Until recently was the current Commander of the Federation Flagship Nibiru. Grandson of Anu (2/3 reptilian), son of Enki, cousin of Inanna. Captured the flagship Nibiru from 2000 B.C.E. until 1999 C.E. Also known as: >> Baal, >> Bael, >> Ra.
MARGIVIEL	Angel, angelic guard.
MARIA	Ascended Master. → Mother Mary.
MARINE	She is for intercommunications on ship of Thonn.

MARKIN, George   → Ontein.

MARLA   Aka Connie Weber.
                         Beautiful blonde extraterrestrial, married by Howard Menger,
                         over 500 years old.

MAROCH   Angel.

MARSIA   A medical student from Sirius, studied on Turellian.

MARY   Ascended Lady Master.
                         Mary of the House of Magdalena was the wife of Yeshua
                         Malathiel.
                         She is of Lyran descent.
                         → Atia, Jesus, Jmmanuel, Mother Mary.

MARY MAGDALENE
                         Is Lady Master Magda.
                         Channel is Gillian MacBeth-Loutan.4
                         → Magda.

MASAR   Spirit of planet Mars.

MASTHO   Genius.

MATAREL   Angel of the Rain.
                         Also known as: Matariel, Mathariel, Matriel.

MATARIEL   Other name of Matarel.

MATHARIEL   Other name of Matarel.

MATHLAI   Angel.

MATREYA   → Maitreya.

MATRIEL   Other name of Matarel.

MATTHEW   Channel is Suzy Ward.

MATTON   He is from an other galaxy.
                         Great Coordinator with Ashtar.
                         Space Master for the Coordination of all Space Volunteers
                         throughout the universe.
                         Member of the Ashtar Command.

MAYA   Mother of Buddha, called Mayadevi, 600 B.C.E.

MAYA OHM MAHATMA
Guardian of the Heart Light of Mt. Shasta.
Incarnations:
>>   Shamra Talia.
Also known as Ariel Excelsis Elohim.

MAYAM   Prince, brother of queen Mu, approx. 9,500 B.C.E.

MEBAHIAH   Angel.

MECK-TAU   Scientist from planet Mars.
                       Member of the Solar Cross.

MEHER BABA   Indian master born in 1984. He was strongly connected with
                       Sufism; he did not speak from 1925 until he left his body in
                       1969.

MEHIEL   Angel.

MELAKIM   Angel of Children's Safety.

MELCHIOR   Master of Alchemy & Science.

MELCHIZEDEK   Lord, Ascended Master, messenger, Ancient Cosmic Being. 2000
                       B.C.E., angel.
                       Though he has lived on Earth, he was not born and did not die.
                       He serves with great authority, love and power on the cosmic
                       level (entire universe).
                       King, Sage of Salem in the time of Abraham, about 2000 B.C.E.
                       "Prince of Peace". Called Sydik in Phoenician mythology.
                       Incarnation of Lord Sananda.

MELECH   Angel of the order of Powers.

MELIA   She is a powerful Master-teacher from Orion.

MELIOTH   Angel.

MELKEJAL   Angel.
                       Other name of Machiediel.

MELORA   Higher dimensional member of Jyoti's soul group. Now merged
                       with Ocala and Bi-La.
                       Channel: Jyoti Alla-An.
                       → Council of Four.
                       → Jyoti Alla-An.

MEMUNEH   Angel.

MENARA   From Lyra.

MERCURY   Ascended Master, god, other name of Thoth.
                      Angel of Progress.
                      Really lived.
                      Incarnations: Hermes Trismegistus.
                      → Thoth

MERESIJM   Angel.

MERIARIJIM   Angel.

MERKIN   Cmdr.
                      → Merku.

MERKU   Cmdr., Scientist from planet Mars
                      Also called Merkin.
                      Member of the Solar Cross.

MERLIN   Great magician, seer-poet, his Celt name: Taliesin.
                      Welsh sorcerer of the 5th century, born about 450 C.E. in
                      Carmarthen, South Wales, Great Britain. Died about 520 C.E.
                      Son of Morvryn.
                      He was Leonardo da Vinci, Tesla.
                      Member of the Planetary Council.
                      Also known as:
                      >>   Myrddin,
                      >>   Taliesin.
                      Channel: John Armitage.

MEROS   Angel.

MESHABBER   Angel.

MESSIACH   Angel.

METATRON   Lord, Cherubim (said to be an Archangel). Ruling angel of the
                      order of Seraphim. Ruling angel prince of the order of
                      Archangels. Chief Elohim, Liberating Angel. Supreme Angel of
                      Death, Angel of Prayer. Prince of the ministering angels.
                      He is light; he is like a step down from God, one who occupies
                      the throne next to the Divine Throne.
                      He has been known as the link between the human and the
                      divine.
                      His superior is Radueriel (Vretil).
                      Subordinates of him are Gabriel, Michael, Uzziel.
                      Head of the Sirian Central Sun Council.
                      Head of the Galactic Federation Council.
                      Overseer & mentor of Light workers of Terra.
                      Is said to have been Enoch.
                      Never was Enoch, he was his teacher.
                      Twin brother of Sandalphon,
                      His female equivalent is Shekinah.
                      He has many other names like:
                      >>   Lad,

>>	Little Iao,
>>	Surya,
>>	Yahoel,
>>	Yofiel.

Channel: Christine Bearse, Laurie Gilmore, Santari Green, Soleira Green, Lauri Gudnason, Debbie Wright.
→ Shekinah.

METH   A guide from Apu.

MIBI   Angel.

MICAH   Great Cosmic Angel.

MICHA   Healer, friend of Tibus.

MICHAEL   Lord, Archangel of the 1ˢᵗ (blue) Ray (Flame) of Protection, Straightness & Power.
Angel of Prayer, Throne Angel.
Ruling angel prince of the order of Archangels.
Ruling angel of the order of Seraphim.
Ruling angel prince of the order of Virtues.
Best known of the Archangels.
Is known for his great power of protection, his mighty sword cuts away anything that no longer serves.
"Prince of Light". Means „Who is like God".
Protector of the Christian Church, Guardian Angel of Israel.
Subordinate of Metatron.
Archangel Gabriel and Michael cooperate with the Time Lords who control physical reality.
Member of the Spiritual Hierarchy.
Also known as Oxoh.
Channel: Isaac George, Ronna Herman, Shepard Hoodwin, Eric Klein, Carolyn Ann O Riley, Lilian Whalley, Debbie Wright.

MICHAL   Angel.

MIDAEL   Warrior Angel.

MIEL   Angel of Mercury.

MIHR   Angel.

MIKAEL   Angel.

MIKAEL ASHTAR Founder & director of the Ashtar Command.
Ashtar's ship is not a mothership, (space for about 1,000 people).
He lives in the 13ᵗʰ universe.
He gets orders direct from the Source.
He had 3 sons on the planet SAKASIA in the first universe (now we are in the 12ᵗʰ universe).
Used the name Ashtar Sheran a long time ago.

MIKHAIL   Archangel.

MIKHAR   One of the celestial Powers.
                      Also known as Mikheus.

MIKHEUS   Other name of Mikhar.

MIKIAH   Channel is Kathryn L. Nesbitt.

MIKIEL   Angel.

MIKOS   Head Librarian from the Library of Porthologos in the
                      underground city of Catharia beneath the Aegean Sea.

MILCHA   Mother of Adam, from country Otlana, Atlantis,
                      8300 B.C.E., later reincarnation as third son of Shiva, Apostle
                      Petrus.

MINIEL   Angel.

MIRA   From the Pleiadian High Council.
                      Member of the Ashtar Command.
                      Channel is Valerie Donner.

MIRACH   Keeper of the Blue Star Energy from the Andromeda star
                      system.
                      Also known as Tua Ur.

MIRI   Angel.

MIRVIN   Key member of the Ashtar Command.

MISHAR   Healer and councilor.
                      Space Commander in the Star Command from Arcturus.
                      Is about 6'4 and 7 ft tall, embracing a wingspan of at least 6 ft.
                      On board works with the high-level councilors by monitoring
                      weather patterns of Earth.
                      → West Star.

MISHKA   Member of the Ashtar Command.

MISTRIS   Female officer from the Leo Constellation.

MITZGITARI   Angel.

MOAKKIBAT   Recording Angel.

MODINIEL   Spirit of planet Mars.

MOFF   Pilot on ship of Thonn (1948).

MON-KA	Other name of Monka.
MONACHIEL	Angel.
NONJORONSON	Urantia Book. Channel George Barnard.
MONKA	Commander of the 7th fleet of the Ashtar Command. Head of the Solar Tribunal on Titan, Saturn. Member of the Solar Cross and the Ashtar Galactic Command. Assistant to Ashtar. Also known as Kadar-Monka, Mon-Ka. → Kadar-Monka.
MORA	Scientist from planet Venus. Member of the Solar Cross.
MORAEL	Angel of Awe & Fear.
MORANAE	→ Morenae.
MORANEY	From Andromeda. Has the ability to travel in time.
MORDAD	Angel of Death.
MORENAE	Male being from Andromeda. 7.5 ft tall, weighs about 450 pounds.
MORIEL	Angel of the Wind.
MORONI	Angel of the Latter-Day Saints. Giver of the Book of Mormon. Gave the prophecies to Joseph Smith in the early 1830's.
MORVICA	Of the Galactic Confederation. Channel: MirRa.
MORVRYN	Merlin's father.

MOSES   Incarnation of Jesus (Sananda), about 1350 B.C.E.
                          Incarnation of Ascended Master Lord Ling.
                          Moses is in fact 2 people:
                          >>   Moab, a Chaldean chief,
                          >>   Prince Sesostres in Egypt.
                          His spirit guides: Aelohin, Ariel.
                          True name: Shemmah (means great shining or Sun of the Night),
                          1500 B.C.E.
                          Came from the civilization Ashan,
                          His mother: Av.Isis.Thimetis, daughter of Ramses I., his
                          grandfather: Pharaoh Seti Ramses I.,   his stepson: Ghesen
                          (Essen) was the founder of the Essener School. Studied the old
                          copies of Neghada (Alexandria) 10 years in the desert of Sinai,
                          (Original = Antulion Chronicles).
                          Traveled to the secret places: Atlas Mountains in Mauritania,
                          Sinai, Hor, Nebo, Gondar, Ethiopia, wandered with 600.000
                          people (not only Hebrews) from Egypt to Sinai.
                          → Filon.

MOTHER EARTH   Also called Virgo.
                          → Gaia, Lady Gaia, Virgo.

MOTHER GAIA   She has long, wavy dark hair, parted in the middle.
                          She is Lady Gaia.
                          → Gaia, Lady Gaia, Virgo.

MOTHER KUMARA   Channel is Marion L. White.

MOTHER MARY   Mother of Sananda.
                          Divine Polarity of the 5th Ray.
                          Was originally an angel, gave birth to the Christ.
                          Wife of Jesse, mother of David.
                          Daughter of Anna & Joachim (initiates of the Brotherhood).
                          Her guardian angel was Selith.
                          Ascended with her body as Mother Mary.
                          Incarnated as:
                          >>   Priestess in the early years of Atlantis,
                          >>   Isis,
                          >>   Kali,
                          >>   Mary, mother of Jesus,
                          >>   Mother Meera.
                          Also known as:
                          >>   Ascended Lady Master Mary,
                          >>   Atia,
                          >>   Blessed Virgin (Mary),
                          >>   Bride of the Holy Spirit,
                          >>   Divine Mother,
                          >>   Immaculate Conception,
                          >>   Kuan Yin,
                          >>   Mother of God,
                          >>   Mother of the World,
                          >>   Our Lady of Fatima,

>>	Our Lady of Guadalupe,
>>	Our Lady of the Rosary,
>>	Quan Yin,
>>	Queen of Angels,
>>	Queen of Heaven,
>>	The Blessed Mother.

Channel: Valerie Donner, Sue Hall, Geraldine Innocente, Annie Kirkwood, Elizabeth Clare Prophet, Carolyn Shearer, Lori Adaile Toye, Andrew Whalley, Helen Whalley, Lilian Whalley, Marion L. White.
→ Atia.

MOTHER MEERA Avatar, incarnation of Mother Mary.
Born Dec. 26, 1960 in Chandepalle, southern India. Living now in Thalheim in Germany. Is believed by many to be an incarnation of Divine Mother.

MOTHER NEBADONIA
"Mother" spirit.

MOTHER SEKHMET
→ Sekhmet.

MQTTRO Angel.

MTNIEL Angel of Animals.

MU Queen of Atlantis, wife of king Atlas, approx. 9500 B.C.E.

MUBASA Co-commander of Upasu Arasatha.

MULLA Intraterrestrial master from the Sierra du Roncador, Matogrosso, Brazil.

MUMIAH Angel.

MUNKIR Angel.

MUPIEL Angel.
Mupiel means „Out of the Mouth of God".

MURDAD Angel.

MUSHABA Ascended Master. 7th/8th dimensional being.

MURIEL Ruling angel of the order of Dominations (Dominions).

MUSLINE Woman officer from Alpha Centauri.

MUTUOL Angel.

MYL-LA N-TROK   KOR supervisor from Mars.
Member of the Solar Cross.

MYRDDIN   Other name of Merlin.

MZPOPIASAIEL   Angel.

NAADAME   Prince over all the angels.

NAAMAH   Angel of Prostitution.
One of the 4 mates of Samael.

NACHIEL   Angel of the Sun.

NADA   → Lady Nada.

NAFRIEL   Angelic guard.

NAHALIEL   Angel.

NAKIR   Angel.

NAKRIEL   Angelic guard.

NANGRIEL   Angel.

NANNAR   Father of Ereshkigal, Inanna & Utu, son of Enlil & Ninlil.

NAOPHIEL   Angel.

NARIEL   Angel of the South Wind.

NARSINHA   Man-Lion Avatar.

NASCIA   Is part of the communication network at the Galactic Center.

NATHANAEL   Angel of Fire and Vengeance. Ruling angel of the order of
Seraphim.

NATIEL   Angel.

NDMH   Angel.

NEBADONIA   → Mother Nebadonia.

NEGONNA   Princess, came allegedly with prince Neosam from planet Tythan
to planet Earth.

NEHINAH   Angel.

NELA   Also known as O-Nee-Sayer-Wann Nela.
Extraterrestrial who was in contact with Martin Riley.

NEMAMIAH	Archangel, guardian angel.
NEOSAM	Prince, came allegedly with princess Negonna from planet Tythan to planet Earth.
NEPHILIM	Other name of Lucifer. Fallen angels of Lucifer.
NERA	She is from Timar in the Dal universe.
NERGAL	Son of Enki, husband of Ereshkigal.
NERIA	Angel. Neria means „Lamp of God".
NERIEL	Angel of the Moon.
NESANEL	Angel.
NETONIEL	Angel of Fame & Glory.
NETZACH	Angel.
NEUMAN	Star Visitor. Channel: Marian MacNeil.
NIN-KHURSAG	→ Ninhursag.
NINGAL	Mother of Inanna & Utu, wife of Nannar.
NINHARSAG	Other name of Ninhursag.
NINHURSAG	Daughter of Anu (king An), mother of Ninurta. In ancient Egypt called Isis. She was a reptilian princess. Pleiadian physician, genetic scientist. Created the Lulus (Apa-Mus), an ape-beast hybrid race on Earth, by using her own DNA. Also called: Nin-Khursag, Ninharsag, Ninmah. → An, Isis. → Sheti.
NINKI	Spouse of Enki.
NINLIL	Wife of Enlil, mother of Nannar.
NINMAH	Other name of Ninhursag.
NINTI	Expert medicine lady of the Annunaki. She is Isis.

NINURTA   Son of Ninhursag & Enlil.

NIRIH   Name of Ashtar on Mawuvia.

NISROC   Angel.

NISROCH   Ruling angel prince of the order of Principalities.

NITHAIAH   Poet Angel of the order of Dominations.

NITIKA   Genius.

NOAH   It was not necessarily his real name.
                       The Incas were the last of Noah's civilization.
                       Noah's ark was a spaceship. He was not the only one who built
                       an ark (but the first one) and it was many times bigger than
                       pictured.

NOAPHIEL   Angel.

NOGANIEL   Angel.

NOKODEMION   Other name of Enoch.

NOSTRADAMUS   Channel: Dolores Cannon.

NOVANCIA   Young Draco warrior.
                       The name is pseudonym which means "as mighty as a star".
                       7 ft tall, dark brown in color, age about 153 years.

NUMU   God Pastor of the old "Kobdas" from Lemuria.
                       His spirit guides: Isis, Orfeo.
                       Daughter: Vesperina.
                       33300 B.C.E.

NUR EL   From Mars.

NURIEL   Angel.

O-NEE-SAYER-WANN NELA
                       Also known as Nela.
                       Extraterrestrial who was in contact with Martin Riley.

O-QUA TANGIN WANN TAN
                       Also known as Tan.
                       Extraterrestrial who was in contact with Martin Riley.

OASPE   Grand Master of Light. He is the overseer at the University of
                       San Tam.

OCALA   Angelic guide.
                       → Council of Four.

OCH	Angel of the Sun, Prince of Alchemy.
ODAM	Other name of Lilith.
ODINA	Wife of Anfion, Atlantis.
OERTHA	Angel of the North.
OESCEVE	A guide from Venus and Morlen (Ganymede).
OFANIEL	Angel of the Moon.
OKMAYA	Spiritual guide of Antulio.
OLEA	A guide from Apu and Morlen (Ganymede).
OLETAMO	A guide from Morlen (Ganymede), in contact with groups in Spain.
OLMEX	A guide from Morlen (Ganymede), in contact with La Coruña, Spain.
OMAEL	Angel.
OMELIEL	Angel.
OMEN	A guide from Morlen (Ganymede), in contact with La Coruña, Spain.
OMMI	A traveler from Nebora.
OMNEC ONEC	Female extraterrestrial from Venus, came to Earth as a child in 1955, born 246 years ago. She was adopted by an American family who just had lost their daughter. Her Earth name is Sheila Gibson.
OMNIEL	Said to be an Archangel.
OMOPHORUS	Angel.
OMRI-TAS	Ascended Master, Ruler of the Violet Planet. Channel: Elizabeth Clare Prophet.
OMSA	God of the Biaviians.
OMUNI	A guide from Morlen (Ganymede).
ONIAC	A guide from Venus.

ONTEIN   Commander. (Dr. Olance Ki. George Markin 1936-1996).
                     He is now serving in the Ashtar Command in the 9th
                     interdimensionality as the commander of the starship U4
                     Stanisfield from the Unity 4 starfleet.

ONZO   Angel.

OPHANIEL   Ruling angel prince of the order of Cherubim.

OPHIEL   Angel of Meditation.

OPIEL   Angel.

ORANIR   Angel.

ORBIDO   From the Jupiter Command.

ORDELAT   A guide from Morlen (Ganymede).

ORFEO   Spirit guide of: Anfion, Buddha, Numu.

ORIARES   Angel.

ORIEL   Other name of Auriel.

ORIPHIEL   Ruling angel prince of the order of Thrones.

ORIS   Elder from Zeta Reticuli.

ORMAEL   Angel.

OROMASIS   Ascended Master.
                     Was a prince of the Fire Element.
                     He always comes surrounded by clouds of fire.
                     His Twin Flame is Diana.

ORTHON   Venusian contact to George Adamski, long haired.
                     Other name of Jesus.
                     → George Adamski.

ORVON   Space Commander from the planet Zelia in the Orion
                     Constellation. He is a cosmic philosopher. His ship is about 45m
                     in diameter, 9m in height. There are 7 lecturers in his craft.

OSAEL   Cherub.

OSANTA   Princess & Goddess of Yore.

OSENY   Cherub.

OSGAEBIAL   Angel.

OSIRIS   Son of king Atlas from Atlantis, approx. 9,500 B.C.E.
                     Older brother of Seth.

OSSIM   A guide from Morlen (Ganymede).

OTHEOS   Most holy angel.

OUESTUCATI   Female angel.
                     Also called „Lady of Chaste Hands".

OUL   Angel.

OUMRIEL   Angel.

OXALC   A guide born in Morlen (Ganymede). A "mind doctor" and
                     expert telepath, graduated as coordinator of guides for Mission
                     Rahma. Lives in Crystal City. Sent a telepathical message to Lima,
                     Peru.
                     → Mission Rahma.

OXIRAM   A guide from Morlen (Ganymede).

OXLAM   A guide from Morlen (Ganymede).

OXMALC   A guide from Morlen (Ganymede), mind doctor and instructor in
                     the university of the city of Morella, in the planet Cerpican.

OXOH   Other name of Archangel Michael.
                     Member of the Spiritual Hierarchy.

PAGIEL   Angel.

PAHALIAH   Angel.

PAIMON   One of the most powerful and dangerous of the Goetian Spirits.

PAIMONAH   Angel.

PALAMEDES   Of the Greeks, other name of Enoch.
                     → Enoch.

PALLAS ATHENA   Lady, Lord of Karma, Avatar.
She has been an Ascended Master for thousands of years.
High-ranking Cmdr. Wife of Ashtar, Ashtar's counterpart.
Goddess of Truth.
"Pallas" is Greek and means virgin.
Greek was really a star language from another (Athena's) universe, Russian incorporates Greek letters. She came from another universe.
Member of the Karmic Board.
Pallas Athena & Apollo were the only 2 avatars, the rest of the Greek "gods" were intergalactic interlopers.
Landed on the Parthenon in a vast Merkaba lightship.
The intergalactic beings (impersonated gods) lived on Mount Olympus.
She was always negotiating in behalf of human beings to try to save them from these arbitrary galactic beings.
→ Council of Four.

PALPAE   Arcturian Ambassador of Light, Love and Peace.

PAMMON   Angel.

PANCIA   Angel.

PANCIMEIA   Prince of Angels.

PANIEL   Angel.

PARAMAHANSA YOGANANDA
India yogi who at Babaji's request came to America in 1920. His guru was Sri Yukteswar.

PARASIEL   Angel of Jupiter, Lost Treasures, Secrets.

PARTASAH   Other name of Lilith.

PASTOR   Angel.

PATHA   Angel.

PATROTA   Other name of Lilith.

PATROZIN   Angel.

PATTENY   Angel.

PAUL the APOSTLE
Incarnation of Hilarion.
→ Hilarion.

PAUL the VENETIAN

Lord, Chohan of the 3ʳᵈ (Pink Flame) of Love & Life.
Ascended Master, ascended April 19, 1588.
Has golden hair and blue eyes.
Worked with El Morya at the time of the building of the pyramids.
He trains Elementals.
Also known as:
>>   Head of cultural affairs in the government of Atlantis.
Before Atlantis sank, he went to Peru.
>>   Artist in the Incan Empire.
>>   Paolo Veronese (Paolo Caliari), (1528 - 1588), Italian Master Renaissance painter.
Channel: Geraldine Innocente.
→ Chohans.

PAULAR

Grand Space Commander from Eurekar.

PAULSON

Grand Space Commander from the Pleiades.

PEACE

Elohim of the 6ᵗʰ (purple/gold) Ray of Brotherhood, Peace.
Twin Flame of Aloha.

PECAL

Member of the Ashtar Command.

PELGHI

7ᵗʰ dimensional being from the Pleiades.
Channel: Jyoti Alla-An.

PELIEL

Ruling angel prince of the order of Virtues.

PELLEUR

Twin Flame of Virgo.

PENAT

Angel, intelligence of Venus.

PENDROZ

Angel.

PERELANDRA

Lord of planet Venus.
Member of the Spiritual Hierarchy.

PERMAZ

Angel.

PERPETIEL

Said to be an archangel.

PESAGNIYAH

Angel.

PETAHYAH

Angel.

PETHEL

Most holy angel.

PETRON

Grand Space Commander from Petomalie. His craft is called Astrona. He is a journalist. He is from the Pleiades.

PHAIAR   Angel.

PHAKIEL   Angel, genius, brother of Rahdar.

PHALDOR   Angel of Oracles.

PHALGUS   Genius of Judgement.

PHANUEL   Archangel of Penance, Angel of Hope.
                         Also known as Raguel.

PHARNIEL   Angel.

PHARZUPH   Angel of Carnal Delights.

PHATIEL   Angel.

PHI-RE   Planetary Archangel.
                         Head of the order of Virtues.

PHILIP   Apostle of Jesus Christ.
                         Member of the Saturnian-Council.

PHORLAKH   Angel of Earth.

PHUL   Lord of the Moon, Supreme Lord of the Waters.

PHYLOS   Tibetan Ascended Master.
                         → Nola Van Valer.

PI-RHE   Virtue.

PISTIS SOPHIA   Female angel. She's said to have procreated the superior angels.
                         Mother of Achamoth, Barbelo.

PLATO   Master.

PLEJA   Pleiadian from Erra.

PLEJAS   Last Pleiadian leader who left Earth in the year 10 C.E.

PNIEL   Angel.

PNIMEA   Angel.

PODO   Other name of Lilith.

POIEL   Angel of the order of Principalities.

POMONA   → Lady Pomona.

PORNA   Angel.

POROSA	Angel.
PORTIA	→ Lady Portia.
PRAJAPATI	The Creator, other name of Savatri.
PRAXIL	Angel.
PREMA BABA	Future incarnation of Sai Baba.
PRESNOSTIX	Angel.
PROCTOR 51	Of Akashic Records. Gentle guide who gives answers to assist us in our quest & thirst for knowledge, understanding & enlightenment. Channel: Maureen Whitaker Clifton.
PRUEL	Angelic guard.
PRUKIEL	Angel.
P'TAAH	Other name of P'tah.
PTAAH	Other name of P'tah.
PTAH	Master from the Pleiades (Erra), over 730 years old. Commander of Cosmic Squadron from the Pleiades, commands 100,000 carrier ships like "Share". Channel: Jani King. → Enki.
PTIAU	Angel.
PURITY	Elohim of the 4th (white) Ray of Hope, Perfection, Purity and Wholeness. His Twin Flame is Astrea.
PYTHAGORAS	→ Kuthumi.
QADOSCH	Angel.
QAFSIEL	Angel of the Moon.
QALBAM	Angelic guard.
QAMIEL	Angelic guard.
QANIEL	Angelic guard.
QUADO	Spiritual healer. Channel is Carrie Hart.

QUAKER   Arcturian. Greeter of newly established human telepaths.

QUAN YIN   Lord of Karma.
                       Goddess of Compassion, Mercy & Grace.
                       Ascended Master, Hybrid.
                       Loved and revered throughout Asia.
                       Also known as:
                       >>   Kanin   (in Bali).
                       >>   Kannon (in Japan).
                       >>   Kuan Shih Yin.
                       >>   Kuan Yin.
                       >>   Quan'Am (in Vietnam)
                       Incarnations:
                       >>   Avalokitesvara, had 357 incarnations.
                       >>   Divine Mother Mary.
                       >>   Sophia.
                       Channel: Caroline Fitzgerald, Helen Whalley, Lilian Whalley.

QUANTRA   Arcturian solar scientist.

QUELAMIA   Throne Angel.

QUETZAL   Pleiadian from Erra.

QUETZALCOATL   Mayan serpent god, Avatar, Star Visitor.
                       Member of the Planetary Council.

QUOARTS   Arcturian lunar scientist.

RA   6th dimensional being.
                       Husband of Isis.
                       Was Marduk.
                       Ra's city was An, also called Anu, Heliopolis, On.
                       → Marduk.

RA'ASIEL X   Angel.

RABIA   Angel.

RACHEL   Female angel known as Air's Lady.
                       Angel of Humor & Self-Confidence.
                       One of the 4 matriarchs.

RACHIEL   Angel, presiding spirit of Venus.

RACHMIEL   Angel of Compassion.

RADHA   Goddess of Beauty, Compassion, Grace and Harmony.

RADUERIEL	Recording Angel, Angel of Muses & Poetry. Creator of the lesser angels. Superior to Metatron. Also known as Vretil.
RAECHEL	Female Zeta Reticulan hybrid, living on Earth. Crash landed in the Nevada desert in 1956.
RAEL	Angel of Venus.
RAGUEL	Other name of archangel Phanuel.
RAGUIL	Said to be an archangel.
RAHAB	Angel of the deep.
RAHDAR	Genius.
RAHMIEL	Angel of Love.
RAHTIEL	Angel of Constellations.
RAISMES of APHRA	
	Incarnation of Thoth. → Thoth.
RAKHANIEL	Angel.
RAKOCKZI	Ascended Master.
RALA	Pleiadian from Erra.
RAM KAR	
RAMA	Avatar. Incarnation of Sai Baba, Vishnu.
RAMAKRISHNA	One of the greatest Hindu Saints, live 1836 - 1886.
RAMALA	Master.
RAMONA	Ascended Lady Master. Also known as: >> Flora, >> Goddess of Flowers.
RAMPEL	Angel of Mountains.
RAMPIAC	A guide from Venus.
RAMSES I.	Seti Ramses I., grandfather of Moses.

RAMU Saturnian Space Brother who was in contact with George Adamski in 1953 and 1954.

RAMUEL Angelic leader, fallen angel.

RANOASH From the Ataien.
Channel: Dorothy Roeder.

RANYA Female warrior from Maldek.
Senior female commander in Lady Athena's Light Forces.

RAPHAEL Archangel of the 5th (emerald, green) Ray.
Archangel of Compassion, Consecration, Dedication, Healing, Love, Prayer, Science, Sun, Travel, Truth.
Throne Angel.
Ruling angel prince of the order of Virtues.
Ruling angel prince of the order of Cherubim.
Ruling angel prince of the order of Archangels.
Works with Master Hilarion.
Raphael means "God has Healed", "Medicine of God".
Channel: Elizabeth Clare Prophet, Jessica Saunders, Jeannie Weyrick.

RASH Angel.

RASHIEL Angel of Earthquakes.

RAUEL Angel of Money.

RAUERIEL Angel of Song.

RAY-ELLA LE-EL Name of Cmdr. Galimai-A.
→ Galimai-A.

RAYNESS, Dr. Member of the Council of 48.

RAZIEL Said to be an archangel.
Which means "Secret of God".
Angel of the Secret Regions and Chief of the Supreme Mysteries.
"Boss" of angel Abigrael.
Ruling angel prince of the order of Thrones.
Also known as Galizur.

REGALIEL Angel.

REGES A guide from Apu.

REHATIEL Angel.

REHEL Angel.

REIVTIP Angel.

REKHODIAH   Angel.

REMIEL   Angel of Karma, one of the holy angels.
                   Said to be an archangel.

REMLIEL   Angel of Awakening.

REQUEL   Ruling angel prince of the order of Principalities.

REQUIEL   Angel of the Moon.

RESH   Other name of Archangel Uriel.

RHAMIEL   Angel.

RHAUMEL   Angel.

RIDIA   Angel of the Rain.

RIDYA   Angel of the Rain.

RIFION   Angel.

RIGEL   Member of the Ashtar Command.
                   He is an officer from Saturn.
                   Also known as angel Anachiel or Ankhiel.

RIGZIEL   One of the holy sefiroth.

RIKBIEL   Chief of the Merkabah Angels.

RIMEZIN   Angel.

RISNUCH   Angel of Agriculture.

RO   From Uranus, visited Earth in 1973, contacted by the apostles in
                   an other sphere on Easter Island, the apostles are higher in
                   hierarchy than Uranus.
                   Channel: P. Leopold.

ROANN   Guardian Being from the Nebula Orion.
                   Channel: Amber Leigh.

ROCHEL   Angel.

ROELHAIPHAR   Angel.

ROREX   Angel.

ROSABIS   Genius of Metals.

ROSENKREUZ, Christian
→ Saint Germain.

ROSINAC   A guide from Venus on the spaceship Tipus.

ROSKAUWSKI   Count. Other name of St. Germain.

ROWENA   → Lady Rowena.

RUBIEL   Other name of Ruchiel.

RUBY   Female Reptoid.

RUCHIEL   Angel of the Wind.
Also known as Ben-Nez, Rubiel, Ruhiel.

RUDOSOR   Angel.

RUHIEL   Other name of Ruchiel.

RUMILAC   A guide from Venus on the spaceship Tipus.

RUSVON   Angel.

RUWANO   Angel.

RZIEL   Angel.

SA ANANDA   Also known as Sananda or Sanandana.
One of the Seven Holy Kumaras.

SA LU SA   Is from the Galactic Federation.
Channel is Mike Quinsey.

SA NA KUMARA   Also known as Sana.
One of the Seven Holy Kumaras.
One of the Seven Sons of Brahma.

SA NA TANA   Also known as Sanatana.
One of the Holy Four, one of the Seven Sons of Brahma.
One of the Seven Holy Kumaras.

SA RA   A Pleiadian who was in contact with Dr. Michael Wolf.

SABREAEL   Angel.

SABRIEL   Virtue.

SACHIEL   Cherubim, Angel of Money, presiding spirit of Jupiter.

SACHLUPH   Angel of Plants.

SADIA	Wife of Bohindra, 8400 B.C.E.
SAGAMEMNON	From Uranus.
SAHAQIEL	Angel of the Sky.
SAHARÓN	King of country Poseidonia, Atlantis. Name of desert Sahara to remember him.

SAI BABA, Bhagavan Sri Sathya

He is an Avatar, Master.
Born Nov. 23, 1926, lives in Puttaparthi, Andhra Pradesh, India.
Incarnations: Rama, Krishna.
Future incarnation: Prema Baba.

SAINT FRANCIS of ASSISI

→ Kuthumi.

SAINT GERMAIN

Ascended Master, Chohan (Lord) of the 7th Ray (Violet Flame).
Born in 1561, some say he was born 1710 in Portugal.
His Twin Flame is Lady Portia.
Prince Francis Racoczy ascended May 1, 1684, from the Rockoczy Mansion in the Carpathian Mountain region of Transylvania (Romania).
It is said that he died in 1784, but was seen in 1789 all over the world.
There exist a lot of false St. Germaine's.
Elihu is his name in celestial realm.
Friend of Lord Kuthumi.
The "Wonderman of Europe" in the 1700's.
He looked the same for 100 years,
Spoke all European languages fluently, had a complete knowledge of History, was a composer, played the violin very well, traveled by thought, fed the poor and worked for peace.
He always dressed in black & white.
He was famous for his amazing skills in medicine and alchemy, especially for transmuting metals into gold.
Member of the Great Karmic Board.
Member of the Solar Tribunal.
Belongs to the Great White Brotherhood, the Brotherhood of the Royal Teton and the Brotherhood of Mount Shasta.
He was also said to be the inventor of Masonry.
Founded Rosicrucianism and Freemasonry in England.
Also known as:
>> Comte de Saint-Germain,
>> Count of Saint Germain,
>> Count Roskauwski,
>> Elihu (celestial realm),
>> God of Freedom,
>> Lord (Chohan) of the 7th Ray,
>> the man who never dies and knows everything,
>> "Uncle Sam",

>> „Wonder Man of Europe",
>> "Wundermann".
Incarnations:
>>   High Priest in Atlantis, 11,000 B.C.E.
>>   Samuel (prophet), 1050 B.C.E.
>>   Saint Joseph (Mary's husband),
>>   Saint Alban (Roman soldier in the 3rd century
          (first martyr of the British Isles)),
>>   Merlin,
>>   Roger Bacon,
>>   Christopher Columbus,
>>   Francis Bacon (wrote under the name of William
          Shakespeare).
As writer he used the names:
>>   Andraes, Valentine,
>>   Burton, Robert,
>>   Cervantes,
>>   Comte de Gabalis,
>>   Marlowe, Christopher,
>>   Montaigne,
>>   Spenser, Edmund.
Channel: ElectRa Ahn, Forenna (Kasandra Clemente), Isaac
George, Godfre, Sue Hall, Lois Hartwick, Jani King, Eric Klein,
Lyara, MA'al, Lori Adaile Toye, Lilian Whalley, Paul Yandeau.
→ Germaine, Rosenkreuz.
→ Chohans.
→ Guy W. Ballard, Peter Mt Shasta, Nola Van Valer.

SAINT GERMAINE

→ Saint Germain.

SAINT PAUL   Apostle, incarnation of Hilarius.

SALEM   The Great Light who identifies himself as ambassador to 44
                        universes.
                        Channel: Diandra.

SALILUS   Angel, genius.

SALMAEL   Other name of Samael.

SAM HII   Ruling Angel of the North Star.
                        Means „Creation of Life".
                        Also known as Shom Hii.

SAMAEL	Archangel, Seraphim, Angel of the Death.
	Dark Angel, has been regarded as evil and good.
	Chief of the Satans, Prince of Demons.
	Chief Ruler of the 5th (7th ?) Heaven.
	Great Serpent with 12 wings.
	Served by 2,000,000 angels.
	Guardian angel of Esau.
	Means „Severity of God".
	His 4 mates were:
	>> Agrat bat Mahlat,
	>> Eisheth Zenunim,
	>> Lilith,
	>> Naamah.
	Also known as: Arimanius, Bilar, Bilair, Bilid, Salmael, Samil, Sammael, Satan, Satanil, Sear, Seere, Seir.
SAMANDIRIEL	Angel.
SAMAX	Chief of the Angels of the Air.
SAMAYASA	Angelic leader, fallen angel.
SAMAZA	Reptilian being from Bootes.
SAMERON	Angel.
SAMEVEEL	Angel.
SAMIL	Other name of Samael.
SAMJANG	Pleiadian from Erra.
SAMMAEL	Other name of Samael.
SAMON	Extraterrestrial (?). Built the ancient stone city Ofir at the mouth of the Amazon River in South America.
	→ Ofir.
SAMPIAC	A guide from Venus, commander of the spaceship Tipus, graduated from the interstellar base in Saturn and coordinator of the Venusian guides.
SAMUEL	Incarnation of Ascended Master Saint Germain.
SAMYASA	Angel.
SANA	From Druar in the Nol System.
SANA	→ Sa Na Kumara.
SANAKA	→ Sanatka.

SANANDA   Lord. Avatar. Ascended Master. World teacher with Kuthumi.
The Great Commander of the Earth Mission.
Commander of the Galactic Federation of Light.
Supreme Commander of the Intergalactic Fleet and spiritual governor of the local universe.
One of the Holy Four, one of the Seven Sons of Brahma.
One of the Seven Holy Kumaras, brother of Sanat Kumara.
Was originally of the Elohim.
Sananda's soul left just prior to the cruzification.
Commander-in-Chief of the Ashtar Galactic Command & Jerusalem Command.
Now he has short hair and still a beard.
Works with Kelemariah in the group of Physicians & Scientists in the Ashtar Command.
Jesus was born about the 20th July.
Jesus & Sananda are 2 different souls, but both carry the Christ Energy.
In a previous life, he has lived as Moses.
Ezekiel was in Sananda's craft.
He walked in the body of Jesus in the 40 days of the desert & Jesus walked out.
He created the order of Melchizedek.
Incarnations:
>> Apollonius of Tyana,
>> Buddha,
>> Krishna,
>> Maitreya,
>> Melchizedek,
>> Mohammed,
>> Quetzalcoatl.
Also known as:
>> Christ Essence
>> Esu,
>> High Christ Consciousness,
>> Jesus,
>> Joshua,
>> Sananda Kumara,
>> The Christ.
Channel: ElectRa Ahn, Jan Eaton, Caroline Fitzgerald, Alec Christos Gabbitas, Sue Hall, Lois Hartwick, Eric Klein, Sara Lyara Estes, David K. Miller, Dr. Norma Milanovich, Nada-Yolanda, Sandi Sheppard, Sister Thedra, Lisa Smith, Lori Adaile Toye, Andrew Whalley, Lilian Whalley, Marion L. White, Debbie Wright.
→ Jesus, Sa Ananda.

SANANDA KUMARA
→ Sananda.

SANANDANA   → Sa Ananda.

SANAT KUMARA Regent Lord of the World. Prince of Light.
(Ancient) teacher of light from Venus.
Lord of the Flame. Planetary logos.
Returned to Venus on Jan. 1, 1956.
Was originally of the Elohim.
Divine Complement of Lady Venus.
Is part reptilian.
White hair, piercing blue eyes, bronze colored skin, around 12 ft tall.
Of the Order of Melchizedek.
Leader of the Orion Humans, Ascended Master.
Head of the Christos Beings, their base is located on Venus.
Leader of the "chain of Venus planets" with Lady Venus.
Has assisted Earth & humanity for millions of years.
Brother of Sananda.
One of the Seven Sons of Brahma.
One of the Holy Four, one of the Seven Holy Kumaras.
Also known as:
>>   Ahura Mazda,
>>   Karttikeya,
>>   Kumara,
>>   Regent Lord of the World,
>>   The Ancient of Days,
>>   The Youth of Endless Summers.
Channel: Brother Philip, Godfre, MA'al, Elizabeth Clare Prophet, Lori Adaile Toye, Lilian Whalley.
→ YaPool.
→ Seven Holy Kumaras.

SANAT-KUMARA Also known as Sanat Kumara.
→ Sanat Kumara.

SANAT-SUJATA → Sujata.

SANATANA Sa Na Tana.

SANATKA Also known as Sanaka.
Chief of the Seven Holy Kumaras.
One of the Holy Four.
One of the Seven Sons of Brahma.

SANATSUJATA → Sujata.

SANDALPHON Archangel, Angel Prince. Angel of Glory, Power, Prayer.
Also known as Alue, was prophet Elias.
Twin brother of Metatron.
Channel: Caroline Fitzgerald.
→ Elohim.

SANDIUS From Uranus, lived before in Egypt 6327 – 6284.

SANGARIAH Angel.

SANGRARIEL	Angel.
SANKARACHARYA	Master.
SANNUL	Angel of the order of Powers.
SANSIRUOUS	He was the first Reptilian to empower the females of his race as warriors.
SANTANAEL	Angel.
SANTON	Grand Space Commander from Cassiopeia from the planet Zel. His experimental spacecraft is Andrena 72.
SARAKUYAL	Angelic leader, fallen angel.
SARAQAEL	Holy angel, Archangel.
SARANANA	Angel.
SARAS	Spirit of planet Earth. Planet Earth was known under that name in the universe.
SARASWATI	Goddess of Art, Science and Wisdom.
SARGON	One of Inanna's favorite husbands. Reigned from 2334 B.C.E. – 2279 B.C.E.
SARIEL	Seraph, Angel of Death, Knowledge. Means „Command of God". said to be an archangel.
SARPHIEL	Angel.
SARQUAMICH	Angel.
SASGABIEL	Angel.
SATAARAN	Genius.
SATAN	Fallen angel, other name of Samael. Also known as Arimanius. → Samael.
SATANIL	Other name of Samael.
SATAREL	Angel.
SATRINA	Other name of Lilith.

SATYA	Pleiadian goddess.
SAURIEL	Angel of Death, Redeemer.
SAVANIAH	Angel.
SAVATRI	Other name of Savitri.
SAVITAR	Other name of Savitri.
SAVITRI	Woman officer from Venus. Angel who has golden hands, golden eyes. Also known as: Prajapati, Savitar, Savatri.
SAVURIEL	Angelic guard.
SAXOS	Angel of Mediation.
SCHACHLIL	Genius.
SCHALTIEL	Angel.
SCHIOEL	Angel.
SCHREWNEIL	Angel.
SCOPTA	From the Spectrum Plane.
SEALIAH	Angel of Vegetation.
SEALTIEL	Archangel of Contemplation, Worship.
SEAR	Other name of Seere (Samael).
SECLAM	Angel of the order of Powers.
SEDEKIAH	Angel of Jupiter.
SEE-VEN	Ascended Grand Master.
SEERE	Very powerful Goetian Spirit. Also known as: Sear, Seir. → Samael.
SEFONIEL	Angel.
SEHEIAH	Angel.
SEIR	Other name of Samael (Seere).
SEKEL	Female angel.

SEKHMET   Lion lady with a lion head and tail, 12 ft. tall.
                       She is from Nibiru. Twin Flame of Lord Alcyone.
                       The last time Sekhmet was on Earth was about 2000 B.C.E.,
                       there she lived about 3000 years in a body.
                       Also known as Mother Sekhmet.
                       Sister of Hathor.
                       Channel: Kara Kincannon, Susan Leland.

SELITH   Guardian angel of Mother Mary.

SEMJASE   Ascended Master of the Pleiades.
                       From high spiritual dimensions of the Pleiades (Erra).
                       Name allegedly invented by Billy Meier.
                       Female Pleiadian, 350 years old (1996).
                       From February 1965 until June 1973 lived with Asket's people in
                       the DAL Universe, she came to Earth in July 1973. On January
                       28, 1975 first contact with Billy Meier. On February 3, 1984 last
                       contact with Billy Meier.
                       Due to her accident on December 15, 1977 Semjase suffered a
                       cerebral collapse in November 1984. She is for about 70 years in
                       the DAL Universe for regeneration of her brain and all PSI
                       powers.
                       Channel: Carol Withrow.
                       → Billy Meier.

SEMUN-IAC   A guide from Venus.

SEPHORA   Wife of Moses, 1500 B.C.E.

SEPHURIRON   Angel.

SERAPH   Angel of Fire.

SERAPIEL   Ruling angel and leader of the order of Seraphim.

SERAPIS BEY Ascended Master.
Lord (Chohan) of the 4th Ray (White Flame).
He has golden hair, amber colored eyes.
Ascended about 400 B.C.E.
It is said he came from Venus.
Hierarch of the Ascension Temple at Luxor, Egypt.
He works with the Seraphim.
Worked in the 19th century closely with El Morya, Kuthumi, Djwhal Khul and other masters to found the Theosophical Society.
Incarnations:
>>   High Priest in the Ascension Temple in Atlantis, 9,500 B.C.E.,
>>   Akhenaton IV, built the temples at Thebes and Karnak,
>>   Amenhotep III (1417 – 1379 B.C.E.), called the "Magnificent", built the temple of Luxor,
>>   Leonidas, King of Sparta, about 480 b.C,
>>   Phidias, Atenas (architect and sculptor), supervised the building of the Parthenon (438 B.C.E.).
→ Chohans.

SERAQUIEL Angel.

SEREF Angel.

SERONIAC A guide from Venus.

SERUF Angel Prince of Fire, Seraph.

SETH Son of king Atlas form Atlantis, approx. 9,500 B.C.E.
Younger brother of Osiris.
Wanted to reestablish the Atlantean Empire.

SETHLANS Angel, one of the Novensiles.

SHAARI Female Commander from Arcturus.
Works in the Star Command as a holographic healer and interdimensional teacher.
Integrated into a human body in 1989.
Channel to: Intergalactic Council of Twelve.
Shaari & Trinity Seminars, P.O.Box 22040, Brentwood Bay, B.C.E., Canada.
Tel: (604) 360-8708.

SHAH JAHAN → Kuthumi.

SHAKZIEL Angel of Water Insects.

SHALGIEL Angel of Snow.

SHAMRA TALIA   Master of Divine Communion from the 12th dimension.
                      Member of the Council of the Rainbow Bridge.

SHANYAN   Stepson of Krishna, son of Malwa.

SHARIVAR   Other name of Sharivari.

SHARIVARI   Angel.

SHARULA   Crown princess, daughter of the Ra & Rana Mu of Telos.
                      Ambassador of the Agartha Network.
                      Resident of Telos (city below Mt. Shasta), age of 267 years
                      (1997.07.02), physically appears to be in her mid 30's.
                      → Sharula Dux.

SHATEIEL   Angel of Silence.

SHAYA   Most ancient conscious entity.
                      King of the World, Divine Lord of Agartha.
                      Ruler of Shambhala.
                      Father of all Buddhas.
                      His feminine expression is WooPaa.
                      → Agartha.

SHCACHLIL   Angel of the Sun.

SHEATZO   Being from Sirius.

SHEKIN   Female aspect of creation, the Holy Spirit.

SHEKINAH   Female Angel of Freedom & Liberation.
                      Angel of the Lord.
                      Female equivalent of Metatron.
                      Female manifestation of God in man.

SHEKTAR   Angel.

SHEMESHIEL   Angel.

SHEMHAMPHORAE
                      Other name of Daniel.

SHETEL   Angel.

SHIDARTA GAUTAMA
                      → Buddha, 600 B.C.E.

SHIMBALA   Father of Devin, died during the first Great War.
                      Former head of the 9D Nibiruan Council.

SHIMSHIEL   Angelic guard.

SHINIAL   Angel.

SHIVA   Lord, destroyer - transformer.
                     Also known as:
                     >>   Holy Spirit,
                     >>   Lord of Love,
                     >>   Mahadeva,
                     >>   Mahesvara,
                     >>   Nataraja,
                     >>   Siva,
                     >>   Vamadeva.
                     Channel Elizabeth Clare Prophet.
                     → Hathor.

SHOM HII   Other name of Sam Hii.

SIALUL   Genius of Prosperity.

SIG-MAR   From Trantor.
                     Member of the Solar Cross.

SIMAEL   Said to be an archangel.

SIMIKIEL   Angel.

SIRAI   Sirian female counselor and exobiologist.

SIRAYA   Lord.
                     Works with Lord Kuwaya.
                     → Supreme Creative Force.

SIRIO   Spiritual guide of Antulio.

SITAEL   Seraph.

SIZAJASEL   Angel.

SIZOUSE   Angel of Prayer.

SKANDA   → Sanat Kumara.

SKREED   Extraterrestrial of an intelligent Insectillian race who was in
                     contact with Martin Riley.

SOCHODIAH   Angel.

SOFIEL   Recording Angel, Angel of Vegetation.

SOHEMME   Angel of the Seal.

SOHIN   Represents the energy of the Life Bearers.
                     Celestial Hierarchy.

SOKKA

SOLAR   From Vega.

SOLARA

SOLARIS KUMARA

Great being of fire who serves on the Planetary Council as an advisor. He represents the Higher Councils of the Universal Spiritual Sun.

SOLEMINE   She is from the Hydra star cluster.

SOLITUM   A guide from Apu.

SOLMEN   Intraterrestrial master from Mt. Shasta, California.

SOLOVIAC   A guide from Venus.

SOLTEC

Commander of one of the key monitoring spacecraft, that patrols for the Ashtar Command, in the Forces of Light. Astrophysicist on his starship - the Phoenix.
Space Scientist & Sun Technician.
He is from the planet Centurus in the Alpha Centauri system.
Contacted Richard Miller in 1954.
From Saturn, member of Space Federation.
Member of Interplanetary Alliance.
Member of the Ashtar Command and the Solar Cross..
Friend of Hatonn, son of Monka.
Channel: Bob Young.
→ Richard Miller.

SOLUZEN   Angel.

SOPHIA

The She-ness of all that is.
Mother of Eve, princess from country Otlana, Atlantis, (8350 B.C.E.).
Incarnation of Quan Yin.
Channel is Gillian MacBeth-Loutan.

SOPHIEL   Recording Angel.

SOQED HOZI   Angel.

SORDAZ

A guide from Apu. Commander of Cerilum, a base of the Confederation (also known as Rumi Suyo) in Huanuco, Peru. He is now in charge of coordinating Venusian guides.
→ Cerilum.

SORIAM   Intraterrestrial master, regent of Lake Titicaca.

SOROMEZ	Intraterrestrial master of Lake Titicaca.
SOSOL	Angel.
SOTHIS	Angel.
SOURCE	God.
SPARTAN	Space Commander from the Pleiades made 13 phone calls to Yashah from the Outer Space.
SPHANO-SAN	→ Beth.
SPHENER	Celestial Power.
SPLENDITENES	Angel.
SRI MAGRA	Ascended Master who held the office „Lord of the World" prior to Sanat Kumara and Gautama Buddha.
SRI YUKTESWAR	Great master. He was one of the few gurus who deserve absolute trust. Was the disciple of Lahiri Mahasaya.
SSNIALIAH	Angel.
ST.GERMAIN	→ Germaine, Saint Germain.
ST.GERMAINE	→ Germaine, Saint Germain.
STANTON	Grand Space Commander from the experimental craft Anstranda 17 from the planet Pacifica from the Orion galaxy.
STIMULATOR	Angel.
STRATEIA	Angel.
SUDDHODANA	Father of Buddha, 600 B.C.E.
SUDOR	Pleiadian from Askal in the Plejaren System.
SUI'EL	Angel of Earthquakes.
SUJATA	Also known as Ambhamsi, Sanat Sujata, Sanatsujata. One of the Seven Holy Kumaras. One of the Seven Sons of Brahma.
SULEIMAN II	Incarnation of Croesus.
SUM	Guide from Apu, in contact with La Coruña, Spain.
SUMMANUS	Angel, one of the Novensiles.

SUNA   Cherub, Seraph.

SUPHLATUS   Genius of Dust.

SUPREME CREATIVE FORCE
                       (God).
                       Consists of three immortal & powerful aspects, of which only
                       two have been revealed: Lord Kuwaya, Lord Siraya.

SURA   Revealing Angel.

SUREA   Lord, the Divine Manifestor.

SUREYA   Other name of Surea.

SURIEL   Archangel, Angel of Death, Healing.

SURNIA   Female extraterrestrial scientist.
                       Member of the Solar Cross.

SURYA   Other name of Metatron.

SUSABO   Angel.

SUSNIEL   Angel.

SUTH   Chief of the Angels of the Air.

SUTKO   Guardian of Cosmic Laws.
                       Member of the Galactic Tribunal on Aldebaran-3. Member of
                       the Solar Cross.

SYTH   Angel.

TABLIBIK   Genius.

TABRIS   Angel.

TAFEL X   Angel.

TAFTHI   Angel.

TAGAS   Angelic prince.

TAHARIAL   Angel of Purity.
                       Also known as Tahariel.

TAHARIEL   Other name of Taharial.

TAHUTI   Ibis god.
                       Channel is Maia.

TALIAHAD	Angel of Water.
TALIDA	From the Lyra System.
TALIESIN	→ Merlin, his Celt name.
TALTO	Other name of Lilith.
TAMAEL	Angel.
TAMIEL	Angelic leader, fallen angel.
TAMLRIS	Great Master of Wisdom, Elder Wise, White Being. Powerful admiral. Androgen of the Sirian Solar Breeds.
TAN	Also known as O-Qua Tangin-Wann Tan. Extraterrestrial friend of Martin Riley.
TANYA	Crewmember of Valiant Thor's ship.
TAR	Angel of the Sun.
TARA	Channel: Sue Hall, Helen Whalley.
TARIEL	Angel of Summer.
TAROT	Angel of Time.
TARQUAM	Angel of Autumn.
TARSHISH	Ruling angel prince of the order of Virtues.
TARWAN	Angel of the Sun.
TASHABA	Entity from the Sirian Star System, catlike.
TAURON	Pleiadian from Erra.
TEBLIEL	Angel of the Earth.
TEEL	Vice-Commander of Victor One from Venus.
TEHUTI	Came from civilization Altea by space ship. Annunaki rebel. Ancient Egypt master architect. First, he built pyramids in Egypt, later in the Americas, China and on other places on the planet. Great timekeeper of the Annunaki created the Mayan Calendar, about 3,000 B.C.E. Also known as Hermes, Thoth.

TEIAIEL   Throne Angel.

TELANTES   Angel.

TELETRON   Sirian expert on Lyran/Sirian culture, galactic Historian.

TEMPAST   Angel.

TEPISEUTH   Angel.

TERATHEL   Angel of the order of Dominions.

TEREC   A guide from Venus.

TERS   From Druan in the Nol System.

TESESHUAN   Channel: Jessica Saunders.

TETRA   Angel.

THALARO   One of the 12 Elders at the Solar Tribunal on Saturn.

THARSIS   Angel of Choices, Decisions.

THEGRI   Angel of Animals.

THEL DAR   Light being that created many of the existing universes.
                       Is Inanna.
                       → Inanna.

THELIEL   Angel.

THEODORA   Member of the Ashtar Space Command.

THEOSOPHIA   Ascended Lady Master.
                       She holds the office of the Goddess of Wisdom.
                       Incarnation: Mary Baker Eddy.

THIEL   Angel of planet Venus.

THIMETIS   → Av.Isis.Thimetis, mother of Moses, 1300 B.C.E.

THONN   Starship commander from Stella (Venus), his ship crashed in
                       Helgoland in a storm (1948).

THOR   God from the galaxy Latania.

THOTH   Angel, Master & Teacher of universal wisdom from the planet
                       Osiran in the galaxy Floreida.
                       Immortal!

Thoth is known as a God of the Egyptians, later adopted by the Greeks and renamed "Hermes." As a God-Being, he was venerated in Egypt from at least 3000 B.C.E. He was given credit for inventing hieroglyphic writing. He was known as the "Scribe of the Gods," and as such, was the recorder of all human deeds. It has also been said through the ages, that the Great Thoth brought to mankind the sciences of law, astrology, anatomy, medicine, chemistry, art, magic, alchemy and architecture. There are certain learned scholars of the past who equated Thoth with the biblical prophet Enoch, saying that they were the same. Iamblichus declared Thoth to have been the author of twenty thousand books, while Manetho credited him with having written more than thirty-six thousand. The Greeks called Thoth "Hermes Trismesgistus," the latter name meaning "Thrice Great."

The ancient Egyptians oftentimes depicted Thoth as Ibis-headed, although he was also portrayed at times with the head of a baboon.

There are ancient texts, which claim that Thoth was the architect of the Great Pyramid of Gizeh. The most famous books attributed to him are "The Emerald Tablets" and "The Pymander."

"As 'Toth-Mus-Zurud,' He came within a vesica of Light, a Merkabah of golden and blue-white fire, from Rigel, through the 'Asefetas' (the Belt of Orion), and descended unto 'Rastaru' (Rastau), the etheric manifold of the plain of Gizeh. He brought the Enochian Table containing the blueprint for the building of the Temple of the Risen One, later to be called the Temple of the Lion, which is now known as the 'Great Pyramid.' He was the Master Architect of this construction, which was begun in the year 10,400 B.C.E. It was completed in 10,348 B.C.E.

In the year 9,160 B.C.E., he entered as Raismes of Aphra for 300 years. After that he reincarnated as Amenophis, architect to Akhenaten, Imenhotep, architect to Zoser, and Hiram Abiff, architect to King Solomon.

He was of pure Orion genetics.

Thoth means "the Grand Communicator". Toth-Mus-Zurud was known in Atlantis as the 'Sword of Orion'. His origin is Ultra-Terrestrial, from the 'Eighth Sphere of Heaven.'

He now dwells with the Central Earth Tribes.

Thoth was a light being and a Priest-King of Atlantis. For many millennia he was the ruler-guardian of Atlantis. He did indeed go to Egypt and was greeted by a cannibal-type of race of beings and he stayed with them and taught them, and the Egyptians considered Thoth a god. Moreover, it was Thoth who constructed the Great Pyramid, and not Cheops or Khufu. Built the sacred city Adocentyn.

Greek name of the ancient Egypt Tehuti.

Light Principle 40 (LP40) will fall between 2015 & 2025.

Thoth & his MERKABAH Group "Chariot of the Sun".

Incarnations:

>>   Raismes of Aphra (9,160 B.C.E.), 300 years old,

>>   Amenophis.
Also known as:
>>   Amenophis,
>>   Cadmus,
>>   Enoch (supposedly),
>>   God Mercury,
>>   Hermes,
>>   Hermes Trimesgistus,
>>   Palamedes,
>>   Raismes of Aphra,
>>   Tehuti,
>>   Thoth-Mus-Zurud,
>>   Thothmus.
Channel: Lois Hartwick.
→ Enoch, Tehuti.
→ Adocentyn.

THOTH-MUS-ZURUD
                    Other name of Thoth.
                    Means "Thoth the Atlantean".
                    He was the "Sword of Orion".
                    He dwelt primarily in Atlantis.

THOTHMUS   Other name of Thoth.
                    → Thoth.

THURIEL   Angel.

THUTMOSE III   → Kuthumi.

TIAMAT   Elohim goddess.

TIBUS   Golden human from a star craft, time traveler from the future.
                    Dark olive skin, large hazel eyes, goldish hair.
                    Channel: Dianne Tessman.

TIEL   Angelic guard.

TILEION   Angel.

TILONAS   Angel.

TINA   Angel, one of the Novensiles.

TIRTAEL   Angel.

TITINAC   Female guide from Venus, mental doctor and physician onboard
                    the spaceship Tipus. She lives in the underwater base of
                    Acqualium, located northwest of Chancay, Peru.

TOBIAS   Channel Geoff Hoppe.

TOMAR	An Arcturian Spiritual leader. Channel: David K. Miller.
TOMIMIEL	Angel.
TORIN	
TORQUAMANDO	Commander.
TORQUARET	Angel of Autumn.
TRANSANKO	Prof. from Atlantis.
TRGIAOB	Angel of Wild Birds.
TRSIEL	Angel of Rivers.
TSAPHIEL	Angel of the Moon.
TUA UR	Other name of Mirach.
TUAL	Angel.
TUBIEL	Angel of Summer.
TUELLA	Channel to Ashtar.
TULATU	Angel of Omnipotence.
TULEO	Science officer, brother of Thonn.
TUREL	Angel.
TURMIEL	Angelic guard.
TUWAHEL	Angel.
TZADIQEL	Archangel who rules Jupiter.
TZADIQUEL	Angel.
TZADKIEL	Angel of Divine Justice. Other name of Zadkiel.
TZAPHQIEL	Angel.
TZEDEQIAH	Angel.
UBAVIEL	Angel.
UGRASENA	Grandfather of Krishna, king of Madura, India, 3000 B.C.E.

UMABEL   Angel.

UMEROZ   Angel.

UNIAH   On board of Victor One.

UNIXITRON   Commander of the Planetary Forces of Liberation.
                              Acts unknown to humankind.

UNIVERSAL DREAMER
                              Is God.

UPASU ARASATHA
                              Commander of a space station of a size of 34 km.
                              Son of Atarsatha from the Pleiades.
                              Tagurer from Sorxerma, his wife is Adaga.

URAKABARAMEEL
                              Angelic leader, fallen angel.

URAKABRAMEEL
                              Other name of Urakabarameel.

URIEL   Lord, Throne Angel.
                              Ruling angel prince of the order of Cherubim.
                              Ruling angel of the order of Seraphim.
                              Archangel of Ministration, Salvation.
                              Archangel of the 6th Ray.
                              Angel of Chance, Fire, Literature, Money, Music, Repentance,
                              Salvation, Transformation.
                              Uriel means "Fire of God", „Flame of God", „Light of God",
                              Sun of „God".
                              Twin Flame is Aurora.
                              Works with Lady Master Nada on the 6th Ray of Devotion to
                              peace.
                              Is said to have given the Kabala.
                              Also known as:
                              >>   Aleph,
                              >>   Auriel,
                              >>   Lamed,
                              >>   Resh,
                              >>   Vau,
                              >>   Yod.
                              Channel: Elizabeth Clare Prophet.

URIRON   Angel.

URPANIEL   Angel.

USIEL   Ruling angel prince of the order of Virtues.

UTU   Twin brother of Inanna, son of Nannar& Ningal, grandfather of
                           Gilgamesh.

UVAEL   Angel.

UWULA   Angel.

UXTAAL   Elder from Uranus.

UZZA   Angel.

UZZIEL   Cherubim, Virtue, Throne Angel. Angel of Earth, Mercy.
                           Means „Strength of God".
                           Works under Gabriel & Metatron.

VAJRAPANI   Channel: Brian Rolfe.

VALDAR   Earth mission leader from the Koldasian system, had contacts in
                           South Africa. Valdar warns Earth not to make the same mistakes
                           taking place in their solar system.

VALEOEL   Said to be an archangel.

VALIANT THOR   Grand Space Commander of Victor One from Venus.
                           Landed 1957 in Virginia. Met allegedly R. Nixon.
                           Frank Stranges claims that he keeps contact with him.

VALLANCE   Space Commander, interdimensional being from the planet
                           Zicona in Orion, does interception in 94 galaxies.
                           Between 7 to 9 ft tall, gold-colored hair, piercing blue eyes, slim,
                           2700 years old (lifespan 3500 years +).
                           Member of the Orion Command Security Unit.

VALOEL   Angel.

VAOL   Angel of the Moon.

VARCAN   Angel of the Air, Sun.

VARTAR   Extraterrestrial intelligence.
                           Channel: John Percival.

VASAIS   Cosmonaut from the Andromeda galaxy.

VASAN   He helps for the re-opening of psychic abilities, of the Starfleet
                           ground personnel.

VASSAGO   Angel.

VASUVEDA   Father of Krishna, second son of king Vado Van Ugrasena of
                           Madura, India, 3000 B.C.E.

VATALE   Prince over all angels and Caesars.

VAU   Other name of Archangel Uriel.

VEGUANIEL   Angel.

VEHIEL   Angel.

VEHUEL   Angel of the order of Principalities.

VEHUIAH   Seraphim.

VEJOVIS   Angel, one of the Novensiles.

VEL   Angel.

VENAJOA   From Venus, she's officer aboard the starship Janus.
                        Member of the Ashtar Command.

VENIBBETH   Angel.

VENOSIA   Woman officer from Venus.

VENUS   Lady Master on Venus.
                        Divine Complement of Sanat Kumara.
                        Spirit guide of Abel.
                        Also known as:
                        >>   Goddess of Beauty,
                        >>   Goddess of Love.
                        Channel: Elizabeth Clare Prophet, Carolyn Shearer.

VEPAR   Goetian Spirit, female demon. Vepar is a creature of the sea and
                        can never leave the sea.
                        Also known as The Serpent Queen.

VERCHIEL   Angel, ruler of the order of Powers.
                        Governor of the Sun.

VERITAN   Comes in the Light of Logic.

VERITILBIA   Lord of planet Mercury.
                        Member of the Spiritual Hierarchy.

VESPERINA   Reincarnation of Vestha, daughter of Numu. 33300 B.C.E.

VESTA   Divine Complement of Helios.

VESTHA   Wife (almost blind) of Juno, 45800 - 45755 b. C.

VEYARES   Commander of the mothership West Star, operates under Ashtar,
                        the Star Command and the Intergalactic Council of Twelve.
                        → West Star.

VICTORIA Elohim of the 7th (violet) Ray.
14 to 15 ft tall.
Her Twin Flame is Arcturus.
Also known as Diana (not the same Diana that is Twin Flame of prince Oromasis).
→ Arcturus.

VINK From Vega.

VIRACOCHA Founder of the Inca dynasty and builder of Cuzco.

VIRGIN MARY → Mother Mary.

VIRGINIA Elohim of the 5th (green) Ray of Constancy, Healing, Truth.
Twin Flame of Cyclopea.

VIRGO Keeper of the Flame of Light burning in the physical cells of all being.
She is Mother Earth.
Her Twin Flame is Pelleur.
Channel: Geraldine Innocente, Elizabeth Clare Prophet.
→ Gaia.

VISHNU Avatar, sky god and protector of the universe.
Lord of the Heart.
Incarnations (10 to 39):
>> Krishna,
>> Rama,
>> Sai Baba.

VISSAEUS Sage being from Andromeda. 4300 years old.

VISTA Lord of Karma.

VIVAMUS Master. Higher Aspect of Sanat Kumara.
"I Am" Presence of the Kumaras.
Information officer for the Elohim.
Channel: Liliane Bader, Barbara Burns, Caroline Fitzgerald, MA'al, David K. Miller, Saemmi Muth, Radha.

VIVENUS Being from Venus.

VOGODA Ascended Master.
Works together with El Morya.

VOHAL Angel of Power.

VOHU MANAH Angel of Milk.

VOIZIA Angel.

VOLTRA   Commander, leading Space Psychologist from planet Venus.
                              Key member of the Ashtar Command. Member of the Solar
                              Cross.
                              Channel Francesca Aleuti.

VRANIEL   Angel.

VRETIL   Archangel of Sacred Books.

VULCAN   Lilith is another great energy, along with Vulcan. These are all
                              beings from old Atlantis and prior to   that   Pangaea   and
                              Lemuria.

VVAEL   Angel.

VYWAMUS   → Vivamus.

WAH, Dr.   A spirit traveler serving in the 49 planes of light.

WALLIM   Angel.

WASHTA   New Sirian Ascended Master from Sirius B.

WATSON, Dr. Norman   (1812 – 1879).
                              Ascended Grand Master from the 11th interdimensionality.
                              Medical Chief Doctor on Ashtar's mothership Athena.

WEATTA   Angel of the Seal.

WENS   A group of beings.

WHITE BUFFALO CALF WOMAN
                              Avatar and Star Visitor.

WILKIRIA   Mother of Antulio, 16700 B.C.E., later reincarnation as
                              Av.Isis.Thimetis 1500 B.C.E.

WINKA   Boy from the galactic underground colony on Mars.

WOODOK   He is the Captain of the starship Crystal Bell. Has landed many
                              times on the volcano Etna in Sicily.

WOOPAA   Divine Lord of Agartha.
                              Feminine expression of ShaYa.

WUNDERMANN   Name of Saint Germain.
                              → Saint Germain.

XANXA   Guide from Apu, replaced by Xendor.

XENDOR   A Terrestrial guide, member of the White Brotherhood. He works in the Blue Base in Peru and is currently replacing the guide Xanxa from Apu.

XENIALAC   A guide from Venus.

XENON   A guide from Cerpican.

XEXOR   Benevolent spirit.

XOZIAN   A guide from Venus.

XYLETRON   Cmdr. of the Intergalactic Fleet.
                          Member of the Ashtar Command.
                          Channel: Lyara.

YABBASHAEL   Angel of Earth.

YAHALA   Angelic guard.

YAHEL   Angel of the Moon.

YAHOEL   Other name of Metatron.

YAHRIEL   Ruling angel of the order of Dominions (Dominations).

YAPOOL   Multidimensional creature.
                          The Solar Giant YaPool is the only child of ShaYa and WooPa. YaPool is a warrior Lord and will be the new king of Shambhala. He belongs to the cosmic consciousness of the ancient Kumara tribe from Sirius.

YARASHIEL   Angelic guard.

YASHAH   (Walter Collins). Owner of Alahoy.
                          Space Commander in the year 1804.

YASHIEL   Angel of the Moon.

YBHAKU

YEFEFIAH   Angel.

YEKAHEL   Spirit of planet Mercury.

YEORGOS   Commander.
                          Channel: Glenda Stocks.

YEPHIEL   Angel.

YESHUA BEN JOSEPH
                          Hybrid. Is Jesus.

YESHUA MALATHIEL

Died at Massada 64 C.E., was not crucified.
Was a blue blood.
→ Jesus.

YISHA   Lord.

YO   On board of Victor One.

YOD   Other name of Archangel Uriel.

YOFIEL   Other name of Iofiel, Metatron.

YOYSIA   Chief Genetics Engineer of the Galactic Federation
                         Sirius A Council.

YROUEL   Angel of Fear.

YUMINALE   Woman officer from Alpha Centauri.
                         Member of the Ashtar Command.
                         One of the Cosmic Virgins.

YUMINALEE   → Yuminale.

YURA   Spirit of Light & Rain.

YURKEMI   Angel of Hail.

ZABKIEL   Ruling angel prince of the order of Thrones.

ZACHAREL   Angel.

ZACHRIEL   Angel of Memory.

ZADKIEL   Archangel of the 7th (violet) Ray (Flame) of Transformation.
                         Archangel of Invocation.
                         Angel of Charity, Gentleness, Solace.
                         Ruling angel of the order of Dominions (Dominations).
                         Also known as:
                         >> Lord Zadkiel,
                         >> Tzadkiel.

ZAFENATPANEACH

Pleiadian from Erra.

ZAGZAGEL   Angel of Wisdom.

ZAHARIEL   Angel.

ZAKKIEL   Angel of Storms.

ZALBESAEL	Angel of Rain. Means: „Heart of God".
ZALIEL	Angel.
ZAMAEL	Angel of Sexual Pleasures.
ZANDRIEL	Lord.
ZANTESE	Draco-Human hybrid. Zantese means "Strength of a Thousand Blooms". Their average lifespan is 500 – 600 years; she is about 5 ft tall, golden-brown scales.
ZAPHKIEL	Said to be an archangel. Ruling angel prince of the order of Thrones. Ruling angel of the order of Dominions (Dominations).
ZARALL	Archangel, Cherub.
ZARATHUSTRA	Ascended Master. Messenger of Ahura Mazda, founded Zoroastrianism in ancient Persia.
ZARENE	Ascended Grand Master.
ZAVAEL	Angel of Whirlwinds.
ZAYDAY	Angel.
ZAZAGEL	Angel.
ZAZEL	Angel.
ZECHIEL	Angel.
ZEENA	Female dimensional time-traveler.
ZEFFAR	Genius.
ZEHANPURYU'H	Angel, higher than Metatron.
ZEIRNA	Genius.
ZEKA	Space Commander sent messages to a telephone answering Machine.
ZEL, Dr.	From San Tam.
ZELNA	Woman officer from Saturn.
ZEN TAO	Master.

ZEND   Father of Zoroaster.
                     Incarnation of Lord Sananda.

ZENDA   Disciple of Krishna, 3000 B.C.E., later incarnation as king
                     Balthazar.

ZENDOR   Son of Ashtar & Athena.

ZEPHON   Cherub, Guardian Prince of Paradise.

ZEPHRON   Archangel.

ZERIEL   Angel Prince of the order of Principalities.
                     also known as Zuriel.

ZERUCH   Angel.

ZETHAR   Angel of Confusion, Immortality.

ZEUS   → Altea.

ZHOSER   → Zoser.

ZIANOR   Angel.

ZIASANDRA   Enoch's name in Sumeria.

ZIDKIEL   Angel.

ZIKIEL   Angel of Comets & Meteors.
                     Also known as Ziquiel.

ZIQUIEL   Other name of Zikiel.

ZIZUPH   Genius.

ZO   Communications supervisor, KOR, Mars.
                     Member of the Solar Cross.

ZOLGUS   Extraterrestrial.
                     Member of the Solar Cross.

ZOLTAR   Ascended Grand Master from Arcturia from the Bootes
                     Constellation.

ZOPHIEL   Archangel, other name of Iofiel.
                     Ruling angel prince of the order of Cherubim.

ZORB   He is the head of the galactic M.A.S.H units within this solar
                     system, located in the Jupiter Command.

ZOROASTER   Master, Teacher of Light.
                       Member of the Planetary Council.

ZOSER   Master of Healing.
                       Master physician for the new millennium.
                       First builder of the pyramid.
                       "Zhoser" means "holy".
                       Incarnations: pharaoh in the 3rd dynasty of ancient Egypt.

ZUHL   Saturnian Space Brother who took George Adamski to a
                       Saturnian mothership in 1953.

ZUPHLAS   Angel of Forests, Trees.

ZURIEL   Other name of Zeriel.

7.2 Messiahs

MESSIAHS (Avatar: Jhasua (Sananda (Jesus)))

1. Juno	45800-45755	Lemuria, Nuculandia
2. Numo	33300	Lemuria, Gegantes
3. Anfion	22300	Atlantis, Otlana
(& Beth [Sphano-San])		
4. Antulio	16700	Atlantis, Zeus
5. Abel	8300	Ethea, Eden
6. Krishna	3000	India, Bombay
7. Moses	1500	Ahuar (Egypt) & Sinai
8. Buddha	600	Nepal, Kapilavastu
9. Jhasua	0	

7.3 Cosmic Beings

Elys
Helios
Kryon
Kumad
Lytton
Mahatma
Melchizedek
Nibiru.

7.4 Chohans

A Chohan is an Ascended Master that focuses the Christ Consciousness of one of the Seven Rays of God's Manifestation.
The Seven Chohans represent the attributes of the Solar Logos and Christ Consciousness of each Ray to Earth's evolution.

1st Ray   (Blue Flame)   represented by El Morya,
                                      residing in Darjeeling, India.

2nd Ray (Yellow Flame)   represented by Lord Lanto,
                                      residing in Grand Teton Mountains, near Jackson Hole,
                                      Wyoming.

3rd Ray   (Pink Flame)   represented by Paul the Venetian,
                                      residing in Château de Liberté, in Southern France.

4th Ray (White Flame)   represented by Serapis Bey,
                                      residing in the Temple of Ascension, in Luxor, Egypt.

5th Ray (Green Flame)   represented by Hilarion,
                                      residing in the Temple of Truth, in Crete, Greece.

6th Ray (Ruby, Purple, Gold Flame)
                                      represented by Lady Nada,
                                      residing in Saudi Arabia.

7th Ray (Violet Flame)   represented by Saint Germain,
                                      residing in the Table Mountain in the Teton Mountain
                                      Range, Wyoming, in India, and in Transylvania,
                                      Romania.

7.5 Ascended Masters

Masters were created at the beginning of the white race. Masters are the children of the Elohim. They are not angels. There are 144,000 Ascended Master.
Individuals that were once embodied on a physical plane (e.g. Earth).
Balanced more than 50% of negative karma and fulfilled their Dharma (Divine Plan).
It is also said that anyone who has lived upon this plane at any time and has gone through a death experience is an Ascended Master.
They live in the 5th dimension and higher.
They are the Orion humans who used the reptilian esoteric knowledge to physically ascend. The reptilians have one way to ascend and the humans have another:
The reptilians way is through abstinence and physical isolation, through long periods of esoteric living they are able to shift their molecular structure and thus disappear into another dimension.
Also known as Ladies and Lords of Shamballa.

Adama, Aeolus, Ashtar, Bartholomew, Buddha, Cazekiel, Chiron, Confucius, Djwhal Khul, Dr. Norman, El Morya, Elijah, Ganesh, Gautama-Buddha, Germaine, Godfre, Goo-Ling (Saint), Hilarion, Jesus, Kinich Ahau, Kristine (Lady), Kuan Yin, Kuthumi, Lady Clarion, Lady Leto, Lady Lotus, Lady Magda, Lady Mary, Lady Nada, Lady Portia, Lady Rowena, Lanello, Lord Lanto, Lord Ling, Maha Chohan, Maria, Maitreya, Mary, Melchizedek, Omri-Tas, Oromasis, Pallas Athena, Paul the Venetian, Phylos (the Tibetan), Quan-Yin, Rakockzi, Ramona, Saint Germain, Sananda, Sanat Kumara, See-Ven, Serapis Bey, Sri Magra, St. Germain, Theosophia, Vogoda, Washta, Watson, Zarathustra, Zarene, Zoltar.

→ Brotherhood of the All, Great White Brotherhood, Council of Light.

7.6 Avatars

In Sanskrit avatar means descent or reincarnation of the same soul in a different body, in
Hinduism avatar is a human incarnation of the Divine.
Each Avatar appears when the world is in crisis.

Adonai, Alpha, Apollo, Babaji, Babalon, Beth, Castor, Diana, Ghamma, Ghimel, Hehalep,
Horos, Jhasua, Jhuno, Kapella, Krishna, Kurma, Lady Guadalupe, Lo Chi (at a pre-
Lemurian time), Mother Meera, Narsinha, Orfeo, Pallas Athena, Pallus, Polux,
Quetzalcoatl, Rama, Regulo, Resay, Sai Baba, Sananda, Schipho, Shedanial, Shemonis,
Thipert, Venus, Virgho, Vishnu, White Buffalo Calf Woman, Zahin.

7.7 Spiritual Hierarchy

SPIRITUAL HIERARCHY (9 Orders)

Control interdimensional energy transfer by the use of interdimensional gates.

1ˢᵗ Sphere:	Angels who serve as heavenly counselors.
	Angels of pure contemplation, govern all creation.

1. Seraphim   Highest order of the highest hierarchy, surround the throne of God.
Singular is Seraph. Also called Angels of Love, Seraphs.
They have 6 wings.
They are mixed beings like the Cherubim.
Higher Reptilian (means „Fiery Serpent"). They're represented by the serpent leader Serapiel.
Ruling princes of this order are:
Camael, Jahoel, Metatron, Michael, Nathanael, Serapiel, Uriel.
6 major Seraphim are:
Ananea, Azuriel, Betea, Cephetas, Ezekeal, Immanuel.
Seraphs are:
Achaih, Abdiel, Cahetel, Chabalym, Chaylon, Eoluth, Gabriel, Jehoel, Jeliel, Metatron, Michael, Nathanael, Salmael, Samael, Samil, Sammael, Sariel, Satan, Satanil, Seir, Seraphiel, Serapiel, Seruf, Sitael, Suna, Uriel, Vehuiah.

2. Cherubim   Also called Cherubs, Hashmallim, Holy Beasts, Ophanim.
Guardians of light and stars.
Keepers of the celestial records.
They are mixed beings like the Seraphim and combine features of bird, snake and human.
Ruling princes of this order are:
Gabriel, Kerubiel, Ophaniel, Raphael, Uriel, Zophiel.
Satan was also a ruling prince.
Cherubs are:
Ardouisur (female), Chabalym, Chaylon, Chayyiel, Cherubiel, Eoluth, Favardin, Gabriel, Hahaiah, Hakamiah, Ham Meyuchad, Lucifer (Satan), Metatron, Ophaniel, Osael, Oseny, Raphael, Sachiel, Suna, Uriel, Uzziel, Zarall, Zephon, Zophiel.

3. Thrones   Companion angels of the planets.

Also called Abalim, Angels of Pure Goodness, Arelim, Auphanim, Chariots, Erelim, Galgallin, Merkaba, Merkabah, Ophanim, Wheels.

Earth angel is Lady Gaia.

Chief of this order is Iofiel (Yofiel, Zophiel).

Ruling princes of this order are:

Japhkiel, Jophiel, Oriphiel, Raziel, Zabkiel, Zaphkiel.

Thrones are:

Ariel, Chayo, Fanuel, Gabriel, Israel, Jophiel, Lady Gaia, Iofiel, Michael, Oriphiel, Quelamia, Raphael, Raziel, Teiaiel, Uriel, Uzziel, Yofiel, Zaphkiel, Zophiel.

2nd Sphere: Angels who serve as heavenly governors.

Angels of the cosmos, govern all the cosmos.

4. Dominions   Serve to integrate the spiritual & the material worlds.

Also called Angels of Leadership, Angels of Mercy, Dominations, Hashmallim, Kuriotetes, Lords, Lordships, Spirits of Wisdom.

Divine bureaucrats that regulate angelic duties.

Ruling angels of this order are:

Baradi'el, Hashmal, Muriel, Yahriel, Zadkiel, Zaphiel.

Dominions are:

Hashmal, Muriel, Nithaiah, Terathel, Zacharael, Zadkiel.

5. Virtues   The are able to beam out massive levels of divine energy.

Also called Angels of Grace, Angels of the Brilliant Ones, Angels of Valor, Malakim, Mights, Splendors, Tarshishim.

Angels who work miracles on Earth.

It is said that they have control over the elements and stars.

Chief of this order is Phi-Re.

Ruling angel princes of this order are:

Barbiel, Haniel, Michael, Peliel, Raphael, Tarshish, Usiel.

Virtues are:

Amael, Asha, Barbiel, Cerviel, Hahael, Hahahel, Haniel, Michael, Peliel, Phi-Re, Raphael, Sabriel, Tarshish, Usiel, Uzziel.

6. Powers   Bearers of the conscience of all of humanity, keepers of the collective history.

Angels of birth and death.

Chief of this order is Camael.

Powers are:

Abel, Camael, Cassiel, Derdekea, Drop, Eth, Gabriel, Geno, Jerazol, Jeu, Kamael, Kemuel, Lucifer, Melech, Mikhar, Mikheus, Raphael, Sannul, Seclam, Sphener, Verchiel.

3rd Sphere: Angels who function as heavenly messengers.

Angels of the world, govern all the world.

7. Principalities

Guardian angels of all large groups, from cities & nations, also human creations such as multi-national corporations.

Their numbers are believed to be countless.

Also called Integrating Angels, Princes.

Ruling angels of this order are:

Amael, Cervihel, Haniel, Nisroch, Requel.

Principalities are:

Daniel, Poiel, Vehuel, Zeriel.

8. Archangels

Also called Archangeloi, Overlighting Angels, Lords of Spiritual Creation.

Messengers of God.

The archangels are believed to command the heavenly army in an ongoing war with Satan and his legion of angels.

Special emissaries of the Principalities.

They can be in many places at one time.

Guardians of people and all living things.

These beings are from a different family from the angels, 8th dimensional beings.

1st Ray, Blue Flame of Faith, Power, Protection, Will,
represented by Michael.

2nd Ray, Yellow Flame of Illumination, Understanding, Wisdom,
represented by Jophiel.

3rd Ray, Pink Flame of Adoration, Compassion, Creativity, Love,
represented by Chamuel.

4th Ray, White Flame of Discipline, Harmony, Purity,
represented by Gabriel.

5th Ray, Green Flame of Abundance, Healing, Science, Truth,
represented by Raphael.

6th Ray, Ruby, Purple, Gold Flame of Ministration, Peace, Service,
represented by Uriel.

7th Ray, Violet Flame of Ceremony, Freedom, Mercy, Transmutation,
represented by Zadkiel.

Ruling princes of this order are:

Barakiel, Barbiel, Gabriel, Jehudiel, Metatron, Michael, Raphael.

Anael, Anthriel, Aquariel, Aramaiti, Armaita, Armaiti, Azra'Il, Azrael, Barachiel, Barbiel, Barkiel, Camael, Cassiel, Chamuel, Elohim, Ezekiel, Gabriel, Galizur, Hananiel, Haniel, Iofiel, Ionel, Israfel, Israfil, Jibril, Jophiel, Mael, Metatron, Michael, Mikhail, Omniel, Perpetiel, Phanuel, Phi-Re, Raguel, Raguil, Raphael, Raziel, Salmael, Samael, Samil, Sammael, Sandalphon, Saraqael, Satan, Satanil, Sealtiel, Seir, Suriel, Tzadiqel, Uriel, Valeoel, Vretil, Yofiel, Zadkiel, Zarall, Zephron, Zophiel.

Following are said to be archangels:

Anael, Aniel, Anthriel, Aquariel, Barakiel, Chamael, Chamuel, Jeduhiel, Jophiel, Metatron, Omniel, Perpetiel, Raguil, Raziel, Remiel, Sariel, Simael, Valeoel, Zadkiel, Zaphiel.

It is said that each Archangel is a fleet of craft.
Archangels are personified Qualities, 8th dimensional beings.
Channel: David K. Miller.
→ Gabriel, Michael, Zadkiel.

9. Angels   People believe in Angels because the Bible says they are real and they are not immortal.
Angels never had physical bodies.
The ones most concerned with the human affairs.
Angels are sub-space aliens that can influence our thoughts and consequently manipulate our actions.
They reproduce like humans (males/females).
They supposedly resemble tall, skinny bats with pointed little ears at the top of their small heads, large black eyes, arms (not wings).
They usually show them as a flickering light, sometimes with a blue hue.
There are many different kinds, with different functions: guardian angels (companion angels).
Angelic guardians regulate the interdimensional Portals.
Normally at least 10 guardian angels per person.
Belong to families or clans.

A'Albiel, Aban, Abariel, Abasdarhon, Abigrael, Abrid, Abuzohar, Acheliah, Adnachael, Adnachiel, Adnai, Adoniel, Aduachiel, Af Bri, Afriel, Afsi-Khof, Aftiel, Agiel, Agrat bat Mahlat, Aha, Ahadiel, Akatriel, Akrasiel, Al Ussa, Alimiel, Alimon, Altarib, Amabael, Amabiel, Amael, Amaliel, Amatiel, Amazarac, Ambriel, Amitiel, Anachiel , Anael, Anafiel, Anahita, Anane, Ananiel, Ankhiel, Anauel, Anfial, Angerecton, Aniel, Anitor, Anixiel, Anthriel, Anunna, Apsu, Aquariel, Aralim, Arariel, Arathiel, Arauchia, Arbatel, Ardarel, Ardousius, Arehanah, Arel, Arella, Arial, Arias, Ariel, Ariella, Arizial, Aramaiti, Armaita, Armaiti, Armers, Armisael, Arzal, Asael, Asaph, Asasiel, Ashriel, Asiel, Asmodel, Asron, Assiel, Ataphiel, Atar, Atel, Attaris, Atuesuel, Atuniel, Auel, Auphonim, Auriel, Ausiul, Ayib, Aymelek, Ayscher, Azacachia, Azael, Azaradel, Azarael, Azazael, Azbuga, Azbugah, Azer, Azkeel, Azliel, Azrael, Babiel, Bagdial, Bahman, Bahram, Balidet, Ballaton, Balthial, Baphomet, Barachiel, Baradi'el, Barakiel, Barbiel, Barchiel, Bardiel, Bareschas, Bariel, Barkaial, Barpharanges, Bartzachiah, Baruch, Batraal, Beburos, Bedaliel, Behemiel, Ben Nez, Betea, Betheuel, Blaef, Boel, Bualu, Burchat, Butator, Cabriel, Cadmiel, Calliel, Caluel, Camael, Cambiel, Cambill, Capabile, Caphriel, Caracasa, Cassiel, Castiel, Cathetel, Cedar, Cephetas, Cervihel, Chaioth, Chamael, Chamuel, Chamyel, Charbiel, Charman, Charms, Charoum, Chasan, Chaschmalim, Chasmali, Chassan, Chassiel, Chayo, Chayyliel, Cheratiel, Cheriour, Chermes, Chokmahel, Chosniel, Colopatiron, Comato, Commissoros, Corabael, Corat, Cruciel, Cupra, Dagiel, Damabiah, Dameal, Damel, Daniel, Darel, Degaliel, Derdekea, Devecia, Dina, Diniel, Donachiel, Donquel, Douma, Doumah, Dracon, Duma, Duchiel, Egalmiel, Eheres, Eiael, Eirnilus, Eisheth

Zenunim, El Adrel, El Auria, El El, Elamiz, Elimiel, Eloa, Elomeel, Elomnia, Elouai, Enediel, Enejie, Ercle, Ertrael, Eschiel, Espiacent, Euchey, Eurabatres, Ezekiel, Ezgadi, Ezrieli, Famiel, Fraciel, Fromzon, Furlac, Futiniel, Gabriel, Gabriella, Gabril, Gabuthelon, Galgaliel, Galmon, Gamiel, Gargatel, Gaviel, Gazardiel, Gedariah, Geliel, Geno, Germael, Gethel, Gibril, Giel, Glmarij, Gotzone, Gradiel, Guabarel, Gurid, Gutrix, Habbiel, Hahael, Hahahel, Hakem, Halliza, Haludiel, Hamal, Hamaliel, Hamatiel, Hamied, Hanael, Haniel, Hannuel, Hantiel, Harabael, Hariel, Harshiel, Harudha, Hashmal, Hashmed, Hayyel, Heiglot, Helemmelek, Helison, Hngel, Hodniel, Hormuz, Humastrav, Husael, Iacoajul, Iadara, Iahmel, Iax, Iciriel, Iedidiel, Iehuiah, Ieiaiel, Ielahiah, Ietuquiel, Iggereth, Ikkar Sof, Imriel, In Hii, Ingethal, Iofiel, Iolet, Irel, Isda, Isheth Zenunim, Ishliah, Isma'Il, Ismoli, Israfel, Ithuriel, Itkal, Itqal, Jahoel, Janiel, Japhkiel, Jariel, Jeduhiel, Jeduthum, Jeduthun, Jehiel, Jehoel, Jehudiel, Jerazol, Jeu, Jhudiel, Jibril, Jomiael, Jophiel, Joustriel, Kabniel, Kabshiel, Kadi, Kadiel, Kakabel, Kamael, Kandile, Kemiel, Kepharel, Kerub, Kerubiel, Kerubim, Kfial, Kmiel, Kokaviel, Korniel, Kotecha, Kutiel, Kyriel, Labusi, Lahriel, Lamach, Lamediel, Larzod, Lazai, Lebes, Lecabel, Lelahel, Leliel, Lepha, Liwet, Logos, Loniel, Lucifer, Luel, Luma'il, Mach, Machidiel, Madan, Madimel, Mador, Mael, Mahadeo, Mahariel, Maion, Maktiel, Malachim, Malaika, Malchidiel, Malkiel, Maltiel, Manakel, Mantus, Manu, Margiviel, Maroch, Mars, Matarel, Matariel, Mathlai, Meachuel, Mebahiah, Mehiel, Melakim, Melech, Melioth, Melkejal, Memuneh, Menrva, Mercury, Meresijm, Meros, Meriarijim, Meshabber, Messiach, Metatron, Mibi, Micah, Michael, Michal, Midael, Miel, Mihr, Mikael, Mikhail, Mikhar, Mikheus, Mikiel, Miniel, Miri, Mitzgitari, Moakkibat, Monachiel, Morael, Mordat, Moriel, Moroni, Mqttro, Mtniel, Mumiah, Munkir, Mupiel, Murdad, Muriel, Mutuol, Mzpopiasaiel, Naadame, Naamah, Nachiel, Nafriel, Nahaliel, Nakir, Nakriel, Nangriel, Naophiel, Nariel, Nathanael, Natiel, Ndmh, Nehinah, Nemamiah, Neria, Neriel, Nesanel, Netoniel, Netzach, Nisroc, Nisroch, Nithaiah, Nitika, Noaphiel, Noganiel, Nuriel, Och, Oertha, Ofaniel, Omael, Omeliel, Omniel, Omophorus, Onzo, Ophaniel, Ophiel, Opiel, Oranir, Oriares, Orifiel, Oriphiel, Ormael, Osael, Osgaebial, Otheos, Ouestucati, Oul, Oumriel, Pagiel, Pahaliah, Paimonah, Pammon, Pancia, Pancimeia, Paniel, Parasiel, Pastor, Patha, Patrozin, Patteny, Peliel, Penat, Pendroz, Perpetiel, Permaz, Pesagniyah, Petahyah, Pethel, Phaiar, Phakiel, Phaldor, Phaleg, Phanuel, Pharniel, Pharzuph, Phatiel, Phorlakh, Phul, Pistis Sophia, Pnimea, Pniel, Porna, Porosa, Praxil, Presnostix, Pruel, Prukiel, Ptiau, Qadosch, Qafsiel, Qalbam, Qamiel, Qaniel, Quelamia, Ra'Asiel X, Rabia, Rachel, Rachiel, Rachmiel, Radueriel, Rael, Raguel, Raguiel, Raguil, Rahmiel, Rahtiel, Rakhaniel, Rampel, Ramuel, Raphael, Rash, Rashiel, Rauel, Raueriel, Raziel, Regaliel, Rehatiel, Rehel, Reivtip, Rekhodiah, Remiel, Remliel, Requel, Requiel, Rhamiel, Rhaumel, Rifion, Rikbiel, Rimezin,Risnuch, Rochel, Roelhaiphar, Rorex, Rubiel, Ruchiel, Ruhiel, Rudosor, Rusvon, Ruwano, Rziel, Sabreael, Sachiel, Sachluph, Sahaqiel, Salilus, Salmael, Samael, Samandiriel, Samax, Sameron, Sameveel, Samil, Sammael, Samuel, Samyasa, Sandolphon, Sangariah, Sangrariel, Santanael, Sarakuyal, Saranana, Saraqael, Sariel, Sarphiel, Sarquamich, Sasgabiel, Satan, Satanil, Satarel, Savaniah, Savuriel, Sauriel, Saxos, Schaltiel, Schioel, Schrewneil, Sealiah, Sealtiel, Seclam, Sedekiah, Sefoniel, Seheiah, Seir, Sekel, Selith, Sephuriron, Seraph, Serapiel, Seraquiel, Seref, Seruf, Sharivar, Sharivari, Shakziel, Shalgiel, Shateiel, Shcachlil, Shekinah, Shektar, Shemeshiel, Shetel, Shimshiel, Shinial, Simael, Simikiel, Sizajasel, Sizouse, Sochodiah, Sofiel, Sohemme, Soluzen, Sophiel, Soqed Hozi, Sosol, Sothis, Splenditenes, Ssnialiah, Stimulator, Strateia, Sui'el, Summanus, Suna, Sura, Suriel, Susabo, Susniel, Suth, Syth, Tabris, Tafel X, Tagas, Tafthi, Taharial, Taliahad, Tamael, Tamiel, Tar,

Tarot, Tarquam, Tarshish, Tarwan, Tebliel, Teiaiel, Telautes, Tempast, Tepiseuth, Terathel, Tetra, Tharsis, Thegri, Theliel, Thiel, Thoth, Thuriel, Tiel, Tileion, Tilonas, Tina, Tirtael, Tomimiel, Torquaret, Trgiaob, Trsiel, Tsaphiel, Tual, Tubiel, Tulatu, Turel, Turmiel, Tuwahel, Tzadiqel, Tzadiquel, Tzadkiel, Tzaphkiel, Tzedeqiah, Ubaviel, Umabel, Umeroz, Urakabarameel, Uriel, Uriron, Urpaniel, Usiel, Uvael, Uwula, Uzza, Uzziel, Valoel, Vaol, Varcan, Vassago, Vatale, Veguaniel, Vehiel, Vehuel, Vehuiah, Vejovis, Vel, Venibbeth, Verchiel, Vhnori, Vohal, Vohu Manah, Voizia, Vraniel, Vretil, Vvael, Wallim, Xexor, Yabbashael, Yahala, Yahriel, Yarashiel, Yashiel, Yefefiah, Yephiel, Yofiel, Yrouel, Yurkemi, Zacharel, Zachariel, Zachriel, Zadkiel, Zagzagel, Zahariel, Zakkiel, Zalbesael, Zaliel, Zamael, Zaphiel, Zavael, Zayday, Zazagel, Zazel, Zechiel, Zehanpuryu'h, Zephon, Zephron, Zeriel, Zeruch, Zethar, Zianor, Zidkiel, Zikiel, Ziquiel, Zophiel, Zuphlas, Zuriel.

7.8 Angels

Angels of the Air	Balidet, Corat, Famiel, Gutrix, Iahmel, Ismoli, Rachel, Suth (Chief), Varcan, Vretil.
Angels of Autumn	Guabarel, Tarquam, Torquaret.
Angels of Creation	Anael.
Angels of the Earth	Arariel, Ashriel, Azarael, Balthial, Furlac, Harabael, Tebliel, Uzziel, Yabbashael.
Angels of Fire	Ardarel, Arel, Atuniel, Azer, Gabriel, Jehoel, Nathaniel, Seraph, Uriel.
Angels of Love	Donquel, Rahmiel, Raphael, Theliel.
Angels of Money	Anauel, Ariel, Rauel, Uriel.
Angels of the Moon	Anixiel, Aymelek, Azaradel, Elimiel, Enediel, Geliel, Iciriel, Kyriel, Neriel, Ofaniel, Qafsiel, Requiel, Tsaphiel, Vaol, Yahel, Yashiel.
Angels of Mountains	Rampel.
Angels of Mysteries	Gabriel, Raziel, Zizuph.
Angels of the North	Oertha.
Angels of Planet Jupiter	Bariel, Sachiel, Sedekiah.
Angels of Planet Mars	Gradiel, Lamach.
Angels of Planet Mercury	Madan, Miel, Phul.
Angels of Planet Saturn	Boel, Maion.
Angels of Planet Venus	Ayib, Eurabatres, Rachiel, Rael, Thiel.
Angels of Prayer	Akatriel, Gabriel, Metatron, Michael, Raphael, Sandalphon, Sizouse.

Angels of the Rain   Matarel, Matariel, Matriel, Ridia, Ridya, Zalbesal.

Angels of Spring   Amatiel, Caracasa, Commissoros, Core.

Angels of Summer   Gargatel, Gaviel, Tariel, Tubiel.

Angels of the Sun   Auel, Nachiel, Och, Raphael, Shcachlil, Tar, Tarwan, Varcan, Verchiel (Governor).

Angels of the Wind   Ben Nez, Moriel, Nariel, Rubiel, Ruchiel, Ruhiel, Rujiel.

Angels of Winter   Amabael, Certari, Ctarari.

Fallen Angels   Akibeel, Amazarac, Armers, Azaradel, Azibeel, Barakaial, Batraal, Danel, Ramuel, Samayasa, Sarakuyal, Tamiel, Urakabrameel.

8. EARTH PERIODS

8.1 Far History

50,000,000,000 B.C.E.	Universe's physical creation was begun by the Time Lords under the direction of the Supreme Creative Force. Birth of Milky Way galaxy. This present creation is the 6th cycle and will run between 50 and 100 billion years.
40,000,000,000 B.C.E.	The galactic Elohim thrust planet Earth into her present position to balance the galaxy and change its shape to spiral.
20,000,000,000 B.C.E.	The Sun appeared and created a proto-Solar system.
4,500,000,000 B.C.E.	Earth was created.
500,000,000 B.C.E.	Begin of Earth like planets by the Sumerian Empire because the star Aldebaran got hotter and hotter and the planets were no longer inhabitable. They also colonized Maldek, Mars, Earth.
400,000,000 B.C.E.	First visit from extraterrestrials from Venus and before from the Pleiades.

PROTOPEOPLE

230,000,000 B.C.E.	Five-fingered protopeople conducted brain surgeries, heart transplants, and liver operations.
206,000,000 B.C.E.	Begin of a Galactic Cycle that is presently ending. First Human life in the Solar System.
200,000,000 B.C.E.	There have been numerous and devastating galactic wars.
120,000,000 B.C.E.	A find by Bashkir scientists is contrary to traditional notions of human history: stone stabs, which are 120 million years old, covered with a relief map of the Ural Region.
113,000,000 B.C.E.	Lyran city on Mars.
75,000,000 B.C.E.	Earth is devastated by nuclear forces.
65,000,000 B.C.E.	Impact of an asteroid on Earth.

60,000,000 B.C.E.	There was found an imprint of a shoe and a foot in a 60,000,000 million year old rock close to the Paluxy River, Texas.
50,000,000 B.C.E.	Orions pass through a black hole portal near Arcturus from the Andromeda Galaxy and settle in the Lyran star system.
40,000,000 B.C.E.	Human race lived in Lyra until the Alpha Draconians arrived; apparently, they were afraid of each other. The Draconians wanted to control their planets, destroyed 3 of the 14 planets and over 50 million Lyran humans were killed.
35,000,000 B.C.E.	There was a firmament of frozen water (ice) above the Earth's surface. It was a huge crystalline shield in two sections, one situated at 15,000 – 18,000 ft, the other a 35,000 – 38,000 ft above the Earth's surface.
35,000,000 B.C.E.	Galactical war.
28,731,007 B.C.E.	The first melding between the primate genes and the human species.
26,000,000 B.C.E.	Dinoid from Bellatrix (Orion) & Reptoid/Reptilian colonies from the constellation of Sagittarius arrive and inhabit Earth.
22,000,000 B.C.E.	Lyran Wars. Explosion creates the Orion Nebula. Refugees go to the Erra system, Hyades and Vega.
18,617,841 B.C.E.	First consciously awakened Man on Earth. Sanat Kumara came with a spaceship from the planet Venus with his 4 Great Lords and 100 assistants. He used his spiritual powers to awake the centers of individuality in the Earth Man (= "missing link"). He called the first consciously awakened man Adam in tribute to the Venusian Lords who belongs to the Adamic Race of Venus. Sanat Kumara changed the sex polarity of Adam from bisexual to unisexual. (Creation of Eve).
18,000,000 B.C.E.	Rise of pre-cetacean.
18,000,000 B.C.E.	Sanat Kumara, Master from Venus, assumed the role of Planetary Logos of Earth.

10,500,000 B.C.E.	5 races were created (133 mill. souls on Earth).

Red Race: lived in Atlantis & America.
Brown Race: lived in the Andes & Lemuria.
Yellow Race: lived in the Gobi Desert.
Black Race: lived in Sudan & Upper West Africa.
White Race: lived along the Black Sea & the Carpathian Mountains.

8,000,000 B.C.E. Destruction of Dinoid / Reptoid group on planet Earth by the Pre-Cetacean civilization, which evolved on planet Earth. Half of the Pre-Cetacean population was evacuated to the Pegasus constellation and to the Cetus constellation. Reptoid/Dinoid refugees fled to planet Maldek.

4,300,000 B.C.E. Colonization of the 4th planet of Sirius B system.
Time of the initial organization of the Galactic Federation by the Sirius B inhabitants with help of the Sirius A inhabitants.

4,000,000 B.C.E. Galactic Federation was formed.

4,000,000 B.C.E. The 3rd planet, called Atarmunk, of the Sirius B solar system Akonowai was settled.

2,500,000 B.C.E. On Earth, there was only a white race. Black beings from the star system Sutarus in the Andromeda galaxy created a second race on planet Earth, a black race.

2,400,000 B.C.E. Allegedly, Maldek was destroyed in a war.

2,000,000 B.C.E. Mars and Venus colonized. Sirians helped create the bodies we have now by adding some of their own DNA. Genetically almost identical.

1,200,000 – 1,000,000 B.C.E.

GREAT GALACTIC WAR /GALACTIC WARS,

Started approximately 1.2 million years ago and lasted for 200,000 years. War started from Orion, in the end vaporized Mikael Ashtar. Many of the Avyonians fled with starship Pelegai to Sirius A.
First planet Avyon was destroyed in the Great Galactic War.
→ Mariaca, Mikael Ashtar.

1,000,000 B.C.E.	At this time, there were four water planets in the Solar System: Earth, Maldek, Mars, Venus. The dark forces of Anchara (Reptoid/Dinoid races) invaded the Solar System, leaving Mars with a very thin atmosphere and destroying her vast oceans, lakes and streams. Venus's atmosphere was altered. Hyperborea was completely destroyed and all Humans were killed. Any remaining life went underground and has stayed there for nearly a million years. Orion base on Mars. → Mars.
900,000 B.C.E.	The Galactic Federation destroyed planet Maldek by a large battle planet that was brought into the Solar System. The Solar System was controlled for 80,000 years by the Reptoid/Dinoid races. Planet Earth returned to Human control approx. 900,000 B.C.E. Human colony founded Lemurian Mother Empire on the Lemuria continent and lasted for 850,000 years.
889,000 B.C.E.	The Greys were captured (while leaving Zeta 1 & Zeta 2) by a group in Orion that was already genetically altered by the Alpha Draconians. → Alpha Draconians, Draconians, Greys.
705,000 B.C.E.	Extensive wars on Maldek.
500,000 B.C.E.	Alleged destruction of Maldek. Atlantis, Yu and Libyan / Egyptian daughter empires founded.
437,225 B.C.E.	Last Great War in the Solar System that included Terra and Nibiru. Queen Suttee of Orion led the invasion.
430,000 B.C.E.	Alalu, former king of Nibiru buried on Mars. (Mars Face!).
387,000 B.C.E.	→ Maldek.
317,000 B.C.E.	Mars base by the Pleiadians, Lyrans, Sirians partially destroyed. Solar System fell to the Orion Group.
275,000 B.C.E.	Star nations created with genetic engineering a hybrid race, which was the first Homo Sapiens.
228,000 B.C.E.	Lyrans landed on planet Erra in the Pleiades.
225,000 B.C.E.	The Pleiadians discovered Earth. They discovered 3 groups of uncivilized people living there; the larger of these groups were light skinned and were of Lyran descent.

210,000 B.C.E.   Marcab Empire, negative Orions.

196,000 B.C.E.   The Pleiadians stayed on Earth until the year 10 AD.

186,500 B.C.E.   Destruction of planet Maldek.

154,000 B.C.E.   First landing of extraterrestrials on planet Earth on the continent of Lemuria.

150,000 B.C.E.   First Lyran conflict.

130,000 B.C.E.   Star nations again bioengineered Homo Sapiens and Homo Sapiens Sapiens was born.

120,000 B.C.E.   Religious manipulation by implants.

115,000 B.C.E.   Our solar system was involved in a war. Part of it was caused by the Pleiadians, who simply left.

111,000 B.C.E.   Moon cities destroyed in a war.

100,000 B.C.E.   The Lyrans developed a race on the lost continent of Hyperborea (South Polar Region). Atlantis – a daughter empire of Lemuria – was founded on a huge island in the Atlantic Ocean. Yü – a daughter empire of Lemuria – was founded, located in Central China and Tibet.
                               → Lemuria.

87,000 B.C.E.   High technology level in the Lyran society on Earth.

77,000 B.C.E.   There was a human form living on planet Mars.

76,000 B.C.E.   First civilization in Lemuria lasted until 24,000 B.C.E.

75,000 B.C.E.   Interplanetary war in the Solar System destroys Maldek, which becomes the asteroid belt. Final destruction of Mars civilization and Mars atmosphere.

60,000 B.C.E.   Visit on Earth by Andromedans from Zenetae for 62 years.

50,000 B.C.E.   Some Pleiadian refugees from the Lyran system come to Earth. The Elders imprison the negative paraphysical entities under Earth's surface, locked in a specific frequency.

47,000 B.C.E.   Pleiadian groups (Atlans) live in peace on Earth. First Atlantis, 70,000 scientists.

38,000 B.C.E.   Nuclear war on Earth, 2,000 refugees flee to the Pegasus system.

31,000 B.C.E.	Pleiadians return and rebuild Atlantis. Slave races are generated. Genetic cloning and crystal technology.
30,000 B.C.E.	Atlantean-Mu wars, 12,000 dissidents leave Earth.
25,000 B.C.E.	The Atlantean daughter empire destroyed Lemuria with the help of renegades from Alpha Centauri and the Pleiades. One of Earth's moons was taken with force field down to the continent of Lemuria to destroy Lemuria.
24,000 B.C.E.	End of the first civilization on Lemuria.
16,300 B.C.E.	During the time of Atlantis, it was possible to see both of the suns in our solar system. The Earth was moved into its current orbit by the Pleiadians.
15,000 B.C.E.	Crystal skulls were made.
11,913 B.C.E.	Last nuclear war on Earth.
11,000 B.C.E.	The Lemurians moved into an existing Galactic Federation facility beneath Mt. Shasta, California, when the Atlanteans attacked them.
10,500 B.C.E.	Destruction of Atlantis.
10,468 B.C.E.	First Great Catastrophe.
10,400 B.C.E.	Descendants from the Atlantean-Mu wars, who left 20,000 years before, led by Arus, return to Earth and engage the Atlanteans. Begin of the construction of the Great Pyramid of Gizeh. Greys use Humans as slaves against the Pleiadians.
10,348 B.C.E.	End of the construction of the Great Pyramid of Gizeh.
10,000 B.C.E.	Begin of Telos before a thermonuclear war. 25,000 escaped the war.
9,500 B.C.E.	Atlantean civilization on Earth is decimated.
9,160 B.C.E.	Thoth takes a human body.
8,200 B.C.E.	After a war, the Grey-Marcab society is fragmented. Mercenary groups continue to subsist on animal and human biological products and experience sensation from human emotional fields.
6,000 B.C.E.	Pleiadians crossbreed with Earth Humanoids. Blonds visit Earth.

4,500 B.C.E.	Acambaro in Mexico, discovered 1944 by Waldemar Julsrud.
4,200 B.C.E.	Start of Mission Rahma.
3,600 – 3,300 B.C.E.	Major Orion influence in the Middle East.
3,166 B.C.E.	Second Catastrophe.
3,056 B.C.E.	The great city Ofir was built by Samon. → Samon.
3,000 B.C.E.	Orion Group leaves Earth.
2,740 B.C.E.	Viracocha founded the Inca dynasty and built Cuzco.
2,039 B.C.E.	Allegedly a man and a woman landed on the Moon and on Mars.
2,000 B.C.E.	Sekhmet lives in the Ancient Egypt for 3000 years in a body.
2,000 B.C.E.	Aryans and alien mining groups' conflict. Nuclear explosion in the area of Pakistan.
1,657 B.C.E.	Probably last occurrence of Planet X in the Solar System.
1,400 B.C.E.	Pleiadians leave Earth.
651 B.C.E.	Most of the Old Testament was constructed of pirated versions of Chaldean texts.

8.2 Earth Periods

PANGAEA

Lilith and Vulcan are beings from old Atlantis and prior to that Pangaea and Lemuria.

HYBORNEA

2,000,000 B.C.E.

First human galactic colony, located in the Arctic Ocean, about the size of Antarctica, completely destroyed some 1,000,000 years ago as part of a general attack on this solar system by the Dinoids/Reptoids from Maldek.
Also called Hyperborea.

1,000,000 B.C.E.

Colonies on Earth (Hybornea), Mars & Venus destroyed by the Dinoids/Reptoids from Maldek. Dinoids/Reptoids regain control over Earth for a period of 80,000 years.
Galactic Federation destroyed Maldek.

HYBORNEA / HIBORNIA / HYPERBOREA

1,000,000 B.C.E.

First Galactic Federation colony on Earth. Complete Lyran/Sirian type of civilization.
First continent encompassing all of the land mass.
Also called Hybornea or Hibornia; lasted 1,000,000 years.
It was devastated by the dark forces of Anchara.

TIAHUANACO

18000 B.C.E.

Tiahuanaco means City of the Dead.

ATLANTIS

15000 –10000 B.C.E.

From 65,000,000 people only survived 2,000,000.
A few different renegades from the Pleiades, Alpha & Beta Centauri came to Earth (after the Flood) as "gods".

10000 B.C.E.

Atlantis sunk in the Atlantic Ocean.
→ Year 2001.

RAMA EMPIRE

13000 B.C.E.

In Northern India and Pakistan. They manufactured their own flying ships, called Vimanas.

MT. SHASTA

10000 B.C.E.	→ Adama, Sharula Dux.
	→ Mt. Shasta.

MEGIDDO

9228 B.C.E.	Town in Israel, close to mount Tabor, meeting-point of the Group of Nine.

EDEN

8300 B.C.E. (Abel).	From: East Mediterranean Sea, Ahuar (Egypt), Caucasus until Baltic Sea, Center at the connection of Euphrates & Hildekel (Tigris), at the lake Evana (Iraq), Neghada (centuries later Alexandria), capital of Ahuar (Egypt).
	Origin of the legend of "Apple & Snake" was Cain's group "The Red Serpent". The member had a ring with a red serpent (devil).

SUMER/SUMERIA

5000 B.C.E.	Early development of Sumer.
4000 B.C.E.	High civilization.
2750 B.C.E.	Gilgamesh rules Uruk.
2350 B.C.E.	Sargon of Agade creates the empire of Akkad, Umma and Sumer.
	→ Sumerian Empire.

UR

6257 B.C.E.	Colony of Atlantis.
	Tower of Babel built 200 years after Khufu, 3000 years later destroyed.
3400 B.C.E.	The second chakra wiring is disconnected for most people on Earth, these blocks from spiritual maturation or evolution.
3313 B.C.E.	Mayan Calendar begins.
3100 B.C.E.	Kali Yuga began (for 6000 years).

INDIA

3000 B.C.E.	(Krishna). 49 towers on the Island of Bombay, (Flamenes of Lemuria). → Lamas).
	Countries: Madura, Golkonda).
2675 B.C.E.	Gilgamesh.
550 – 479 B.C.E.	Gautama Buddha.
500 B.C.E.	Sanskrit itself was codified.

EGYPT

13000 B.C.E.	Vast megalithic metropolis, reaching several levels below the Gizeh plateau.
11000 B.C.E.	Great pyramid built (150 years before destruction of Atlantis), built by civilizations of Hoova, Ashan, Altea, Myrex.
5000 B.C.E.	Great pyramid finished.
4500 - 3000 B.C.E.	Prehistoric time, descend from the race of Tolsteka, Atlantis, half-gods; Shior is the name of Nile.
3500 - 3000 B.C.E.	The other 2 great pyramids built.
3000 B.C.E.	Unification of Empire, pharaoh: Ka, Narmer.

2950 - 2770 B.C.E.
(*1. Dynasty*),
Abydos, Memphis,
Pharaoh: Aha, Djer, Wadj, Dewen, Anedjib, Semerjet, Qa'a.

2770 - 2640 B.C.E.
(*2. Dynasty*),
Abydos, Memphis,
Pharaoh: Hetepsechemui, Raneb, Ninetjer, Peribsen, Chasechemui.

2640 - 2575 B.C.E.
(*3. Dynasty*),
Memphis,
Pharaoh: Nebka, Djoser, Sechemchet, Huni.

2575 - 2465 B.C.E.
(*4. Dynasty*),
Memphis,
2575 - 2551 Snofru,
2551 - 2528 Cheops,
2528 - 2520 Djedefre,
2520 - 2494 Chephren,
2490 - 2471 Mykerinos,
2471 - 2467 Schepseskaf.

2465 - 2325 B.C.E.
(*5. Dynasty*),
Memphis,
2465 - 2458 Userkaf,
2458 - 2446 Sahure,
2446 - 2427 Neferirkare,
2420 - 2396 Niuserre,
2396 - 2388 Menkauhor,
2388 - 2355 Djedkare (Asosi),
2355 - 2325 Unas.

2325 - 2155 B.C.E.
(*6. Dynasty*),
Memphis,
2325 - 2300 Teti, Userkare,
2300 - 2268 Pepi I.,
2268 - 2254 Merenre I.,
2254 - 2160 Pepi II., Merenre II.,
        Antiemsaf, Nitokis.

2155 - 2134 B.C.E.   (*7./8. Dynasty*),
Memphis, many only short time pharaohs.

2134 - 2040 B.C.E.   (*9./10. Dynasty*),
Herakleopolis, Thebes,
2134 - 2040 Cheti(Achthöes), Merikare.

2134 - 1991 B.C.E.   (*11. Dynasty*),
Herakleopolis, Thebes, Lischt,
2134 - 2118 Mentuhotep I., Antef I.,
2118 - 2069 Antef II.,
2069 - 2061 Antef III.,
2061 - 2010 Mentuhotep II. (Nebhepetre),
             Mentuhotep III. (Seanchkare),
1998 - 1991 Mentuhotep IV. (Nebtauire).

1991 - 1785 B.C.E.   (*12.Dynasty*),
Thebes, Lischt,
1991 - 1962 Amenemhet I.,
1971 - 1926 Sesostris I.,
1929 - 1892 Amenemhet II.,
1897 - 1878 Sesostris II.,
1878 - 1841 (?)Sesostris III.,
1844 - 1797 Amenemhet III.,
1798 - 1789 Amenemhet IV.,
1789 - 1785 Nofrusobek.

1785 - 1650 B.C.E.   (*13.Dynasty*),
Thebes, Lischt,
about 54 pharaohs.

1715 - 1650 B.C.E.   (*14.Dynasty*),
Delta of Nile, Nehsi & other small kingdoms.

1650 - 1540 B.C.E.   (*15./16.Dynasty*),
Auaris, Thebes, (Hyksos),
1650 - 1640 Salitis, Scheschi, Yakobher,
1620 - 1610 Chian (Chajan),
1595 - 1550 Apopi,
1550 - 1540 Chamudi.

1650 - 1551 B.C.E.   (*17.Dynasty*),
Auaris, Thebes,
1640   Antef,
1580   Tao I.,
1570 - 1560 Tao II.,
1555 - 1551 Kamose.

1540 - 1295 B.C.E.	(*18.Dynasty*),
	Thebes, Memphis, Ramses-town,
	1540 - 1515 Ahmose,
	1515 - 1494 Amenophis I.,
	1494 - 1482 Thutmosis I.,
	1482 - 1479 Thutmosis II.,
	1479 - 1457 Hatschepsut,
	1479 - 1425 Thutmosis III.,
	1427 - 1401 Amenophis II.,
	1401 - 1391 Thutmosis IV.,
	1391 - 1353 Amenophis III.,
	1353 - 1336 Amenophis IV. / Echnaton,
	1336 - 1327 Semenchkare, Tutanchamun,
	1326 - 1322 Eje,
	1322 - 1295 Haremhab.
1500 B.C.E.	Ramses I., worked with black magicians, gave the order to kill all the Hebrew male children, to kill the baby Aton-Moses.
1295 - 1188 B.C.E.	(*19.Dynasty*),
	Thebes, Memphis, Ramses-town,
	1295 - 1293 Ramses I.,
	1293 - 1279 Sethos I.,
	1279 - 1213 Ramses II.,
	1213 - 1202 Merenptah,
	1203 - 1196 Sethos II.,
	1196 - 1190 Amenmesse, Siptah,
	1190 - 1188 Tausret.
1188 - 1070 B.C.E.	(*20.Dynasty*),
	Thebes, Memphis, Ramses-town,
	1188 - 1184 Sethnacht,
	1184 - 1153 Ramses III.,
	1153 - 1146 Ramses IV.,
	1146 - 1142 Ramses V.,
	1142 - 1135 Ramses VI.,
	1135 - 1129 Ramses VII.,
	1129 - 1127 Ramses VIII.,
	1127 - 1109 Ramses IX.,
	1109 - 1099 Ramses X.,
	1099 - 1070 Ramses XI.
1070 - 945 B.C.E.	(*21.Dynasty*),
	Tanis, Thebes, Bubastis,
	1070 - 1044 Smendes,
	1040 – 990 Psusennes I.,
	993 - 984 Amenemope,
	978 - 960 Siamun,
	960 - 945 Psusennes II.

945 - 722 B.C.E.   (*22.Dynasty*), (Bubastides),
                          Tanis, Thebes, Bubastis,
                            945 - 924 Scheschonk I.,
                            924 - 887 Osorkon I.,
                            862 - 833 Osorkon II.,
                            839 - 814 Takeloth II.,
                            814 - 763 Scheschonk III.,
                            763 - 758 Pimui,
                            758 - 722 Scheschonk V.

808 - 715 B.C.E.   (*23.Dynasty*),
                          Tanis, Thebes, Bubastis,
                            808 - 783 Petubastis,
                            760 - 750 Osorkon III.,
                            740   Takeloth III.,
                            730   Rudjamun.

725 - 712 B.C.E.   (*24.Dynasty*),
                          Tanis, Thebes, Bubastis,
                            725 - 718 Tefnacht,
                            718 - 712 Bocchoris.

712 - 664 B.C.E.   (*25.Dynasty*),
                          (kings of Ethiopia),
                               - 740 Kaschta,
                            740 - 713 Pianchi,
                            712 - 698 Schabaka,
                            698 - 690 Schebitku,
                            690 - 664 Taharqa,
                            664 - 656 Tanutamun,
                            671 - 664 (Assyrian occupation).

664 - 525 B.C.E.   (*26.Dynasty*), (Saïtes),
                            672 - 664 Necho I.,
                            664 - 610 Psammetich I.,
                            610 - 595 Necho II.,
                            595 - 589 Psammetich II.,
                            589 - 570 Apries,
                            570 - 526 Amasis,
                            526 - 525 Psammetich III.

525 - 404 B.C.E.   (27.Dynasty),
                          (Persian dominion).

404 - 399 B.C.E.   (*28.Dynasty*),
                            404 - 399 Amyrtaios.

399 - 380 B.C.E.   (*29.Dynasty*),
                            399 - 393 Nepherites I.,
                            393   Psammuthis,
                            393 - 380 Hakoris,
                            380   Nepherites II.

380 - 343 B.C.E.	(*30. Dynasty*),
	380 - 362 Nektanebos I.,
	362 - 360 Teos,
	360 - 343 Nektanebos II.
343 - 332 B.C.E.	(second Persia dominion)
332 - 30 B.C.E.	(Greek dominion),
	Alexander the Great, Ptolemäens)
30 B.C.E. *- 642* C.E.	(Roman & Byzanz dominion).

NEPAL

600 B.C.E.   (Buddha).
               Capital Kapilavastu, race of Sakyas.

ALEXANDRIA

               Ptolomeo, founder of Alexandria.
               Base for the Greek philosophers: Aristotle, Plato, Socrates.
0 B.C.E.   Filon of Alexandria in the time of Jesus.

PERSIA

               The old masters took their wisdom from Tibet & Nepal (copies of the Antulion Chronicles) & from the disciples of Krishna (Zenda Avesta).

CHINA

               Colony of Atlantis.

SUMER

               Colony of Atlantis.

EGYPT

               Colony of Atlantis.

GREECE

               Colony of Atlantis.

STONEHENGE

               Built by the 24 Civilizations (12+12).

8.3 Lemuria

LEMURIA

900,000 B.C.E.	The Lemurians arrived on planet Earth. Second human galactic colony on Earth by the Galactic Federation, about the size of Asia, located in the middle of the Pacific Ocean, was founded, duration about 850,000 years, destroyed some 25,000 years ago by attack from continent of Atlantis.
500,000 B.C.E.	The family of Anu (specifically Enki & Ninhursag) created a race of beings here on Terra (Earth) to work for them - us, they combined their own DNA with that of Homo erectus.
100,000 B.C.E.	They developed daughter empires. The most important were Atlantis and Yü. → 900,000 B.C.E. → Planet Mu.

LEMURIA/LEMUR/MU

Lemuria is also known as Mu.
Land mass lying in the Pacific Ocean from the United States to South America.
The Andes of Peru were part of the Lemurian civilization.
The majestic Haleakala crater in Maui, Hawaii is one of the last remnants of Lemuria.
They lived in caves hiding from the Dinosaurs.
Men were 5 ft tall, women a few inches shorter.
The black people are of Lemurian descent.
Lilith and Vulcan are beings from old Atlantis and prior to that Pangaea and Lemuria.
The Elders of Lemuria (Thirteenth School) moved their headquarters prior to the cataclysm to Tibet. They allegedly established the Great White Brotherhood.

76000 B.C.E.	First civilization. Allegedly there was one language and one government.
45800 B.C.E. (Juno)	Nuculandia, port: Cape Tronador.
33300 B.C.E. (Numu)	Mirtaymari, capital of the "Gegantes", they came from Titan, third moon of Saturn, last king of the Hakiosaris in Gegantes, origin of the race of Tolsteka.
35000 B.C.E.	Many civilizations came from Arcturus, Lyra & Pleiades.

AKSU

32000 B.C.E.   Culture destroyed by war.

8.4 Atlantis

ATLANTIS, MU, LIBYA/EGYPT

500,000 B.C.E.   Lemurians founded the colonies Atlantis, YU (Central China & Tibet) & Libya/Egypt.

450,000 B.C.E.   Last major war on Earth, since that lives a reptilian race (serpent race) underground, they are basically hyperborean in nature. They have control on the planet at depths from 100 to 200 miles down. When people go into the inner earth, they enter via the poles.

250,000 B.C.E.   The astronauts (Anunnaki) in Africa mutinied.
                         Creation of the Lulus (primitive worker-race).

ATLANTIS

There were many civilizations on planet Earth before Atlantis.
There were other populated areas on the planet at this time, but Atlantis was the center of civilization. The people were hundreds of years old.
There were three empires:
>>   Old Empire: 400,000 B.C.E. – 25,000 B.C.E.
       coexisted with Lemuria.
>>   Middle Empire: 25,000 B.C.E. – 15,000 B.C.E.
>>   New Empire: 15,000 B.C.E. – 10,000 B.C.E.
It's real name was Poseid or Poseidon.
Thoth was a light being and a Priest-King of Atlantis. For many millennia. He was the ruler-guardian of Atlantis.
Lilith is another great energy, along with Vulcan.
These are all beings from old Atlantis and prior to that Pangaea and Lemuria.
Thoth is a very great and wonderful being of light. Thoth is in the process of returning in the fullness of his being. He is more than Enoch and others.
→ Thoth-Mus_Zurud.

32000 B.C.E. - **10850** B.C.E.

3rd Earth galactic colony, located in the mid Atlantic Ocean, sunk 12,000 years ago.
There were 144,000 elders in Atlantis
Atlantis = (Atlantis + Lemuria + Mu), Mu came from planet Ashan. Dolphins are incarnated people from Atlantis.
→ Planet Mu.

25000 B.C.E.   Atlantis destroyed Lemuria (by destroying the 2nd moon of Earth, by using force fields) in a catastrophic shower of moon-meteors.
Yu Empire went underground and form today the Kingdom of Agartha & Shamballah.
Atlantis forms 10 ruling districts, each with its own king.

22300 B.C.E. (Anfion). Orozuma, capital of Otlana.

22000 B.C.E.   → Vailixi.

16700 B.C.E. (Antulio) Manh-Ehtel (means source of the stars), capital of Zeus, language Tolsteka.
Destroyed by war. After the destruction of Atlantis they escaped to China & South America, but most of those who escaped by aircraft flew to India, Tibet, Egypt, Chaldea, Sumer & parts of North America & some small islands.
Large Island 77,000 SQM.
Pleiadians lived on a mountain called Atlas (Step Pyramid).
Moved records of wisdom to temples of Egypt. Many pharaohs were leaders of Atlantis: Imhotep, Tutankhamen, and Ramses.
An asteroid imbedded itself in the ocean floor (Puerto Rico Plateau).
Earth experienced a polar shift of 2 degrees.

11000 B.C.E.   First major Atlantean wars.

10840 B.C.E.   Final destruction of Atlantis.

9600 B.C.E.   Sinking of Atlantean landmasses, after the Great Crystal (primary energy force on Atlantis) exploded.

8.5 Recent History

Year 450	Merlin's birth in Carmarthen, South Wales, Gt. Britain.
Year 469	King Arthur's birth.
Year 493	Beginning of Camelot.
Year 520	Merlin's death.
Year 1500	Draconian Reptiloids and Rigelian Greys try to conquer Procyon and fail.
Year 1717	→ Freemasonry.
Year 1748	All human souls incarnating on Earth since 1748 have the Zeta seal distortion within their 4th DNA strand.
Year 1902	In the year 1902 Guardian groups began poking holes in Earth's Zeta Frequency Fence.
Year 1926	Time traveling Zetas began interacting between several Earth governments.
Year 1930	Guy W. Ballard had an encounter with St. Germain on the slopes of Mt. Shasta.
Year 1931	The Greys got on Earth, but they did time travel that it looks like they have been here for thousands of years.
Late 1930's	The Zetas began their hybridization program.
Year 1941	First UFO came down in the ocean west of San Diego and was retrieved by the Navy.
Year 1947.06.24	Kenneth Arnold, a civilian pilot observed 9 flying disc-shaped aircraft flying over the Cascade Mountains in the State of Washington.
Year 1947	The United States, the Soviet Union and Great Britain became involved with the Greys. In the locker of one of the landed UFOs were found human parts. Near the South Pole, the crews of two separate aircrafts witnessed a huge opening in the ice cap where there was a dense green forest, clear lakes with temperatures in the mid 70s.
Year 1948	Several discs crashed.

Year 1950   There lived allegedly about 1500 space people in America.

Year 1952   First contact with the Ashtar Command.

Year 1953   Contact was made with aliens. Astronauts found a bunch of space ships going around the Earth.

Year 1954   Eisenhower met with the Greys. An agency MJ-12 was brought into effect. In May, treaty with the Greys was signed at Holloman AFB in California by the United States government (NSA). Exchange of technology for studying humans by Greys.

Year 1956   Jamisson Neruda's father discovered a crashed UFO in the jungle of Bolivia.

Year 1958   The NSA astronauts and the Russians were on the Moon.

Year 1959   First landing by the NSA black government on Mars.

Year 1961   Moon became colony of the NSA. The facility is as large as New York State. The structures on the surface were designed by JPL.

Year 1964   A huge underwater metallic, cylindrical shaped object has been found on the floor of the North Atlantic, about   60 miles long and gave off strong energy fields that distorted navigational and electronic instruments.

Year 1964   First Soviet piloted alien vehicles were flown.
                       Full contact with extraterrestrials was made in June 1964.

Year 1968   Base "Eve" was completed.

Year 1969   First man on Moon.
                       A confrontation between Americans and Soviets at the lunar base Luna broke out. The Soviets attempted to take over the base Luna.

Year 1974.01.22   Spaceships landed in the desert of Chilca, south of Peru.
                       → Mission Rahma.

Year 1983   First spotting of Planet X.

Year 1986   → 6ᵗʰ Root Race.

Year 1989   (February/March).
                       The Draconians invaded Mars and destroyed the human colony. Base "Eve" destroyed by the Orion Group and Draconian forces.

Year 1994   Illuminati secretly moved their world center to New Zealand.

Year 1997.09   In September of 1997 Aurigan Dracos came through the star gate opening and launched a serious attack on Earth, but they were intercepted by a group of other races, including Andromedans, Capellan female warrior Dracos, Taygetan Pleiadians.

Year 1998.04.04   Armageddon took place. This battle took place on the 4th dimension (astral plane).

Year 2000   Passing from 3rd to 4th dimension.

8.6 Predictions

Year 1999 – 2003   Massive destruction all over the world, population decreases to
                           about 80%.

Year 2001   The Muons from planet Myton, located in the Pleiades star
                           system, carrying 1000 space scientists, will land their spacecraft in
                           an area of the Caribbean Sea, that was part of Atlantis.

Year 2001.12.25   A large meteor about the size of a football field will hit the ocean
                           in the Middle East and will destroy everything in this part for
                           several hundred miles.

Year 2002   3rd World War in the Middle East.
                           Implementation of the New World Order.
                           Earth will enter in the 5th dimension.

Year 2002.02.21-24   UFOs will be appearing worldwide during the Olympics.

Year 2002.03   Earthquake will shake the California coast shelf loose and will
                           virtually eliminate the state of California.

Year 2003 (Spring)   In Spring Nibiru (Planet X) will pass Earth again after 3600
                           years. Now called „2001 KX76". Planet X (the 10th planet) orbits
                           between the Sun and its dark twin.

Year 2003.07   There is a high probability of a magnetic pole shift.

Year 2003.08.12   All aliens have to leave planet Earth until that date, by force if
                           necessary. ET influence will end.

Year 2003   There is a strong probability that they will take away the Moon.

Year 2003   Planet X will pass Earth.
                           → Planet X.

Year 2004   Arriving of the Sirius-B armada in our system.
                           There will be one humanity, one planet composed of all.

Year 2005   The Earth will have its true reality formed. It will join the
                           sisterhood of planets. The capital of New Jerusalem will be in
                           Omaha, Nebraska. Omaha will become the financial, spiritual
                           and economical capital of the world.
                           → New Jerusalem.

Year 2005 – 2006   End of World War III.
                           Start of a new World Order dominated by India (Hindustan).

Year 2006	We will see a whole new way of perfection. There will be plants on Earth that will give life and sustenance as never before seen. Starvation on the earth – all those things will be gone.
Year 2007	Everyone will have full memory of who they are, who they were, where they come from and what they want to do. DNA coding (memory of all 22 races) will unlock. There will be total balance and harmony, and they will still be in their physical bodies.
Year 2008	The new race of humans will begin to design their new reality of life on this planet as they intended it to be when they first came here from the stars. There will be one government system. The most powerful banks, computer manufacturers and software companies will merge to create the OLIN technology, which will become the standard operating system of all the world's computer-based systems. The oceans could rise at least 200 feet between 1996 and 2008.
Year 2009	From 2007 to 2009. 17-degree pole shift: >> North America is supposed to be on the equator. >> Saudi Arabia becomes the new North Pole.
Year 2010	End of Kali Yuga. The planet will hold its space in the great council of planets and become a part of the universal enlightened sisterhood and brotherhood of humanity and keepers of the light circles. It has happened on many planets and it is expected to happen on many other planets.
Year 2011	Released of all karma.
Year 2011	Something big will happen. Our sun will undergo a 180-degree pole shift. Man will live up to 225 years. Change to the 6th interdimensionality. Birth of the 5th Golden Age.
Year 2011-2022	Start of intergalactic communication.
Year 2012	Earth completes the final part of her ascension to a 5th dimensional state of existence. The ascension process will be completed.
Year 2012.12.21	End of the Mayan Calendar.
Year 2013.12	Third density as we know it will cease to exist.
Year 2013.12.03	Between 435 and 510 million people will move into 5th density.
Year 2015 – 2025	Light Principle 40 (LP40) will fall.

Year 2016   The OLIN technology will know the preferences and interests of every individual linked to its network, and by the year 2016, it will be more common than telephones in the late 20th century.

Year 2017   The Zetas plan to repopulate planet Earth following 2017 with the Zeta-human hybrids.

Year 2022   Man will live up to 900 years.

Year 2027   Earth will be absolutely interwoven into the Galactic Association of Worlds, as an equal member.

Year 2032   Man will live up to 3000 years.

Year 2033-3033   5th Golden Age. (4th was Atlantis, 3rd was Lemuria, 2nd was Excalibur). There will be no birth during 1000 years.

Year 2040   There will be discovered a huge planet in the Solar System.

Year 2060   End of the world predicted by Sir Isaac Newton.

Year 2097   The Earth will strictly be for masters.

Year 3000   There will be discovered another planet in the Solar System.

Year 3497   The Earth will give up its spirit and allow the outer portions to go into complete destruction of intermolecular change.

Year 4230-6443   The Zeta/Draco Alliance has successfully overtaken the human world culture.
                         → 6th Root Race.

Year 6000   There will be discovered the sixteenth and last planet in the Solar System.

9. APPENDIX

9.1 Abbreviations

AAAS	American Association for the Advancement of Science
AAF	Army Air Forces
ABMA	Army Ballistic Missile Agency
ACCET	Academy of Clinical Close Encounter Therapists
ACERN	Australian Close Encounter Resource Network
A.D.	Anno Domini
ADC	Air Defense Command
AEC	Atomic Energy Commission
AFB	Air Force Base
AFIS	Air Force Intelligence Service
AFOC	Air Force Operations Center
AFOSI	US Air Force Office of Special Investigations
AFSS	Air Force Security Service
AGSO	Australian Geological Survey Organization
AIAA	American Institute for Aeronautics and Astronautics
AISS	Air Intelligence Service Squadron
AMC	Air Material Command
AP	Associated Press
AMORC	Ancient Mystical Order Rosae Crucis
APRG	Aerial Phenomenon Research Group
APRO	Aerial Phenomenon Research Organization
ASA	Army Security Agency
ATIC	Air Technical Intelligence Center
ATIC	Aerospace Technical Information Command
AVIONICS	Aviation Electronics
BC	Bilderberg Council
B.C.	Before Christ
B.C.E.	Before the Common Era
BG	Bilderberg Group
BMDO	Ballistic Missile Defense Organization
BT	Black Triangle (UFO)
CAUS	Citizens Against UFO Secrecy
CBU	Committee of Brazilian UFO Researchers
C.E.	Common Era
CE I	Close Encounter of the First Kind
CE II	Close Encounter of the Second Kind
CE III	Close Encounter of the Third Kind
CE IV	Close Encounters of the Fourth Kind
CEES	Close Extraterrestrial Encounter Syndrome
CFR	Council On Foreign Relations
CI	Counter Intelligence
CIA	Central Intelligence Agency
CIC	Counter Intelligence Corps
CME	Coronal mass ejection/explosion
CNES	French Space Agency.
CNN	Cable News Network
COG	Continuity of Government Project

COMINT	Communications Intelligence (NSA)
CPU	Central Processing Unit
CS	Combat Support
CSA	Covert Security Agency
CSC	Central Security Control (USAF)
CSETI	Center for the Study of Extra-Terrestrial Intelligence
CSICOP	Committee for the Scientific Investigation of Phenomenon
CSS	Combat Service Support
CUFON	Computer UFO Network
CUFOS	Center for UFO Studies
DARPA	Defense Advanced Research Projects Agency
DEA	Drug Enforcement Agency
DEGUFO	Deutschsprachige Gesellschaft für UFO-Forschung (German UFO research society)
DEO-INTEL	Department of Energy Intelligence
DEPT	Department
DHS	Department of Homeland Security
DIA	Defense Intelligence Agency
DIS	Defense Investigative Service
DISCO	Defense Industry Security Command
DNA	Defense Nuclear Agency
DOD	Dept of Defense
DOE	Department of Energy
DSM	Diagnostic Statistical Manual
E/M	Electro-Magnetic
EADS	European Aeronautic Defense & Space Company
EBE	Extraterrestrial Biological Entity
ELF	Electro-Low-Frequency
ELF	Extreme-Low-Frequency
ELMINT	electromagnetic intelligence
EM	Electromagnetic
ESA	European Space Agency
ESP	Extra Sensory Perception
ET	Extraterrestrial
FAA	Federal Aviation Administration
FAB	Brazilian Air Force
FBI	Federal Bureau of Investigation
FEMA	Federal Emergency Management Agency
FF	Foo Fighter
FOIA	Freedom of Information Act
FSRI	Florida Space Research Institute
FTC	Federal Trade Commission
F.U.	Flying Unknowns
FUFOR	Fund for UFO Research
GPS	Global Position System
GSW	Ground Saucer Watch
HAARP	High-frequency Active Auroral Research Project
HF	High Frequency
HP	Holographic Portal
HST	Hubble Space Telescope
HUMCAT	Humanoid Catalogue
IAC	Identified Alien Craft

IAS	Institute of Aerospace Sciences
ICBM	Intercontinental Ballistic Missile
ICUFOR	International Center for UFO Research
IF	Intruders Foundation
IFO	Identified Flying Object
IGU	Intergalactic Union
INEL	Idaho National Engineering Laboratories
IPRI	Instituto Peruano de Relaciones Interplanetarias
IPU	Interplanetary Phenomenon Unit
IRIS	Incorporated Research Institutions for Seismology
IUR	International UFO Reporter
JCS	Joint Chiefs of Staff
JIC	Joint Intelligence Committee
JINR	Joint Institute for Nuclear Research
JPL	Jet Propulsion Laboratory
KBO	Kuiper Belt object
KBR	Kabardino-Balkaria Republic
KGB	Komitet Gosudarstvennoy Bezopasnosti
KSC	Kennedy Space Center
LANL	Los Alamos National Laboratories
LBJ	Lyndon B. Johnson
LCC	Launch Control Center
LINEAR	Lincoln Near Earth Asteroid Research
LLNL	Lawrence Livermore National Laboratories
LMC	Large Magellanic Cloud
Maj.	Majestic-12
MAJCOM	Majestic Community
MAJI	Majority Agency for Joint Intelligence
MAJIC	Military Assessment of the Joint Intelligence Committee
MDA	Missile Defense Agency
MI	Military Intelligence
MIB	Men in Black
MID	Military Intelligence Division
MILABS	Military Abductions
MIRACL	Mid-Infrared Advanced Chemical Laser
MIT	Massachusetts Institute of Technology
MJ-12	Majestic-12
MMPI	Minnesota Multiphasic Personality Inventory
MPC	Minor Planet Center
MUFON	Mutual Unidentified Flying Object Network
NACA	National Advisory Committee on Aeronautics
NARA	National Archives Records Administration
NASA	National Aeronautics & Space Administration
NATO	North Atlantic Treaty Organization
NAVSPASUR	Naval Space Surveillance System
NBC	National Broadcasting Corporation
NCS	National Security Council
NDE	Near Death Experience
NEA	Near Earth Asteroid
NEO	Near Earth Object
NEST	Nuclear Emergency Search Team
NIC	National Intelligence Council

NICAP	National Investigations Committee on Aerial Phenomena
NIDS	National Institute of Discovery Sciences
NIS	Naval Investigative Service
NMCC	The National Military Command Center
NMD	National Missile Defense
NORAD	North American Aerospace Defense Command
NPIC	National Photographic Interpretation Center
NPO	National Program Office
NRO	National Reconnaissance Office
NRO	National Reconnaissance Organization
NSA	National Security Agency
NSAM	National Security Action Memorandum
NSC	National Security Council
NSTC	National Science and Technology Council
NSW	New South Wales
NTR	Nevada Test Range
NUFOC	National UFO Conference
NUFORC	National UFO Reporting Center
OBE	Out of Body Experience
OOBE	Out of Body Experience
OIC	Officer in Charge
OPEC	Organization for Petroleum Exporting Countries
OSI	Office of Special Investigations
OSIR	Organization for Scientific Investigation and Research
OSS	Office of Strategic Services
OTS	Office of Technical Services
OVNI	Objeto Volador No Identificado
OWL	One World League
PA	Privacy Act
PEER	Program for Extraordinary Experience Research
PRG	Paradigm Research Group
PSE	Psychological Stress Evaluator
PSYINT	Parapsychological Intelligence
PSYOP	Psychological Operation
PTSD	post-traumatic stress disorder
RAAF	Roswell Army Air Field
REM	Rapid Eye Movement
RF	Radio Frequency
RFID	Radio Frequency Identification Device
RUFORS	Russian UFO Research Station.
SAC	Special Agent in Charge
SAIC	Science Applications International Corp.
SDI	Strategic Defense Initiative ("Star Wars")
SDIO	Strategic Defense Initiative Office
SETI	Search for Extraterrestrial Intelligence (founded 1984)
SMDC	Space and Missile Defense Command
SNL-W	Sandia National Laboratories-West
SRI	Stanford Research Institute
TC	Trilateral Commission
TLC	Trilateral Commission
UAO	Unidentified Aerial Object
UCAF	Unmanned Combat Air Vehicle

UCP	Universal Confederation of Planets
UFO	Unidentified Flying Object
UFOCAT	UFO Catalogue (from CUFOS)
UFORC	UFO Reporting Center
UFORIC	UFO Research Institute of Canada
ULATT	Unidentified Lenticular Aerodyne Technology Transfer
UPI	United Press International
US	United States
U.S.A	United States of America
USAF	United States Air Force
USCIB	United States Communications Intelligence Board
USO	Unidentified Submarine Object
VLT	Very Large Telescope
VRE	Virtual Reality Experiences
WA	Western Australia

9.2 Bibliography

Abductions

Cannon, Dolores,   "Between Death and Life: Conversations with a Spirit",
                             1993,1995,2001,
                             "Legacy from the Stars", 1996,
                             "The Custodians, Beyond Abductions", 1999,2001,
                             "The Convoluted Universe", 2001,
                             Ozark Mountain Publishers, P.O.Box 754, Huntsville, AR
                             72740.

Fowler, Ray,   "The Andreasson Affair", Prentice Hall, Englewood Cliffs, N.J.,
                             1979.

Freudenstein, Werner,

                             "UFO-Entführung auf der Alm", Germany.

Fuller, John,   "The Interrupted Journey", Dial Press, New York, 1966.

Hayes, Anna,   "Voyagers, The Sleeping Abductees", Wild Flower Press, USA,
                             1998.

Hopkins, Budd,   "Missing Time", Marek, New York, 1981.

Jacobs, David M.,   "Secret Life: First Hand Accounts of UFO Abductions", Simon
                             & Schuster, New York, 1992.

Mack, John E.,   "Abduction: Human Encounters With Aliens", Scribners, 1994.

Randles, Jenny,   "Alien Abductions", New Brunswick, 1988.

Riley, Martin,   "The Coming of Tan", second printing,
                             Histority Productions, 91 River Rd., Stockton New Jersey 08559.

Strieber, Whitley   "Communion – A True Story", Avon Books, 10 East 53rd Street,
                             New York, New York 10022-5299, 1988.
                             "Confirmation: The Hard Evidence of Aliens Among Us.", St.
                             Martin's Paperbacks, 175 Fifth Avenue, New York, N.Y. 10010,
                             1998.

Turner, Karla,   "Alien Abductions in the Gingerbread House." 1993.

Walton, Travis   "Fire in the Sky: The Walton Experience", Marlowe & Company,
                             632 Broadway, Seventh Floor, New York, New York 10012,
                             USA, 1996.

Aliens / UFO's

Adamski, George,   "Inside the Space Ships", Abelard-Schuman, Inc., 404 Fourth
                             Ave., New York 16, N.Y., USA, 1955

Bender, Albert K.,   "Flying Saucers and the Three Men", Neville Spearman Limited,
                             London, UK, 1963.

Boylan, R. J.   "Close Extraterrestrial Encounters: Positive Experiences With
                             Mysterious Visitors.", Wild Flower Press, Tigard, OR.

Candyce, Valerio,   "Cattle Mutilations in Northern New Mexico", TAOS Magazine,
                             1979.

Commander X,   "The Ultimate Deception", Abelard Productions, Inc., 1990.

Dolan, Richard M.,   "UFOs and the National Security State", Hampton Roads
                             Publishing Company Inc., 1125 Stoney Ridge Road,
                             Charlottesville, VA 22902, 2002.

Estes, Sara Lyara,   "Operation Terra".

Friedman, S. and D. Berliner,
                             "UFO Crash at Corono", Paragon, New York, 1992.

Hall, Richards   "A Documented History of UFO Sightings, Alien Encounters
                             and Coverups", Aurora Press Inc., Santa Fe, New Mexico, USA,
                             1988.

Hesemann, Michael,   "UFOs: Die Beweise", Munich, 1990.
                             "UFOs: Die Kontakte", Munich, 1990.

Hopkins, Budd,   "Intruders: The Incredible Visitations at Copley Woods, Random
                             House, New York, 1987.

Jacobs, David M.,   "The Threat", Simon & Schuster, 1997;
                             "The UFO Controversy in America", Indiana University Press,
                             Bloomington, 1975.

Jay, David   "Flying Saucers have landed!", World Publishing Co., Cincinnati,
                             Ohio, 1970.

Jeffrey, Kent,   "Santilli's Controversial Autopsy Movie", MUFON UFO
                             Journal, Seguin, Texas, USA, no. 335, March 1996.

Kerr, Roger,   "History of the Council of Six", 1999.

Ki, Olance,   "Valiant Thor Speaks", Alahoy Publications, Canyonville, OR
                             97417, USA, 1995.

Larkins, Lisette,   "Talking to Extraterrestrials", 2002, "Calling On Extraterrestrials", 2003, "Listening to Extraterrestrials", 2004, Hampton Roads Publishing Company, Inc., 1125 Stoney Ridge Road, Charlottesville, VA 22902, USA.

Leir, Roger K. Dr.,   "CASEBOOK: Alien Implants", Dell Publishing, 1540 Broadway, New York, New York 10036, 2000.

Lorgen, Eve,   "The Love Bite – Alien Interference in Human Love Relationships", Greenleaf Publications, 2000.

Mantle, Philip,   "The Roswell Film Footage", UFO Times, BUFORA, Batley, England, no. 36, Jul/Aug 1995.

Marss, Jim,   "Alien Agenda, Investigating the Extraterrestrial Presence Among Us", Harper Paperbacks, 10 East 53rd Street, New York, N.Y. 10022-5299, 1997, 1998.

Milanovich, Norma J.,   "We Are the Arcturians".

Miller, David K.   "Connecting with the Arcturians", Prescott, AZ, USA.

Montgomery, Ruth,   "Aliens Among Us".

Morehouse, David,   "Psychic Warrior", St Martin's Press, New York, 1996

Moulton Howe, Linda,   "Glimpses of Other Realities Volume II: High Strangeness", 1998.

Nichols, Preston B., **Moon** Peter,   "Encounter in the Pleiades: An Inside Look At UFOs", Sky Books, Box 769, Westbury, New York 11590-0104, 1996, 2003.

Nidle, Sheldon,   "Selamat Ja!"; "You Are Becoming a Galactic Human". "Your First Contact", PAO, Pukalani, USA.

Oswanta, Yashah,   "Divine Guidance From the Space Brothers", Alahoy Publications, Vancouver, British Columbia, Canada, 1987.

Pereira, Patricia L.   "Songs of the Arcturians (The Arcturian Star Chronicles, Vol 1)", 1996.
"Eagles of the New Dawn (The Arcturian Star Chronicles, Vol 2)", 1997.
"Songs of Malantor (The Arcturian Star Chronicles, Vol 3)", 1998.
"Arcturian Songs of the Masters of Light (The Arcturian Star Chronicles, Vol 4)", 1999,
Beyond Words Publishing, Inc., 20827 N.W. Cornell Road, Suite 500, Hillsboro, Oregon 97124-9808.

Randle, K. and **Schmitt** D.,
"UFO Crash at Roswell", Avon, New York, 1991.

Royal Holt, Lyssa,   "The Prism of Lyra",
"Preparing for Contact",
"Visitors from Within".

Scully, Frank,   "Behind the Flying Saucers", 1950.

Sitchin, Zecharia,   "The Wars of Gods and Men", New York, 1985.

Starr, Jelaila,   "We Are the Nibiruans", Granite Publishing, Columbus NC, USA.

Stokes, Trey,   "Special Effects: The Fine Art of Fooling People", *UFO Times*, BUFORA, Batley, England, January 1996.

Story, Ronald D.,   "The Encyclopedia of Extraterrestrial Encounters", 3540 – 32nd Avenue North # 114, St. Petersburg, Florida 33713 USA.

Stringfield, Leonard,   "The UFO Crash Retrieval", 1980.

Tuella,   "Ashtar: Revealing the Secret Identity of the Forces of Light and Their Spiritual Program for Earth",
"Project World Evacuation".

VonKeviczky, Colman,
"Autopsy of a Human-like 'Freak' Body", New York, USA, 23 October 1995.

Wachter, Hanspeter,   "Der Roswell-Film", *Magazin 2000*, Neuss, Germany, no. 110, May 1996.

Wendelle, Stevens,   "UFO … Contact from Reticulum", 1989.

Wolf, Michael Dr.   "Catchers of Heaven", Dorrance Publishing, USA.

New World Order / Conspiracy

Coleman, John,   "Illuminati in America", World in Review (2533 N. Carson St, Carson City, NV 89706), USA, 1992

Commander X,   "The Ultimate Deception", Abelard Productions, Inc., 1990.

Crockett, Arthur,   "New World Order".

Good, Timothy,   "Above Top Secret", London, 1987.

Greer, Steven M. M.D.,

                              "Disclosure" Book, "Extraterrestrial Contact" Book, Disclosure Project, P.O.B 2365, Charlottesville VA 22902, USA.

Marss, Jim,   "Crossfire: The Plot That Killed Kennedy", 1989; "Rule by Secrecy", 2000.

Roads, Duncan,   NEXUS MAGAZINE (Head Office), PO Box 30, Mapleton Qld 4560 Australia.

Ruppert, Michael C.,   Former LAPD officer, is Editor/Publisher of *From The Wilderness* newsletter. PO Box 6061-350, Sherman Oaks, CA 91413, USA.

Springmeier, Fritz,   "Bloodlines of the Illuminati", Ambassador House (PO Box 1153, Westminster, CO 80030), USA, 1999

Remote Viewing

Akwei, John S.,   "Covert Operations of the US NSA", *NEXUS* Magazine, vol. 3, no. 3, 1996.

Brown, Courtney,   "Cosmic Voyage: A Scientific Discovery of Extraterrestrials Visiting Earth", Penguin Books, 1996.

Buhlman, William,   "Adventures Beyond the Body", Greenleaf, 1996; "The Secret of the Soul", Greenleaf, 1996.

Forsyth, Richard,   "Room with a Remote View", *Encounters*, issue 10, August 1996.

Marss, Jim,   Psi Spies, 1995/2000.

Vistica, Gregory,   "Psychics and Spooks", *Newsweek*, 11 December 1995.

Spirit World

Altea, Rosemary,   "You Own the Power", P.O. Box 1151, Manchester, VT 05254.

Belsey, Ashian,   "Mirrors of Eternity".

Blavatsky, Helena P.,   "Isis Unveiled", New York Herald, 1877.

Cannon, Dolores,   "Conversations with Nostradamus", Vol 1, 1996,
                              Ozark Mountain Publishers, P.O.Box 754, Huntsville, AR 72740-0754,
                              "Conversations with Nostradamus", Vol 2, 1990,
                              America West Publishers, P.O.Box 2208, Carson City, Nevada 89702,
                              "Conversations with Nostradamus", Vol 3, 2001,
                              Ozark Mountain Publishers, P.O.Box 754, Huntsville, AR 72740-0754,
                              "They Walked With Jesus", 2001,
                              Ozark Mountain Publishers, P.O.Box 754, Huntsville, AR 72740-0754.

Chaney, Earlyne,   "Secrets from Mount Shasta", Astara Online Bookstore.

Chaney, Robert,   "Akashic Records", Astara Online Bookstore.

Cooper-Oakley, Isabel,
                              "Comte de St. Germain", Theosophical Publishing House, 1912.

Cori, Patricia,   "Atlantis Rising, The Struggle of Darkness and Light", iUniverse.com, Inc., 5220 S 16th, Ste. 200, Lincoln, NE 68512, 2001.

Cota-Robles, Patricia Diane,
                              "What on Earth Is Going on?", The New Age Study of Humanity's Purpose, P.O. Box 41883, Tucson, AZ 85717, USA.

Dean, Michael,   "The Return of Merlin", Global Communications, New Brunswick, USA, 1994.

Dombrowski, Bev (Dranda),
                              10956 Green Street, Space 217, Columbia, CA 95310, USA.

Fischer, Linn,   "Angels of Love & Light", The Temple of The Presence, P.O.Box 17839, Tucson, Arizona 85731-7839, USA.

Groves, Campbell,   "Appolonius of Tyana", Chicago, USA, 1968.

Herman, Ronna,   "On Wings of Light",
                            "Personal Message from AA Michael", 6005 Clear Creek Drive,
                            Reno NV 89502, USA.

Herzog, Roberta S.,   "The Akashic Records", 2004.

Ki, Olance,   "Lest These Days Be Shortened", Alahoy Publications,
                            Canyonville, OR, USA, 1996.

King, Godfre Ray,   "Unveiled Mysteries", Saint Germain Series Volume 1 – 4, The
                            Temple of The Presence, P.O.Box 17839, Tucson, Arizona
                            85731-7839, USA.

Marciniak, Barbara,   "Bringers of the Dawn-Teachings from the Pleiadians",
                            Bear & Company Inc., Santa Fe, New Mexico, USA, 1992.

Meade, Marion,   "Madame Blavatsky – The Woman Behind the Myth", New
                            York, USA, 1980.

Moulton Howe, Linda,

                            "Mysterious Lights and Crop Circles", LMH Productions,
                            Jamison, PA, USA, 2002.

Mumford, Dr. Jonn,   "A Chakra & Kundalini Workbook", 2nd Edition, Llewellyn
                            Publications, St. Paul, MN, USA, 1995.

O'Riley, Carolyn Ann,   "The Journey Within".

Oribello, William Alexander,

                            "Sacred Magic", Inner Light Publications, New Brunswick, NJ,
                            USA, 1992.

Prophet, Elizabeth Clare,

                            "The Great White Brotherhood: In the Culture, History and
                            Religion of America, Amazon.Com.

Prophet, Mark L. & **Prophet**, Elizabeth Clare,

                            "Cosmic Consciousness", Amazon.Com.

Robbins, Dianne,   "Telos: The Call Goes Out from the Hollow Earth and the
                            Underground Cities", Onelight.Com Publications, P.O. Box
                            10945, Rochester, NY 14610 USA, Mt. Shasta Publishing,
                            Mt.Shasta, CA 96067-1509, 1996, 2000, 2001.

Rother, Steve,   "Welcome Home, The New Planet Earth", Lightworker
                            Publications, 2002.

Sutphen, Tara,   "Blame It on Your Past Lives", Valley of the Sun Publishing,
                            Malibu, CA, USA, 1993.

Tessman, Diane,   "The Transformation", Inner Light Publications, New
                            Brunswick, NJ, USA, 1983/1988.

Predictions

"The Years 2001 – 2007",   "The   Year   2011".   Alahoy
Publications, Canyonville, OR, USA.

Space / Planets

"Spaceflight Now: The Leading Source for Online Space News",
Pole Star Publications Ltd., 2001/2002.

Announcement

High resolution, color prints, signed by the artist, of the paintings in this book and more, will be available soon.

Yeva's CD "Space 11-11" will also be out before the end of the year 2005.

 Watch for details at   www.yevasuniverse.com

About the Author

Rolf Waeber was born (1955) and educated in Switzerland. His intensive computer studies landed him in the technological field. Since 1973 he has worked as a mainframe computer analyst and programmer. He speaks fluent German, Spanish, and English and understands French and Italian. In 1994 he left Switzerland and lived for five years in Ecuador, South America, where he worked temporarily as a translator and tourist guide.

He went on many tours in the highlands where he had a close encounter with the Inca culture. It was one of countless, unforgettable experiences. Due to scorching heat all climbing had to be done at night, walking and "resting" in the daytime. Sometimes he would walk non-stop over twenty-two hours, covering up to one hundred kilometers. Solo, he climbed numerous mountains and felt on top of the world when he reached the summit of Mt. Chimborazo, 6310 meters. The high of touching the black velvet sky sequined with shimmering stars did not last, as Rolf Waeber had to return to Switzerland in November of 1999, due to political upheaval in the Andean community.

Whether in Ecuador or Zurich Switzerland, each with their own charms and challenges or wherever the roads will take Rolf Waeber, he will always find a daring endeavor. Walking with bare feet on burning charcoal at a temperature around 800°C and mastering this with bravour, is just one example. He is a passionate hiker, on burning coals or not. He loves nature on earth and elsewhere. At an early age Rolf indulged in science fiction, later science facts, and the combination of it all opened the door to other worlds, from parapsychology to extraterrestrial. As a member of German and American UFO groups, he has attended international meetings, but there is one important meeting Rolf Waeber is dreaming of. You, the reader, take a guess.

Y. Tierney

Printed in the United States
by Baker & Taylor Publisher Services